Missing Jesus?

DEDICATED

to all Southern Africans of the past and the present who are faithful disciples of Jesus here.
You are all my heroes!

ABOUT THIS BOOK

You will love how this guidebook leads you on the exciting journey of getting to know Jesus better. You will come to appreciate the relevance of Jesus to all dimensions of life today – including the social, spiritual, religious, economic, political, relational and ecological realities. John Wessels has developed and taught the contents of this guidebook in courses since the year 2000. Over the years he has often re-written, enlarged and refined the guidebook. Now, nineteen years after the start of this project, he has decided it is ready for publication.

The guidebook can be used as a comprehensive journey of discipleship for individuals, small groups or congregations. It may also be divided into three separate shorter studies in the following way: 'Jesus rediscovered!' (six-week journey), 'The Kingdom Consciousness Movement' (nine-week journey), 'Salvation rediscovered' (six-week journey).

Instructions for all these and more options are given in the guidebook and supported by the website: www.missingjesus.net

ABOUT THE AUTHOR

John Wessels is passionate about Jesus! He fervently believes that Jesus and his Kingdom are the hope Southern Africa needs now. He believes that Christians, both local congregations and small groups, should be spending much more time getting to know Jesus and the meaning of his life, ministry and teachings. That is what this book is about!

John is an ordained minister in the Methodist Church of Southern Africa and has been the minister of congregations in East London, Buffalo Flats, Sea Point, Observatory, Brackenfell, Rosebank and Linden. He grew up in East London and enjoys long-distance trail running and any time he can get in the mountains. John is married to Angela and they have two children, Ashlynn and Luke.

MISSING JESUS?

Finding the Shepherd we lost

JOHN WESSELS

PORCUPINE PRESS
Johannesburg

All rights reserved. No part of this book may be reproduced or transmitted in any form or by any means, electronic or mechanical, including photocopying, recording, or by any information storage and retrieval system, without permission in writing from the copyright owner and the publisher.

© John Dalling Wessels 2019

The parable *'The Inventor'* in Anthony De Mello's *'The Prayer of the Frog'* is reproduced by courtesy of Gujarat Sahitya Prakash

Excerpts from *The Rainbow People of God: The Making of a Peaceful Revolution*, are quoted by courtesy of Desmond Mpilo Tutu

Published and distributed by
Porcupine Press in 2019
P O Box 2756
Pinegowrie, 2123
Gauteng, South Africa
www.porcupinepress.co.za

ISBN: 978-1-928455-38-7
ISBN: 978-1-928455-52-3 (POD: Ingram Spark)

Illustrations by Sandy Lightley
Cover design and page layout by wim@wimrheeder.co.za
Set in 11 point on 15 point, Minion Pro

Printed by **novus** print, a Novus Holdings company

CONTENTS

Foreword	9
Preface	14
How to use the book	18
Acknowledgements	27

PART 1 – LOST

1. **Missing Jesus. What happens when you lose the Shepherd?**   32
   Crisis: Jesus is missing from the lives of many people, Christians, churchgoers and church structures.

2. **Community**   52
   God's intention in creation was, and still is, community.

3. **Division**   72
   Sin divides.

PART 2 – FOUND BY THE SHEPHERD

4. **Who is Jesus of Nazareth?**   89
   God the Word became human as Jesus of Nazareth.

5. **Jesus' Birth and Ministry**   114
   Restoration: Jesus' birth, life and ministry re-establish the state of community that was lost in the fall.

6. **The Kingdom Consciousness Movement**   129
   Good news: The reign of God has arrived and you are invited to change your whole life according to that great news.

7. **What Jesus Practised**   149
   Jesus' ministry: Jesus' ministry was characterised by compassion, faith and forgiveness – all of which were transformative for those who received.

8. **The Kingdom has come! Jesus teaches Kingdom Consciousness**   166
   Jesus' teaching: Submitting to God's reign is a life-giving choice and involves a transformation of consciousness and behaviour.

9. **Jesus valued sharing and not greed** — 189
   Exploring Jesus' teaching about money and possessions.

10. **Jesus valued people and not prestige** — 209
    Exploring Jesus' teaching about honour.

11. **Love steps across boundaries** — 227
    Exploring Jesus' teaching about solidarity.

12. **Loving service is the most powerful force in the world** — 245
    Exploring Jesus' teaching about power.

13. **Hope of the world** — 260
    The 'Already' and 'Not Yet' reality of God's reign.

14. **Jesus' death and resurrection** — 278
    Sealed: Jesus' death and resurrection seals the state of community that was restored in his birth, life and ministry.

PART 3 – FINDING THE SHEPHERD

15. **Entrusting yourself to the Shepherd** — 306
    My faith: I am transformed when I personally respond to Jesus in faith.

16. **Who is the Holy Spirit? Jesus continues His Mission** — 328
    The Spirit of Jesus: The Holy Spirit is the One who is the presence and power of Jesus with us.

17. **The Holy Spirit in my relationship with God and the community** — 344
    The Holy Spirit accomplishes my unity with God and a community life amongst people.

18. **The Holy Spirit in my relationship with my environment and myself** — 362
    The Holy Spirit accomplishes a life-giving relationship with my environment and a oneness with myself.

19. **Receiving the Holy Spirit** — 386
    The Spirit of transformation: We need to actively invite the Holy Spirit to work in us and through us to experience Resurrection Life.

20. **The Prayer of the Kingdom**   **400**
    The Lord's Prayer sums up Jesus' call to live with Kingdom Consciousness.

21. **Intimate Life with the Shepherd**   **416**
    The spiritual disciplines: These are the means by which I entrust myself to Jesus the Good Shepherd on a daily basis and experience his provision and protection through them.

Epilogue	**448**
Appendix 1: Ideas of the Atonement	**450**
Appendix 2: The great omission in the Great Commission	**459**
Recommendations	**462**
The 'Missing Jesus?' Website	**466**
Bibliography	**467**
About the author	**472**

Missing Jesus?

FOREWORD

People are looking for Jesus, not doctrine.

A foreword of compiled recommendations by Allan Boesak, Mamphela Ramphele, Njongonkulu Ndungane, Yvette Moses, Albert Nolan, Faith Whitby, Derek Morphew and Trevor Hudson.

John Wessels' *Missing Jesus* truly is a gem of a book, a gift to clergy and lay persons, to teachers and students of the Word, a joy to read and will no doubt be a joy to work with. This is a guidebook, but not a 'how to' book or a spiritual DIY book, rather it is journeying book, inviting us on a journey to find the Jesus we have missed – not properly seen or understood, misread and misinterpreted. And what a fascinating journey this is! The thorough research behind this book and the theological and biblical knowledge are obvious, but not in a way that would hamper non-theologians. Rather they are woven into the fabric of the work, breathe through every sentence, authenticate the thinking like leaven in good bread. So page after page is a discovery, a delightful lesson, an invitation to find more. At the root, at the core, and through it all is Jesus. The author's love for Jesus and the Bible is unabashed, his treatment of the material intellectually honest, his understanding of the relevance of the Bible and the message of Jesus to the challenges facing the church and our societies is spot on, his approach to the reader highly respectful. A delightful book.

PROF. ALLAN BOESAK
Pastor, academic, activist and author of *The Tenderness of Conscience: African Renaissance and the Spirituality of Politics* and 18 other titles.

This book is a contribution to our public discourse that could not have come at a better time. We are a nation of majority believers of many faiths with an emphasis on 'personalised salvation' rather than the radical ministry of 'the word made flesh' or the core principles of the Ubuntu we profess!

This book challenges all people of faith to confront the inequities in our social relationships at all levels that stand in contradiction with the faiths we profess. The power of the book's point of departure that *'God is a foundational force and energising power that makes life possible'* enables the reader to align the biblical creation story with the science of evolution.

The presentation of God as Love present in all creation, and Jesus as the 'word made flesh' to model this Love at four levels: of God, between humans, within the self, and of the environment and nature, provides a practical way of living our faith in obedience to the Love imperative.

The core message would be particularly appealing to those like me who were brought up in communities with a value system encapsulated by *Ubuntu*. The Ubuntu notion that a human being is always in communion with other human beings, as well as with the spiritual and natural world, resonates with the Love imperative at the core of all major religions.

The humiliating poverty endured by the majority of our fellow citizens challenges us to live the core values of our faiths and of Ubuntu as set out above. The interactive exercises at the end of each chapter are useful tools for consciousness raising essential for personal, communal and social healing to reconcile the physical, spiritual and natural in our lives. Ubuntu is an ideal medium to bind us together as a nation. This should be required reading for all seeking to live their beliefs.

DR MAMPHELA RAMPHELE
Academic, activist and author of *Dreams, Betrayal and Hope* and 18 other titles.

I am delighted to recommend *Missing Jesus* for the use of Christians, both those new to the faith and those who have regarded themselves as such for many years. *Missing Jesus* is a comprehensive, thought-provoking contribution to the literature of our faith that will deepen the spiritual life of anyone who reads it, or uses it as a study guide. Leaders of our churches will at times find the guide somewhat uncomfortable in the challenges it presents to that institution.

The author correctly describes it as a 'guidebook'. A guide is something that 'indicates the way', and this book will certainly show the reader, in a very practical manner, how to live a more spiritually fulfilling life. I particularly enjoyed the emphasis on community and relationships; this is, of course, of particular relevance to those of us living in Africa and our understanding of ubuntu. The use of stories to illustrate examples follows in the footsteps of Jesus who told many stories or parables as a way of helping his listeners understand what he was saying. In the same way, the author is able to clearly communicate complex spiritual truths in a straightforward and accessible way.

This guidebook is suitable for individual or group use, and will provide a suitable framework for several months of group study, or even individual use. The structure of discussion, revision, reflection and application at the end of each chapter has been intelligently compiled, and will provide an excellent basis for group Bible study.

I have no hesitation in recommending this guidebook to Christians who desire to grow their spiritual lives both in relation to God, their communities, the societies in which they live, and themselves.

THE MOST REVD NJONGONKULU NDUNGANE
Archbishop Emeritus of Cape Town and author of *A World with a Human Face: A Voice from Africa.*

The Shepherd Psalm (Psalm 23) has probably been one of the most widely read Psalms, yet little used in our understanding of discipleship. Using the concept of Jesus as the Shepherd, John provides an insightful framework in this resource book, *Missing Jesus*, calling us to understand who Jesus is, how we might be drawn into a relationship with Him, how to nurture this through spiritual disciplines, in order that we might participate meaningfully in His life in the world around us. What struck me is the simplicity of the text, while at the same time dealing with complex, foundational doctrines and practices of our Christian faith. His insightful illustrations that do justice to the South African context as well as our Wesleyan framework make this a relevant resource for our churches in our Southern African context. In the pre-read of this book, I have been personally challenged in many areas of my faith, using the thought provoking personal reflection questions, and would recommend this as a timely gift to our church as a whole in our desire to equip members in their ongoing discipleship journey in relationship with Jesus, our Good Shepherd.

REVD YVETTE MOSES
Methodist minister, Acting Bishop and Bishop elect of Cape of Good Hope Synod

In the 1970s when I became a university chaplain I tried to teach the Catholic students Christian Doctrine. I failed. They were bored to tears. Eventually I came to the conclusion that they were not interested in any kind of doctrine. This made me realise that of course Christian faith after all is not basically about doctrines. Christian faith is about a person: Jesus of Nazareth. So I began a series of talks about Jesus as a person: his life, his struggles, his aims and his significance for us in South Africa today. That was an unbelievable success. Later it became a book: *Jesus Before Christianity*.

John Wessels has now taken this one step further. His analysis of just how much Jesus is missing from the preaching and practices of the Christian Churches today is very revealing – and indeed shocking. Christians seem to conform much more to the dominant culture than to the practice and preaching of Jesus. John shows us how Jesus' practice centred on compassion for all who suffer while his teaching centred on the Kingdom or Reign of God and its values. We don't hear much of that in our Churches.

What we have here is a comprehensive guidebook for all who preach or teach in the Churches which will enable us to find the missing Jesus, the Shepherd we had lost. I can recommend it without reservation.

FR. ALBERT NOLAN
Academic, theologian and author of *Jesus before Christianity* and 8 other titles.

It has been said 'If you can, do. If you can't, teach.' This guidebook demonstrates that in the Christian life, one can only teach out of a lifetime of 'doing'. John holds together a vast scope of work (content) and a depth of insight, as well as finding practical ways in which this resource can be used in a variety of ways to enable growing discipleship. The work is theologically sound, and also accessible to readers at a number of levels. John encourages his readers to build an authentic relationship with Jesus Christ, rather than be 'consumers' of religion. Rowan Williams, in his book *Being Disciples: Essentials of the Christian Life*, defines a disciple as one who learns '… how to be a place in the world where the act of God can come alive'. He also reminds us that discipleship '… is not an intermittent state; it's a relationship that continues'. This guidebook is an invaluable resource in enabling individuals and communities to find and be found by Jesus, to grow into deeper and more meaningful relationship as disciples, and to journey in participating with God in the realisation of the reign of God in the world. I highly recommend it.

REVD FAITH WHITBY
Methodist Minister and Bishop elect for Central Synod of the Methodist Church of Southern Africa.

As one of those tasked to assist with peer review, I can claim to have read this work quite thoroughly. It was a pleasure to read it, for a number of reasons.

I agree with the central thesis of the 'missing Jesus'. Protestant Evangelicalism has tended towards a reductionist view of the gospel. Generally, it begins with Paul and then reads the gospels with Pauline lenses, landing on the cross as the essential core (the passion narrative with a brief introduction idea). This means that the Kingdom of God mission and message of Jesus is largely ignored. This work brings an important theological corrective.

The elevation of the Christus Victor approach to the atonement matches some important trends in contemporary theology. The rediscovery of Jesus' mission and message of the kingdom does have such implications, important implications!

I found the journey of discipleship approach really helpful. This is a discipleship/theology, or theology-through-discipleship.

The way the book 'lands' on the spiritual disciplines is also commendable. This is a theology-through-discipleship leading to spiritual formation, an intentionally crafted and refreshing combination of approaches.

DR DEREK MORPHEW
Academic Dean of the Vineyard Institute and author of
Breakthrough: Discovering the Kingdom, and 17 other titles.

Over the past few years it has been a privilege to witness John pour his life into writing *Missing Jesus*. On its pages he has distilled his own many years of academic study, faithful ministry in the local congregation and personal walk with God. Now he offers us a wonderful and practical resource that explores the radical message and mission of Jesus and how we can follow him in the power of the Spirit within our complex Southern African context. Like any good teacher, he has clothed his rich theological insights in simple and accessible language. Almost each page sparkles with fresh insight, pastoral relevance and down-to-earth application. More than this, he has also gone to great lengths to make this book a journey-resource for both individuals and small groups, as well as for seasonal and year-long courses in the local congregation. As I went through the contents, I found my appetite to discover the missing Jesus both whetted and satisfied. In a day and age when 'consumer Christianity' has become an accepted norm for church life, we need thoughtful voices of integrity that keep calling us back to explore and to embrace the Christ-following way. John is one of those voices and we are indebted to him for this labour of commitment and love.

TREVOR HUDSON
Methodist Pastor and author of *Friendship with God – How God's Offer of Intimate Relationship can Change Your Life* and 29 other titles.

PREFACE

This is a book about our relationship with Jesus. If you are reading these opening words then you probably have a relationship with Jesus already. So why would you read this book? To answer that, I invite you to reflect on these questions:
- If a curious person, knowing you are a Christian, asked you to give an overview of Jesus' teaching and practice and the meaning of it all, would you have much to say?
- How much detail do you know of Jesus' teaching and preaching?
- Perhaps you know that the theme of love was important to Jesus, but are you able to explain Jesus' very distinctive teaching on who to love, why love and how to love?
- Do you know that Jesus spoke most about the Kingdom of God, and if so are you able to explain why this Kingdom is so important?
- How does Jesus fit in with God's intention in creation?
- What is the relationship between Jesus and the Holy Spirit – and why is the Holy Spirit so important in your relationship with Jesus?
- How do you follow Jesus today?

These questions are important in your relationship with Jesus and are just a few of the ones that are studied in this book. Many are neglected by Christians even though they are all essential. This book will help you to fill in many of the missing pieces of your relationship with Jesus. I think that is a very good reason to read on.

If you are not in a relationship with Jesus – a special welcome to you! I feel particularly excited that you are reading this book. Thank you for giving me an opportunity to present Jesus to you. You will certainly be able to make an informed decision about your relationship with Jesus whilst reading this book. I hope you continue reading.

If you are in a relationship with Jesus then I am sure that you view that relationship as very important in your life. You might say that it is the most important relationship in your life, defining and determining all other aspects of your life. This book will help you to honour that good conviction through helping you to understand, experience and participate in the life that Jesus offers the world.

We can only be in a relationship with the Jesus we know. Could it be that you are in a relationship with a part of Jesus, not the whole? Could it be that there is a lot of Jesus that is missing for you and needs to be found? This book will help you enormously with finding the missing Jesus in your life, as the journey of writing it helped me and continues to grow me. Along the way you will also discover, as I did, that some of the Jesus you have believed in is the kind of person Jesus called to repentance! This will be because our beliefs have actually been informed by the ideals of our culture rather than in the life and ministry of Jesus of Nazareth.

There are so many dynamics and dimensions that make up our relationship with Jesus – following and learning, repentance and transformation, grace and obedience, worship and friendship, realism and discipline, thinking and living, meaning and purpose, personal and social, God and creation, today and eternity and many more. All of this is included in this book! So if you want to grow in anything that has been mentioned in this and previous paragraphs then this is a book for you.

Don't skip over the most important words in this guidebook! I am frequently amazed at how powerful the words of scripture are, how they speak 'into' my spirit and mind, how the 'aha' moment happens in reading them. The quotations from the Bible are therefore the most important part of this guidebook and I appeal to you to read them all – even if you are very familiar with your Bible. If you are not familiar with your Bible then a huge smile has come to my face as I type this – you are in for a treat!

Please read the following text – it sums up my passion for the themes of this book. This text is an eloquent celebration of Jesus Christ and his message. Allow these words to sink into your consciousness – it will then be clear that to have Jesus 'missing' in our lives is to have lost hope for any point or meaning to life. Savour these words, even if they are familiar, and appreciate that there is great depth of living truth here:

> *He is the image of the invisible God, the firstborn of all creation; for in him all things in heaven and on earth were created, things visible and invisible, whether thrones or dominions or rulers or powers—all things have been created through him and for him. He himself is before all things, and in him all things hold together. He is the head of the body, the church; he is the beginning, the firstborn from the dead, so that he might come to have first place in everything. For in him all the fullness of God was pleased to dwell, and through him God was pleased to reconcile to himself all things, whether on earth or in heaven, by making peace through the blood of his cross.* Colossians 1.15-20

I have pursued a deeper and more real relationship with Jesus whilst writing this guidebook. The almost two decades it has taken have been plenty of time to journey with this content and in which to discover dynamics and dimensions that seemed almost impossibly precipitous mountain passes. As it approaches finalisation I know that I will spend the rest of my life trying to catch up to authentically living some of its most challenging content.

The themes of discipleship have already brought about very significant changes to my journey with Jesus. The most difficult has been Jesus' insistence that I put the Kingdom of God first in my life. He teaches us to seek God's Kingdom on earth as it is in heaven – and South Africa is the earth on which I was born and where I have needed to pursue discipleship. The journey of this guidebook has run parallel to the journey of the very difficult birthing of a new South Africa. We have journeyed from the very deep dark place of a brutal, deceitful and unjust state where every aspect of national life needed radical transformation. The journey to a new land has not been easy at all and has followed a track that has been dangerous, exhausting, complex and distressing. It has also been a journey with beautiful views, wonderful travel companions and energising developments. It has been a journey that has been healing for some and tragic for others. We have too slowly resolved some injustices but have also punctured our fuel tank with great corruption and gashes of greed.

God wants his kingdom to come and his will to be done in South Africa, and this would certainly bring her the good life she longs for. But progress in this journey will not happen without a high price being paid of selfless and courageous discipleship – and therein has been my struggle. I have often found the cost too high and the desire for more pleasant and comfortable journeys too great. Jesus' call to grow God's Kingdom requires a commitment to our country that is far higher than any nationalism or patriotism and will ultimately bring a far greater blessing to our land of birth. I needed to pray a great deal and needed light and insight for making decisions on so many levels. All along, the call to discipleship here, rather than somewhere else, was unambiguous. I have failed in many ways to be the kind of disciple needed in this land, but the call to be on the journey never leaves me and I continue to be on the path. I pray that Jesus' Spirit will help us gain traction for his Kingdom here because that will be the best light by which to see the great beauty of this land and her people.

A PRAYER FOR THE JOURNEY

You will only grow if you are willing to quest for truth in a courageous and thorough way. There are many difficult questions that we face when we quest for truth. We need to be very prayerful in the journey. But know this also, searching for truth is not going to reassure you about the validity of all the things you currently believe. Some of your current beliefs may be revealed as half-truths. All of us are challenged and transformed in the journey of seeking truth.

Many years ago I found this prayer and adapted it slightly and have used it as a prayer in most of the sessions of all the groups that I have led in teaching the contents of this guidebook. I offer it now to you and your journey:

> *From the cowardice that shrinks from new truth,*
> *from the laziness that is content with half-truths,*
> *from the arrogance that thinks it knows all the truth,*
> *O God of Truth, deliver us.*
> *We ask this in the name of Jesus,*
> *the One who is the Way, the Truth and the Life. Amen*[1]

---

[1] This is a traditional Kenyan prayer, according to Joni Rodgers (https://www.goodreads.com/quotes/574568-there-s-a-traditional-kenyan-prayer-from-the-cowardice-that-dares). I have added the last sentence.

HOW TO USE THE BOOK

This book is meant to be experienced as a travel guide for explorers of the landscape of faith. You will see that it is loaded with information – not the kind of light read you can curl up comfortably with. On the contrary, it is meant to inspire you to put on your pilgrim shoes and explore pathways Jesus has led us on, discovering life as God intended it.

This guidebook can be read as any other non-fiction book is read – as an individual's journey of learning. You don't have to 'do' the book with other people. It is designed to be used for a number of possible journeys both long and short. The following options are designed to fit the needs and aspirations of different group sizes as well as individuals.

1. TRAVELLING ALONE

And after Jesus had dismissed the crowds, he went up the mountain by himself to pray. When evening came, he was there alone.
(Matthew 14.23)

The journey of this guidebook can certainly be followed by a reader on their own. You could journey slowly, reading just a few paragraphs a day. Or you could read more quickly and discipline yourself to cover a chapter a week.

Remember that you can use any of the shorter options or seasonal journeys too.

More information is available on the website.

2. AS A CONGREGATIONAL COURSE

'Therefore every scribe who has been trained for the kingdom of heaven is like the master of a household who brings out of his treasure what is new and what is old.' (Matthew 13.52)

I love this saying of Jesus because it expresses the exciting experience of inspiration that every preacher and teacher for the Kingdom has. It is not easy to describe, but it has to do with sparks of connection leaping between the pages of scripture and the current context. Analogies and metaphors come to mind that will bring home the teachings of Jesus. Inspiring stories are noticed and retold that reveal the current value and power of these 2000-year-old

Kingdom teachings. It is a very dynamic experience that is enhanced by the interaction with the hearer who asks questions (or shares stories and insights) which lead to further insights, inspirations and connections. In this experience we all realise that it has been a gift and a grace from Jesus' Spirit who is present giving birth to a Kingdom Consciousness.

The congregational course invites you to be part of such an experience in your local church. You have probably experienced courses that have been run – now you may use this guidebook to run a *Missing Jesus? Finding the Shepherd we lost* teaching series. What follows is a summary of the steps you can follow to run this teaching series in your congregation. More help is available on the www.missingjesus.net website.

Step 1. Decide who will teach the course.

Begin by choosing a teacher for the course. It doesn't have to be your minister, priest or pastor, as long as the person has good foundational knowledge of scripture and theology and has the gift of teaching.

Having someone known to your congregation personally teaching the content is the most real way for a congregation to journey through any discipleship material. I have found that it is weaker if the congregation must watch a video recording and listen to stories that are from contexts very far removed from their own. This is one of the main reasons why I have not included much of my own illustrative material in this guidebook. To put it differently, the content of this guidebook is for the most part undressed and needs to be given its clothes by the teacher that is presenting the content. This guidebook also functions like a textbook that often contains more information than is strictly necessary for the course. The teacher/leader decides what to focus on in the lesson and the participants can read up on the extra information before or after the lesson.

Step 2. Decide who will be responsible for the administration of the course.

The number of people attending will determine how many administrative and logistical people you need.

Step 3. Decide on the course dates.

The full journey will take between 17 and 21 weeks. If you go away to do the Holy Spirit chapters on a weekend retreat (which is highly recommended) then the journey can take 17 weeks. If you do one chapter a week then the journey will take 21 weeks. The venue for the Holy Spirit weekend should be booked.

There are also options for only doing a portion of the book rather than the whole book (see below).

Step 4. Decide on the programme format.

Decide on whether you will have a meal together at the beginning. Will you include worship? It certainly is best to at least have a refreshment break between the teaching session and the small group discussions.

Step 5. Start advertising and open the registration process for the course.

A useful information flyer about the book and course can be downloaded from the website.

Step 6. Choose small group facilitators and train them.

The best way to do the course is to allow for small group discussion after the teacher has presented the content of the chapter. The training needed for these small group facilitators is simple and will only require a two-hour session with them. This training is also available on the website.

Step 7. Purchase the guidebook for each participant.

Each member of the group should have their own guidebook. It will be very difficult to follow and engage with the contents without owning your own copy. You will find that there is so much content in the guidebook that you will want it available to you as a resource for future reference. I have written this guidebook as an attempt to be thorough about the foundations of Christian discipleship, therefore it should be reread every few years.

Please contact me, John Wessels, for the purchase of the guidebooks at info@missingjesus.net and via the www.missingjesus.net website. I can also currently be contacted at john@trinitylinden.org.za, or wesselsfamily@cybersmart.co.za and 011-8881740/1/2. If these details change then please contact your nearest Methodist Church to locate me in the Methodist Church of Southern Africa's directory. I can also be contacted to give advice on the use of the guidebook.

Step 8. Launch well.

Pay attention to reminders to participants, logistics for the launch, payment processes, etc.

Step 9. Run the course and intensify the prayers for the journey.

Pay special attention to feedback from small groups.

Step 10. Review and evaluate the course.

This course is an excellent way to make disciples and can therefore be run annually or even more than once a year (depending on the size of your church). When you review the course you can also identify which of the participants could be good small group facilitators for the next course.

3. SMALL GROUP GATHERING

> 'For where two or three are gathered in my name,
> I am there among them.' (Matthew 18.20)

Think about the verse above. Jesus is found to be amongst those who meet together in his name. To gather in his name is to gather as those who desire to be part of the Jesus movement in this world. Jesus is no longer 'missing' in such a group, but is present, particularly when there is a genuine desire to follow him as our Shepherd.

This section will give you advice and guidelines for using this guidebook as a book to study in a small group setting (Bible Study Group, Cell Group, Home Group, Class Meeting, Fellowship Group, Small Group, Discipleship Group, Connect Group, etc.) What follows is a summary of the steps you can follow to use the guidebook in a small group journey. More help is available on the www.missingjesus.net website.

Step 1. Download the latest information flyer from the website.

Share this information with your small group in order to decide about whether this is a good time for your group to follow this journey.

Step 2. Purchase the guidebook for each participant.

See Step 7 under 'As a congregational course' above.

Step 3. Decide on your weekly format for the study.

You are a group that already has an established flow to your gatherings. The journey through this guidebook should try and fit into that which is familiar to your group. It will quickly become evident that you need a lot of time in each gathering to read parts of the guidebook together and to discuss the content so that it is understood and appreciated. You may well need to abbreviate your usual time of fellowship for the duration of this study. If you are a new group then I propose the following simple and helpful structure for a gathering – the 'Four W's' of Welcome, Worship, Word and Works.

Step 4. Decide how long you will take to journey through the guidebook.

This guidebook is intended to serve as a journey of enabling each participant to understand, experience and participate in discipleship. The foundations for Christian discipleship are an enormous field of study, so the journey cannot be accomplished in a convenient six weeks. The longer a group takes, the better.

The quickest journey through this guidebook for a small group will be a journey of 21 weeks, although many participants have found this to be too quick. A journey of 21 weeks will depend on each participant reading the chapter before you meet as a group. Your group time will then be devoted to the suggested Bible Study and to discussing what has been read in the chapter. The small group leader may select a few paragraphs of importance to read as a group during the meeting.

If a group cannot dedicate 21 weeks but is committed to learning about discipleship then the only option would be to study a part of the book instead of the whole book. I give some guidelines for such an approach a little later in this section, under 'Shorter alternatives for both Small Groups and Congregational courses'. Guidelines for those groups that are prepared to spend longer than 21 weeks on this journey are given under 'Anno Domini' below.

4.   *ANNO DOMINI*: 'A YEAR OF THE LORD'

> *You crown the year with your bounty;*
>   *your wagon tracks overflow with richness.*
> *The pastures of the wilderness overflow,*
>   *the hills gird themselves with joy.*
> *The meadows clothe themselves with flocks,*
>   *the valleys deck themselves with grain,*
>   *they shout and sing together for joy.* (Psalm 65.11-13)

A small group may prefer to journey slowly and carefully through the content of this guidebook. This may well be the best way to really appreciate the content. You would simply do this by only reading as many pages as is comfortable each time you meet. If you read six pages a week then the guidebook would take you one year to complete. That would be a special year of study!

There will be more information for this option on the website.

5. SHORTER ALTERNATIVES FOR BOTH SMALL GROUPS AND CONGREGATIONAL COURSES.

This guidebook can be divided into three separate studies in the following way:

'Jesus rediscovered!' (Six-week journey)

Discover Jesus in fresh and exciting ways in this six-week small group study! In this journey participants will rediscover God's intention in creation and will understand what went wrong with God's plan. It will become clear how deeply and profoundly Jesus offers life to the world. Participants will be impressed that we are not only saved by Jesus' death, but also by his birth, life, ministry and resurrection. A powerful call to find the Shepherd we lost will be impressed upon each participant.

In this 'Jesus rediscovered' journey you will travel through chapters 2, 3, 4, 5, 14 and 15. See the website for more details of this journey.

'The Kingdom Consciousness Movement' (Nine-week journey)

This is a breakthrough study in the Kingdom of God and is a must for any person who desires to be a disciple of Jesus today! In this nine-week small group study participants will receive a thorough unpacking of Jesus' ministry of establishing the Kingdom of God.

In this 'The Kingdom Consciousness Movement' journey you will travel through chapters 5 to 13. See the website for more details of this journey.

'Salvation rediscovered' (Six-week journey)

Discover and experience the life-changing journey of entrusting yourself to Jesus and His Spirit! In this six-week small group study participants discover the personal transformation that is graciously given by God through faith, his Spirit and the spiritual disciplines.

In this 'Salvation rediscovered' journey you will travel through chapters 15 to 21. See the website for more details.

It will be essential that participants own the whole *Missing Jesus? Finding the Shepherd we lost* guidebook for any of the above three mini course options.

6. SEASONAL JOURNEYS

For everything there is a season, and a time for every matter under heaven. (Ecclesiastes 3.1)

The content of this guidebook cannot be absorbed in only one reading and you will be greatly enriched by having ways in which you reread some of it. Below I suggest how you may occasionally use the three main seasons of spiritual preparation as times to re-engage with the themes. I have more guidelines for these journeys on the website.

Finding Jesus in Advent

Journey with chapters 2 to 5. There are four weeks of advent and you could do one chapter a week.

Finding Jesus in Lent

Option 1: Journey with chapters 6 to 14. There are 40 days to Lent (excluding Sundays) and you could read about four pages a day.
Option 2: Lent is a time in which we seek to grow and deepen in our relationship with Jesus. To do this you could deepen your use of the spiritual disciplines during Lent. For this I suggest you follow chapters 20 and 21 and learn to practise the Lord's Prayer as suggested and also some of the other disciplines.

Finding Jesus and His Spirit between Easter and Pentecost

Journey with chapters 15 to 19. There are 50 days from Easter Sunday to Pentecost Sunday. Due to the central importance of the Trinity, I suggest you continue this journey through to Trinity Sunday, which is the Sunday after Pentecost. That would make it a 57-day journey. You would only need to read two pages a day.

USING THE 'GOD SPOKE TO ME ...' PAGES

Each chapter ends with a 'God spoke to me ...' page. This is a space to write notes about your special experiences whilst reading the chapter. These may be 'aha' or 'wow' moments. They may be moments of a deep sense of calling. They may be moments of personal conviction. They may be a place to record resolutions you take for your Christian journey. The idea with the 'God spoke to me ...' page is not to summarise the chapter for yourself, but rather to make sure you record the personally significant moments for you in the chapter. We often presume we will remember noteworthy things – but we frequently forget them. Jesus referred to this in his parable of the sower in which for various reasons seeds which God sows in our lives do not take deep root and bear fruit (Matthew 13.1-23; Mark 4.1-20; Luke 8.4-15.)

A GUIDEBOOK FOR THE WHOLE OF YOUR CHRISTIAN JOURNEY

I have written this guidebook with an intention of giving you, the pilgrim, a discipleship resource that will be useful to you for the rest of your life. I have tried to be comprehensive, thorough and practically useful in a long-term way. This also helps you understand why this book is longer than the average Christian book.

This is meant to be the kind of book that you refer to often to re-orientate yourself to the major features of the Christian landscape, or to read up and then explore parts of the landscape that have not yet seen your feet. Every Christian needs a guidebook leading them through the foundational truths of the faith movement started by Jesus. It is amazing to me that there are so few Christians who have such a book. I do hope and pray that this guidebook will provide you with the information, inspiration, guidance, foundational studies and direction you need to understand, experience and participate in the life that Jesus offers you and the world.

The Bible is the real guidebook for our journey through life – but this does not mean that other books are not necessary to help us find our way. My aim in this guidebook is to highlight the most important themes of scripture, especially of the teachings of Jesus. You will notice therefore that I include many quotations from scripture. Once I have helped you to discover the major themes of scripture, especially of the teachings of Jesus, you will notice that your appreciation and grasp of all of the Bible is greatly enhanced.

ACKNOWLEDGEMENTS

When we sit through all the rolling credits at the end of a movie we are amazed at how many people it takes to make one. This guidebook is no different. I hope to be able to give credit to the many people who have helped to make it possible.

Work on this guidebook has been ongoing since the year 2000 and in all that time I can truly say that Angela, my wonderful wife, has been incredibly supportive of the project! Angela has a wonderful, gentle, wise and sincere way of encouraging, supporting and advising me in this work. She also has a tremendous way of being practically helpful in support of the project itself and also in keeping home life sane while I have worked on various aspects of the guidebook and course. What has really amazed and blessed me is that her generosity of spirit has not waned as the re-writing project got to be a bit like Jack's beanstalk, and just grew and grew. I am truly blessed to have Angela in my life. As Ashlynn and Luke, our two children, have grown up they have also become supportive and encouraging in very special and endearing ways. Thank you Angela, Ashlynn and Luke for all your support in the years of 'Cornerstone for Life' and now 'Missing Jesus'. Your lives, more than anyone else's, have been affected by this project and I am so grateful for all the ways in which you have supported me.

My mom's support for this project and my ministry in general has been equally intense. She was intimately familiar with this guidebook's predecessor, 'Cornerstone for Life', because in those early days when this project was home produced and printed on the church photostat machine she served as one of the proof readers. Although she passed away in 2014 at the time that 'Cornerstone for Life' was starting to transform into 'Missing Jesus' the name Moira Wessels still belongs to the heartbeat of this guidebook.

I am an African writing from a South African perspective seeking to be particularly relevant to Southern Africa. I am unable to name all of the teachers, writers, books and preachers who formed me as a preacher, teacher and writer. This guidebook has been mostly shaped by Southern African thinkers, writers and books. This has been intentional – my desire has been to make a resource book for discipleship here that has been developed here. This is a Southern African stew. The following Southern Africans have been particularly important resources in the writing of this guidebook – Albert Nolan, Allan Boesak, Brian Gaybba, Desmond Tutu, Trevor Hudson, Tinyiko Maluleka,

Njongonkulu Ndungane, Teddy Sakupapa, Rothney Tshaka, John W. de Gruchy, Derek Morphew and Alan Storey.

The nature of this guidebook has also required me to use scholarship and resources from other parts of the world – all my resources are listed in the bibliography.

I am grateful to Media Associates International which is a Christian organisation for encouraging and empowering Christian writers and editors. I have benefited from one of their workshops, their webinars, the network they offer and the advice they give.

In 2017 the following Home Groups were part of piloting the guidebook as a small group resource. I am very grateful to the following leaders of those groups for their enthusiastic involvement and critique: Karl Weber, James Baker, Val Ochse, Londeka Mabaso, Denise Erasmus, Liz Theron, Johanna Denning, Peter Witbooi and Cathy Shimmin.

In 2018 I put my manuscript through a peer review process. I am so grateful to the following colleagues and theological thinkers who gave an enormous amount of time and attention to critiquing the manuscript: Alan Robinson, Andrew and Sandy Sieborger, Alan Storey, Donald Cragg, Vusi Vilakati, Sikawu Makubalo, Refilwe Tawana, Steve Briggs, Margaret Rundle, Maurice Adams, Mandy Hackland, Trevor Ruthenberg, Wayne Bower, James Massey, William Loader, Dimitri Stathoulis, Christian Williams, Everhard Etsebeth, Bill Webster, Delme Linscott, Musi Losaba, Purity Malinga, Mark Eccles, Louis Peters, Themba Gamedze, Derek Morphew, Roger Scholtz, Ike Moloabi, Dave Newton, Devin Fleetwood, Festus Marumo, Lea Marumo, Simon Prins, Rob Theunissen, Alan Bester, Brian Burger, Smanga Bosman, Alan Molyneux, Gcobani Vika.

I wish to express my grateful appreciation to the leaders of the Methodist Churches I have served who have supported me in this project. Up to this point this has been Sea Point Methodist, Brackenfell Methodist, Rosebank Methodist and Trinity Methodist, Linden.

I continue to be really grateful and dependent on the prayer support that I receive for this project. The following people have been part of a long-standing group of intercessors: Angela Wessels, Bob and Maryke Douglas, Michelle Douglas, Val Hardisty, Judy Steele, Val Pallister, Geoff Pallister, Patti Dwyer, Gail Steyn, Meryl Wright, Noreen Mackenzie, Denise Erasmus, Tshabedi Lekeka, Rob Theunissen, Thembi Mngomezulu, Ann De Vaal, Lesley Smithers, Sandra Stirling, James Steele and Alice Kent-Brown. As always in ministry there are more people praying for me than I know about! I mention these names only because they have pledged to pray in response to email updates I have sent them on a regular basis. You can be sure that many of them will continue praying for this project beyond the publication of this guidebook. I will continue to send them updates and things to pray for as this ministry unfolds.

Sandy Lightley's illustrations animate the text in wonderful and humorous ways. They also endear the reader to the developing drama. I am so grateful for the way in which she has put her skill at the service of this book project.

Writing this guidebook is one thing, but producing it is quite another and really does require an experienced team to do it well. The people of Porcupine Press were this team for me and I am very grateful to them. Visiting the headquarters of Porcupine Press feels a bit like being part of an underground movement plotting for renewal in society. Within an ordinary town house complex, inside Gail and David Robbins' unit, I found this movement's hub in two people incredibly committed to supporting and developing grassroots authors in Southern Africa. They believe in books and the upliftment and enlightenment that comes through them. Gail is the monarch overseeing in detail the whole production process. Frances Perryer was the editor and according to Gail had 'the most important job' in working on my manuscript. Wim Rheeder designed the cover and every bit of layout between the covers. Valda Strauss went through everything again as a proofreader. I am very grateful for the skill and heart each one of the team put into this guidebook.

Producing, printing and presenting this book in all its formats was an enormously costly exercise and was dependent on a number of financial donors. Without Justin Mason, the Matlala family, Brigid Schrieder, six other couples and one individual the book's retail cost would have needed to be doubled. I do ask you the purchaser to join me in my prayers of thanks for these important providers. Both you and I have been blessed by them.

I am so grateful for the generosity of Allan Boesak, Trevor Hudson, Derek Morphew, Yvette Moses, Njongonkulu Ndungane, Albert Nolan, Mamphela Ramphele and Faith Whitby for the recommendations that have graced the opening of this guidebook. They are faithful disciples of Jesus in Southern Africa and beyond and as such are my heroes. All of them are also high-profile leaders and have many requests on their time. It has therefore been enormously encouraging to me that they have been so very generous in the way in which they have supported this new resource for Christian education.

At the time of going to print I am working with Mark Becking on building the website for this guidebook. Mark has been an enthusiastic supporter of this guidebook since I met him five years ago and I am very grateful for all the support he has given me and most especially for the building of the website and securing the domain name.

These acknowledgements would not be complete for me without acknowledging that I feel that I have received from God so much more than I have been able to share in this guidebook. By this I am trying to say that although this book has been an enormous amount of work I am just a small tick on the great elephant-sized reality of God and God's great love for this world and how that love has come to us in Jesus and his Spirit. 'Acknowledge' is too small a word for that – no word is big enough.

All the passages of scripture are taken from the NEW REVISED STANDARD VERSION of the Bible.

PART 1

LOST

1

MISSING JESUS
WHAT HAPPENS WHEN YOU LOSE THE SHEPHERD?

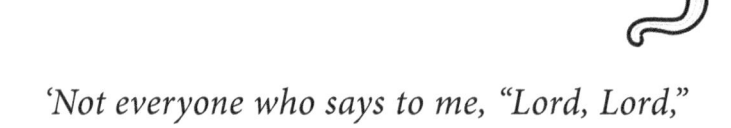

*'Not everyone who says to me, "Lord, Lord,"
will enter the kingdom of heaven, but only the one
who does the will of my Father in heaven.'*
(Jesus, recorded in Matthew 7.21)

Let me tell you a parable:

After many years of labour an inventor discovered the art of making fire. He took his tools to the snow-clad northern regions and initiated a tribe into the art – and the advantages – of making fire.

The people became so absorbed in this novelty that it did not occur to them to thank the inventor who one day quietly slipped away. Being one of those rare human beings endowed with greatness, he had no desire to be remembered or revered; all he sought was the satisfaction of knowing that someone had benefited from his discovery.

The next tribe he went to was just as eager to learn as the first. But the local priests, jealous of the stranger's hold on the people, had him assassinated. To allay any suspicion of the crime, they had a portrait of the Great Inventor enthroned upon the main altar of the temple; and a liturgy designed so that his name would be revered and his memory kept alive. The greatest care was taken that not a single rubric of the liturgy was altered or omitted.

The tools for making fire were enshrined within a casket and were said to bring healing to all who laid their hands on them with faith. The High Priest himself undertook the task of compiling a Life of the Inventor. This became the Holy book in which his loving kindness was offered as an example for all to emulate, his glorious deeds were eulogised, his superhuman nature made an article of faith. The priests saw to it that the Book was handed down to future generations, while they authoritatively interpreted the meaning of his words and the significance of his holy life and death. And they ruthlessly punished with death or excommunication anyone who deviated from their doctrine.

Caught up as they were in these religious tasks, the people completely forgot the art of making fire.[1]

That line, 'Caught up as they were in these religious tasks, the people completely forgot the art of making fire' describes a people who have missed the whole point of their religious existence. This is an important parable for Christians. Take a moment to reflect on what it says to you. Could it be that Jesus is missing in a similar way in your life? Read the following observations about Christianity. How true do you think they are? Do you also think that Jesus is missing, to varying degrees, in the lives of many Christians, church-goers and church structures? Do you have observations of this problem that are not in the list below?

---

[1] Anthony de Mello, *The Prayer of the Frog*, p. 7f. Story used with permission of publisher.

The teachings of Jesus are scantily known and poorly understood by many Christians. Jesus' public ministry included an enormous amount of teaching. So many forget that he was known as *Rabbi*, or 'Teacher'. He is certainly the most influential and best known of all Jewish rabbis and sages. Yet the content of this major aspect of Jesus' ministry is often neglected by many Christians. By this I mean that his teachings are rarely studied, systematised, known, followed or applied by Christians. Jesus, as teacher, is missing from their Christian faith. Such Christians are far from the flock that is faithful to Jesus the teaching Shepherd.

Christianity's identity in society has often been in clear violation of almost everything Jesus stood for. Pause a moment and appreciate how people in society know who Christians are. People are known to be Christians by the group they belong to. These groups would be characterised by certain rituals and forms of belonging. As we reflect on this we realise that the group's identity may not actually be closely aligned with the teachings of Jesus at all but may still be understood by society as Christian because they have called themselves a 'church' and 'Christian'. The group and all the individuals have the identity of being 'Christian' and society understands this – even though no attention may have been paid to Jesus and his teachings. These individuals and groups will of course use the name 'Jesus' in their gatherings but will decide for themselves what meaning to give to him. One may say that Christianity is defined in society sociologically, not theologically. Here we understand how it can be so easy to be identified as Christian while missing Jesus.

It is good to appreciate that an individual can gain an enormous amount of power in certain contexts with the title 'Christian' and related titles such as 'Pastor', 'Reverend', 'Bishop', 'Prophet' and 'Apostle'. Individuals can use this power of identity in society in ways that are completely anti-Jesus.

This reality has led to history showing that Christianity and Christians have done things that are in complete violation of what Jesus stood for. Many of these actions were atrocities that were committed in the name of Jesus. Jesus was 'missing' even though his name was present. The Church's Inquisition of the 13th to 19th Century tortured and executed several tens of thousands of people for not holding to an orthodox Christian faith. The Crusades of the 11th to 16th Century brutally killed between one million and three million people, most of them Muslims, or believed to be Muslims. The crusaders carried the cross as their emblem and believed they were serving Jesus in this feudal conquest. The Thirty Year (1618-1648) war in Europe was fought largely as a religious war between Protestants and Catholics. This war reduced the population of some European countries by between 25 and 40%. Add to these such awful acts as the Holocaust (six million Jews killed),

Rwandan Genocide (nearly one million killed) and Colonial and Apartheid rule – all carried out by self-proclaimed Christian countries.

At present the Central African Republic is in a black hole of a civil war. I call this war a 'black hole' because it is not broadcast to the world and no one is interested in it. It is a war that has Christian and Muslim militias fighting each other – including tactics such as machete attacks. A civil war currently being fought in the name of Jesus! These are just a few appalling examples of how far Christians have often strayed from their Shepherd.

We are now experiencing a growing trend of the abuse of church members through increasingly absurd and even life-threatening religious practices. Some church members are now forced by their pastors to eat snakes, rats, dog food, underwear and who knows what else. Pastors spray insect repellent (Doom) onto their congregants as an act of healing. These pastors do these things to assert, demonstrate and increase their power over the people who attend their church. There is no doubt that the dehumanising poverty and systemic neglect of some townships combined with both the ignorance and desperation of church members is the toxic cocktail that makes such absurd religious practices possible. Professor Rothney Tshaka, commenting on this, states that:

> 'Life-threatening faith practices become ubiquitous when discord between faith and reason is encouraged. What cannot be left out in this equation is the subject of abject poverty which drives the exploitation of the most vulnerable in society and the wretchedness that then abounds. These young leaders at grassroots level, upon realising the spiritual vacuum created because of the encouragement of the imbalance between faith and reason, now become drones that feed on the most vulnerable.'[2]

The gulf between such practices and Jesus of Nazareth is astronomically wide. In a phrase that is current, Jesus would say to this and many other violations of his ministry mentioned in this chapter, *'Not in my name!'*

Many of the crises we face in the world are because Christian leaders conform themselves to the demands of political, social and economic systems that are in violation of Jesus' teachings. I focus on leaders here because there should be no overlooking of the way in which the crises of poverty, environmental degradation, corruption, abuse of power (to name a few of our many crises) are the direct result

---

[2] Tshaka, T., 'From Marikana to believers eating snakes, ants, underwear and rats cheerfully – black theology of liberation in a time of empire and life-threatening faith praxis', in Welker, M., Koopman, N., Vorster, J., *Church and Civil Society: German and South African Perspectives*, pp. 201-202.

of choices made by leaders to advance systems and goals that are in complete violation of Jesus and his Kingdom. Yet this is done in the name of Jesus! So many leaders in Southern Africa and the Western world blatantly profess themselves to be Christian and arrogantly seek support from Christian constituencies.

Tinyiko Sam Maluleke has written insightfully of how we as Christians need to take ownership of the problems of distressed Africa, for this is also a predominantly Christian Africa. He asks the question:

> 'On the one hand we have a picture of a distressed and a distressing Africa, on the other, we have the picture of a massively Christian continent. How can this "tension" be resolved? … These situations must force us to think introspectively and honestly about the possible culpability of Christianity and Christian churches in some of the crises that Africa is facing.'[3]

This is particularly tragic when we had hoped we were entering a phase of justice in the 'new South Africa'. Unfortunately we have found that many of the core political, social and economic injustices of the 'old South Africa' are repeated in the 'new'. The faces of the leaders have changed but the new faces are repeating the ungodly ways of the previous leaders. This is true of leaders in politics and business. The focus on leaders here is entirely appropriate since their choices affect so many lives for so many generations. Repentance in this single group can make an enormous difference to an exponentially great number of people. We have Christian leaders who want to be followed but they are not following their shepherd.

In South Africa there has been much talk of 'State Capture'. What we are talking about here and in other parts of this chapter is 'Church Capture'.

In subtle but serious ways too many Christians hold to beliefs and lifestyles that are exploitative, unjust, ungracious, greedy, oppressive, pre-tentious, judgemental, unloving, narcissistic, lazy, violent and expedient. There are Christians to whom one or more of these descriptions apply and they possibly do not know that these are the beliefs and lifestyles that Jesus called to repentance. For Christians to realign ourselves with Christ, we need to pause and ask ourselves the question, 'How did we arrive here?' Sheep of this flock are actually far from Jesus the good Shepherd. Rather, the flock that is faithful to Jesus understands, experiences and participates in the life that he offers the world.

Christians generally conform to a dominant culture more than to the kingdom of God. Jesus would certainly want us to be non-conformist

---

[3] Maluleka T.S., 'Christianity in a Distressed Africa: A Time to Own Up', in *Missionalia* Vol. 26, No. 3 (November 1998), pp. 332-335.

to a consumeristic, pleasure-seeking and materialistic culture. Jesus would certainly want us to be non-conformist to the dominating and ladder-climbing practices that we are taught from childhood. Jesus would certainly want us not to conform to a society that just wants us to fit in and not make a fuss about injustices and violations of God's will, and not to conform to the narrow self-serving agendas of both political parties and media, even though those two are themselves often at odds with each other.

Here is a small, significant and often overlooked example. In this world of consumerism and pleasure seeking, the 'Holy Land', perhaps the most lethally divided place in the world, is rather a religious theme park that is visited by Christians who make no attempt to be a witness for Jesus' community-building kingdom. Christian tourists are content and delighted to have walked where Jesus walked – forgetting that following him is about following his ways.

Sheep are known to just unthinkingly follow where their nose leads them – how many of us Christians have our noses too deeply in the world of comforting pleasures to even notice that we have become separated from Jesus the Shepherd.

The current sins that the church 'names and shames' are almost all sins that are determined by the agendas of certain toxic pressure groups. Jesus certainly turned the spotlight onto sin in his day such as hardness of heart, unforgiveness, materialism, consumerism, greed, hoarding, pretentiousness and domination. These sins continue to be prevalent both inside and outside of church, but are mostly overlooked. But behaviours that Jesus never focused on as sin, but which he certainly would have encountered, are 'named and shamed' as sin today. Unusual sexual orientation is certainly the most obvious example of this tragic dynamic.

I mean 'tragic dynamic' because of the way in which brutality towards LGBTQI+ persons is worse in Africa than anywhere else in the world. At its most extreme expression there are gangs of Christian thugs who practise the horror of 'corrective rape' in the name of Jesus against lesbians. At the heart of such excessive focus on unusual sexual orientation is the dynamic of global homophobic pressure groups who find it convenient to use the church to further their aims. A simplistic selective and non-contextual reading of scripture is used and combined with swindling us into believing that LGBTQI+ lifestyles are 'un-African'. Homophobia is in fact one of the defining features of African Christianity and global pressure groups are glad to have Africa as their bulwark in their fight against LGBTQI+ people. Christianity is growing exponentially in Africa but the type of Christianity that is developing is being driven by a virulent form of neo-fundamentalism rather than by any real attention to Jesus and his teachings.

Many Christians are too attached to their theological label. Jesus would certainly want us to keep our inner freedom alive to be able to be faithful to the Kingdom rather than the demands of boxes like fundamentalist, conservative, liberal, liberationist, charismatic, reformed and evangelical. Jesus is of course violated if we are more deeply attached to labels like Methodist, Roman Catholic, non-denominational, independent, etc. For the sake of the Kingdom, Jesus would even want us to be able to work outside of a religious box altogether.

These labels make Christianity a deeply divided religion. Surely the mere factual reality of our deep divisions is a sign that we are missing Jesus. Surely Jesus would be a uniting influence if we were all following him more closely?

It is sobering to see that history shows that every church grouping that has chosen to honour its label rather than the truth has eventually awoken to find itself far from Jesus' way and in need of a long journey back to him. In South Africa the Dutch Reformed Church (DRC) was a theological defender of apartheid. This put it at odds with the other Reformed Churches in South Africa, all of which would later unite to become the Uniting Reformed Church in Southern Africa (URCSA). In 1982 the World Alliance of Reformed Churches (WARC) declared that apartheid was a heresy. This prompted a long journey of repentance for the DRC that now, 37 years later, is not complete in that the DRC and the URCSA are still unable to become one united denomination. The sticking point is the acceptance of the Belhar Confession, in which racial unity and defence of the oppressed is plainly supported.

Christians have often been irrelevant and wishy-washy. This is inconsistent for people who follow Jesus, who initiated God's reign on this earth. Surely God's reign makes for a lot of good in this world! The reign of God is about all the dimensions of human liberation in the here and now. This human liberation is the heavenly fire that Jesus came to bring on earth – but is missing in so many ways in a Christianity that has become dull, bland and tame. It is in these sins of omission (failing to do the good we should do as followers of Jesus) that we are exposed as missing Jesus.

An awareness of this is found in the press statement released by the Zimbabwe heads of Christian denominations in the wake of the military takeover of government and the house arrest of President Robert Mugabe. In this statement the church leaders acknowledge that the country is in a crisis that cannot only be blamed on the economy and the politicians. In the statement they say:

> 'The church has lost its prophetic urge driven by personality cults and superstitious approaches to socio-economic and political challenges...

> We all need to go before God and ask God to forgive us for ways in which we have contributed to the situation through neglect or wrong action.'[4]

It is a horrible thing to wake up and find that you have betrayed the Shepherd and that your own life and context are suffering terribly because of that.

Professor Rothney Tshaka writes movingly about this crisis when he reflects on a talk he gave to the Christian Youth Movement of the Uniting Reformed Church in Southern Africa. As I share some of what he wrote, please note his call for the urgency of the teaching ministry of the church, precisely because of the way in which congregants' beliefs do not appreciate the relevance of Jesus' ministry to the concrete realities of poverty:

> In that address I argued for the importance of having a teaching ministry for our church. That ministry, in my opinion, would entail providing opportunities for our congregants to be educated as we minister to them. To begin to see the relationship between the material and the spiritual and to eventually come to the realisation that poverty is in fact not God ordained and that it is not by God's design that most that are poor happen to be black. More significantly, I argued, context and historicity play vital roles as we strive towards that teaching ministry. I referred to the Easter celebrations which had become one of the key Christian events in our church calendar and reminded my audience of the disgusting objective of crucifixion which was essentially aimed at silencing those who dared to challenge delinquent hegemonies in their societies. I was very surprised, even disturbed, to realise that the perspective that I gave challenged the so-called spiritual perspective of the crucifixion which for them had nothing at all to do with politics.[5]

Wow – those words certainly wake us up to realise that following Jesus closely would lead to the very opposite of wishy-washy and irrelevant.

Church life is generally caught up with maintaining itself as an institution. An institution can be a very demanding entity. Congregations and denominations require large amounts of time and resources to be maintained. They do a lot of good and are mostly a valuable part of the community, which

---

[4] 'Zimbabwe heads of Christian Denominations – Zimbabwe between a crisis and a Kairos (Opportunity): The Pastoral Message of the Churches on the current situation date 15th November 2017'. This three-page letter bears the logos of Zimbabwe Council of Churches, Zimbabwe Catholic Bishops Conference, Evangelical Fellowship of Zimbabwe and UDACIZA.

[5] Tshaka, R.S., 'A perspective on notions of spirituality, democracy, social cohesion and public theology', in *Verbum et Ecclesia* Vol. 35, No. 3, 2014, Art. #1336, p. 2.

does mean that a lot of the time and resources are well spent. Very little time however is spent making disciples, or on studying the teachings of Jesus. An enormous amount of time is spent looking after the requirements of the organisation. It would be a mistake to think that it is wrong that the Jesus movement formalised itself into an institution. A movement will always need to organise and structure itself if it is to survive.

This institutional life is a necessary burden that the church must bear with a spirit of servanthood. But the problem is that often the maintenance of the institution becomes the goal of the institution. To the extent that the church becomes consumed by the institutional project, to that extent Jesus becomes missing.

As a minister of a local congregation I have intimate daily experience of this problem from the inside. All of us ministers, pastors and priests start out with a calling to lead people to Jesus but we end up facing a thousand other unrelenting needs, problems and agendas that easily make us lose our way.

Whenever church leaders critically reflect on our faithfulness as the church, the awareness arises that we are 'missing Jesus', his message and purpose in the life and work of the church. An example of this arose when church leaders gathered to reflect on the 30th Anniversary of the South African Kairos Document. Their conviction was found in their statement which they released on 20th August 2015 in which they made the following observation:

> 'We have reached a new moment of truth, a new Kairos. We recognize how the coming of Jesus and his teaching about a new kingdom and a new reign against the Roman empire of his day has completely passed us by. We lament that, by and large, the church of today has become distracted from this mission of preparing the way for God's reign.'

We are sheep who know that we have lost touch with our Shepherd!

Many Christians and churches have views that have the effect of trapping Jesus within their narrow definitions. The problem here is serious but difficult to describe and even more challenging to solve. We encounter the problem when churches try and define who is 'saved' and who is 'damned'. The effect of these views often results in the reality that Jesus is reduced to the criterion for belonging to the 'saved' – that is, 'You must believe in Jesus to be saved.'

It is not a problem to assert the importance of a personal response to Jesus – read on and you will be more convinced than you may previously have been of this vital response to Jesus. Nor is it a problem to assert that we find salvation in Jesus. It is however a serious problem when we give the world the impression that Jesus is merely the criterion of belonging to the saved. The view that Jesus came to earth to be the criterion for deciding who is 'saved' and who is 'damned' is very problematic. Such a view is sectarian and is completely the opposite of the focus and intention of Jesus' ministry.

As this guidebook will make clear, Jesus' mission cannot be reduced to the confines of any institution, even if that institution is the church. People who have reduced Jesus to the key name in a church's dogma are not actually following the real Jesus; they are following a caricature of him. The Jesus they are following is a misrepresentation and a distraction from the real Jesus. When this happens in the life of the church it has lost the Shepherd.

In our digital age Christians are able to create their own profile of Christian spirituality and this profile often excludes discipleship of Jesus. In a digital age people can be much more selective about the kind of Christian spirituality they expose themselves to. People are also able to be more selective about whose sermons and teachings they listen to – and even if they want to listen at all. In this way their own use of their Bible apps enables them to develop their personal ideal profile of their faith.

Research into the kind of Christian spirituality that has developed in this context shows that people have tailored a spirituality that satisfies their own needs and leaves discipleship of Jesus out of the profile. Rev. Dr Pete Phillips, as Director of CODEC Research Centre for Digital Theology at the University of Durham, has highlighted this in research that tracks the favourite Bible verses used and shared on Bible apps where they have noticed that there is a tendency

> 'to shift into what we call a therapeutic spectrum, in other words they tend to be verses which are saying nice things about people, lots of love and health and happiness and so on …. It means that people are following a kind of cultural agenda … it is less doctrinal, … (these verses are) a wealth of click-bait which is nice and airy and fairy, lots of platitudes about what the Christian faith is about, certainly no reference in the top verses that are being shared to what Jesus did in history. So you end up with a kind of Godless Jesus-less Christianity which is actually an oxymoron. You cannot have Christ-less Christianity. We are moving much more to a spiritualisation of this, rather than it being seen as a religion…. There has always been a strand of Christianity which is about therapy, about making people whole, there is a core strand to that, but if that becomes the only strand then I think we have lost something.'[6]

---

[6] This is a verbatim quote from an interview with Dr Phillips in 'Religion in a Digital Age – How technology is changing belief, faith and religious practice', a Manuela Saragosa Business Daily podcast on the BBC World Service. Aired 23rd August 2017.

Simply put, the digital age is developing a personalised form of Christian spirituality that is missing Jesus! Have you noticed this?

Too many Christians believe that Jesus came to earth simply to die on the cross. As a result of this belief they do not take his teachings and ministry seriously since, in their view, those are minor details.

Such a reduction of Jesus' life and ministry is the result of a very high-altitude view that looks down on the Jesus event as a cosmic sacrifice for sins, so that those who believe in him can be forgiven and go to heaven when they die. From that high altitude life on earth has no real significance except to be the place where one makes a decision for Jesus – a decision that enables that person to spend eternity in heaven, which is the only place that has significance. In essence Jesus is nothing more than a name that must be believed in. In this view one is almost entirely missing the meaning of Jesus' birth, life, ministry, death and resurrection.

For many people, including Christians, Jesus is missing from the list of the world's most intelligent people. Is this perhaps part of the reason why Jesus as teacher is ignored by many? If Jesus was regarded as someone of robust intelligence, knowledge, insight and wisdom then it would follow that you would become a student of his teachings. If what Jesus said was regarded as the most important teachings on dealing with life as it 'really' is, then you would eagerly be a lifetime disciple of all that he said. Generally however Jesus is regarded as brave but not brilliant. The first disciples however were different – they were so impressed with the brilliance and richness of Jesus' teachings that they were radical in their learning and applying and untiring in their passing on of the teachings. For too many, Jesus is a brave sheep rather than a brilliant shepherd, and so they are not bothered with following him.

There are many who seek a New Age type of spirituality because Jesus has not been introduced to them as real hope for the world and their lives. Jesus has not been presented to them as relevant and vital for the world and their lives, nor as a real-life personality dealing with real-life issues. Jesus is therefore missing from their lives.

For many, this lack, combined with their distaste for religion, has led them to seek spirituality without religion. This is a common quest today, but many have found it to be unsatisfactory and may now have very little meaning that holds their life together. This quest for spirituality has led many to pick and choose from different religions and spiritualities and so end up with a buffet of practices that have no unifying foundation and also minimal spiritual value. If you find some echo in your journey with what I have just described I do hope that you will read on. My task is not to get you into religion but rather to show how a relationship with Jesus leads to abundant life.

Even those who have never been Christians need to return to the Shepherd they lost. We humans have our start with God and so in a profound way we all do come from God. Life begins in union with God; we begin life as the result of the will of God and we begin life as God's project. With this insight then we understand life as a journey of returning to God, a journey of seeking that unity and oneness with God that we all knew in our beginning. We all inevitably lose our unity with God and need to return to God. This is why it is appropriate to speak of 'finding the shepherd we lost' even if we have never been a Christian.

Many have a longing for Jesus to be experienced as closer to them. Many years ago I noticed that I went through periods of intense longing for Jesus, for his nearer presence. I noticed that this feeling would always be most poignant on Ascension Day – when we remembered Jesus' ascension to the right hand of the Father. I thought to myself, 'What is there to celebrate in Jesus leaving us?'

As I spent time reflecting on these feelings I realised that I needed to get to know Jesus better and so I decided to begin a journey of frequent and disciplined reading of the Gospels. As I did this Jesus became so much more familiar and real to me. The Holy Spirit has worked in rewarding ways through my journey of seeking to get to know Jesus better. Over the years I have encountered many others who are missing Jesus in this particular sense of the phrase – they are longing for Him. This guidebook, combined with your own attention to the Gospels, will be used by the Holy Spirit to make Jesus the Shepherd a near and living presence for you.

AN INVITATION TO SEEK JESUS

Are there some observations of missing Jesus that I left out that you would want to add? Could you recognise some of these in your life and in the society around you? On their own each of the above aspects of missing Jesus are serious enough, but altogether they amount to a fundamental crisis in Christianity – especially Christianity in Southern Africa. Surely, nowhere and in no one person do all of these problems combine at once – but we can unfortunately recognise all these observations as true to varying degrees.

It is time to see the opportunity in the crisis – that Jesus has opened our eyes to these matters so that we may turn to him in fresh ways. Awareness of a crisis is always a gift, doubly so if one has received the awareness before all of the disastrous consequences have happened. There is time to repent – not merely to avoid disaster, but rather to be able to experience the life that Jesus offers the world.

G.K. Chesterton observed that 'The Christian ideal has not been tried and found wanting; it has been found difficult and left untried.'[7] There is so much powerful truth to this statement and so much that is central to this guidebook.

Jesus does expect us to seek him as our Shepherd. We are humans, not sheep! We have intelligence and can take responsibility if we are far from our Shepherd. In fact Psalm 8 affirms that people were created *'a little lower than God, and crowned (them) with glory and honor. You have given them dominion over the works of your hands; you have put all things under their feet'*. The language of 'sheep' and 'Shepherd' are of course metaphors and should not be taken to absolve us of our responsibility as intelligent humans.

The common thread in all of the observations above is the lack of obedience to the actual teachings of Jesus. At its worst, Christianity seems to be an amorphous religion that sees the practical application of Jesus' teachings to be irrelevant or unnecessary. It is then a religion that bears his name but not his character. Such distance from Jesus accounts for the way in which some individual Christians have so little life, love or hope to offer in the home or society.

The word 'missing' by definition means 'absent from the proper or accustomed place'.[8] In each of the situations above Jesus was not allowed to take up his proper place as Lord. Finding him therefore means that we allow him to take up his proper place as Lord.

The subheading of this guidebook, 'Finding the Shepherd we lost', has been a little controversial because some people are uncomfortable with the idea that we can lose Jesus as a shepherd. They also believe that Jesus is the one who looks for lost sheep – we are not the ones that look for a lost shepherd. Of course the shepherd is not lost, it is we who have wandered from the shepherd or rebelled against him.

Yes, it is true that Jesus is constantly looking for the lost sheep. However, Jesus does teach that we can lose the shepherd and it is a teaching that we need to always keep ourselves conscious of. The following are some examples from our Bibles about the important role we have to 'find' Jesus:

- John the Baptiser made it clear that we have a responsibility to prepare a path for Jesus by way of repenting of our waywardness (Luke 3.1-20).

---

[7] The G.K. Chesterton website says that this comes from his book *What's Wrong with the World*, 1910. I accessed this quote from https://www.chesterton.org/quotations-of-g-k-chesterton/ on 26/6/2018.

[8] *The New International Webster's Comprehensive Dictionary of the English Language*.

- When Jesus called disciples he used the phrase 'follow me'. That is clearly a responsibility he was giving them in relation to himself – namely that they had to follow him and his teachings closely (Matthew 4.19; 8.22; 9.9; 19.21; John 1.43; 12.26; 21.19).
- Jesus laments that the towns of Chorazin, Bethsaida and Capernaum had not repented even though his deeds of power had been done in them (see Matthew 11.20-24 and Luke 10.13-15). Jesus the shepherd had come to these towns but they had not changed their ways in order to be faithful to him.
- The parable of the prodigal son is a story about a rebellious and irresponsible son who eventually comes to his senses and returns home to his father. Core to this story is the need for the son to come to his senses as a necessary precondition for his return home.
- In one of his Judgement Day descriptions Jesus separates us into two groups in the same way that a shepherd separates sheep from goats (Matthew 25.31-46). The sheep are the ones welcomed into the Kingdom and eternal life, while the goats are sent to eternal punishment. The sheep are those who have faithfully followed Jesus the Shepherd, while the goats are those that have not. It is acceptable then to assert that many have lost Jesus as Shepherd because Jesus makes the same point in this judgement day teaching!
- Jesus uses the metaphor of sheep running away from him the shepherd when he predicts that the disciples will desert, deny and even betray him during his arrest and trial. Just because Jesus is the shepherd does not guarantee that a sheep does not get separated from the shepherd. In the span of history it is clear that many Christians have repeated the desertion, denial and even betrayal of Jesus that the first disciples did. Matthew 26.31: *Then Jesus said to them, 'You will all become deserters because of me this night; for it is written, "I will strike the shepherd, and the sheep of the flock will be scattered."'* And John 16.32: *'The hour is coming, indeed it has come, when you will be scattered, each one to his home, and you will leave me alone.'*
- This 'missing Jesus' theme is also a message that the ascended Jesus gives to John the Apostle on the island of Patmos in a vision. Having appeared to John in a vision the first message that Jesus gives to John is for the people in the Church in Ephesus who have lost him and fallen away from following him. In very moving words Jesus says, *'You have abandoned the love you had at first. Remember then from what you have fallen; repent, and do the works you did at first.'* (Revelation 2.4-5).
- Later on in the same vision there is a message for the church in Laodicea

who are believers who have drifted far from radical discipleship. In the language of this vision they have become lukewarm and Jesus stands knocking at the door of their lives longing to enter again. Clearly these are sheep who need to find the shepherd they lost. Often Christians think that the famous image of Jesus standing and knocking at the door of our lives applies to non-Christians, but in this passage we see that it first applied to Christians.[9]

To say that Jesus is missing is not the same as saying that he is absent. God is omnipresent, which is a fancy word to say that God is always and everywhere present and available. But God is present and mostly ignored and often rebelled against. In this sense it is important to assert that Jesus is present but not followed and is therefore missing as our Shepherd.

---

[9] Revelation 3.14-20: *And to the angel of the church in Laodicea write: The words of the Amen, the faithful and true witness, the origin of God's creation: 'I know your works; you are neither cold nor hot. I wish that you were either cold or hot. So, because you are lukewarm, and neither cold nor hot, I am about to spit you out of my mouth. For you say, "I am rich, I have prospered, and I need nothing." You do not realize that you are wretched, pitiable, poor, blind, and naked. Therefore I counsel you to buy from me gold refined by fire so that you may be rich; and white robes to clothe you and to keep the shame of your nakedness from being seen; and salve to anoint your eyes so that you may see. I reprove and discipline those whom I love. Be earnest, therefore, and repent. Listen! I am standing at the door, knocking; if you hear my voice and open the door, I will come in to you and eat with you, and you with me.'*

The role of all leaders in the church is to be the 'elder' who must 'tend the flock of God that is in your charge' – a metaphor that implies that sheep can stray from Jesus, who is the 'chief shepherd'. This guidebook is my attempt as an elder to bring sheep back to their shepherd.[10]

When we find the Shepherd we lost we discover that what has happened is that we have been found by him. Any awareness of being lost, any desire for growth, any quest for truth, any dissatisfaction with current discipleship and any awareness that one may be missing the full influence of Jesus – this is all given to us by the Holy Spirit. Any finding, any discovery, any answers, any understanding, any growth, and any transformation – this too is given to us by the Holy Spirit. This guidebook celebrates that the journey of finding the Shepherd we lost is really a journey of being found by the Good Shepherd who is always seeking out the lost sheep.

In closing, ancient wisdom says, 'The most important thing is to not forget the most important thing!' What is the most important 'thing'? To remain close to Jesus our shepherd. This book is offered to you as a guide for that journey.

---

[10] 1 Peter 5.1-4: *'Now as an elder myself and a witness of the sufferings of Christ, as well as one who shares in the glory to be revealed, I exhort the elders among you to tend the flock of God that is in your charge, exercising the oversight, not under compulsion but willingly, as God would have you do it – not for sordid gain but eagerly. Do not lord it over those in your charge, but be examples to the flock. And when the chief shepherd appears, you will win the crown of glory that never fades away.'*

Missing Jesus?

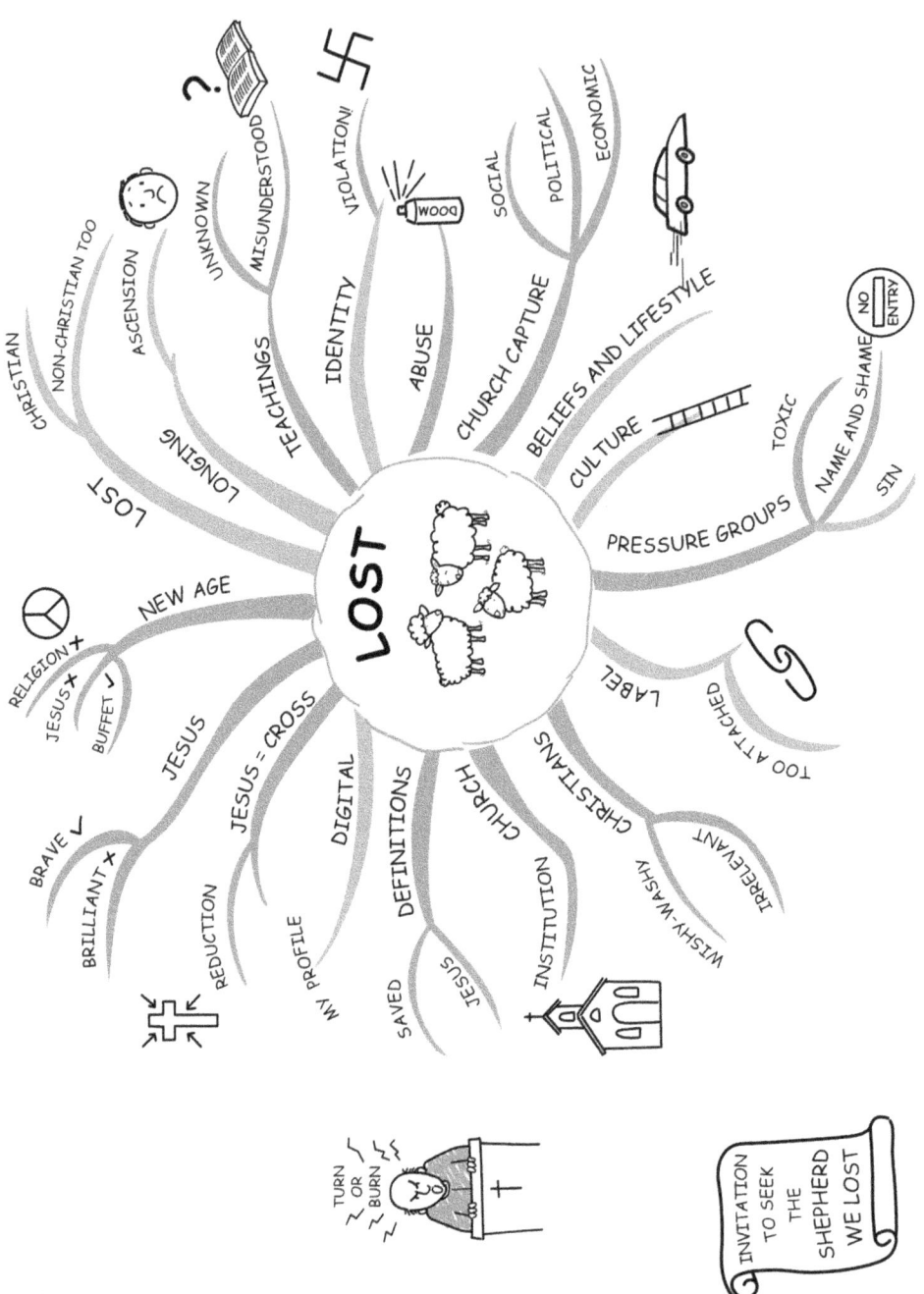

SUGGESTIONS FOR DISCUSSION, REVISION, REFLECTION AND APPLICATION

(These questions are intended for group work, but can easily be adapted for personal use.)

1. What is the most important message to you in this chapter? (Remember to also make a note of this on your 'God spoke to me' page.)
2. Icebreaker question: What are your hopes as you start this journey through this guidebook?
3. Turn to Matthew 16.13-20:
   a. What stands out for you as you read this passage?
   b. Peter is confident, '*You are the Messiah*'. In what ways is Jesus hope for the world today?
   c. Who do you know who carries the kind of confidence Peter had? Tell the group about this person.
   d. What obstacles are in the way of you fully living the hope Jesus offers the world?
4. Below are a variety of suggestions and questions to aid your appreciation of this chapter. Do not attempt to do all of them! Choose those that are most appropriate to your unique situation and/or group. The questions are designed to help variously with revision, understanding, appreciation, reflection or application of the content.
   a. In what ways has this chapter prompted you to think about how closely or distantly you follow Jesus?
   b. In what ways are you personally aware of distance from Jesus? Perhaps you experience this as a deep longing for a closer relationship and walk with Jesus?
   c. Why has Jesus become missing in the lives of so many people, Christians, churchgoers and church structures in history and in the world today?
   d. What is Jesus' proper place in our lives and in the world? Answer this question in your own words and convictions.
   e. How can God be omnipresent but Jesus be missing?
   f. What criteria would you use to discern whether something done in Jesus' name really is true to Him?

g. What would you add to this chapter's listing of the ways in which Jesus is missing in the Christians, church and society of today?
h. What do you consider to be the most serious way in which Jesus is missing in society today?
i. Speak about the ways in which Jesus may be missing in your life.
j. How would you describe your present longing (or lack of longing) to follow Jesus?
k. Who gets the credit if I do follow Jesus again?

GOD SPOKE TO ME ...

2

COMMUNITY

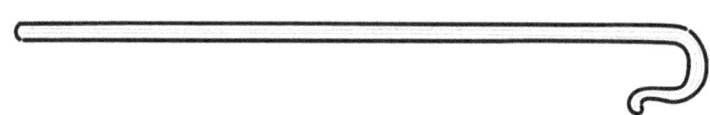

God is Love. (1 John 4.16)

Before the beginning, before anything that exists came into being, there was only God. This was not a lonely existence!

Why do I say this? Why do I want to start the journey of the guidebook at a place that is even before the beginning? The reason is that there is something very important to appreciate about God. Many of our problems exist because this core truth is overlooked by believers and non-believers alike.

Please come with me on a journey of finding God.

BEFORE THE BEGINNING THERE WAS COMMUNITY
Not an old man with a white beard sitting on a throne!

One thing you can be very sure of is that God is not an old man with a white beard sitting on a throne in heaven. God is much closer, more real, substantial and essential than that. This makes it difficult; God is so close and so fills every part of life that it is difficult to point and say 'that is God'.

There is a story that really helps us to realise this. The story starts with a father and son sitting on a rocky ledge next to a stream, when the father points to the stream and says, 'Without water we will die – it is essential for life'. A fish is swimming below the rocky ledge that the father and son are sitting on and this little fish hears the conversation and realises that he himself does not know what water is, nor where it is. So the fish starts a quest to find water. He looks for it all day, everywhere, even going into deep tunnels in the stream and nearly getting eaten by the eel that lived there. At one point the fish even tried to get out of the stream and look for water on the rocky ledge where the father and son had sat, but fortunately for the fish he couldn't get that right. Eventually, that night the fish returned to his mother all in a panic: 'Mama, Mama, what's water? I must find water or I'll die!'

Now, if the mother fish was truly wise then she would have been able to tell her child that he lives immersed in water, and the reason he misses it is not that it is so far away but, paradoxically, so close. But the baby fish would be very fortunate indeed if his mother had the eyes to see that.

For the sake of my point may I say that most fish spend their whole lives thinking that water is something separate from them, something unseen and distant, intangible and mysterious, something belonging to another realm of being.[1]

Do you see what I am showing you? In that last line replace the word 'fish' with 'people' and 'water' with 'God': Most people spend their whole lives thinking that God is something separate from them, something unseen and distant, intangible and mysterious, something belonging to another realm of being.

As a start, I invite you to search for God without going anywhere. Just think about your experience of life so far and think about how you have thought about that experience. You do not even have to be a person who believes in God to see what I will point out. Firstly, you would agree that there certainly is a foundational force and energising power that makes life possible. Everything seems to be held together in unity, order and regularity, even though there is also much spontaneity which seems to come from the same force that determines the order. Have you noticed this?

Secondly, you would agree that there is also a source from which values come. Things like truth, learning, goodness, care, justice, love and beauty are definite realities. These realities seem to come from some power or wellspring. History is filled with a revealing force that has brought this to light. This revealing force has been at work in both 'secular' and 'sacred' quests for learning. Have you noticed this?

Thirdly, you would agree that people have potential for more than their current level of existence. Latent within them, unrealised in their living, are possibilities for growth, survival, achievement, victory and greater wholeness. Not only do these exist but there seems to be a force that entices them toward these possibilities. Part of this dynamic is a force that moves us toward co-operation with others and therefore these possibilities for growth and greater wholeness are not only possibilities for individuals but also for nature and society. There is definitely a force of connection at work in life. Have you noticed this?

---

[1] Cynthia Bourgeault, in her book *Mystical Hope: Trusting in the Mercy of God*, p. 20, imagines this fish who says, 'Mama, Mama, what's water? I gotta find water or I'll die!' I have developed the above story around it.

Friends, what you have noticed is God – God who is real, foundational and essential to life. This is God who is part of life, not separate from life; God who is seen and experienced by all. God is not invisible, intangible and distant. This is God who is part of our realm of being.

I realise that it needs faith for you to agree to labelling these realities as 'God'. I realise that if you are not a person of faith you may not want to agree with the previous paragraph. I do however invite you to stay with us for our journey of 'finding God'.

In the observations above we have not only noticed God – but we have noticed God as three persons! We have noticed that God is Trinity. We have noticed that God is three distinct forces and dynamics that make life as we know it possible. These three forces are known as the three persons of the Trinity. These three persons are intimately related to each other in the reality that God is. This may seem difficult to grasp now, but I hope it will become clearer as we continue our journey.

For now I point out that in the first instance above we were observing God as creator and origin of life. In the second instance above we were observing God as revelation and the eternal Word. In the third instance above we were observing God as Spirit and animator of life.

Microscopes and telescopes

I invite you to continue this journey as we now look at life through microscopes. Amazingly we discover a trinity of reality at the core of life. The most basic building block of the entire physical universe is the atom. The atom is an orbiting structure of three particles – proton, electron and neutron – in constant interaction with one another. In this journey I invite you to note not only the reality of the threeness but also of how essential the interplay between the proton, electron and the neutron is. In this guidebook we will come to appreciate fully that relationships are core to the life God created.

We discover that relationships are the foundational nature of reality when we look through telescopes too. The pattern that we find in atoms is repeated in the universe. In the universe the pattern of parts orbiting and relating to each other is repeated amongst the planets, stars (suns) and even galaxies. Everything is relational to everything else.

Turkish Delight

Now let us continue this journey of finding God by going back in time. Let us go back in time to the fourth century in eastern Turkey and pay attention to what a group of theologians known as the Cappadocian Fathers are saying.[2] They are the ones who have done the most advanced thinking on the nature of God and it is thanks to their philosophy that we have the description of God that we call the 'Trinity'.[3]

Did you know that the doctrine of the Trinity is not described in our Bibles? In fact very few doctrines are described in our Bibles. The work of theologians is to try and make coherent sense of what the Bible describes. The doctrine of the Trinity is our best explanation for the way in which God is described and experienced in our Bibles.

The Cappadocian Fathers helped us to understand that God is three persons, traditionally known as Father, Son and Holy Spirit. All have their own identities and are in a loving relationship with each other. God has an inner life of three persons whilst having a single nature which is inseparable and undivided. The three are defined by their relationship to each other and so are one in the most profound and deepest way. Technically the Fathers described God as one Divine Substance, but three Divine persons. In other words, God is one Being but three persons.

From the Cappadocian Fathers and other theologians of the first 500 years of Christianity we have come to understand the following about the three persons of the Trinity. The first person is the source of all that exists. This is God the creator. The first person is referred to as Father, Love, Unbegotten Origin of all else and sometimes Mother. The second person is the one who reveals the will of the creator and executes the Creator's will. The second person is referred to as Son, Beloved, begotten expression of all the Father is, Word, Redeemer and Jesus. The third person is the Spirit of love between the first and the second person and also their love for all that is created. The third person is referred to as the Holy Spirit, Spirit of God, Spirit of Jesus, or simply Spirit, Lover, Advocate, animator of life, Love-bond between Father and Son, Love-bond of the Father and the Son for all that exists and also the Love-bond where it exists between parts of creation.

The greatest gift of the Cappadocian Fathers is their mystical description of the relationships between the three persons and how this results in a profound oneness. They have helped us to understand that the three persons love each other and give themselves to each other to such an extent that they are one

---

[2] The Cappadocian Fathers were Basil the Great (330-379), who was Bishop of Caesarea; Gregory of Nyssa (335-395), who was Bishop of Nyssa and Gregory of Nazianzus (329-389), who became Patriarch of Constantinople. They were all born in Cappadocia.

[3] The doctrine of the Trinity was finalised in the fifth century. The creed is commonly known as the Athanasian Creed.

through the act of loving self-giving. Through sharing themselves so fully in the person and work of each other they are united by their love into a single loving community and identity. God is the eternal community of oneness. God is an eternal community of Love.

This is why it is so appropriate that John defined God as 'love' – see 1 John 4.16: *'God is love, and those who abide in love abide in God, and God abides in them.'* The divine community that God is would break down if God were not love. This active community of love is also the reason why the word 'God' is sometimes best understood as a verb rather than a noun.

Deep within the reality of God as Trinity we are able to appreciate why God's love is so multidimensional. The Father's love is expressed in being the *source* of all that exists and of all that is good. The Son's love as the eternal Word is expressed through *revealing* the nature and will of the creator. The Spirit's love is expressed through the *bonding* character of love.

Wow – what delight! Pause and say a prayer of worship.

The core of reality is communal

We really have now found God! We have discovered that God is a real force and presence and person who has brought all that exists into being and who is at work in this world as revelation to humanity and a profound life force amongst all life forms. Earlier, when we looked through our microscopes and telescopes, we noticed that the core of reality is relational. This makes complete sense because the core of God is relational. What we are seeing is a family resemblance between God and God's creation. What we are seeing is that both science and spirituality have discovered that relationality is the core of reality. We live in a Trinitarian universe, one where the infinite energy of relationships is the ultimate reality. All of this we have discovered in our theology and science since Bible times. It would be good to end this search with three more steps back in time, this time in our Bible to see how they experienced God then.

What Jesus knew

We stop first at Jesus. I want to briefly mention just one passage now. In John 14.8-31 we read how Jesus speaks of his oneness with God, who he refers to as 'Father'. For example, he says:
- *'Whoever has seen me has seen the Father'*
- *'I am in the Father and the Father is in me'*
- *'I will do whatever you ask in my name, so that the Father may be glorified in the Son. If in my name you ask me for anything, I will do it'*

- 'I will ask the Father, and he will give you another Advocate, to be with you forever. This is the Spirit of truth'
- 'The Advocate, the Holy Spirit, whom the Father will send in my name, will teach you everything, and remind you of all that I have said to you.'

Together in those few verses it is clear that there are three persons to this divine community and that they are working together. If you would like to read more passages from Jesus' ministry that have a strong Trinitarian flavour then read:
- At Jesus' baptism (Matthew 3.13-17, Mark 1.9-11, Luke 4.1-13) we see Father, Son and Holy Spirit as different persons in the story.

- Jesus speaks of Father and Spirit in one verse in John 15.26.
- John 16.12-15 powerfully makes the close relationship of the three persons of the Godhead clear.
- John 17.11, Jesus prays to the Father that the disciples *'may be one, as we are one'*.
- Matthew 28.19, Jesus commissions the disciples to make disciples, he instructs them to baptise these new followers into the Trinitarian faith: *'Go therefore and make disciples of all nations, baptizing them in the name of the Father and of the Son and of the Holy Spirit.'* Clearly Jesus wants us to be a people who know that God is Community.
- John 20.21-22, Jesus again witnessing to Trinity, this time after the resurrection.
- If you would like to read passages that refer to the Trinity in our own lives then see Romans 5.1-5; 8.12-17; 15.30; 1 Corinthians 6.11; 12.4-6; 2 Corinthians 1.21-22; 3.3; 13.11-13; Galatians 4.6; Ephesians 4.3-6; 2 Thessalonians 2.13-17.

What Abraham saw

Our next stop in our journey back in time in our quest to find God (which is like a fish trying to find water) is a fascinating stop. We go back at least 2000 years before Jesus to watch Abraham receive a visit from God. Genesis 18 tells us *The LORD appeared to Abraham by the oaks of Mamre, as he sat at the entrance of his tent in the heat of the day.* But what has fascinated so many people is that this appearance of the Lord to Abraham involves three men! *He looked up and saw three men standing near him. When he saw them, he ran from the tent entrance to meet them, and bowed down to the ground. He said, 'My lord, if I find favor with you, do not pass by your servant. Let a little water be brought, and wash your feet, and rest yourselves under the tree. Let me bring a little bread, that you may refresh yourselves, and after that you may pass on – since you have come to your servant.'*

Even here, so deep in the Old Testament, is this reference to God as a community of three![4] Throughout this appearance the author refers to these three men as 'LORD' (all the letters capital, which is the English way of writing Yahweh).

Three thousand five hundred years after this event, the Russian iconographer Andrei Rublev made an icon of this scene and named it 'The Trinity'. It is the most famous of all icons and is also the most profound way in which the Trinity has ever been visualised.

---

[4] Our stance in this reading of Genesis 18 is not to say 'The writer believed in the Trinity'. Rather our stance is to stand in awe at the way in which God appeared as three men to Abraham whilst at the same time God was making Abraham the spiritual father of monotheism (belief in one God).

Last stop is at the beginning

Our last stop is to note something very interesting at the beginning of our Bible. In Genesis 1.1 we meet God as creator, *In the beginning when God created the heavens and the earth.* Then interestingly in the second verse we meet God as Spirit! We read, *...the earth was a formless void and darkness covered the face of the deep, while the Spirit of God swept over the face of the waters.* And then in the third verse we meet God as Word as he speaks creation into being! We read, *Then God said, 'Let there be light'; and there was light.*

Now we quickly admit that the author in the original literary context would not have been trying to convey the idea of Trinity here. We are reading 'Trinity' into this as Christians. Having said that, I think it is amazing and important that the core three different persons of the triune God can be seen beneath the surface of the opening three verses of our Bible![5]

I hope you have enjoyed this journey of discovering God. In this journey we have discovered that the core of God is relational. God is the eternal community of oneness. God is a community. So, before the beginning there was Community! Before creation there was Community – the Community that God is. Eternally there is the Community of God.

IN THE BEGINNING COMMUNITY CREATED COMMUNITY
Creation, the work of infinite Love

God is love and is therefore a giver, and because he is infinite, his giving is done on a scale of infinity. God gave by lovingly, joyfully, creating the universe. It is a work of art, a marvel, an incredible expression of God's intimate and expansive genius.

Creation is truly marvellous as a functional unit (ecosystems) and amazing in its diversity (9 000 flowering plants in the Cape Floral Kingdom!) and awe-inspiring in its expressiveness (many birdsongs go well beyond the demands of biological necessity). It is precious in its experience (the experience of love!) and mysterious in the sense of transcendence (our awareness of the 'more' of life) and the excitement of being human ('A human being is an understanding potentiality-for-being'[6]) and my sense of the beauty of it all. Why does this all exist? What is the purpose and meaning of creation?

---

[5] Also, it is fascinating that in Genesis 1.26 and 11.7 God refers to himself as 'us' and 'our'. Also, in Genesis 1 the word that is translated 'God' is a plural word '*Elohiym*' but is correctly translated as 'God', not 'Gods'. In the original context these verses are not referring to trinity here. They would not have had that concept of God. I am pointing to their intuition of God as a community, a plurality, whilst being monotheists.

[6] Ross Snyder, *Inscape*, Abingdon Press, Nashville and New York, 1968, p. 9.

Creation was the moment when matter came into being, and is therefore also the beginning of time. This matter that came into being is the result of the will of God and therefore in some ways reflects God's being. God expressed himself through creation without limiting himself to creation. Later God became human in Jesus, but about 13.5 billion years ago God's being was first reflected in God's creation. God's being is reflected in God's purpose and intention in creation. That intention (purpose) was to create community on earth, as God is Community in heaven. This is the truth at the core of Genesis 1.26, *Then God said, 'Let us make humankind in our image, according to our likeness … So God created humankind in His image, in the image of God he created them; male and female he created them.'* (Note that the word 'humankind' in this verse is the English translation of the Hebrew word *'Adam'*.) A human being on their own does not reflect the image of God! Only community reflects the image of God.

In the previous section you will have read my reference to the scientific understanding of our origins (13.5 billion years ago). In a moment we will together look closely at the description of our origins given in the book of Genesis. Can we hold both science and scripture together? Nobel physicist Frank Wilczek draws our attention to a core principle in existence that I think can help us profoundly in this part of our journey together in this guidebook. I propose that we appreciate that the truth of one does not negate the truth of the other.

Science is discovering the physics of beginnings and scripture reveals the purpose of our existence. I listened recently to Krista Tippett's interview with Frank Wilczek in which he describes the notion of complementarity as something that he treasures deeply. Complementarity says that there can exist two deep propositions about the same reality and that seem to be opposed but are in fact both true and complementary. He says that the essence of complementarity is 'that you have to view the world in different ways to do it justice, and the different ways can each be very rich, can each be internally consistent, can each have its own language and rules, but they may be mutually incompatible. And to do full justice to reality, you have to take both into account.'[7] We are going to try to appreciate both Genesis and science. So in the spirit of complementarity we turn now toward Genesis 1 to 3.

The Genesis account of creation is in the literary form of a cosmological narrative which is an ancient way of telling deep truths in the form of a sacred story.[8] The deep truths are entirely true without the story having had to happen in the way it is told. The creation stories of Genesis are genius revelations of God's intention in creation and as such need to be respected and honoured as the most important part of the wisdom lineage in scripture.

---

[7] Complementarity is a notion that Wilczek learned from the great Danish physicist and philosopher Niels Bohr, who pioneered quantum mechanics and was Einstein's interlocutor. Wilczek says: 'In ordinary reality and ordinary time and space, the opposite of a truth is a falsehood. But deep propositions have a meaning that goes beyond their surface. You can recognise a deep truth by the feature that its opposite is also a deep truth.' He points out that light is both a particle and a wave and that it is 'sometimes useful to think of it one way and at other times useful to think of it another way. Both can be informative in different circumstances, but it is very difficult – in fact, impossible – to apply them both at once.' The interview recording and transcript can be found at the onbeing project website. It is the interview of June 14th 2018. I accessed it on this link on 20th June 2018: https://onbeing.org/programs/frank-wilczek-why-is-the-world-so-beautiful-jun2018/

[8] The technical term 'myth' is sometimes used for this literature form of cosmological narrative. If you come across that term please don't confuse the common usage of the English word 'myth' with what is being referred to here. In English it is common to use the word 'myth' to mean something false. When talking about the literary form, 'myth' refers to the most important of all literary forms, namely our sacred stories in which God is the chief character, and are stories that convey our deepest insights into truth. This is why I use the term 'cosmological narrative'. 'Myths' are about theological truths, not scientific truths. 'Myths' do tell historical truth – not in the sense of a specific date or time, but in the truth about why things (history) have turned out as they have.

Human beings live by stories. We understand ourselves, our past, present and future in stories. Our fears, hopes and beliefs are all carried in story form. We dream and daydream in narrative, we love and hate in narrative. This is not just because we enjoy stories or because they are easy to remember, but narrative is actually the central function of our minds.

Genesis 1 to 3 are sacred stories that are the result of revelation aimed at answering questions like: Who are we, and where did we come from? Was there a purpose in our creation? How is everything meant to fit together? What about God? Where does God fit into the picture?

Let us take a journey through Genesis 1 and 2 and see the community that God created. It is worth remembering now that our journey in science earlier revealed how relationships are the foundational reality – that everything is in relationship with everything else. (I suggest you spend time reading Genesis 1 and 2 now before reading further in the guidebook.)

In the beginning Community created friendship (community, unity and harmony) between God and humanity

The reader of Genesis 1 is given a special sense of God as an artist starting off with nothing, a formless void, and into that nothingness he calls forth, one by one, pieces of creation, each beautiful on its own, but each contributing to a greater whole and a greater beauty called life. The love and delight of this creator artist saturates the scene for the reader.

Then on the sixth day God calls a special part of creation into being – something that is going to be more than just part of life on the canvas of creation – a being with whom God can have a relationship! These human beings[9] will bear a similar image to God and have a similar nature – and God is doubly delighted with this piece of creation. Remember God's nature is relational (Trinity) – so human beings are created to also be relational and one of those relationships is the relationship between God and humans.

The reader reaches Genesis 2.4 and notes that the scene now changes – God here is not calling the pieces of creation into being – God is personally in the scene of creation and we witness God forming a man from the dust of the ground.[10] God's personal involvement becomes even more intimate in that he then bends over this body and breathes into his nostrils the breath of life which

---

[9] The Hebrew word is 'Adam', which can be plural or singular, depending on context. In this instance it is clearly plural, referring to humanity.

[10] Again, the Hebrew word is 'Adam', but in this instance the story makes more sense if we imagine it singular but representative of all men. The word 'ground' is 'Adamah' – 'Adam' is therefore literally 'earth creature' or 'creature of the soil'.

then brings this new being to life.

A short while later we witness an even deeper intimate involvement as God reaches into the man (who is fortunately asleep), pulls out a rib and forms a woman out of it. This intimacy then becomes a special relationship between Adam, Eve and God as they enjoy walks together in the garden of God's presence.[11] The human community that God created is not separate from God, but is included in the divine Community like one big happy family.

Any reader of scripture will be impressed with the ongoing relationship that exists between God and humanity. Psalm 8 is a psalm of creation and celebrates that humanity is given special responsibility and may be seen as God's favourite part of his whole creation. Parts of Psalm 8.3-6 read: *When I look at the heavens ...what are human beings that you are mindful of them? ... Yet you have made them a little lower than God, and crowned them with glory and honor. You have given them dominion over the works of your hands...* These verses are also quoted in Hebrews 2.6 and 7.

Much later in scripture we are given front row seats to Jesus' own passionate prayer before dying, which is built on the sure knowledge that God's plan for humanity was no more and no less than unity between humanity, Father, Son and Spirit! Jesus prays that we *'... may all be one. As you, Father, are in me and I am in you, may they also be in us, so that the world may believe that you have sent me.'* (John 17.21)

In the beginning Community created friendship (community, unity and harmony) amongst people

The reader of Genesis 1 is impressed by the unity between people that was intended in the beginning. It is clear that humans (plural), men and women together, reflect the image of God. Indeed because God is a community of unity it is only as a community that a person can reflect the image of God. When Genesis 1 tells of us being created in the image of God it is certainly not saying that somehow we look like God! It is only through good relationships of unity that I can begin to reflect anything of the image of God.

For the reader of Genesis 2.18-25, a very different scene is played out before us. Here we hear God saying that something is not good in his creation – something is missing. What we see is that God's creation is not complete until the man is in community – *It is not good for the man to be alone.* So a mate was made for man for the very purpose of creating community. The organic unity

---

[11] Genesis 3.8-10 speaks of God walking in the garden in such a way as to imply that Adam and Eve used to enjoy walking with him.

amongst people is further underlined by the phrase that we are all bone of each other's bone, flesh of each other's flesh.

Note that the woman is there to help him out of his aloneness, not to be his servant. She is not helping him because he has too much work to do, she is rescuing him from aloneness. She is created as his friend, partner and ally. They were created equal to serve each other. Just as there is no domination in the Trinity (Divine Community), so is there no domination in the human community.[12]

Genesis 2 ends with the description of this man and woman's nudity – which is an added detail giving the reader a vivid impression that absolutely nothing separated this man and woman. We are given a picture of no physical, psychological, spiritual or emotional barriers between them.

In the beginning Community created friendship (community, unity and harmony) between people and their environment.

The person listening to Genesis 1.26 and 28-30 hears that humanity is charged with taking care of creation (this is what 'dominion' means in this context). Similarly in Genesis 2 the man is put in the Garden of Eden to look after it. As we have listened to the story of creation we have been able to see with the mind's eye how God has lovingly taken delight in each part of his masterpiece of creation. When he creates humans he does so with a purpose of us being caretakers for the rest of creation – the love of the whole scene should make it obvious that we are not placed in a relationship of exploitation to the rest of God's creation. So we are clearly placed in the world to be in a good, loving and caring relationship with our environment.

We hear also that we have been given fruit to eat. So creation will care for us while we will care for creation. It is a relationship of mutual hospitality. Interestingly, pain did not exist in this state because no conscious being was given or taken as food.

To appreciate the vital importance of our relationship with our environment we need to realise that the whole of creation and everything in it is humanity's 'environment'. Our environment includes nature (soil, water, sea, air, plants, mineral resources, animals, plants and plant kingdoms, ecosystems, etc.) but also the structures that we ourselves have created (economic systems, social systems, political systems, countries, cities, towns, farming, buildings, media, cultures, schools, hospitals, etc.). All of this makes up our 'environment'.

---

[12] For a very interesting explanation of this see Gilbert Bilezikian, *Community 101: Reclaiming the Local Church as a Community of Oneness*, Zondervan, Grand Rapids, Michigan, 1997, pp. 19-25.

Our environment's importance is in the reality that it is essential to us humans. We cannot live without it. We are bodily creatures completely dependent on our environment. As indicated earlier, 'Adam' means 'creature of the soil' – which is very much the same as 'creature of the environment'. Certainly life for humans is impossible without the hospitality of our environment. It is essential to see that God's intention in creation was a relationship of mutual hospitality between humanity and our environment.

In the beginning Community created friendship (community, unity and harmony) in each person's relationship with themselves

The first creation story ends at the beginning of Genesis 2 with a precious gift that is a vital part of a person's friendship and kindness towards themselves – rest. Embracing rest is one of the most important signs that you are your own best friend.

The second creation story ends with the words *And the man and his wife were both naked, and were not ashamed.* I believe this is a wonderful image of being completely at home with oneself – of having nothing to be ashamed of, of not wanting to hide anything. Shame is the result of being at odds with oneself, of disappointing oneself. If there is no shame then you are at peace and harmony with yourself.

TOV – THE FOUR RELATIONSHIPS OF LIFE ARE *TOV*

What a beautiful plan – friendship with God, each other, creation and myself. Throughout this guidebook I will refer to these four relationships as the 'four relationships of life' – namely, our relationship with God, our relationship with each other, our relationship with our environment and our relationship with ourselves.[13]

---

[13] The four relationships of life are very important in *Missing Jesus?*. I am indebted to my theology professor, Brian Gaybba, for this teaching. I have since come across other teachers who also speak of these four areas of relationships, although some leave out the relationship with our environment. It is of course essential that the relationship with our context/environment be included.

We have seen that God has revealed to us that his intention was and is friendship (community, unity, harmony) in these four relationships of life. This is God's plan and this is the state that God declares to be 'good': *God saw everything that He had made, and indeed, it was very good.* (Genesis 1.31). Genesis 1 is precious in the way in which it gives us insight into God's delight in his creation. Seven times God is heard to say that his creation is 'good' in that opening chapter of our Bibles! The Hebrew *'tov'* translated as 'good' is a word that conveys more than just the English word 'good' – one needs to understand synonyms like 'delectable', 'delightful' and 'desirable' to get the right feel for what God is saying about his creation.

St Thomas Aquinas (1225-1274) gives expression to some of the wonder of this, 'Because the Divine could not express itself in any single being, the Divine created the great multiplicity of beings so that the perfection lacking to one would be supplied by the others. Thus the whole universe together participates in and manifests the divine more than any single being whatever.'

It is important to also appreciate that we owe God our allegiance because God has created us. We will have freedom to rebel if we wish, but that would be a violation of what we owe God. This is an important point to remember, especially later when we focus on Jesus who teaches that God reigns and that we owe God our allegiance.

God achieved God's purpose in creation, but when you look around you, you see a different reality at work too. What is this all about? That takes us to our next chapter.

Indeed creation does not start with a problem, it starts with a foundational oneness, goodness and blessedness. Our Bibles do not open with original sin but with original blessing![14] God does not start the story of life with a problem, with a negative, with a crisis – rather God starts with a success, a blessing, an uninterrupted union. God would not have declared it good if it were not so.

---

[14] Original Blessing is a term coined by Matthew Fox in his book *Original Blessing: A primer in Creation Spirituality*.

Missing Jesus?

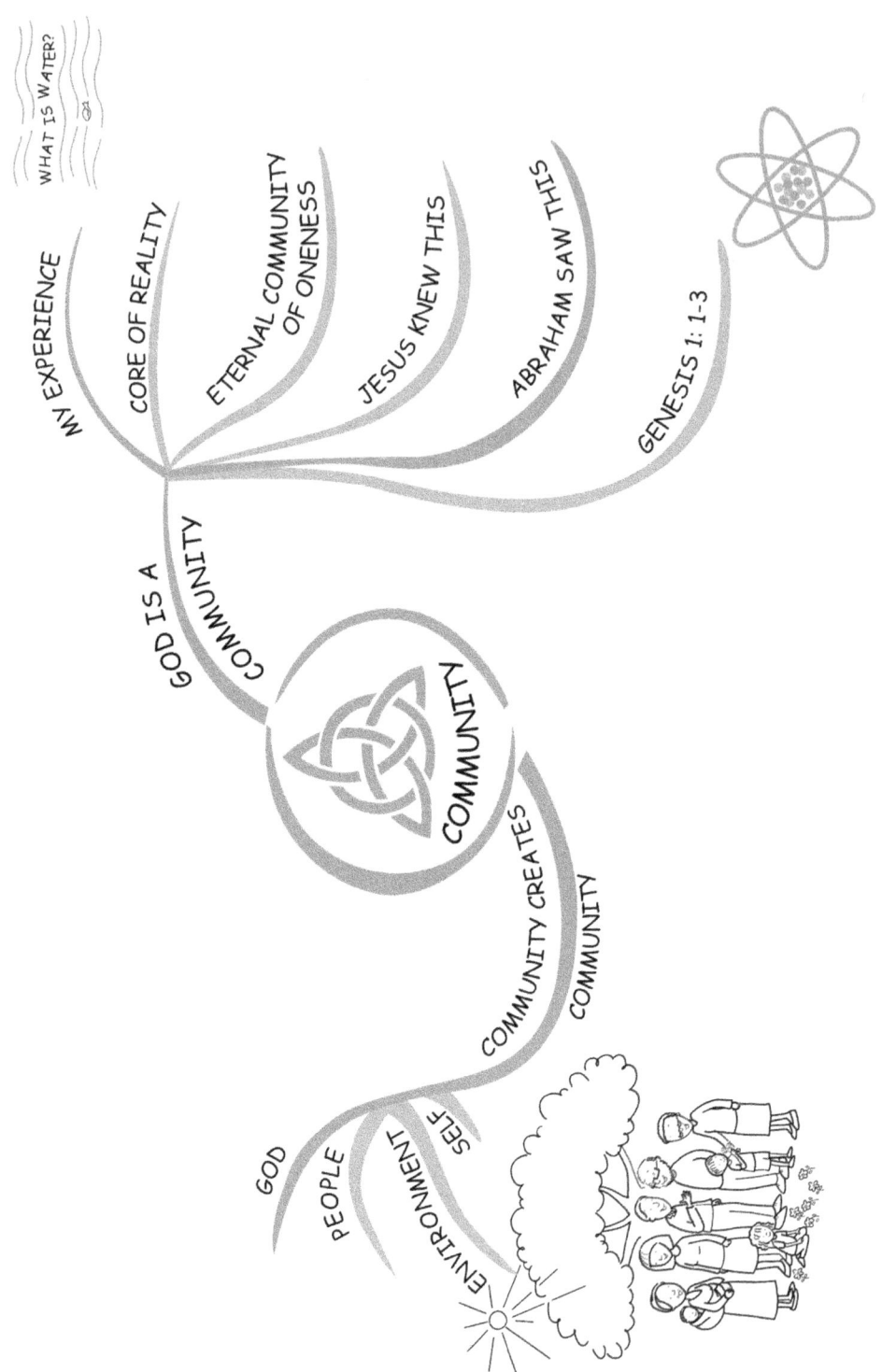

SUGGESTIONS FOR DISCUSSION, REVISION, REFLECTION AND APPLICATION

(These questions are intended for group work, but can easily be adapted for personal use.)

1. What is the most important message to you in this chapter? (Remember to also make a note of this on your 'God spoke to me' page.)
2. Icebreaker question: If you could choose to meet any historical figure (besides Jesus) who would you choose to meet, and why? (The question must be answered quickly. As a group, do not spend longer than 5 minutes in total on this question.)
3. Read Genesis 1.1-2.3 and answer the following questions:
   a. What does this passage say about God? What are the characteristics of God revealed here?
   b. Why did God create? What purpose do different aspects of creation have?
   c. What does this passage say about humans? What is our purpose?
   d. What does this passage say about the relationship between God and humans? What is that relationship meant to look like?
   e. What can we learn from this that might be helpful to us in the future?
4. Below are a variety of suggestions and questions to aid your appreciation of this chapter. Do not attempt to do all of them! Choose those that are most appropriate to your unique situation and/or group. The questions are designed to help variously with revision, understanding, appreciation, reflection or application of the content.
   a. Why do we say that God is a Community?
   b. Why do we say that God created community?
   c. What are the four relationships of life?
   d. Can you think of any aspect of life excluded from the four relationships of life?
   e. How do you feel about talking about our relationship with God as a friendship?
   f. Name someone who seems to most enjoy harmony in all four of the relationships of life? How do they manage to live that way? What impact does it have on the people around them?

g. What is most special about the four relationships of life for you?
h. How do you respond to the idea that we were created for friendship with God?
i. How do you respond to the idea that we were created for friendship with other people?
j. How do you respond to the idea that we were created for friendship with the environment?
k. How do you respond to the idea that you are created for friendship with yourself?

GOD SPOKE TO ME ...

3

DIVISION

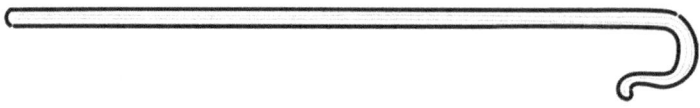

The man and his wife hid themselves from the presence of the LORD God (Genesis 3.8)

AFTER THE BEGINNING CAME REBELLION

The Bible should have ended at Genesis 2. Each one of us could have memorised the whole Bible! But Genesis 3 then tells us of another beginning, the beginning of rebellion.

There are two ways in which God's plan for creation is fulfilled. God as Creator has determined that these two ways relate to the other two persons of the Trinity:

We are invited to live by his Spirit, the Spirit of Love. God's desire in creation is that we lovingly give ourselves to God, other people, the rest of creation and ourselves. Although there are no instructions about this in Genesis 1+2 it should be very obvious that the only way in which community is maintained is through loving relationships. A deeper reading of the instruction to *Be fruitful and multiply, … have dominion* reveals that this is an instruction to build community through loving servanthood.[1] In this way we will be our true selves, our authentic selves and the people God created us to be.

We are invited to live by the Word of God. The Word of God is the second person of the Trinity, who exists to reveal the will of the Creator. The world was created through the Word and, in the creation story, we received our do's and one don't through the Word. We are called to be obedient to the Word.[2] The

---

[1] See Gilbert Bilezikian, *Community 101: Reclaiming the Local Church as a Community of Oneness*, pp. 25-27.

[2] I will never forget reading the startling opening words of Dietrich Bonhoeffer's *Ethics* (a book that he never finished because of his martyrdom under direct order from Hitler). 'The knowledge of good and evil seems to be the aim of all ethical reflection. The first task of Christian ethics is to invalidate this knowledge.' He goes on to speak of Christian ethics as the pursuit to know God and God's revelation (Word), which was the knowledge we had before the fall. Knowledge of good and evil is part of our fallen state.

instructions given are designed to sustain the community that God had created.

God's plan for creation is therefore fulfilled by **love** and **obedience**. The two are intricately linked, to love means to obey God, and to obey God means to love. A breakdown of the one will lead to a breakdown of the other.

To sin is to violate love or obedience. This is what happened. The one 'don't' – to not eat from the tree of the knowledge of good and evil – was disobeyed. The first sin was a sin of disobedience, which was by implication a failure in love, and the result was the breakdown of the community that God had created. This is powerfully brought home in 1 Peter 2.8: *'They stumble because they disobey the word ...'*

The temptation for which humanity fell was the temptation for a greater degree of self-sufficiency and for the allurement of independence. Humanity thought that to be 'like God' meant to know what God knows, to have knowledge so that they could decide for themselves what was right and wrong and not have to depend on the revealed will of God. In this way it was a quest for independence and separateness from God. It was a sin that protested against humility in the presence of God. It was greed – in spite of having been given so much they wanted more. It was a refusal to trust in the wisdom of God.

Humanity was created to enjoy a blissful innocence of naturally knowing and trusting God. This innocence was lost through their disobedience and was replaced by knowledge of wrongdoing, shame, guilt and alienation.

The potential for this sin lay in our God-given ability to choose. We are created with freedom to love or not to love, to obey or not to obey the will of God. God did not want us to be robots who love and obey without freedom. Love and obedience are only real if they are freely given. Freedom makes true love possible! Our freedom is a gift that lights the way to the greatest of all realities – Love. God created us for community but with the freedom to choose to be independent, separate, divisive, selfish, hurtful or hateful.

The reality of division does not turn the reality of community into a fiction. The reality of division does not annihilate the reality of community. Both are real. The pursuit of community is not unrealistic. In the beginning God created community with the freedom to choose separateness. It is all about choice.

AFTER REBELLION CAME THE BEGINNING OF DIVISION

I have shown how we were created for friendship (community, unity and harmony) in the four relationships of life. To sin is to betray our authentic being, to fall away from our true self, to orientate ourselves away from our authentic being. Scripture tells us of these choices and their consequences.

Genesis 3 tells of the cataclysmic divisiveness of sin (I suggest you first read through Genesis 3 now):

Sin is divisive in our relationship with God. Sadly we have to watch how the man and woman hide away from God instead of enjoying their usual evening walk together. When asked, they admit to having become strangely scared of God. A little later we see how they are removed from this special garden of God's presence. What should have been an intimate trust-filled relationship has become one marked by fear, division and distance.

Sin is divisive in our relationship with each other. Almost immediately downstream of sin we see the man and the woman blaming each other for what has happened. This quickly picks up momentum and escalates into domination of the man over the woman for he now 'rules' her.[3] Things go quickly from bad to worse: in the very next chapter we see that Adam and Eve's children fight and Cain kills Abel (Genesis 4.1-8). What should have been a loving intimate relationship between equals has become one characterised by mistrust, distance, domination and violence.

---

[3] Those who believe that it is God's original will for men to rule women are reminded here that it was not God's intention in creation. Such dynamics of domination are part of the fall and the result of it.

Sin is divisive in our relationship with the rest of creation (environment). Genesis 3.15-19 describes a whole litany of hostility, pain, and great difficulty in the man and woman's relationship with the rest of creation. Even working the land for food is now filled with difficulty and hardship. We hear that an animal had to lose its life because of this sin because the man and the woman are clothed with leather. A special hostility starts between snakes and humans, but it soon spreads to our relationship with all animals. After the flood we read in Genesis 9.1-7 that humanity becomes the fear and dread of all animals because as a further result of sin they have become humanity's food. What should have been an arena of mutual hospitality has become one of hostility.

Sin is divisive in our relationship with ourselves. In the story this is the most immediate impact of sin as the man and the woman become aware of their nudity and are ashamed of themselves. Innocence is lost and cover-ups begin. The covering up only gets more elaborate as time moves on – within a few verses the fig leaves that they first used are replaced with leather clothing. We see here the end of that state of inner harmony and peace.

SIN – SUCH A SMALL WORD FOR SUCH A BIG PROBLEM

As humans we would be wise to face how this sacred story reveals us humans and our sin to be the problem in the world. We have sown sin and reaped a whirlwind of division.

In ways that cut us to the heart we have been shown in Genesis 3 what sin is and that the effects of sin are alienation, division, disharmony, distance and the wrecking of the community that God had created. This alienation, division, disharmony and distance would lead to more sin, resulting in deeper alienation, division, disharmony and distance and so it would go on. Brian Gaybba summed it up so well – 'Sin divides and (if left unchallenged) destroys all that it divides.'[4]

The Apostle Paul understood at very deep levels that sin results in our loss of life in union with God. To lose this life in union with God is to lose the force of Life itself and to be sucked into the force of death, destruction, division, decay and attrition. It is this death that Paul refers to when he says in Romans 6.23: *'For the wages of sin is death.'* We will all die physically, but for some physical death is swallowed up by Life and union with God, for others physical death multiplies the terror of alienation from God. The only remedy would be for God to personally heal the alienation, division, disharmony and distance.

---

[4] This is a phrase that Prof. Brian Gaybba often used in our Systematics Theology class. This theme is unpacked in his book, *God is a Community: A General Survey of Christian Theology*. See especially pp. 145f.

Sin caused such a beautiful plan to go so wrong and it lays the conditions for sin to increase and continually make matters worse. Let me help us to understand sin a little better.

God is Love, God is Loving Community, and humanity – the crown of God's creation, was created to reflect that loving community. We were called to love, which means that we were shown the will of God. We were given free will by God, which means that we were given the choice to obey or disobey, love or not love. Sin was and is the decision to disobey and alienate rather than obey and love. Simply put – my sin is all the ways in which I fail to love God, my neighbour, the world I live in and myself.

We were each born with original sin. This does not mean that we were born guilty; it means that we were born into a broken relationship with God. This broken relationship is not God's ungracious judgement on us but is the consequence of the sin of the world we are born into. We are all born into this broken relationship and are all in need of reconciliation with God. This would apply to 'good' people and 'bad' people. Original sin also means that personal sin is inevitable for each of us. Original sin is, as I shall show, both corporate and personal, both resulting in actual sinning in each of the four relationships of life.

Let us look a little more closely at alienation in the four relationships of life today. It may be helpful to you to use the acronym GOES to remember the four relationships of life – God, Others, Environment, Self.[5] As we look now at alienation in the four relationships, note how our sin, and the way in which we co-operate in our sinning in society, has meant that sin has taken on a life of its own and has also become the objective reality of evil in this world. Please also note how this has introduced so many levels of forces that lead to death in society. We will see later in this guidebook how God deals with sin, evil and death.

Division in our relationship with God

In the words of Isaiah 59.2, *Your iniquities have made a gulf between you and your God.* This continues to be the experience of many today. Current examples are:
- Every human gets caught up with attachment to superficial things because we have missed the real life-giving experience of union with God.
- Every human quests for happiness in false, temporary and inappropriate things because we have not found an eternal joy to sustain us.

---
[5] My thanks to Maurice Adams for this acronym.

- Every human is overly preoccupied with 'what do people think of me?' This is because we are not in touch with God's loving embrace of each of us.
- Many fear God and get very nervous when the topic God comes up in conversation.
- Sin has made it difficult to perceive God's active presence in the world, thus making atheism possible.
- Many believe in the existence of God but do not experience a daily life-giving relationship with Him.
- Without a good relationship with God the door is opened to much sin because the person does not recognise the value of following life as it was meant to be lived (as revealed in Jesus).

Imagine how much more fulfilling and meaningful life would be for us if we had greater union with God. Imagine how much less suffering we would impose on others.

Division in our relationship with one another

This arena offers examples that are both corporate and personal aspects of original sin. Current examples are:

- The world is full of all manner of divisiveness (class divisions, social divisions, prejudices, xenophobia, war, etc.). This divisiveness can spring up quite quickly and become polarised and entrenched, resulting in a sudden loss of a sense of community.
- We live in a world in which many evil people are in positions of power and influence.
- It is important to focus on the issue of war and military spending here. Note that it costs about the same to arm and train one soldier as it does to educate 80 children, to build one bomber as it did to wipe out smallpox over a 10-year period, to launch the latest nuclear-missile submarine as it does to build 450 000 modest homes. The money required to provide adequate food, water, education, health and housing for everyone in the world has been estimated at $17 billion a year. It is a huge sum of money … about as much as the world spends on arms every two weeks… 'Every gun that is made, every warship that is launched, every rocket fired signifies, in a final sense, a theft from those who hunger and are not fed, from those who are cold and are not clothed.'[6] A more recent single South African example would be to note that it would cost R400 million to provide all of our schools with textbooks – something we are not able to do – yet we spent R1.17 billion on the research and development of the Rooivalk helicopter.
- The global response to HIV/AIDS has generally been characterised by selfishness, greed, competitiveness and opportunism. South Africa is the worst hit country in the world and our democratically elected government has failed horribly in addressing this humanitarian crisis.
- So much of the world's 'togetherness' is not for the purpose of building community but merely convenience.
- The high rate of divorce causes suffering that often lasts for generations.
- The children of many dysfunctional families do not receive the love and acceptance they need.

Imagine how much less suffering there would be in the world if people related to each other in a loving and compassionate way!

---

[6] President Eisenhower of USA said these words and quoted these amounts in 1961!

Division in our relationship with our environment

In speaking of 'environment' or 'rest of creation' I do not only mean the natural world, but also the world we have built around us (social structures, economic systems, political systems, cities, countries, buildings, shops etc.). The care-taking mandate God gave was to lovingly mould the world. We should have moulded a world that was a testimony to love, a world that would have enabled us to become fully alive and loving as humans. Instead, most of what has been built is a testimony to selfishness. It is in this arena that the devastating determined power of sin is perceived. We see also how the effects of sin can continue after individual repentance. This arena offers good examples of the corporate aspect of original sin. Current examples are:

- Economic systems, both local and global, mainly benefit the 'haves' and impoverish the 'have nots' further. At the turn of the century in South Africa the richest 10% of the population controlled 50.1% of the wealth of the economy and the poorest people only had access to less than 1% of the economy, with 57% of the population living below the poverty line. Poverty does not just happen, but is rather the result of systems that make some poor and others rich. This evil of economic systems is demonstrated by how quickly a small new black economic elite were able to gain enormous wealth for themselves with no benefit to the poor. 'The first four years of black majority rule produced a surprising number of new, black "empowerment achievers" who are worth millions. By 1999, 33 black-controlled organisations had been listed on the Johannesburg Stock Exchange and by late 1998 the value of black-controlled corporations was around R48 billion. All this new wealth is concentrated among the aristocracy of the new political ruling class. Meanwhile, the misery of the vast masses of poor people is growing. There is no doubt that the greatest enemy South Africa is facing is poverty.'[7]
- Ecological crisis in the world. Ecology is the relationship between living things and their environment. We are currently in an environmental crisis because we humans forgot that we are part of an ecosystem in which we need to be in a good and sustainable relationship with our earth. One simple but devastating illustration of this is right outside my window now. A small part of the writing of this guidebook has been done at a retreat centre outside of Johannesburg at the Cradle of Humankind area. The Bloubankspruit runs through the grounds of the retreat centre. It is always special to hear the sound of the stream gently bubbling along and it looks so inviting on a hot day. But the river is a desert of life – there are no fish, frogs or birds hunting or any significant stream

---

[7] Allan Boesak, *The Tenderness of Conscience: African Renaissance and the Spirituality of Politics*, p.53. For an excellent reflection on economics in South Africa read the whole of chapter 2 and 3.

ecosystem. The water's acid levels are so high that it is barren water. What a contradiction in terms – 'barren water'! Raw and untreated acid from mining upstream has been intentionally drained into the water. Those who warned us in the past that we would have environmental wastelands because of our poisoning of ecosystems have been proven correct!
- Social structures that force people to be separate and unequal.
- Those in power use indoctrination to mould the attitudes of citizens so that the destructive and divisive social structure is accepted and propagated.
- Many diseases and illnesses have been caused by the destruction of our natural environment. We poison our oceans and rivers, we spew toxins into the air we breathe, we take a chance with dangerous levels of radiation in our environment, we have depleted the protective ozone layer, we recklessly feed antibiotics and hormones to animals in mass food production, we remove the lungs of the planet through deforestation etc. These are just some of the reasons why our environment is unsafe to live in and unsafe to live off.
- Many people struggle with addiction – which is an experience of being dominated by an item in their environment. This is certainly as much a problem in my relationship with my environment as it is a problem in my relationship with myself. In this regard we can understand the profound wisdom of God's command to have dominion over creation. God is saying that the right relationship with creation and its gifts is to appreciate and treasure them without becoming possessive or becoming controlled by them. An alcoholic does not have dominion over alcohol but is rather dominated and controlled by alcohol and their dependence on it. This is what the problem of greed is all about too, in that greed is impotence to control an appetite. This is why Paul in 1 Corinthians 6.12-20 makes it clear that he should not be dominated by the stomach, food or sexual appetites.

Imagine how much less suffering there would be in the world if people cared for the environment and also built social structures that were a testimony to love.

Division in my relationship with myself

Originally there was meant to be an inner harmony within us, with all our desires, appetites, intentions, aspirations, abilities and faculties pressed into the service of love. But that harmony is no more. Paul powerfully describes the battle that has replaced it in Romans 7.14-25. This arena offers good examples of the personal aspect of original sin. Current examples are:
- Many suffer from an inner emptiness and inner restlessness.
- A great gulf exists between who we were meant to be and who we are.

- When appetites and desires are not controlled by love then they become a competing mass of demands always seeking their own satisfaction. This results in a lot of hardship for ourselves and others.
- We struggle to love and be loved.
- Inner alienation causes irresponsible behaviour. Irresponsible behaviour causes death and injury in 'accidents'.
- We do not care for our own bodies, taking little or no physical exercise, eating foods that are not good for us (unfortunately often ignorantly), and falling prey to substance abuse. Some persist in unhealthy lifestyle habits even after the destructive effects have started to take a toll on the body and mind.
- Some are so driven that they will not even give themselves the rest they need. They cannot see that the Sabbath is not a law to keep but a grace to receive.

Imagine how much less suffering there would be in the world if we as people were inwardly able to love and receive love.

SOME IMPORTANT ADDITIONAL OBSERVATIONS ABOUT BEGINNINGS

My first additional observation is inspired by a cartoon that caught my eye. In the first frame a jaded philosopher says, 'Sometimes I'd like to ask God why he allows poverty, famine and injustice when he could do something about it,' only to be asked, 'What's stopping you?' In the next frame a chastened figure admits: 'I'm afraid God might ask me the same question.' I thought it made its point very well, challenging shallow thinking about these themes.

Further important observations are:

Sin, evil and deadly forces of destruction are objective realities that need to be opposed. We will see in this guidebook that God in Jesus comes to battle these objective realities and will be victorious over them. It is important at this stage to observe the necessity for this work of God in Jesus.

Don't point a finger at Adam and Eve. I hope that this journey has made it clear that we may not point a finger at 'Adam and Eve' and blame all our problems on them. It should be clear that when we point a finger at them there are three fingers pointing back at us. Their sin is our sin; it is reflected in our sin all the time. Sin happens through our choice. Our choice is possible because God gave us freedom to choose. God's desire is that we choose to love God, each other, our environment and ourselves.

It was not meant to be this way. I hope that this point has become crystal clear. It is a point we easily forget. What we live in is a world that was not meant to be. God did not create it this way – God created a very special community.

We have messed it up. It is important to realise this. Deep down is the question: 'What is the point of a life of so much struggle and suffering?' We must realise that this is not how life was meant to be. God's intention (purpose) is being violated continuously by enormous numbers of people.

God does not always get God's way. Another important truth has been made clear in this chapter, one that we find great difficulty in accepting. I have often stated it this way: God does not always get his way. Many people glibly state the opposite: the phrase 'If it's God's will it will happen', or 'God is in control', is often heard. But from the beginning of time we see much that clearly violates the will of God: one need only think of the frequent faithlessness of the people of Israel, the people's rejection of Jesus, the Crusades, the Inquisition, the Holocaust, Apartheid and the Rwandan genocide. In this we hear history's long groan that says 'God does not always get his way'.

We need to admit that God is not in control of every life event. God's gift of freedom to us does mean that God has let go of control of events. It is God's will that we be free to rebel against Him. In this sense, and in this sense only, are the 'bad things' that happen God's will. Bad things do not happen because God has willed them and certainly not because of God's control, but bad things are caused by people who are, by God's will, free to do bad things. Ultimately our conviction is that God's will shall win through. There are also many signs of the obvious superiority of God's will in life today. Our task is to choose life – even if a rebellious world makes that a costly choice for us.

Hope is for real. We should also realise that if God had abandoned the world completely then the world would have ended long ago. God and love are not absent from the world. God did not abandon humanity. It is part of God's character to persist in love. There is so much sinfulness, yet there is also so much love, and it is the presence of this love that is a quiet but magnificent testimony to God's mercy, God's love and God's saving presence. In fact God got busy right away fixing what humanity had messed up. This course will make God's redemption action clear.[8]

MISSING COMMUNITY

This chapter has shown how we were created for community by Community (the triune God). Through the foolish and selfish use of our God-given freedom we have broken community in ways that are so global and entrenched that we are unable to fully remedy the situation.

---

[8] In this course I will not deal with God's plan as it unfolded in the Old Testament. Daniel Erlander's book *Manna and Mercy* presents these themes so very well. This can be purchased at mannaandmercy. capetown@gmail.com, or aslowwalk@gmail.com.

The title of this guidebook is 'Missing Jesus', but we see now that before we were missing Jesus, we were missing community. It is because of the breakdown of community that Jesus comes to us. That is the story for the rest of this book. I pray that it is a life-giving journey for you.

Missing Jesus?

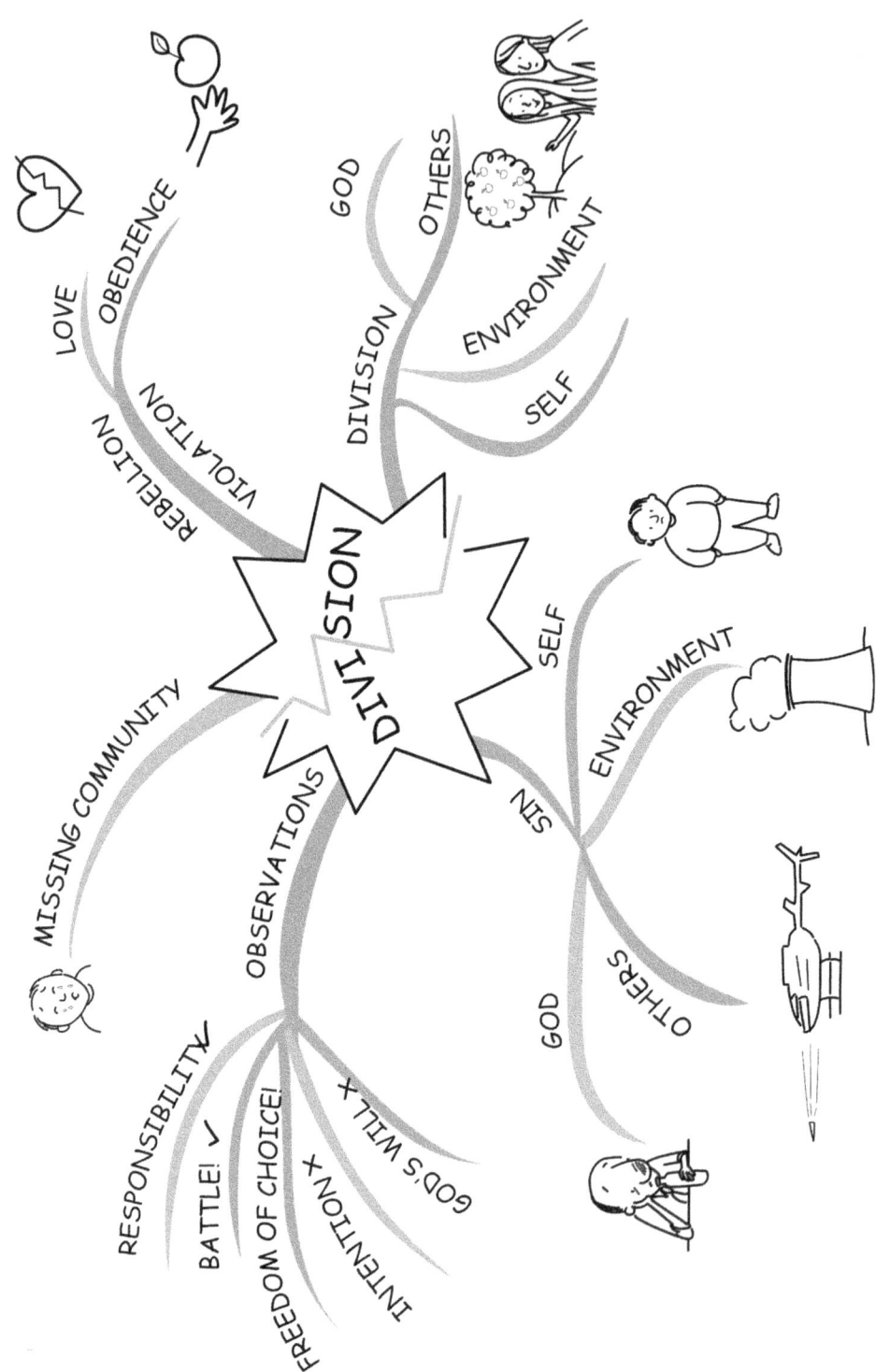

SUGGESTIONS FOR DISCUSSION, REVISION, REFLECTION AND APPLICATION

(These questions are intended for group work, but can easily be adapted for personal use.)

1. What is the most important message to you in this chapter? (Remember to also make a note of this on your 'God spoke to me' page.)
2. Icebreaker question: If you could rid the world of one thing, what would it be? (The question must be answered quickly. As a group, do not spend longer than 5 minutes in total on this question.)
3. Read Genesis 3.1-13 and answer the following questions:
    a. What is the overall impression you get from this passage about the causes of sin?
    b. Discuss your answers to this question above and then try and come to some agreement about the deep nature of temptation and sin.
    c. What are the consequences of sin?
4. Below are a variety of suggestions and questions to aid your appreciation of this chapter. Do not attempt to do all of them! Choose those that are most appropriate to your unique situation and/or group. The questions are designed to help variously with revision, understanding, appreciation, reflection or application of the content.
    a. What went wrong with God's plan for creation?
    b. What is sin?
    c. What is original sin?
    d. What examples would you give, from your own personal experience, of alienation in the four relationships of life today? What is your experience of alienation in the four relationships?
    e. What grieves you most about alienation in the four relationships of life?
    f. Can we blame Adam and Eve for the state of the world today?
    g. Respond to the statement – 'God is in control'. Do you agree? Why/why not? Does it bother you? Do you hope that it is true?
    h. Someone says to you – 'I cannot be held responsible for sin in my life because it is not my fault that I was born into a fallen world.' What would you say to them?
    i. What do you need to do to become more loving?

j. In what areas of your life do you disobey God's will? What are you going to do about it?
k. Do you have hope that God's purpose for creation will ever be fulfilled? Do you feel hopeful? Do your head and your heart perhaps give two different answers? Give reasons for your answer. In your answer give thought to what scripture says about this.

GOD SPOKE TO ME …

PART 2

FOUND BY THE SHEPHERD

4

WHO IS JESUS OF NAZARETH?

And the Word became flesh and lived among us, and we have seen his glory, the glory as of a father's only son, full of grace and truth. (John 1.14)

In the second chapter we came to understand that God's intention for creation was community in all four of life's relationships – friendship with God, each other, creation and oneself. In chapter three we saw how humanity's sin shattered God's intention with cataclysmic divisions in those four relationships of life.

In this, the fourth chapter, we begin to understand who Jesus of Nazareth was and is and how Jesus restores that which was lost through sin. It is the remarkable event of God becoming a creature in his own creation. We will also find out how reliable our information about him is.

WHO IS JESUS FOR ME?

Let me begin with my own personal statement of belief about Jesus:

Jesus is a person, in whom I experience God come to me. Jesus has been real to me for as long as I can remember. I know too that he walked this earth about 2000 years ago. I have read what he taught and agree with many who heard him teach that his teachings are the hope of the world. I know, as I say, that he is God come to us. It amazes me that God should become human; it makes me sit up and take notice. I notice that his mission was to make sure that people knew that God loved them, forgave them, and wanted them to have a new life in his Kingdom, which they didn't have to wait for because he brought it with him. I know that if I lived then, he would have made this clear to me personally.

I know that he was killed as a result of this mission. I know that he rose from the dead. I know that in all this he blazed a trail of reconciliation between God and humanity, amongst the peoples of this world and within people. I know these things in an intimate, lived and experiential way, not merely as a set of ideas, because not only are they recorded in scripture but Jesus also makes them known to me every day.

That is who I believe Jesus to be. Do I, and others who believe such things, have any evidence for such beliefs? Where does the evidence come from? How reliable is it? What does the source material really say?

It is important to lay this foundation because we will be learning a lot about Jesus and his Kingdom in this guidebook – we must have confidence in the historical roots of the things we learn.

WHO IS JESUS FOR THE GOSPEL WRITERS?

The most important documents about Jesus are the writings of the Christian sacred scriptures, specifically the New Testament and especially the Gospels of Matthew, Mark, Luke and John. These are not the only source materials, but they are the richest.

John 1.1-18 gives a powerful description of Jesus as a being who is both divine and human. It is an important passage, and so I will use it as the key passage for our work of understanding who Jesus is.

> *In the beginning was the Word, and the Word was with God, and the Word was God. He was in the beginning with God. All things came into being through him, and without him not one thing came into being. What has come into being in him was life, and the life was the light of all people. The light shines in the darkness, and the darkness did not overcome it.*
>
> *There was a man sent from God, whose name was John. He came as a witness to testify to the light, so that all might believe through him. He himself was not the light, but he came to testify to the light. The true light, which enlightens everyone, was coming into the world. He was in the world, and the world came into being through him; yet the world did not know him. He came to what was his own, and his own people did not accept him. But to all who received him, who believed in his name, he gave power to become children of God, who were born, not of blood or of the will of the flesh or of the will of man, but of God. And the Word became flesh and lived among us, and we have seen his glory, the glory as of a father's only son, full of grace and truth.*
>
> *(John testified to him and cried out, 'This was he of whom I said, "He who comes after me ranks ahead of me because he was before me".') From his fullness we have all received, grace upon grace. The law indeed was given through Moses; grace and truth came through Jesus Christ. No one has ever seen God. It is God the only Son, who is close to the Father's heart, who has made him known.'*

It will be helpful to look at the above passage in two parts: Jesus as divine, and Jesus as human.

Jesus as divine

In the first part, John 1.1-13, we see that John is absolutely clear, emphatic and thorough in asserting the divinity of Jesus. I would summarise this part as follows: John starts by identifying which person in the Trinity Jesus is, namely the Word, that the Word was always part of God, i.e. that there never was a time when he was not. That creation was without exception made 'through' him, and because of this he is its 'light'. It is important for us to believe in Jesus as God, and through that living belief we become children of God.

Essentially what John and the other New Testament writers were convinced of was that Jesus was from God and part of God in such a special way that he needed to be viewed as divine. Their writings show that many of the people who heard Jesus preach, experienced his healing and enjoyed his friendship, believed him to be of God and part of God in the profoundest way possible.

Let us very briefly reflect on some of the highlights of the faith of the New Testament writers about Jesus, particularly his divinity. Mark (the earliest Gospel) records Jesus claiming to be *'Lord of the Sabbath'* and that John the baptiser, who prepared the way for Jesus, was preparing the *'way of the Lord'*. In Matthew Jesus is called *'God with us'* in three places (Matthew 1.23, 18.20, 28.20). We get a very clear insight into Luke's view of Jesus in the sermon he records of Peter on the day of Pentecost (Acts 2, where Jesus is *'Lord'* and the one who pours out God's Spirit, and that the saving name of God is now *'Jesus'*). John has a thoroughly spiritual and symbolic way of speaking about Jesus and is persistent throughout his gospel about Jesus' closeness and oneness with the Father (God). Paul, whose writings are earlier than the Gospels, uses the Old Testament's divine and lofty wisdom language when he speaks about Jesus (Philippians 2.6-11; Colossians 1.15-20 are two of many examples). What is also important about Paul is that many of his writings are the oldest of Christian literature and that in many places Paul is quoting formulas of the early church, thus going back to the very beginnings of the Jesus movement, such as 1 Corinthians 8.6: *Yet for us there is one God, the Father, from whom are all things and for whom we exist, and one Lord, Jesus Christ, through whom are all things and through whom we exist.*

At the time of Jesus, Judaism's language about God was more fluid than it later became when under the influence of rigorous Aristotelian metaphysics. In fact Jewish thinking always had a more narrative quality about it – where truths came through stories, events, experiences and personalities rather than from logical constructions. Of particular importance is the way in which the wisdom and the logos (word) of God were portrayed as aspects of God but personified distinctly. What happened in the early church was that Jesus came to be viewed as the incarnation of these divine aspects (wisdom and logos) of God. In later centuries this view of Jesus' divinity would be developed to be coherent with the metaphysics of Plato – but in its earliest forms it was the Jewish belief in the story that the wisdom and logos of God had personally come to us in Jesus.[1]

There were incidents in which Jesus was actually worshipped and/or revered as a man in special union with God. Here are just two examples:[2]

---

[1] For a fuller discussion of this see Craig S. Keener, *The Historical Jesus of the Gospels*, pp. 279-282.

[2] Also see Matthew 8.2; John 9.35-38; Matthew 14.25-33; John 20.27-29; Acts 2.36-42.

Simon Peter declared that he believed Jesus was part of God and God's special agent in the world:

> *Jesus said to them, 'But who do you say that I am?' Simon Peter answered, 'You are the Messiah, the Son of the living God.' And Jesus answered him, 'Blessed are you, Simon son of Jonah! For flesh and blood has not revealed this to you, but my Father in heaven.'* (Matthew 16.15-17)

Quite remarkably, one of the executing soldiers declares that *'Truly this man was God's Son!'* (Mark 15.39)

It is important that we today appreciate that many years ago, when Jesus walked this earth, some people who got to know him concluded that this man needed to be worshipped as someone who was part of God!

Why did many come to believe this? Different people would have had different reasons, but one common reason would certainly have been their experience of Jesus as someone in whom the presence of God profoundly rested. They encountered in him more than what one senses when one meets a holy or godly man.

Another reason for such beliefs in Jesus was that he did claim to have a uniquely close relationship with God, whom he called Abba. He described that he was in a very intimate and profoundly real relationship with God as Father and he as Son. This relationship was so close that he could talk of himself as being on the divine side, rather than the human side, of the universal divine–human relationship.

Jesus' teaching about himself: Jesus did talk about his own identity, even though he was a self-sacrificial and selfless person. Let us look at some specific examples of this now:

When the Samaritan woman at the well spoke about the awaited-for messiah, Jesus responded and said, *'I am He.'* (John 4.26)

'I am the bread of life. Whoever comes to me will never be hungry, and whoever believes in me will never be thirsty.' (John 6.35)

You will note that all of these teachings begin with the words *'I am'*.[3] For the Jewish listeners the use of this phrase would have been a startling assertion that Jesus was directly from God. The Jewish people's name for God was 'Yahweh' which means 'I am', or, 'He who is' or, 'I am who I am'![4] Jesus used this term in very direct ways too: *'You are from below, I am from above; you are of this world, I am not of this world. I told you that you would die in your sins, for you will die in your sins unless you believe that I am.'* (John 8.23). In fact, Jesus once drove the point home by saying *'Very truly, I tell you, before Abraham was, I am. So they picked up stones to throw at Him, but Jesus hid Himself and went out of the temple.'* (John 8.58-59)

Such statements are prominent in John's Gospel, but are not absent from the other gospels. See for example: *'Whoever welcomes me welcomes the One who sent me.'* (Matthew 10.40)

---

[3] For more 'I am' sayings see John 8.12; 10.7; 10.11-14; 10.36; 11.25-27; 13.13; 14.6; 15.1.

[4] In Exodus 3 Moses is told at the burning bush that God's name is *'I am'*. See also Deuteronomy 32.39 and Isaiah 43.10.

Jesus demanded a loyalty from his disciples far higher than any other rabbi or teacher at the time. A rabbi in Jesus' day may demand that a disciple be prepared to relinquish family ties for the sake of the Torah and a radical philosopher may demand such loyalty to philosophy – but Jesus declares that such radical loyalty is due to himself![5]

Jesus' ministry of forgiving people for their sins was only possible because of his experience of oneness with God and that the oneness enabled him to speak and act for God. Jesus' own self-understanding and consciousness was such that he believed that he could forgive sins in an ultimate way (ie. in a way that only God can). Here is one powerful example:

> *When Jesus saw their faith, he said to the paralytic, 'Son, your sins are forgiven.' Now some of the scribes were sitting there, questioning in their hearts, 'Why does this fellow speak in this way? It is blasphemy! Who can forgive sins but God alone?' At once Jesus perceived in his spirit that they were discussing these questions among themselves; and he said to them, 'Why do you raise such questions in your hearts? Which is easier, to say to the paralytic, "Your sins are forgiven," or to say, "Stand up and take your mat and walk"? But so that you may know that the Son of Man has authority on earth to forgive sins'—he said to the paralytic—'I say to you, stand up, take your mat and go to your home.' And he stood up, and immediately took the mat and went out before all of them; so that they were all amazed and glorified God, saying, 'We have never seen anything like this!' (Mark 2.5-12)*

Jesus was often opposed for breaking Sabbath regulations. He had various reasons for not honouring the regulations as laid down by Jewish legalism, but two of his reasons had to do with his own authority and identity being superior to the Sabbath! See for example Matthew 12.1-8.

In some instances when Jesus teaches about judgement day he speaks of himself as both the judge and the criteria for judgement. We see that we are judged for how we treated him in suffering people! This is again a proclamation that places Jesus on the divine side of the divine–human relationship. (see Matthew 25.31-46)

The deadly impact of Jesus' claim to this special closeness with God: The religious rulers believed Jesus had gone too far too often in speaking and

---

[5] Mark 1.20; Mark 15.40-41 and Luke 8.2-3 (the women mentioned are disciples leaving their family obligations for they were not wives to any of the male disciples); Matthew 10.37; Luke 14.26; Matthew 8.21-22; Luke 9.59-60.

acting on God's behalf. They believed they needed to have him executed for blasphemy. Part of their motivation for this was the fact that many people had come to accept these claims of Jesus and had come to view him as the Messiah, God's special agent in whom the hope of the world is fulfilled.

One instance is described for us as follows: *For this reason the Jews were seeking all the more to kill Him, because He was not only breaking the Sabbath, but was also calling God His own Father, thereby making Himself equal to God.* (John 5.18. See the following references for other instances in Jesus' life where people want to kill him because of the way in which he spoke about himself and the high beliefs people were placing in him: Luke 4.16-30; John 10.31-39; John 8.58-59.

And then under oath, at his trial, before his judges, Jesus admitted to being God's special son and agent, in spite of the mandatory death penalty for such a claim. *Again the high priest asked Him, 'Are you the Messiah, the Son of the Blessed One?' Jesus said, 'I am'.* (Mark 14.61-64)

Craig Keener sums it up in this way, 'The issue is not that later Christologies exalt Jesus in contrast to early sources that do not (though later ones like John are clearly more developed). The issue is instead that it is difficult to find any early Christian source that says much about Jesus that leaves him as a mere earthly Messiah. (Even James, which deals little with Christology, speaks of 'our glorious Lord Jesus Christ'.)[6]

Many writers go on at this point to examine evidence from Jesus' life to support the notion of his divinity. This is a mistake. It is the fundamental mistake of forgetting that God's intention is that we come to understand what God is like by looking at Jesus. We are dependent on the revelation of Jesus to gain insight into the nature of God. It is a mistake therefore to superimpose onto Jesus our preconceived ideas of God. By his words and deeds Jesus himself changed the content of the word 'God'. Jesus helps us understand who God is.

Jesus as human

In the second part of the passage that forms our framework for this chapter, John asserts the humanity of Jesus. I would summarise John 1.14-18 as follows: The moment in history had just happened when the second person in the Trinity, the Word, became human flesh. The Jewish covenant of law was succeeded by the grace received in this incredible act of God himself becoming human. John mentions the name Jesus for the first time and then says that we can only know God through Jesus.

---

[6] Craig S. Keener, 'The Historical Jesus of the Gospels', p. 280. Read pp. 268-282 for a thorough discussion of the early understandings of Jesus' divinity.

It is important to now ask: What was the foundation for the belief in Jesus' humanity?

Jesus – a man of history recorded in the New Testament: One aspect of the foundation is found in the books of the New Testament. In the first sermons about Jesus, Peter makes it clear that he and the disciples were eyewitnesses to the events, *'We are witnesses to all that he did both in Judea and in Jerusalem.'* (Acts 10.39. Peter asserts this again in 1 Peter 5.1 and in 2 Peter 1.16)

John, one of Jesus' disciples, writes in a letter of the physicality of Jesus and his encounter with that physicality:

'We declare to you what was from the beginning, what we have heard, what we have seen with our eyes, what we have looked at and touched with our hands, concerning the word of life — this life was revealed, and we have seen it and testify to it, and declare to you the eternal life that was with the Father and was revealed to us — we declare to you what we have seen and heard so that you also may have fellowship with us; and truly our fellowship is with the Father and with his Son Jesus Christ. We are writing these things so that our joy may be complete.' (1 John 1.1-4)

And in his Gospel John writes, *'Now Jesus did many other signs in the presence of his disciples, which are not written in this book.'* (John 20.30)

Luke makes it clear that his research on the life of Jesus was dependent on eyewitness accounts. (Luke 1.1-3)

It is also interesting to note that both Peter and Paul said to the enemies of the Jesus movement that they, the opponents of Jesus, were eyewitnesses themselves of the things that Christians stood for (Acts 2.22; Acts 26.24-28). They would not have dared say this to opponents if they were trying to be misleading.

These first preachers and writers were clear that, despite their elevated views of Jesus being 'God with us' in such a special way, Jesus was an ordinary human whom they had known well. No one at the time of Jesus came to believe that this man was of a different species to other humans. Jesus was accepted amongst his peers as a fellow human being. The Gospels also show us that Jesus' own self-understanding was that he was a human like anyone else. There is no evidence that Jesus thought that his closeness and oneness with God changed his humanity in any way.

The struggles with accepting the full humanity of Jesus, which emerged in the centuries after his earthly ministry, would have surprised those who knew him. They knew Jesus to be fully human; there was no doubt in their minds. What they have written about him makes it clear that he was fully human. He grew in his mother's womb. He was born and developed from baby through toddler, childhood and adolescence to manhood, just as other bodies grow. He learned (Jesus had a human mind and therefore had to get to know most things through learning and thinking. There were however some things that God revealed to him, e.g. John 15.15). Jesus' knowledge of some things was limited (for example in Mark 5.30-33, Matthew 24.36, Matthew 8.10 we see that Jesus' knowledge had limitations and certain things surprised him. In other words, Jesus is shown to have a human mind, not a divine mind.) He worked. He was a Galilean Jew who spoke with a Galilean accent. He needed to pray. He needed to obey God. He ate and drank. He felt the pangs of hunger and thirst. The strain of ministry exhausted him. He sat beside a well to rest. He fell asleep on a cushion in a boat. He cried. He got angry. He felt indignant. He felt disappointed and rejected. He loved. So gruelling was his very human agony in the garden of Gethsemane that his sweat is described as looking like great drops of blood. He needed support in his hour of agony. He was killed, and when pierced blood and water came out of him (which is the separation of clot and serum after death). His body was then bound in grave-clothes and placed in a rocky tomb.

Jesus – a man of history recorded in non-Biblical sources: The second part of the foundation of the belief in Jesus' humanity is found in the writings of other historians who are not part of the New Testament. Some of these writers were not Christians but were in no doubt about the fact of Jesus as a real man.

Cornelius Tacitus, Lucian of Samosata, Flavius Josephus, Suetonius,

Plinius Secundus, Tertullian, Thallus, Phlegon, the Letter of Mara Bar-Serapion, Justin Martyr, Polycarp, Eusebius, Irenaeus, Ignatius, Justin, Origen and the Jewish Talmuds are some of the non-Biblical 1st and 2nd Century references to Jesus. Some of them are Christian writers, others are Jewish and others Gentile non-Christian.[7] It is worth noting that Jesus does appear in the writings of Roman historians more than any other 'messianic' or prophetic leader of Palestine.[8]

The *Encyclopaedia Britannica* uses 20 000 words in describing Jesus. The description takes up more space than was given to Aristotle, Cicero, Alexander, Julius Caesar, Buddha, Confucius or Mohammed. Concerning the overwhelming independent secular (non-Christian) accounts of Jesus of Nazareth, it makes this conclusion: 'These independent accounts prove that in ancient times even the opponents of Christianity never doubted the historicity of Jesus, which was disputed for the first time and on inadequate grounds by several authors at the end of the 18th, during the 19th, and at the beginning of the 20th Centuries.'[9]

The Gospel writers present us with Jesus who is fully a man, who is not a different species of being from other humans, yet is at the same time part of God in a very unique way. Let us try and appreciate and make sense of how we understand Jesus as divine and human.

JESUS AS FULLY GOD AND FULLY HUMAN

I remember a relative saying to me after she had watched Mel Gibson's *The Passion of the Christ,* that Jesus would not have survived the crucifixion ordeals as long as he did if he had been a normal human being. In this film Jesus' brutal crucifixion is presented in its blow-by-blow sadistic violence and my relative believed that a 'normal' human being could not survive that as long as Jesus did. She had come to believe that Jesus was not really a human like other humans. She supposed that Jesus was different, that his experience of physical violence was not the same for him as it would have been for us. For her there was something superhuman about Jesus.

Jesus as Avatar?

In my experience of teaching on these matters I have found that many Christians today believe that Jesus was not a normal human being – that his divinity somehow changed his humanity. Christians, and some others, view Jesus as

---

[7] These historical figures are quoted in Josh McDowell's *Evidence that Demands a Verdict,* pp. 81-87.

[8] Craig S. Keener, *The Historical Jesus of the Gospels,* pp. 66-67.

[9] *Encyclopaedia Britannica,* 15th Edition, 1974.

someone who looked human and behaved like a human but was not really a human; rather he was God in human appearance. This idea is fairly common and many Christians think that they honour Jesus through this kind of belief. This belief would make Jesus an avatar.[10]

Many people cannot comprehend that Jesus had normal human needs and feelings, that it was necessary for him to have faith, that he was tempted, that he needed to pray, that he needed to obey God. Further, many cannot accept that Jesus had certain limitations in his ideas, likes and dislikes determined by the era and culture he was living in. Further, it is difficult for many to accept that Jesus had limitations in his knowledge, that he could not have known everything and that he had to get to know things through learning and thinking.

Throughout Christian history it has been acknowledged that certain other Christian beliefs make the idea of the full humanity of Jesus difficult to accept. For example: How is it that he is both fully human and fully divine? Surely his divinity changes his humanity, or his humanity changes his divinity? It is difficult to understand Jesus as fully human and at the same time believe in the virgin birth. How does a human walk on water? If he is divine then how can he die on a cross? These are extremely challenging questions, but throughout Christian history it has been regarded as essential that we understand Jesus as fully human.

You thought 'Avatar' was a strange title – now try these ...

Because this is such a challenging and important matter it took the early church a long time to refine and define its understanding of Jesus' identity. Christianity quickly became a faith movement and then religion that was more 'Greek' than its 'Hebrew' roots. The Greek world view was that of Plato and so Jesus had to be understood within that frame of reference, which was very different from Hebrew thinking. In this context, in the history of the early church it became a matter of great importance to define the right beliefs about Jesus, and of course to define the wrong beliefs. The wrong beliefs were labelled as heresies.

The battle against heresies about Jesus' identity was at its most intense in the 4th and 5th Centuries and most of the issues were resolved then. The councils, creeds and resolutions that ended the debates then, have become the yardstick of Christian thinking and belief. The best known of the heresies were:

---

[10] An 'avatar' is a concept in Hinduism in which the deity appears in the form of a human. The deity is not really a human but just appears to be a human. Many westerners know the term 'avatar' from the science fiction film of that name in which humans remotely control Na'vi bodies to interact with the natives of Pandora. In that movie the Na'vi bodies being controlled are avatars in that they look like Na'vi and behave like Na'vi but are not really Na'vi.

- 'Adoptionism' (Jesus was a man who was adopted as the 'Son of God')
- 'Arianism' (denied Jesus' divinity and eternal nature)
- 'Docetism' (Jesus' physical body was an illusion)
- 'Nestorianism' (emphasised Jesus' humanity to such an extent that he was separate from the eternal Word)
- Monophysitism (the most nuanced of them all, making the attractive, but highly problematic, proposal that Jesus was a compound of humanity and divinity and thereby something slightly different from both humanity and divinity).

The most important councils seeking resolution of the divided theologies were Nicaea in 325 AD, Ephesus in 431 AD and Chalcedon in 451 AD. Let us try to understand the Chalcedon resolution now.

Resolution

Let me share some of the text of the Council of Chalcedon with you:

> Therefore, following the holy fathers, we all with one accord teach people to acknowledge one and the same Son, our Lord Jesus Christ, at once complete in Godhead and complete in humanness, truly God and truly human, consisting also of a reasonable soul and body; of one substance (homoousios) with the Father as regards his Godhead, and at the same time of one substance with us as regards his humanity; like us in all respects, apart from sin; as regards his Godhead, begotten of the Father before the ages, but yet as regards his humanity begotten, for us men and for our salvation, of Mary the Virgin, the God-bearer (Theotokos); one and the same Christ, Son, Lord, Only-begotten, recognized in two natures, without confusion, without change, without division, without separation; the distinction of natures being in no way annulled by the union, but rather the characteristics of each nature being preserved and coming together to form one person and subsistence, not as parted or separated into two persons, but one and the same Son and Only-begotten God the Word, Lord Jesus Christ; even as the prophets from earliest times spoke of him, and our Lord Jesus Christ himself taught us, and the creed of the Fathers has handed down to us.

This statement of the Council of Chalcedon in 451 AD, describing the union of the divine and human natures in the person of Jesus, has been accepted ever since then as the way in which we as Christians may picture Jesus as a man who has two natures. We have in Jesus therefore a person who was both fully human and fully divine. His divinity did not make him into a superhuman, nor did his humanity made him less divine.

The Chalcedon statement helps to define the Christian belief, but it doesn't go a long way to help us to understand what is being said. Let me try and help a little more. In essence, Jesus is in every respect a human like any other human – yet he lives in complete union with God. Jesus was born in complete union with God, and throughout the living of his life that union never diminished and would have deepened as a lived experience. The Gospels show us that Jesus nurtured, savoured, explored and enjoyed this union with God.

We live in a world which need not be so Platonic. African philosophy, quantum physics and the Trinitarian perspective all appreciate relationships and connections. In this regard it is important to appreciate that Jesus' own understanding of his divinity is clearly a relational understanding (Jesus understands himself as a human in relational union with God, who is his Father, and in this union is his self-understanding of divinity), not an ontological understanding. (Ontology is about 'being'. Jesus is clear that he is not a different sort of being.)

Jesus would not have thought of himself as 'I am God', because for him the word 'God' meant 'the Father'. Jesus never thought of himself as 'the Father', but rather knew – as his whole lifestyle of prayer shows – that he was in a relationship of oneness with the Father.[11]

Similarly we may also say that Jesus' insight into his divinity was a matter of consciousness rather than ontology. Jesus lived with an awareness of his 'divinity' in the sense of a lived awareness of his oneness with God the Father. This awareness (consciousness) did not make any difference to the nature of his human being – it did not make him into a different species of human. Essentially orthodox Christianity is asserting that 'God' was not in Jesus' DNA any more or any less than God is in our DNA.[12]

It is this union with God that enabled Jesus to face temptation without falling into sin. It is our alienation from God that leads us to sin, and that sin further alienates us from God. So we see that sin is not inherent in the very

---

[11] Another Gospel reference of importance in this regard is Luke 18.18-19 where Jesus clearly shows that he does not think of himself as 'God': *[18] A certain ruler asked him, 'Good Teacher, what must I do to inherit eternal life?' [19] Jesus said to him, 'Why do you call me good? No one is good but God alone'.*

[12] In this paragraph I have, in very few words, described the best way I know to understand Jesus being both God and Man. If you like philosophical debate, a good book to read would be T.V. Morris's *The Logic of the God Incarnate*, Cornell University Press, 1986.

nature of a human being, it is our alienation from God that causes our sin. We are of course born into a world alienated from God – and for this reason we all sin, not for the reason of having sin in our nature. Jesus shows us that to be fully human is to be sinless. Jesus shows us that we too, as adopted children, may know union with God, oneness with God. It is in this unity that we truly die to sin, and are born again to new life in Jesus.

Does this theology have any relevance for Christians living today?

I indicated earlier that I have encountered in people a lot of misunderstanding about Jesus' identity. I have also noticed that misunderstandings about Jesus' identity have led to people missing out on some of the blessings of his incarnation (embodiment). My passion in this guidebook is that you should not be amongst those who are 'Missing Jesus'. I hope that this section is helping you to be amongst those who do not miss out on the remarkable blessings that come with clearer appreciation of the truth about Jesus.

We should appreciate again that the starting point in this theological reflection is the witness of the New Testament writers. They who had known Jesus had come to believe in Jesus' human nature and in Jesus' divine nature. Like Christians before us, our task is to keep faith with the New Testament writers' convictions.

Throughout the church's journey it has experienced Jesus as alive; also that relationship with God is entered into through relationship with Jesus. This was ongoing experiential confirmation that Jesus, who had been a human, was also completely part of divinity.

Throughout Christian history it has been a priority to challenge and expose understandings about Jesus that did not keep faith with the New Testament convictions of Jesus' full humanity and divinity. What is the relevance of having the right understanding? Let me share some important reasons:

It is important to value that God did not just make as if he was coming to us as a human, but that he really did come as one of us. For God the Son (Word) to look human but not really be human would be a kind of devious divine trick played on us. Such a charade would not benefit us or God's dealings with us at all. A right understanding leads us to appreciate that in Jesus we have received a genuine and full incarnation of God the Son (Word).

Christian discipleship is all about following in the footsteps of Jesus, living according to his example and teachings. If Jesus was not fully human, like you and me, then it would be unfair to expect us to be his disciples; to resist sin and to love as he did. If Jesus was superhuman then it would have been far easier, perhaps not difficult at all, to resist sin and to love fully.

We would not need to praise Jesus for his love and sinlessness if he was not a full human being, because his love and resistance to sin may have been done on strengths that we do not have and will never have because we can never be superhumans.

We should realise that God would not have achieved anything in salvation history if God had come to us as a once-off separate species of being (a human-looking being with greater powers than normal humans). God's dealing with humanity would not be enhanced by God becoming a different-from-human species. God's relationship with humanity would not have made any progress if Jesus was something different from fully human.

Jesus' victory is also God's victory. Because God himself has come to us in Jesus we appreciate that the victory over sin, evil and death is God's victory. Scripture wants us to be clear that God is at work in Jesus – that although Jesus is fully human, God is at work in him and through him. The reconciliation that has been achieved between God and humanity has been God's achievement. Paul says this memorably in 2 Corinthians 5.19: *'in Christ God was reconciling the world to himself'*. The victory over sin, evil and death that Jesus wins is the atoning work of God. Gustaf Aulén draws our attention to the heart of this matter when he says, 'The Incarnation is the necessary presupposition of the Atonement, and the Atonement the completion of the Incarnation.'[13]

---

[13] *Christus Victor: An Historical Study of the Three Main Types of the Idea of the Atonement*, Gustaf Aulén, SPCK Classics, London, 1931, p. 151.

My own personal answer to the question of the relevance of this theology is that I am encouraged in my own discipleship to seek communion and intimacy with God, for I know that it was this oneness with the Father that also enabled Jesus to love himself, other people and his environment (four relationships of life). I know and experience God as real the more I put my faith in God. Through a growing and deepening surrender to God I experience my own transformation into Christ-likeness by the work of God's Spirit.

In closing this section it is my delight to share a very beautiful illustration with you which helps to bring some of the points home in a very inspirational way:

> It is as if Shakespeare should want to communicate with Hamlet. He can't do it, because Shakespeare and Hamlet live in different worlds, different universes. Shakespeare is a real person, Hamlet exists only in the world of the play. So how could genuine communication ever be possible? Well, what if Shakespeare wrote himself into the script of the play, created a new character, called William Shakespeare, who would speak and act in the same way that the real-life Shakespeare spoke and acted. Then Hamlet could know Shakespeare: we could even say that Hamlet could have a personal relationship with his creator. So with Jesus, God has written himself into the text of the human drama, giving himself lines and actions that demonstrate to us what God is like in terms we can understand, and making it possible for us to relate to God in a way that simply wasn't possible any other way. And the Christian claim, John's claim, is that when God did that, the name by which he was called was Jesus.[14]

WHERE DOES OUR INFORMATION ABOUT JESUS COME FROM?

Most of our detailed knowledge of Jesus comes directly to us from the New Testament section of our Bibles. There are references to Jesus by other historical figures of the time but they do not give much detail at all. I would like to briefly address the 'trust' issues – namely questions like, 'Can we trust the writers of the New Testament, especially the writers of the Gospels?' and 'Do we have reliable copies of what they wrote?'

The search for historically reliable information about Jesus is called 'The Quest for the Historical Jesus'. In this research there are a variety of things

---

[14] I received this quote many years ago in email correspondence and have forgotten the source. The correspondent said that it came from William Temple but I have not been able to verify that.

researchers look for in the literature to decide which can be trusted to give us true information about Jesus. The following are some of the things researchers look for:

- Any piece of writing is written from a certain perspective and has a purpose and agenda. At times the 'agenda' may cause the writing to distort the events described so much that one does not trust the historical reliability of what is contained. In other words the writing is believed to be too much the work of propaganda. The Gospels are narratives constructed about Jesus with the agenda of encouraging faith in Jesus. Research has shown that the Gospels' agenda has not so deformed or fabricated the original events that we cannot rely on their presentation of those events.
- Comparison to other similar literary forms. The Gospels can be seen as examples of biography and historiography in ancient times and researchers must certainly compare them to those types of literature. Encouragingly, the latest research into the Gospels as surviving books of those literature types have shown that they are extremely reliable.[15]
- Internal coherence. Scholars look for internal coherence within a book and between the books of the New Testament.
- Primary sources. Scholars look favourably on books written by eyewitnesses or at least those who interviewed eyewitnesses. The written records of Jesus' teachings were compiled within a decade of his death, and the first Gospel completed within about 40 years. In other words, the Gospels are based on either the writings of eyewitnesses or the interviewing of those eyewitnesses, or both. This is much more reliable than other ancient biographical works (e.g. the biography of Plato was only completed 400 years after his death).
- The bibliographical test. Unfortunately no original manuscripts are available and so researches must 'test' the reliability of the copies. We can trust our sources if there are many ancient copies available, if there is little or no variation between those copies and if the time gap between the original and the oldest copy is small. The New Testament is quite remarkable in this instance, as you will see in the following table:

---

[15] Craig S. Keener, *The Historical Jesus of the Gospels*, pp. 71-161.

Author	When written	First copy	Time span	No of copies
Plato	427-347 BC	900 AD	1 200 yrs	7
Aristotle	384-322 BC	1100 AD	1 400 yrs	49
Homer (Iliad)	762 BC	300 BC (fragment) 1059 (full manuscript)	460-1 700 yrs	643
New Testament	40-100 AD	125 AD (full manuscript is 350 AD)	25-300 yrs	24 000

(There are only 400 words in your entire Bible where there are some variations amongst the ancient manuscripts. These words have a footnote to give you an alternative reading of the word or phrase.)

- The 'criterion of dissimilarity' – a saying by Jesus that is dissimilar to Jewish context of the time is likely to be authentic.
- The 'criterion of embarrassment' – a story that would have been embarrassing to the early Christian Church is likely to be authentic (e.g. baptism of Jesus by John).
- 'Multiple attestations' – the same event or saying repeated by a variety of authors is of course reliable.
- External verification – here researchers look for other historical sources that substantiate the accuracy, reliability and authenticity of NT books. The NT books pass this test too in that there are many references in the writings of the Church Fathers (100 A.D. onwards) that refer to the reliability of the content and authors of the NT books. Further, a vast amount of archaeological discoveries substantiate NT events, sites and descriptions.

The Gospels, and the rest of the New Testament, emerge from these tests as literature we can trust.

In research for this guidebook I read one of the most recent and thorough volumes in the quest for the historical Jesus – namely Craig S. Keener's comprehensive *The Historical Jesus of the Gospels*. Like him I am confident in following a maximalist approach to accepting information about Jesus from the Gospels. In other words, we can rely on the historical accuracy of most of what we read in the Gospels.

The quest for the historical Jesus has been extremely fruitful and interesting in the last 60–70 years due to the discovery of the Dead Sea Scrolls (1947-1990) which opened up to the world insights about Second Temple Judaism (the Judaism of Jesus' day). Since the Holocaust Jews and Christians have dialogued far more than ever in history and this has been extremely fruitful in discovering the Jewishness of Jesus.

I rely equally on all four of the Gospels. In so doing I am not ignoring the reality that John's Gospel is more theological in nature and at times gives precedence to its theological message rather than history. John's Gospel also communicates a lot with symbols and signs. It is however interesting in some instances that John gives historically reliable information that the other Gospels don't record (for example, recent excavations have revealed a separate route for cattle to get into the temple – only John refers to cattle in the temple[16]).

All four Gospels have a theological message and that message – from those who wrote the most reliable information about Jesus – is vitally important. These Gospel writers were not just telling us of historical events, they were telling us of the meaning of those events – and herein is the life-giving message for us all.

Don't miss the point!

The value of the Christian faith rests on Jesus, not in the belief or behaviour of Christians. Jesus is the Shepherd the world needs, the true foundation of Christianity. Do not allow Christians who have Jesus missing from the foundation of their lives to distract you from seeing Jesus for the authentic person he was, or cause you to lose faith in the true foundation!

Let us be personal

In this chapter you have read of what many people who met Jesus in his earthly ministry came to believe about him. You have also read that through faith in Jesus many people ever since then have experienced a relationship with God. You cannot read these things without making a personal decision about these matters – you either need to decide that you too will have faith, or that you will not have faith in Jesus.

Jesus liked to ask *'Who do you say that I am?'* (Luke 9.20). That is a question he asks you now, as you read this sentence. You do need to answer.

---

[16] *The Historical Jesus of the Gospels,* Craig S. Keener, William B. Eerdmans Publishing Company, Grand Rapids, Michigan, 2009, p 291.

I started with the beginning of John's book; let me end with his ending:

> *Now Jesus did many other signs in the presence of His disciples which are not written in this book. But these are written so that you may come to believe that Jesus is the Messiah, the Son of God, and that through believing you may have life in His name ... The disciple who is testifying to these things and has written them, we know that his testimony is true. But there are also many other things that Jesus did; if every one of them were written down, I suppose that the world itself could not contain the books that would be written.* (John 20.30-31; 21.24-25)

I invite you to take a step of faith in Jesus, if you have not yet done so. This step of faith is still necessary, even though there is so much evidence. It is not a step into the dark; it is a step into the light!

Missing Jesus?

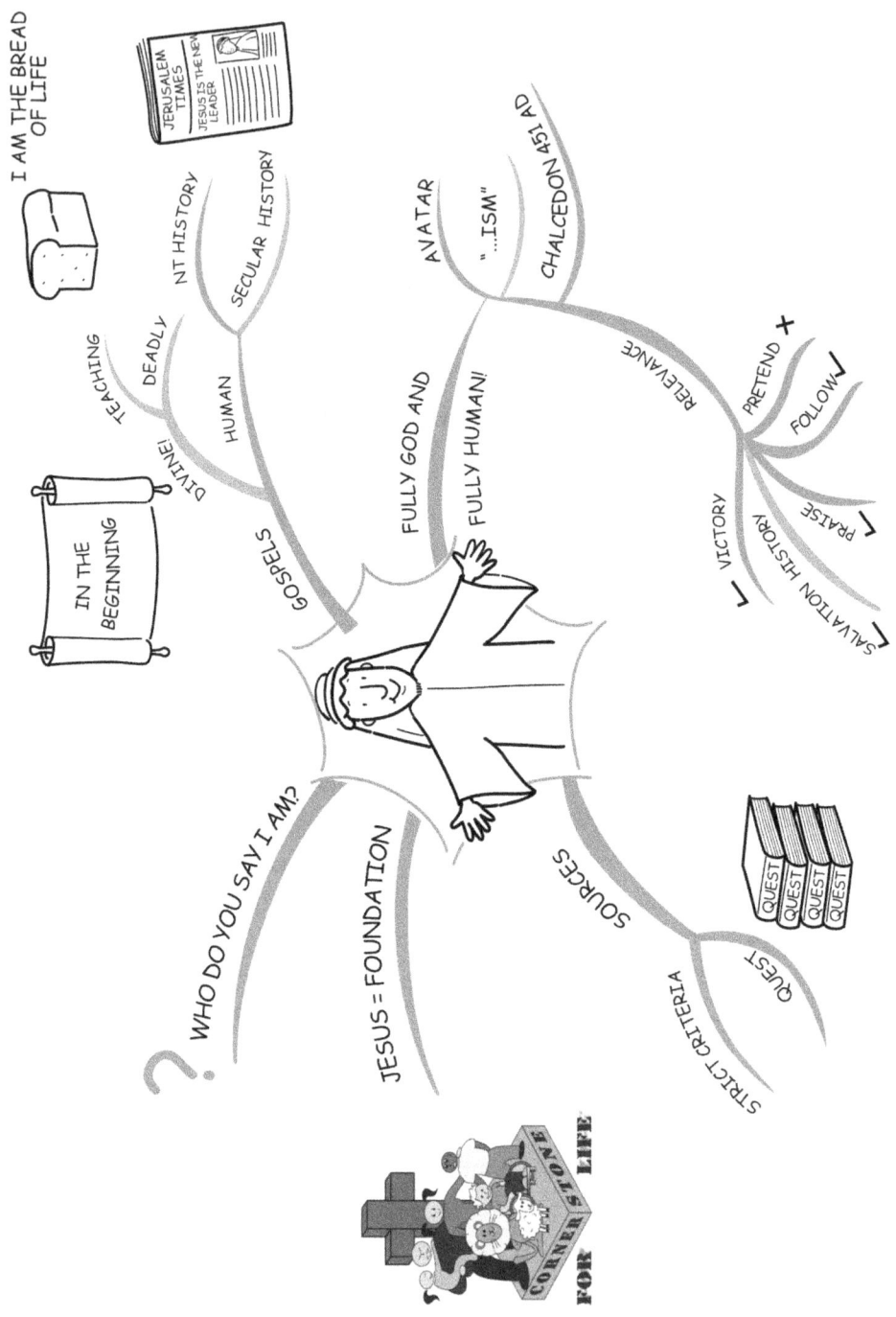

SUGGESTIONS FOR DISCUSSION, REVISION, REFLECTION AND APPLICATION

(These questions are intended for group work, but can easily be adapted for personal use.)

1. What is the most important message to you in this chapter? (Remember to also make a note of this on your 'God spoke to me' page.)
2. Icebreaker question: Tell the group what an item of clothing you are wearing says about you. (The question must be answered quickly. As a group, do not spend longer than 5 minutes in total on this question.)
3. Read John 1:1-18 and answer the following questions:
   a. What did this passage mean for the people who first read it? What was the impact on them? What questions did it raise? What would have been difficult for them? What was good news for them?
   b. What does this passage mean for us today?
   c. What does this passage mean for you now?
4. Below are a variety of suggestions and questions to aid your appreciation of this chapter. Do not attempt to do all of them! Choose those that are most appropriate to your unique situation and/or group. The questions are designed to help variously with revision, understanding, appreciation, reflection or application of the content.
   a. What are our reasons for saying Jesus of Nazareth was divine?
   b. What do you personally think and feel is the most compelling reason to assert Jesus' divinity? What makes you certain that he is divine?
   c. What evidence do we have to say that Jesus was human?
   d. Do you personally have any difficulty in asserting Jesus' full humanity?
   e. Does this theology have any relevance for your own Christian living today?
   f. Revisit the illustration about Shakespeare and Hamlet. What impact does this illustration have on your feelings? On your thoughts?
   g. Is the Bible in your hands an accurate translation of the original writings of scripture? Give reasons for your answer.
   h. Respond to the following statement: 'God became human in Jesus to give the world a special message. We must pay close attention to what he said and did.'

    i. Do you agree?

    ii. Are Christians in general paying close attention to what Jesus said and did?

i. Pierre Teilhard de Chardin said, 'By virtue of the Creation and, still more, the Incarnation, nothing here below is profane for those who know how to see.' Allow this statement to sink in and shape your worldview. Are there any reflections you have now?

Three important matters to reflect on during this coming week:

1. Jesus liked to ask *'Who do you say that I am?'* (Luke 9.20). If your answer has not included a personal entrusting of yourself to Jesus as the Messiah and Son of God then I invite you to pray the following prayer now:

Dear Jesus, I hear you knocking at the door of my life to come in and be my Lord and Saviour.
I now open the door and invite you in.
Please forgive me for my sins that separate me from you.
I want to be in a good relationship with you.
I trust you now.
Through you Lord Jesus I want to die to sin and be born again to a new life with you.
I pray this prayer in the powerful name of Jesus, Amen.

2. What would you say in your personal statement of belief about Jesus? (Perhaps you would like to actually take time to write your own statement this week.)
3. Take a few minutes to imagine meeting Jesus of Nazareth. Perhaps you meet him at the local well. Together you find some shade and get to spend a few minutes together. Take time to place yourself fully in the scene using all five senses. Let the man Jesus be very real to you. What do you say to him? What does he say to you? What impresses you about him? What surprises you about him?

GOD SPOKE TO ME ...

5

JESUS' BIRTH AND MINISTRY

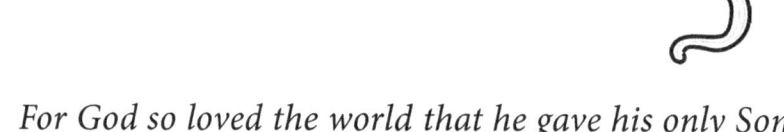

For God so loved the world that he gave his only Son, so that everyone who believes in him may not perish but may have eternal life. Indeed, God did not send the Son into the world to condemn the world, but in order that the world might be saved through him. (John 3.16-17)

Life changed as a result of the person Jesus of Nazareth. The world was a different place after his short life. What were some of the things that changed? Jesus succeeded in changing for the good the fundamental balances of power in the battle between good and evil. Jesus gave to the world a new picture of God: the profound yet shocking revelation of God as self-sacrificial love. The tide of humanity's relationship with God turned and an era of reconciliation and growing closeness was started. The remarkable, and of course essential, feature of this turning tide was its inclusiveness of all peoples of every tribe, race and nation. Thereby good community life was achieved amongst many previously divided people. A spirit of entrapment was lifted from humanity and things that had been rare became abundant – especially transformation of people and healing. Understanding of true power shifted from domination to servanthood. A whole new consciousness of God's reign was born and this consciousness brought remarkable change to people, communities and even nations and cultures.

Jesus' gift to the world was much more than a new religion and a fresh start to the calendar!

How was this all achieved? The remainder of this guidebook will make this clear to you.

What Jesus has done is restore the potential for abundant life that was God's intention in creation. In the second chapter we came to understand that abundant life is experienced in God's intention for creation, which was community in all four of life's relationships. We then saw how sin breaks community through its divisiveness in all four of the relationships of life. We came to understand that sin divides and that if it is left unchallenged it will destroy all that it divides. This fifth chapter will show how Jesus overcomes these divisions and in so doing makes a different reality possible for us all. This different reality that is made available to us is his gift to us, given in his birth, ministry, death and resurrection. This different reality is the restoration of community in the four relationships of life.

JESUS' BIRTH – UNITY BETWEEN GOD AND HUMANITY RE-ESTABLISHED

Through being born as a human child in this world God became part of humanity and thus created a unity between the divine community and humanity. In his very being, as the Word made flesh, Jesus the Christ unites God and humanity. What this means is that God is part of humanity forever and that this bond cannot be broken. Jesus turns the tide against the divisiveness of sin. Jesus brings into being a state of unity between God and humanity. Nothing can break the available unity that Jesus has achieved.

Clear and present manger

The song 'Mary's boy child', which Boney M made famous, captures the truth that the incarnation lays the foundation for us to be saved from our division from God.

> *Hark now hear the angels sing,*
> *a new king born today*
> *and man will live for ever more,*
> *because of Christmas Day.*
> *Trumpets sound and angels sing,*
> *listen to what they say*
> *that man will live for ever more,*
> *because of Christmas day.*[1]

---

[1] The words I have posted here are the original lyrics of the song which was first sung by Harry Belafonte. This original version is slightly different from the Boney M version. The words here were accessed from https://www.lyricsmode.com/lyrics/h/harry_belafonte/marys_boy_child.html on 4/8/2019.

Missing Jesus?

Most Christians focus on Jesus' death as the moment of Jesus winning our salvation, but this song sings a profound truth that we are saved from the consequences of sin because of Christmas day! This does not suggest that Good Friday is unimportant – rather it is vital for us to see that in the incarnation, celebrated at Christmas, God is made part of humanity forever.

Remember that the effect of sin was division in the four relationships of life – Jesus is then a saviour in everything that he does to bring community and unity back to those four relationships.

Core to the event of God coming to us in Jesus is to say that God is not 'out there' but is truly near and present to humanity. Jesus, in becoming human, makes it clear that union with God does not come through escaping the human condition, but in and through the human condition too.

To say it slightly differently, Jesus overcomes the dualistic view of a strict separation between the spiritual and the so-called non-spiritual in which non-spiritual dimensions of life are viewed as unfavourable to spiritual dimensions of life. For God to become a human being in such a simple and humble way (amongst the poor and without the comforts that money can buy) is a very special message about the ideal way in which humanity in our simplicity can be one with God – it is saying that being human is not the problem.

God coming to us in Jesus means that God becomes personal – God becomes a person – and our relationship with God moves from holding ideas about God (first cause, omnipresent, omniscient, etc.) to falling in love with God. We fall in love with a person, we don't really fall in love with abstractions. It is this fact that makes for Christianity's popularity – that it is about a personal relationship with God come to us in Jesus.

God coming to us in Jesus is an act of great hospitality. God becomes human so that he may personally welcome us into a relationship with himself. God becomes human so that he may personally host our lives.

Consummation

The New Testament has another very special way of broadcasting this good news about the restored community with God made available to us in Jesus' birth. It does this by picking up on the Old Testament understanding that God wanted Israel to be his bride. Jewish people were familiar with this metaphor for it was found in many of the great writings of the Hebrew Scriptures. Marriage became the Biblical image for the kind of unity that is possible between God and humanity, between God and a human being.

We have the remarkable life story and writings of Hosea whose own marriage was a symbol of God's persistent love as a husband for his unfaithful bride (see Hosea chapters 1-3). This same theme is the sustained metaphor for God's love for Israel and Israel's unfaithfulness that starts in Jeremiah 2 and is carried through many of the following chapters. The love story of the metaphor is beautifully developed in Ezekiel 16. The passion and intimacy of the metaphor is erotically described in the entire book of Song of Songs. Isaiah also uses the metaphor in Isaiah 54.4-8 and in 62.1-5.

The New Testament writers came to see that the Old Testament was essentially speaking of a metaphorical betrothal (engagement) that was then fulfilled in a metaphorical marriage and consummation of marriage in Jesus' coming into the world. This seems to be Jesus' own understanding because he refers to himself as a bridegroom and that his coming ushers in a wedding feast:

> Then the disciples of John came to him, saying, 'Why do we and the Pharisees fast often, but your disciples do not fast?' And Jesus said to them, 'The wedding guests cannot mourn as long as the bridegroom is with them, can they? The days will come when the bridegroom is taken away from them, and then they will fast.' (Matthew 9.14-17. This saying of Jesus is repeated in Mark 2.18-22 and Luke 5.33-39).

Jesus also clearly enjoyed telling parables in which the Kingdom of God/Heaven is likened to a wedding feast – in Matthew 22.1-14 we hear a parable that starts: *The kingdom of heaven may be compared to a king who gave a wedding banquet for his son.* Matthew 25.1-13 is a different parable, but also about the Kingdom being likened to a wedding event: *Then the kingdom of heaven will be like this. Ten bridesmaids took their lamps and went to meet the bridegroom.* Other references of Jesus' teaching using the parable of a wedding are Luke 12.36, Luke 14.7-11. It is also significant that John's Gospel records the first sign of Jesus' identity and mission at a wedding (John 2.1-12).

John the baptiser understood Jesus to be the bridegroom and himself as the 'best man' at the wedding:

> 'You yourselves are my witnesses that I said, "I am not the Messiah, but I have been sent ahead of him." He who has the bride is the bridegroom. The friend of the bridegroom, who stands and hears him, rejoices greatly at the bridegroom's voice. For this reason my joy has been fulfilled. He must increase, but I must decrease.' (John 3.28-30).[2]

Paul understands Jesus' coming in this way too, when he uses the description of the two-in-one-flesh quality of marriage, to describe the unity of Jesus and the church (believing humanity): *'For this reason a man will leave his father and mother and be joined to his wife, and the two will become one flesh. This is a great mystery, and I am applying it to Christ and the church.'* (Ephesians 5.31-32).

A consistent feature of the Old Testament metaphor of God's people as the bride is that the bride is unfaithful, so unfaithful that she is often described as a whore! We realise that God's act, as husband, of going ahead and marrying this unfaithful bride is an act of incalculable forgiveness on God's part. God is saying to humanity 'I forgive your betrayal and I want to be one with you.' Did you realise that the incarnation is such a beautiful and generous act of forgiveness?

---

[2] The best man in Jewish weddings at the time of Jesus waited at the door of the bridal chamber where the marriage had to be consummated before the feasting began! It would be a moment of great joy when the best man heard the groom's voice and could announce that the festivities may begin.

Many Christians think that God was only willing to forgive our sins after Jesus' death on the cross. But surely the greatest act of loving forgiveness is God's birth in this world that had rejected him so often. Therefore, forgiveness of sins becomes a reality already with the incarnation, not just after Jesus' death. God was not waiting for Jesus to die a terrible death before he would be prepared to forgive sins.

Jesus himself made this clear to us when he granted forgiveness of sins in his ministry. He told people there and then that they were forgiven; he did not say that they had to wait for his death before they would be forgiven. Jesus comes as God's gracious act and testifies to the grace of God throughout his ministry. (I will unpack this aspect of Jesus' ministry much later in this guidebook. If you would like some Scripture references to look at now you may turn to Matthew 6.12, Luke 15.2, and Mark 2.15. There are parallels ('parallels' refers to when there is a similar story in another Gospel) in Luke 7.34-50; Luke 11.37; Luke 14.1; Luke 14.12-13; Luke 15.1; Luke 19.1-10; Luke 23.34; Mark 2.1-12, Matthew 9.2-8.)

Take some time to read John 8.1-11 in conjunction with Ezekiel 16. You see then how Ezekiel 16 is enacted in John 8. Jesus is clearly the one through whom God forgives humanity. Jesus' incarnation is an act of forgiveness, his ministry is a ministry of forgiveness, his dealing with this woman caught in adultery is an enactment of the great forgiveness that Ezekiel prophesied. Ezekiel 16.63 predicts that people would be confounded by God's act of forgiveness. You may feel confounded (mystified and frustrated) by such gracious forgiveness. You may prefer to hold onto the theory that God needed Jesus to die a gruesome death before he would forgive the world!

John the baptiser understood that Jesus' presence in this world re-establishes unity between God and humanity for all who would desire this gift. This is why John also practises a ministry of forgiveness of sins:

> *John the baptizer appeared in the wilderness, proclaiming a baptism of repentance for the forgiveness of sins. And people from the whole Judean countryside and all the people of Jerusalem were going out to him, and were baptized by him in the river Jordan, confessing their sins.* (Mark 1.4-5; see also Matthew 3.6; Luke 3.3).

I believe that the centrality and prominence of this wedding theme is underlined by the fact that the book of Revelation portrays a wedding as one of the closing scenes of that book. This is the marriage supper of the Lamb and I believe that it is the Spirit's way of saying to us, 'Yes, through Jesus there is a marriage that takes place between God and humanity!':

> *Then I heard what seemed to be the voice of a great multitude, like the sound of many waters and like the sound of mighty thunderpeals, crying out, 'Hallelujah! For the Lord our God the Almighty reigns. Let us rejoice and exult and give him the glory, for the marriage of the Lamb has come, and his bride has made herself ready; to her it has been granted to be clothed with fine linen, bright and pure'– for the fine linen is the righteous deeds of the saints. And the angel said to me, 'Write this: Blessed are those who are invited to the marriage supper of the Lamb.' And he said to me, 'These are true words of God.'* (Revelation 19.6-9)

Essentially this vision gives insight into an ongoing marriage feast in heaven that is taking place right now and will reach its fulfilment in the culmination of all things.

I pray that you are blessed by the overwhelming character of God's love come to us in Jesus, whose birth re-establishes unity between God and humanity as a reality available to all. I am not discounting the role of Jesus' death and resurrection at all. We will see later that Jesus' death was essential to seal the unity that was re-established in his birth.

JESUS' MINISTRY RE-ESTABLISHES FRIENDSHIP IN THE FOUR RELATIONSHIPS OF LIFE

When God became human in Jesus the most powerful force in the universe was unleashed, namely self-sacrificial love. God's love for us brought God to the point of sacrificing the unlimited realm of heaven for the limited realm of earth and humanity. This was an enormous sacrifice and in so doing activated the most potent form of love, namely sacrificial love. The potency of this love was seen in Jesus' ministry and would culminate in the sacrificial giving of his human life in a gruesome execution.

Jesus' life and ministry can be summed up with one word – love. Jesus loved all people all the time, not just some people some of the time; and this ministry of love made it clear that God loves all people, not just some people. As my friend Alan Storey often repeats, 'Jesus lived to love'. Religious leaders wanted to force Jesus into their mould, which presented God as selective in his love, but Jesus resisted their pressure and thus angered them.

In order to make God's love for all clear, Jesus emphasised a love for those that society rejected. Jesus showed a special love and attention for abandoned and marginalised peoples. In the Gospels they are described as 'sinners'. 'Sinners' was a term used to describe outcasts from society and would have included the poor, prostitutes, tax collectors, robbers, herdsmen, money lenders, gamblers, the uneducated, those that don't pay their tithes and those who were negligent about all the regulations of Jewish law. These people were rejected by religious authorities; therefore they were rejected in the name of God.

In the world view of Jesus' day people were poor because God had rejected them and people were wealthy because God had approved of them. So it was important for religious leaders to reject the poor because that showed that they agreed with God. However, Jesus saw it as very important to befriend them, in the name of God. The term, 'friend of sinners', given to Jesus by his opponents, was an insult aimed at preventing people from taking him seriously.

The unity between God and humanity that had been restored by Jesus' birth, was therefore protected through his life and ministry. Not only was it protected, it was deepened to become a friendship. Jesus' friendship with all people was an experience, and an offer, of friendship with God. His teachings revealed to us what it means to be God's friends. Jesus made it clear that we could also share in the special relationship he enjoyed with God as his Father.

It is important to realise that if Jesus had not loved all people all the time it would have meant that God's love had been overpowered by sin. The fact that Jesus remained steadfast in his love means that the unity between God and humanity was maintained and strengthened by his life and ministry. ***Jesus' ministry re-established friendship between God and humanity as a reality available to all.***[3]

Jesus' ministry also laid the foundation for good community life between people. He taught us to love all people all the time; to value sharing rather than greed; to value people rather than prestige; and to give our lives to loving service, which Jesus instituted as the most powerful force in the world. Not only did Jesus teach this, he also established it by calling 12 disciples and moulding them and other followers into a community.

It amazed and inspired the Apostle Paul to reflect on the effect Jesus had on the relationships between Jew and Gentile. In the world of that day you were either a Jew or a Gentile (non-Jew), and the hatred between these two groups ran very deep. But in Jesus the hostility between the two groups could be broken down because of his remarkable ministry of grace for all, both Jew and Gentile, and then him being faithful to death for that ministry. Ephesians 2.11-22 includes statements such as ...*in His flesh He has made both groups into one and has broken down the dividing wall, that is, the hostility between us ... that He might create in Himself one new humanity in place of the two, thus making peace.* ***Jesus' ministry re-established friendship between people as a reality available to all.***[4]

Jesus' ministry also set people free from the effects of sin within themselves. Jesus enabled the inner divisions that trapped people in their past, and held them in bondage to sin, to be overcome. The experience of God's love and forgiveness through Jesus enabled people to overcome sin, leave behind all things and follow him. He enabled all their faculties to be unified into the service of love. ***Jesus' ministry re-established friendship with ourselves as a reality available to all.***[5]

---

[3] This theme will be developed further in this guidebook but if you wish to read some passages that relate to it then please see Matthew 5.43-45; Luke 15.3; Matthew 11.19; Luke 7.39; Matthew 22.34-40; Mark 2.5-12.

[4] At this point I have given an extremely brief summary of Jesus' teachings on the values of God's reign. They are so important that this course will deal with them in detail during later chapters on the Kingdom of God / Reign of God. If you wish to immediately look at some passages that present this aspect of Jesus' ministry then please see the following: John 15.12-13; Mark 10.17-22; Luke 14.7-11; Matthew 18.3; Mark 10.42-44; Matthew 5.43-44; Mark 3.31-35; Mark 3.14; Luke 9.1; Matthew 10.1-4; 1 Peter 2.9; Matthew 28.19; Colossians 3.11.

[5] The contents of this paragraph will be further explored later but if you wish to see some passages that present this aspect of Jesus' ministry then please see the following: John 5.14; Matt 4.18-25; Mark 2.13-17; John 15.5; Mark 5.1-20 in which Jesus exercises his authority over a man's inner life, thus enabling him to be in his 'right mind'.

Jesus was very attentive to our relationship with both the natural environment and our human-made environment. In doing so he was demonstrating a way of people living in harmony with the natural environment. He was at home in creation (his 40-day retreat in the wilderness area when he was *'with the wild animals'* (Mark 1.13) demonstrates this most profoundly). He was very attentive to all that we can learn from parts of creation such as birds and plants.

Jesus' ministry also dealt with the social structures of his day. He presented the Kingdom of God as a social structure with the kind of values that, if applied, would make social structures hospitable to humans. He envisioned community between people and their environment. He spoke of God's care for us through the natural world. He taught that human-made structures should also care through the values of sharing rather than greed, people rather than prestige, and love being the power of the powerful. Jesus' teaching was clearly perceived as a threat to the status quo of his day. Jesus dealt with injustice through non-violent direct action rather than the more common responses of blind submission or violent overthrow.[6] **Jesus' ministry established the way of life-giving communion between people and the environment.**[7]

THIS CHAPTER IN A NUTSHELL

The birth, life and ministry of Jesus continue to have a profound effect on our lives. What he achieved then is an achievement for all time. I hope this is clear to you. Ever since Jesus was *born* God became physically part of humanity's world and in so doing overcame the division between God and humanity that had begun with sin. In his *ministry* Jesus re-established friendship in the four relationships of life, showing and teaching the way of love and obedience.

The reality of friendship (communion, union, reconciliation) that I have described is not a theological interpretation of Jesus' ministry that was noticed after the event; on the contrary, the religious and political authorities noticed it as it was happening and opposed it in increasingly determined ways. Jesus was not left to carry on his ministry unhindered but faced increasingly hostile opposition. Jesus' response to this opposition was crucial, for it would either make or break the friendship that he had established. That drama would culminate in him giving his life to his opponents.

Christians and the world know about Jesus' death and think that it was his

---

[6] *Jesus' Third Way* by Walter Wink is a now famous study of Jesus' teachings.

[7] These themes will be explored in detail in various parts of this guidebook. If you wish to read some passages that present a little of these important themes of Jesus' ministry then please see: Mark 10.17-22; Luke 14.7-11; Matthew 18.3; Mark 10.42-44; Matthew 5.43-44; Matthew 28.19; Colossians 3.11. These themes will be unpacked in detail in chapters 6 to 13.

death that won a new reality of forgiveness for our lives. I trust that you can see that as too limited a view. We will have a closer look at Jesus' death and its significance, along with his resurrection, later in this guidebook.

But before we get there we enter into a very exciting stage in our journey. We now enter into a deeper appreciation of the detail of what Jesus taught, how he ministered and lived. This detail is generally missing from people's knowledge of Jesus. Finding this detail is the journey of finding the Shepherd we lost.

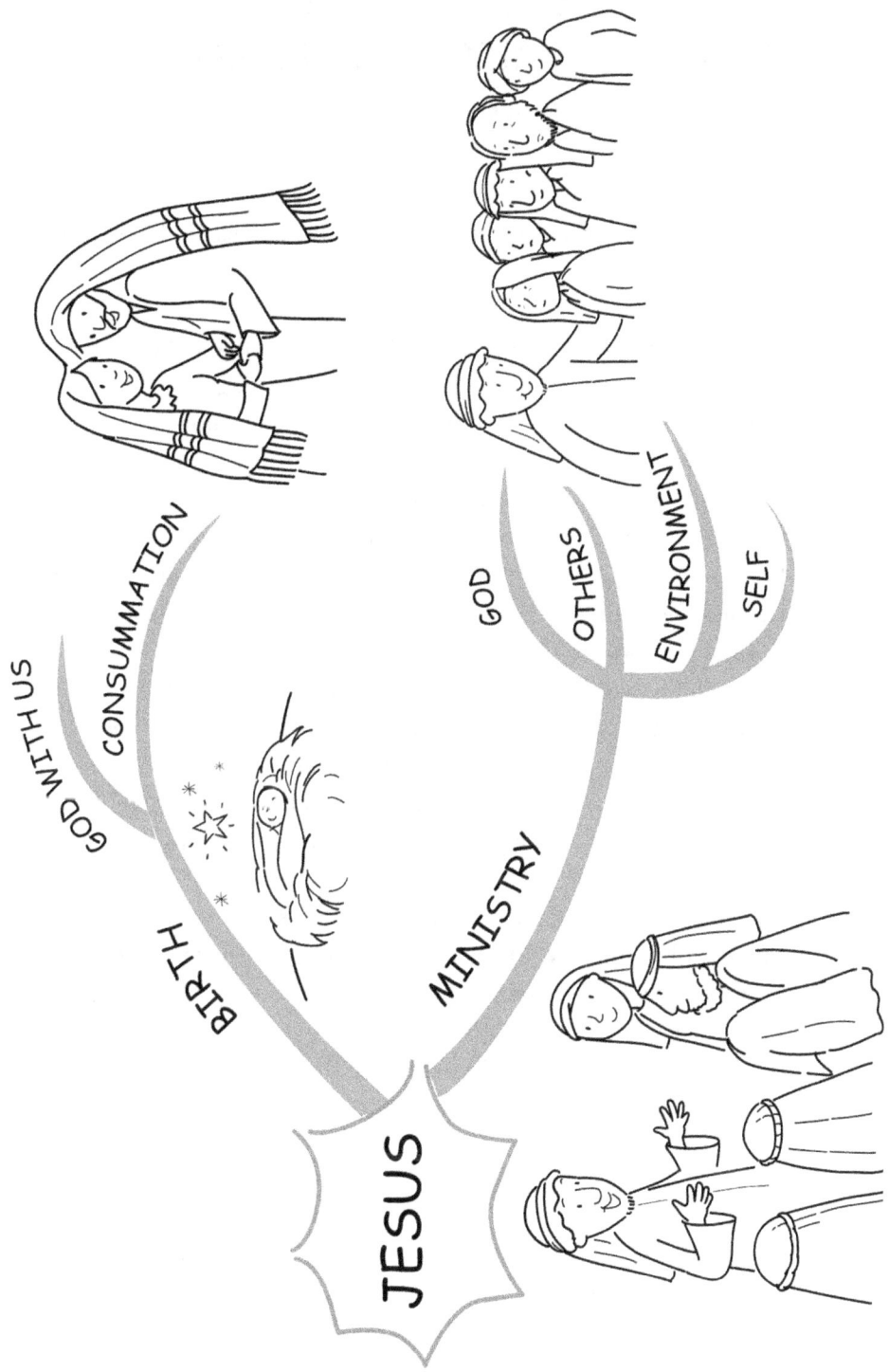

SUGGESTIONS FOR DISCUSSION, REVISION, REFLECTION AND APPLICATION

(These questions are intended for group work, but can easily be adapted for personal use.)

1. What is the most important message to you in this chapter? (Remember to also make a note of this on your 'God spoke to me' page.)
2. Icebreaker question: What is your earliest happy memory of Christmas? (The question must be answered quickly. As a group, do not spend longer than 5 minutes in total on this question.)
3. Read Matthew 1.18-25 and answer the following questions:
    a. What impact did this story have on those who first heard it or read it?
    b. Discuss and reflect on all that you find meaningful in the passage.
    c. What do the words 'God is with us' mean to you?
    d. What do the words 'God is with us' mean to the world?
4. Below are a variety of suggestions and questions to aid your appreciation of this chapter. Do not attempt to do all of them! Choose those that are most appropriate to your unique situation and/or group. The questions are designed to help variously with revision, understanding, appreciation, reflection or application of the content.
    a. The opening paragraph of this chapter attempts to describe some of the ways in which reality has changed because of Jesus. Re-read the paragraph and reflect on it together. What would you add to the list?
    b. If someone were to say to you: 'God sent his Son to the world to die for our sins', what would you like to say to this person?
        i. What do Christians lose out on if they only focus on Jesus' death? Try and make a list.
    c. How are we saved by Jesus' birth? Try and answer this in your own words.
    d. Christian teaching has mostly overlooked the life-changing consequences of Jesus' birth. Now that you have journeyed through this chapter and given the subject attention, what impresses you most about the focus?
    e. How are we saved by Jesus' ministry? Try and answer this in your own words.

f. Because of Jesus, friendship with God is truly possible! How does that make you feel?
g. Because of Jesus, friendship can characterise relationships between all people! Where true friendship exists it is a sign of what is possible in all relationships. What are the qualities of friendship amongst people? Can those qualities be part of all relationships? What is the best possible relationship between humans?
h. Because of Jesus, friendship with yourself is possible! How do you feel about the war with yourself ending? How do you feel about being your own best friend? How can Jesus help you with this?
i. Because of Jesus, friendship with our environment is possible! Are you a friend of the earth? What would it mean for you to become a friend of the earth? Social structures can be life-giving! Describe life-giving social structures. What can you do to make some of this true?

GOD SPOKE TO ME …

6

THE KINGDOM CONSCIOUSNESS MOVEMENT

'The time is fulfilled, and the kingdom of God has come near; repent, and believe in the good news.' (Mark 1.15)

JESUS – MISSING IN PLAIN SIGHT

I now take you into the wonderful world of the detail of Jesus' ministry. This is recorded for us in the Gospels according to Matthew, Mark, Luke and John. There in plain sight is the account of much of what Jesus stood for, what he sought to achieve, what he was burdened to pass on to those who would listen, what he was delighted to be true to, what moved his heart, the influence he passed on, what he was prepared to die for and the impact he had on people and society.

Yet it is the content of this ministry, which he passed on in both his practice and his teachings, which is so unfamiliar to Christians.

The phrase 'The Kingdom of God' or 'The Kingdom of Heaven' is the term Jesus used to encapsulate all that he had come to share. I use the phrase 'The Kingdom Consciousness Movement' as a synonymous term because it helps our modern mind to better appreciate the immediacy of 'the Kingdom'. I will explain all of this shortly.

How well do you know Jesus' teachings on the Kingdom of God? If an interested person asked you: 'I have heard Jesus was a teacher – please summarise his teaching themes for me' or if they asked: 'What are the core values of Jesus' Kingdom?' or 'How do I live according to the Kingdom?' can you answer these questions? Surely the answers should be at the tip of your tongue? But most Christians are just not able to answer these questions with any degree of satisfactory detail, coherence or confidence.

The next eight chapters, including this one, focus on 'The Kingdom Consciousness Movement'. These chapters will enable you to understand Jesus' ministry of teaching, preaching, healing and the general lifestyle choices he made. I will distil much of this information into core values that were at the heart of Jesus' ministry. These values are then the core values of the Kingdom of God.

If you apply what you learn in these chapters you will come to know the joy of God reigning in and through your life. It is a very sad truth that these values are a neglected part of a Christian's understanding and lifestyle. One of the reasons is that they are not taught enough or written about enough. One of the main purposes of this guidebook is to fulfil this need.

What is at stake here is not getting a better score in a Bible knowledge quiz. Rather what is at stake is the integrity of your relationship with Jesus as your Lord and Saviour. It is probable that you do not believe in many things that Jesus taught you to believe in. It is also probable that you believe a lot of things about Jesus that are not true. Further it is probable that the Jesus you call Lord and Saviour may be very different from Jesus of Nazareth. The Jesus you believe in may even be the kind of person Jesus of Nazareth called to repentance! I firmly believe that this is the case with many Christians today.

Jesus certainly welcomes us into the Kingdom when we place our faith in him but then his Kingdom must enter us – and this is a life-changing experience that too few Christians have allowed to happen. They have entered the Kingdom but they have not let the Kingdom enter them. Jesus would say to us 'You have been welcomed into the life of the Kingdom – now welcome the Kingdom into your life'. John Warwick Montgomery helps bring the absolute importance of these issues home with these words: 'If our "Christ of faith" deviates at all from the Biblical "Jesus of history," then to the extent of that deviation, we also lose the genuine Christ of faith.'[1]

In 2002 Michael Cassidy, the well-known evangelist and founder of Africa Enterprise, made the following very important observation:

> One of the more astonishing anomalies of Africa is that we can have a continent of 378 million professing Christians, with 25 000 or more coming into the church daily through biological growth or conversion, and yet our continent seems to slide away more and more into social, political or economic declension. How can this be? Surely that many Christians should be making a major difference. Yet we don't seem to be. I have long puzzled over this. And surely one has to pause and ask for the reason. Finally it struck me. We have preached more a Salvationist theology than a Kingdom theology. We have taught people how to get converted and be born again and find salvation and say 'Hallelujah, Praise God!' but we have not taught them a Kingdom theology and how to live under the kingly rule of Christ.[2]

---

[1] John Warwick Montgomery, 'The Shape of the Past', Bethany Fellowship, 1975, p. 145.

[2] *Theologically Speaking – June 2002*, by Michael Cassidy.

This statement affirms the title I have given to this guidebook. It agrees that the true Jesus is missing in many Christians' lives! Many so-called Christians are not really part of the flock that distinguishes them as followers of Jesus the Good Shepherd. They may well call themselves 'Christian' but their identity in society does not coincide with Jesus' teaching.

At a more sinister level there are those who call themselves 'Christian' because it is a useful label to gain power in society. They will call their groups 'churches' in order to attract people. They may take onto themselves the titles of Christianity such as 'Pastor', 'Reverend', 'Bishop', 'Prophet' and 'Apostle' in order to increase the power of their identity in society. Their motivation in all of this may range from exploitation to money laundering to hate crimes.

This guidebook is all about becoming part of the flock who understand, experience and participate in the life that Jesus offers the world. This will be a journey of yielding to Jesus who is the good shepherd seeking you out as you read this guidebook.

My aim in the next eight chapters is to present the content of Jesus' ministry clearly and concretely.

JESUS THE WISDOM TEACHER
Jesus the Rabbi and Sage

Yes – Jesus was a profound thinker and wisdom teacher! Jesus seems to embrace two identities as a wisdom teacher of his day – both that of rabbi and that of sage.

The Gospels often refer to Jesus as *Rabbi*. A rabbi was a teacher, particularly a teacher of the Law (Law refers to the Law of Moses, namely the *Torah*). Each rabbi had developed their own particular interpretation of the law and taught that interpretation and called disciples to learn and practise that interpretation. Rabbis were vigorous in their debates with each other about interpretations. A rabbi's own interpretations normally fitted within larger schools of Jewish thought – e.g. liberal or conservative. In the Gospels we see Jesus living out the role of rabbi in teaching, in debating the law with legal experts and in interpreting the law for the people.

Both sages and rabbis used rhetorical forms of proverbs, riddles, hyperbole, parables and rhetorical overstatement, which was typical of the wisdom tradition. Like other sages, Jesus opted for an evocative and engaging teaching style designed to arouse transformative responses rather than provide systematic formulae on which to build theological systems. Like other sages,

Jesus also created public drama through actions designed to evoke a response from a certain target amongst the spectators.[3]

Sages, and to a slightly lesser degree rabbis were the great thinkers of that time. For us, that awareness, combined with the many references in scripture to Jesus' times alone in wilderness areas and on mountains, makes it easy to imagine Jesus in deep thought over long periods of time.

Jesus the Thinker

Jesus thought deeply, compassionately and prayerfully about many things. He thought about his context and all the social, political and economic dynamics in that context. Jesus thought about the state of the Jewish religion. Jesus studied and memorised all of the Jewish scriptures. Jesus thought about the other religious practices of the day. Jesus thought deeply and came to an understanding of human existence, Jesus analysed the values of the society of his day. Jesus thought deeply about knowledge, its sources and its power to help or hinder. Jesus came to a profound understanding of the role of language to shape a life-giving relationship to context. Jesus analysed how people were responding to their context. Jesus thought about lessons from history. Jesus thought about all the ways in which people were trapped in their thoughts and spirits. Jesus was also concerned with the matters that the philosophers of his day were paying attention to, which were the great questions of, 'Is there a God and how does this God relate to the world?' and 'What does it mean to lead a truly human life?' Jesus thought about human existence and the question of 'the good life', namely, 'Which life is the good life? Who has the good life?'[4]

---

[3] Craig S. Keener, *The Historical Jesus of the Gospels*. In pages 186-195 Keener distils the results of research, showing Jesus to be sage and rabbi – particularly a sage. In pages 14-32 he reviews contesting views of what kind of sage Jesus could have been.

[4] In *The Divine Conspiracy*, pp. 111-112, Dallas Willard points out that 'As outstanding thinkers before and after him have done, Jesus deals with the two major questions humanity always faces. First there is the question of which life is the good life… The second question … concerns who is truly a good person.' Also read his footnote # 1 on page 443, which refers to Jesus' philosophical standing amongst the great names in the history of philosophy.

Jesus thought about all of this and came up with a theory and practice that would be life-giving for his hearers and for all who, as his disciples, would teach and practise his tradition. Jesus' teachings didn't just fall from heaven and flow through his mouth, rather they were the result of extensive, compassionate and prayer-filled reflection. It is important to realise that Jesus was an advanced thinker and that he came up with a strategic response to his assessment of the situation.

Jesus was a philosopher who gave us a way of thinking and living that is far more life-giving than any philosophy before or after him. Jesus' philosophical legacy is actually far more useful, relevant, astute and truthful than that of any of the great names one could think of (e.g. Socrates, Plato, Aristotle, Descartes, Nietzsche, Kant, Marx, Wittgenstein, Russell, etc.).

Further, it is important to appreciate that Jesus' teaching ministry is part of his battle against the forces of sin and evil. Sin and evil are the powers of darkness that keep people trapped in the shadows of ignorance and Jesus is determined to flood the world with the light of truth. His teachings are the result of deep thought over an extended period of time before and during his ministry. It is probably true that his most intense time of prayerful thinking was during his forty-day retreat in the Jordanian wilderness.

Christians could have avoided overlooking Jesus' profound contribution as a thinker if we had only paid more attention to the tradition in which Jesus placed himself. As I said earlier, Jesus placed himself within the tradition of wisdom teacher, functioning in society as a rabbi and sage. The Old Testament has a rich stream of wisdom literature, most notably Ecclesiastes, Job and Proverbs – but also parts of the Psalms and the Prophets. This wisdom literature was the pioneer work that flourished in the vocation of the rabbi whose task it was to interpret the law and the lore of Judaism. That wisdom tradition gave many great books of wisdom to the world – none however exceeding the surviving records of Jesus' teachings.

The important thing to appreciate about the wisdom tradition is that it is not aimed at passing on information, but rather at being a catalyst for transformation – particularly transformation of consciousness (which is where all transformation must start). I listed some of the deep questions that Jesus paid attention to as a thinker – to these must be added the questions he addressed himself to as a wisdom teacher: 'What does it mean to die before you die? How do you go about losing your little life to find the bigger one? Is it possible to live on this planet with a generosity, abundance, fearlessness, and beauty that mirror Divine Being itself?'[5]

When you put all these many questions of life together, that Jesus was dealing with personally and then sharing in such an advanced and transformative way, then one is quite frustrated with ourselves as Christians for not having taken his teachings more seriously. One is also quite dismayed at how much has been lost in human history through our neglect of so helpful and wise a teacher. We can only imagine what a better place the world would be if it had engaged more deeply with his teachings.

Jesus the Stirrer

As we take a close look at Jesus' teachings we notice that he was not a rule maker. He was not presenting the world with a new static set of laws, rules and regulations. Rather there is something much more dynamic in his teachings and what he was seeking to achieve in them. It is best to understand Jesus the teacher as a provocateur, or in common slang, a stirrer. He is provoking us to ever greater heights of love, stirring us to ever wider practices of grace.

---

[5] Cynthia Bourgeault, *The Wisdom Jesus: Transforming Heart and Mind*, p. 24.

Jesus' sayings are not rules to live by but challenges to live into. You have never arrived at a place of full complete accomplishment of his teachings, since there is always more to strive for. Take one example: *'Love one another. Just as I have loved you, you also should love one another.'* (John 13.34). Do not see this as an impossible ideal placed on us, rather see it as a provocation to grow step-by-step, by trial and error learning, into your best possible fulfilment of this teaching. In this, Jesus is stirring us to find and use our strengths in pursuing faithfulness. In this lifelong quest for faithfulness our weaknesses are exposed to ourselves – not for the purpose of us feeling bad, but rather stirring us to be open to further transformation by God's grace.

Let us not for a moment think that Jesus' wisdom was completely lost to the world. Far from it! Christianity has defined so much of Europe, its colonies and the whole western world, that it is impossible to tell them apart. Of course a lot of what Christianity has determined as a culture has not been faithful enough to Jesus. Where culture has submitted to Jesus there certainly has been transformation of society and betterment of the world.

Please read chapter one again if you think that I am overlooking the wrongs of Christianity. W.E.H. Lecky, who has perhaps studied the historical development of the western world's morals more than anyone else, said that the teachings of Jesus were 'the most powerful moral lever that has ever been applied to the affairs of man.'[6] Further, whole libraries all over the world are full of books that are systematic theologies and commentaries based in part on the teachings of Jesus. Certainly no other thinker has been more influential – even though the most profound depths of his wisdom have not been appreciated yet.

Jesus walked the talk

Jesus lived what he taught; he embodied it, which does mean that there was a congruence, authenticity and integrity to his thinking and teaching. This is worth appreciating in comparison to some of the other great thinkers of human history who were in some cases disappointing people in their personal lifestyles. Some were hateful or hedonistic – few actually lived noble lives. An embodied truth is worth double a truth that sits only on paper or in the mouth and is not reflected in the lifestyle of the philosopher.[7]

---

[6] This is quoted in Dallas Willard, *The Divine Conspiracy: Rediscovering our Hidden Life in God*, p. 147. Dallas further points out a similar comment from the contemporary historian Michael Grant. Dallas also points out how even Nietzsche asserted the indispensable role of Jesus to civilization. He further points out how some of the most influential minds were profoundly Christian, including Kant and Hegel.

[7] Bertrand Russell was filled with hatred, according to Dallas Willard in *The Divine Conspiracy: Rediscovering our Hidden Life in God*, p. 205. Philosophers of Greece had lovers for sexual convenience and adventure – this includes Socrates (see https://classicalwisdom.com/five-reasons-socrates-terrible-husband/ accessed 25/6/2018).

We would be wise to take our cue from the disciples who had first-hand experience of Jesus – they were so confident about the wisdom of Jesus' teachings that they dedicated the rest of their lives to spreading that word – and were even prepared to suffer martyrdom rather than be restrained. The disciples were so confident that they went as far as to say that in Jesus *are hidden all the treasures of wisdom and knowledge.* (Colossians 2.3)

It is a profound sadness for the world that Jesus is not taken more seriously as a thinker and wisdom teacher. It is a significant loss that his name is missing from the list of great philosophers the world has known. It is a tragedy that there are Christians who are not students of his teachings. Those who believe that Jesus came to the world to die on the cross and who thereby pay little attention to his teaching ministry are desperately impoverished.

JESUS THE MIRACLE WORKER

The Gospels include many stories of what are popularly called miracles. 'Miracles' refer to Jesus' works of power in which healing took place, demons were cast out, the dead were raised, the storm was calmed and the multitudes fed. His healing miracles included restoring sight to the blind, healing the sick, making the lame walk, cleansing lepers and restoring hearing to the deaf.[8]

This was such an important dimension of Jesus' ministry that Peter made a point of referring to it in the first sermon of the early church. In Acts 2.22 he says, *'Listen to these words, fellow-Israelites! Jesus of Nazareth was a man whose divine authority was clearly proven to you by all the miracles and wonders which God performed through him. You yourselves know this, for it happened here among you.'*[9]

These miracles are signs of important characteristics of Jesus and the Kingdom that is established through His ministry. Firstly, all of these deeds of power are done because Jesus is deeply moved by compassion to act in this way. These miracles are beautiful stories of incredible blessings that happened to the beneficiaries. Too often talk of 'signs and wonders' takes the focus off of Jesus'

---

[8] We can be confident about the descriptions of Jesus as miracle worker because: 1) the Gospels show that they used early sources which testify to the miracles of Jesus. 2) Acts and the Epistles refer to Jesus' healing ministry. 3) Mark would hardly have invented the idea that Jesus could not heal where faith was lacking. 4) There are many writings of rabbis and the Greek philosopher Celsus of the 1st and 2nd Century who refer to this aspect of Jesus' ministry. They assign his power to sorcery. 5) It is very rare that a person of antiquity had a reputation for miracles. 6) Josephus, the Jewish historian, reports that Jesus did 'startling deeds'. 7) Miracles help account for Jesus' popular following. For more discussion on historicity of Jesus as miracle worker see Craig S. Keener, *The Historical Jesus of the Gospels*, pp. 241-245.

[9] American Bible Society, 1992. *The Holy Bible: The Good News Translation* (2nd ed., Ac 2:22), New York, American Bible Society. I used the Good News Bible here because it refers to 'miracles' whilst the NRSV refers to 'deeds of power'.

overriding love at work for that particular person on that particular day. But the Gospels are clear that the miracles first took place as acts of an all-powerful love focused on the recipient. One precious example is Jesus' healing of the two blind men in Matthew 20.29-34:

> *As they were leaving Jericho, a large crowd followed him. There were two blind men sitting by the roadside. When they heard that Jesus was passing by, they shouted, 'Lord, have mercy on us, Son of David!' The crowd sternly ordered them to be quiet; but they shouted even more loudly, 'Have mercy on us, Lord, Son of David!' Jesus stood still and called them, saying, 'What do you want me to do for you?' They said to him, 'Lord, let our eyes be opened.' Moved with compassion, Jesus touched their eyes. Immediately they regained their sight and followed him.*

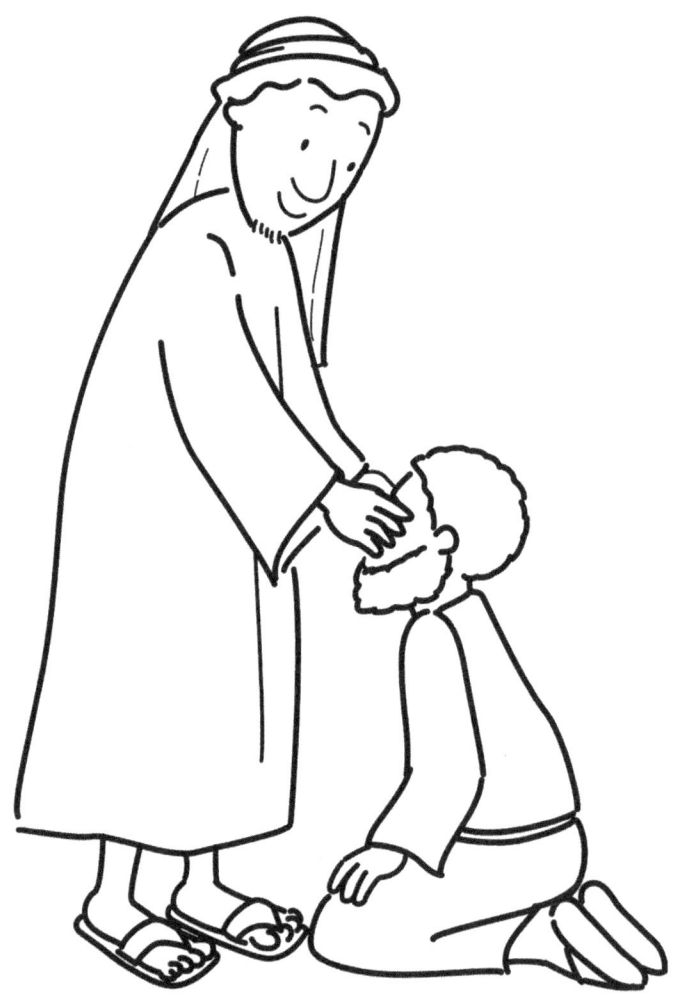

Secondly, these miracles are signs that God's Kingdom has come and that in his reign there will be an end to suffering, disaster, death and evil. The miracles give us windows through which we may look into the Kingdom of God and see what it is like. Miracles continued to play this role in the early church, throughout church history and today. Here is a reference to this in Acts 8.13: *Even Simon himself believed. After being baptized, he stayed constantly with Philip and was amazed when he saw the signs and great miracles that took place.*[10]

Thirdly, these miracles are signs that Jesus really is the agent through whom the Kingdom of God is established. They are signs for Jews that he is the Messiah. This was highlighted in the Acts 2.22 quote at the beginning of this section where Peter asserts that Jesus' miracles prove his divine authority. In the following account we see that Jesus' miracles prompted people to welcome him into Jerusalem as the Messiah/King of Israel:

> *...after throwing their cloaks on the colt, they set Jesus on it. As he rode along, people kept spreading their cloaks on the road. As he was now approaching the path down from the Mount of Olives, the whole multitude of the disciples began to praise God joyfully with a loud voice for all the deeds of power that they had seen, saying, 'Blessed is the king who comes in the name of the Lord! Peace in heaven, and glory in the highest heaven!'* (Luke 19.35-38)

At this point you may be wondering – why didn't Jesus cure all diseases and raise all the dead and drive out all the demons in His day? This is an important question about the coming of the Kingdom and will be dealt with in some detail in chapter 13 when we focus on the 'already' and 'not yet' reality of the Kingdom. In essence we need to appreciate that the Kingdom of God has come in Jesus but fulfilment of God's reign is still developing and will come in the future.

JESUS THE PROPHET

Jesus' ministry would have reminded many of the Hebrew prophets. Jesus made it clear that his healings, exorcisms and teachings showed that a new order had arrived with him. To be an agent of a new order is a strongly eschatological (end times) motif and is a distinctive feature of prophetic ministry.

Jesus acted like a prophet in many ways. Amongst the most outstanding of these prophetic acts were:

---

[10] Craig Keener has made a comprehensive study of miracles in the New Testament and in history in his two-volume book *Miracles: The Credibility of the New Testament Accounts*.

- He experienced revelations from God and then shared these.
- His pronouncement of judgement on the temple like Jeremiah had done; like Jeremiah too he did this with a dramatic symbolic act.
- He chose twelve disciples as the nucleus of his renewal movement, an act consistent with the prophetic restoration of the people of Israel.
- He announced judgement on the Jewish people of the day if they failed to repent.
- He spoke about the future in many end-time sayings which referred to the dramatic end of the current political situation and to a later culmination of history in his own second coming.
- He was a spokesperson for God about the events of his day.[11]

It is also important to note that the oldest surviving Christian documents are Paul's letters to the Thessalonians. In these two letters there is a very strong expectation of the end times that would be culminating in Jesus' second coming. The most obvious explanation of this is that Jesus' own ministry had led people to believe in the imminence of the end times. These letters were written about 20 years after Jesus' execution and are very closely linked to the eschatological material in the Gospels, even though the Gospels were finalised decades later.

The impact Jesus had on people was very similar to the impact of the Hebrew prophets – a bold agent of God breaking into history with his words and symbolic actions.

JESUS THE MESSIAH

Earlier we saw that Jesus' miracles were signs for Jews that he was the Messiah who would bring God's reign into this world. Let us explore this dimension of Jesus' ministry now.

Jesus certainly saw himself as someone through whom God was at work and that a new dispensation had arrived with him. In this self-understanding Jesus goes further than a prophet because a prophet would not have viewed himself as personally central to the new dispensation. The prophet would not have expected people to follow himself, nor would the prophet have viewed himself as a key criterion for the judgement of the people of Israel. Jesus therefore does not see himself as one eschatological prophet among many. In these aspects then we see Jesus taking on the role of the Messiah.

The Greek term for the Messiah is 'Christos' and is almost always translated into English as 'Christ' (there are only six occasions on which the term 'Christos'

---

[11] For a detailed discussion on Jesus the Prophet see Craig S. Keener, *The Historical Jesus of the Gospels*, pp. 238-255.

is translated as 'Messiah'). It refers to the one 'anointed' by God as a special agent to bring God's Kingdom on earth. There are 50 references to Jesus as Christ in the Gospels. There are a staggering further 460 references to Jesus as Christ in the rest of the New Testament.

It is clear that the Jesus movement understood Jesus to be the Christ. What must be appreciated is that this title would have attracted persecution from the Romans because it was clearly a title for a king of a rival kingdom. It is inconceivable that the followers of Jesus would have taken such a dangerous title for their leader if Jesus had not presented himself as such. Remember also that the title is most meaningful for Jews and not for Gentiles but came to be completely accepted by the Gentiles as the correct title for Jesus. They would have got this title from the Jewish followers of Jesus who got the title from Jesus himself.

In the Gospels Pilate has Jesus executed on a charge of treason and has the inscription 'King of the Jews' placed on the cross (Mark 15.2, 9, 12, 26). This reveals the danger of the title 'Christ' and clearly shows that Jesus was prepared to go through with the role and its consequences.[12]

JESUS THE SHEPHERD

Jesus really did fulfil the roles of sage, rabbi, healer, prophet and Messiah. But he also went much further than these identities. Jesus witnessed to being more than an earthly figure; he witnessed to such a closeness to God and to being such a special agent of God that the followers soon came to worship him as divine. Worship of Jesus as divine emerged very early in the Jesus movement and could only have emerged so suddenly and early as a result of Jesus' unique witness about himself.

So if Jesus both fulfilled and transcended these roles – is there one role or metaphor that can capture all that Jesus wants to be for us? Further, it will be clear in these Kingdom Consciousness chapters that Jesus wants people to be impressed by the all-inclusive significance of his ministry. By this I mean that Jesus wants people to understand that his significance is earthly and heavenly, religious and political, relational and economic, personal and social. I believe that the metaphor and role of 'shepherd' is offered to us by Jesus as the most inclusive way of relating to him and his relationship with us.

Jesus calls himself *'the good shepherd'* in John 10.11 and in that chapter describes all the sacrificial ways in which he serves as a good shepherd.[13] Emperors and kings were referred to metaphorically as shepherds in those days

---

[12] For a more detailed discussion of Jesus as Messiah see Craig S. Keener, *The Historical Jesus of the Gospels*, pp. 256-267.

[13] Jesus also uses the shepherd metaphor for himself in Matthew 10.6; 15.24; 18.12-14; 25.32-33; 26.31; Mark 14.27; Luke 15.3-7. The early Jesus followers called Jesus *the great shepherd of the sheep* (Hebrews 13.20), *the Shepherd and Guardian of your souls* (1 Peter 2.25) and *the chief Shepherd* (1 Peter 5.4).

and so people were familiar with the political dimensions of the metaphor. The Jewish hearers would have been familiar with the description of God as their shepherd and so would have been able to hear Jesus' role as God in our lives.[14] Further, to underline both religious and political dimensions, the prophets of the Old Testament had said that the metaphor of a good shepherd would be used for the Messiah who would restore God's Kingdom.[15]

The beauty of the metaphor of shepherd is that it conveys the gracious gift to us of someone who will lead us, provide for us and protect us. It makes it obvious that we need to entrust ourselves to the leadership of the shepherd and stay close to him. It makes it clear that the nature of our relationship with Jesus needs to be a relationship of trust and loyalty through following him. A shepherd is not someone we can be associated with in name only. A shepherd is not just a romantic and endearing pious notion but is rather an all-embracing and defining leader to be followed in the grit, grime and glory of human society.

---

[14] Psalm 23 and Ezekiel 34 are the most prominent but see also Psalms 28.9; 74.1; 77.20; 78.52-53; 80.1; 95.7; 100.3; 121.3-8; Isaiah 40.11; 49.9-10; Jeremiah 23.1-4; 31.10; 49.19-20; 50.17-19; Micah 4.6-8; 7.14.

[15] Jeremiah 3.15; 23.4; Ezekiel 34.23; 37.22; 37.24; Zechariah 13.7

Every person does need a leader. These are the people we look up to and emulate. These are the people we learn from and follow. Sometimes we are conscious of who and what we follow, sometimes we are not. Sometimes we are intentional in our choice of leader, sometimes we are not. Choosing good and life-giving leaders is one of the most important decisions in life.

Dallas Willard, the American philosopher and professor in phenomenology, was a Christian and a passionate writer in the field of spiritual formation. He was once asked by a doctoral student, 'Professor, why do you, an intelligent, thoughtful and well educated man, follow Jesus?' to which Dallas replied, 'Tell me, who else do you have in mind?'[16]

Willard's question asks us to carefully consider who would be a better person to follow than Jesus. I found it to be very helpful to think about that question. I invite you to pause a moment and consider your own answer.

THE KINGDOM OF GOD, THE REIGN OF GOD AND THE KINGDOM CONSCIOUSNESS MOVEMENT

> *'The time is fulfilled, and the kingdom of God has come near; repent, and believe in the good news.'* (Mark 1.15)

Jesus started his ministry with these very important words. The term 'Kingdom of God' referred to the Jewish expectation of the Reign of God on earth after the arrival of the Messiah. Jesus' announcement that the Kingdom of God is 'near' is also often translated as 'at hand' and the idea conveyed is that God's reign has begun and you may become part of it. A simple example is if you ask someone: 'Please hand me that book' and they hold it out to you: the book is 'near' and 'at hand' and you can take hold of it and accept it.

In essence the astonishing good news Jesus is proclaiming is: 'I have brought the Kingdom of God and you are invited to change your whole life according to that great news.' I will quite often refer to 'the Kingdom Consciousness Movement' and 'the Reign of God', rather than the 'Kingdom of God'. I do this because I believe it helps us to realise that God's reign in our lives is more important than any other kingdom (country, allegiance) we may belong to. This is a new consciousness with which to live.

It is very important that we don't have an 'other-worldly' idea about God's reign. It is something that has started in this world and it is our calling to live

---

[16] Trevor Hudson personally told me this story. It is also found in Trevor's book *Invitations to Abundant Life: In Search for Life at its Best*, pp. 179-178.

according to that reign. Living according to God's reign has spiritual, social, political, relational and cognitive implications and thus calls for a whole new consciousness in living.

In these chapters about 'The Kingdom Consciousness Movement' we see that Jesus was the One through whom the Kingdom of God came to this world. We will also see that he was true to God's Reign in the world of his day and how in so doing he became life and hope for the world then and now. As we find and follow this Shepherd we experience the incredible blessing of the life that Jesus offers the world. God's Reign continues to be 'at hand' for all who will repent.

You have a very special journey awaiting you through the next chapters. You will gain the dignity of knowing what your leader is passionate about. You will learn what life can look like if Jesus' teachings are followed. You will gain insight into a new world order that was Jesus' vision. You will see where you fit in.

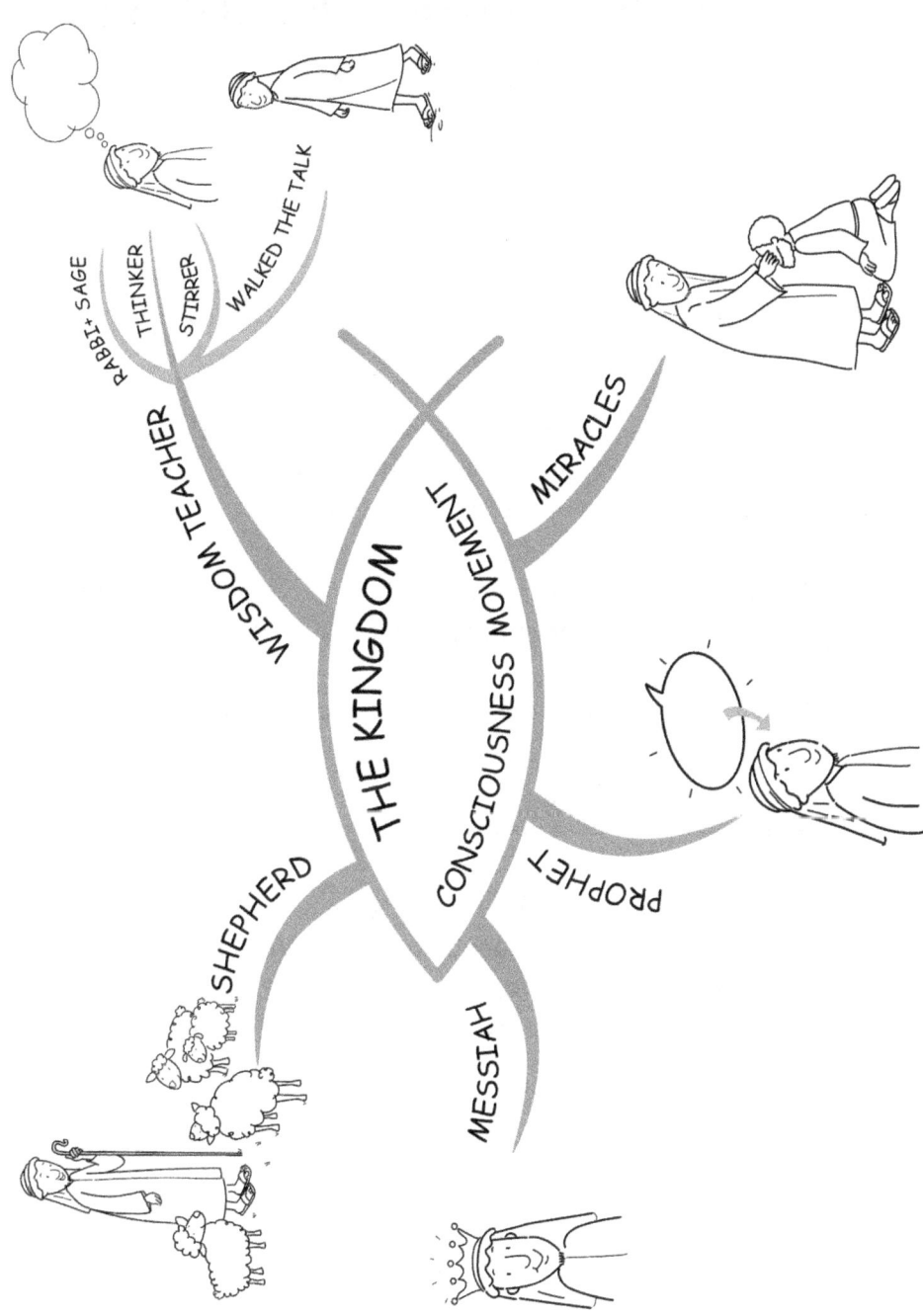

SUGGESTIONS FOR DISCUSSION, REVISION, REFLECTION AND APPLICATION

(These questions are intended for group work, but can easily be adapted for personal use.)

1. What is the most important message to you in this chapter? (Remember to also make a note of this on your 'God spoke to me' page.)
2. Icebreaker question: As a child, what did you wish to become when you grew up? (The question must be answered quickly. As a group, do not spend longer than 5 minutes in total on this question.)
3. Read Mark 1.14-15; Matthew 4.12-17; Luke 4.14-15 and answer the following questions:
    a. Why do you think Jesus' message was called the good news of God?
    b. What do you think people experienced as particularly 'good' in the news?
    c. What does this moment tell us about God and his relationship with the world?
    d. Is a call to repentance good news too?
    e. What would be good news for society today?
    f. What good news would you like to hear from God?
    g. What does it mean to 'believe' in the good news?
4. Below are a variety of suggestions and questions to aid your appreciation of this chapter. Do not attempt to do all of them! Choose those that are most appropriate to your unique situation and/or group. The questions are designed to help variously with revision, understanding, appreciation, reflection or application of the content.
    a. Do you know the teachings of Jesus well? Can you summarise and systematise them? Are you able to give an overview of the teachings to someone who may ask? If you are not able to answer these questions informatively then ask yourself 'How is it that I cannot answer?', 'What have I neglected to do in my Christian journey?' 'Do I think I should be able to answer, or is it only some people who need to know this information, and I am not one of those people?'
    b. Respond to the statement 'The Jesus you believe in may be the kind of

person Jesus of Nazareth called to repentance!' As you think about that statement, what are your feelings? Is there some truth to the allegation? Where might be the differences between the two ideas of Jesus?

c. Try and name some characteristics of the Jesus that 'others' believe in but that you believe are not true characteristics of Jesus.
d. Read again the observation from Michael Cassidy. Is this only a problem in Africa? What difference would it make to Africa if we followed a Kingdom theology?
e. How did you respond to Jesus being described as a thinker? Did it surprise you? What new learning did you most enjoy there? Could it inspire you to be a student of Jesus the thinker?
f. How did you respond to Jesus being described as a stirrer? Does that idea offend you? What for you is Jesus' most provocative and challenging teaching?
g. Which of the identities for Jesus were new learnings for you: Wisdom Teacher (sage and rabbi), healer, prophet, messiah and shepherd? With which one have you normally identified Jesus?
h. How do you respond to Dallas Willard's question 'Who would be a better person to follow than Jesus?'
i. Do you 'follow' Jesus? What difference does that make to your life?

GOD SPOKE TO ME ...

7

WHAT JESUS PRACTISED

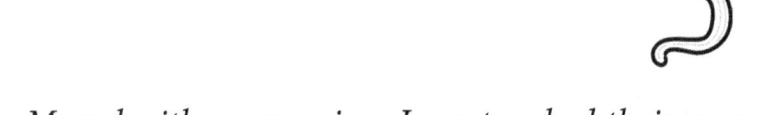

*Moved with compassion, Jesus touched their eyes.
Immediately they regained their sight and followed him.*
(Matthew 20.34)

Two adult bachelor brothers shared a house. They were both known as Dr Jones, since the one ran a medical practice and the other was a preacher with a PhD in Theology. When the phone rang and the person asked for Dr Jones they used to enjoy replying with the question, 'Which one do you want, the one who practises or the one who preaches?'

In this chapter we focus on Jesus' practice, in chapters 8 to 13 we will focus on the content of his preaching.[1] These two dimensions of Jesus' ministry obviously fit together in the establishing of the Kingdom Consciousness Movement.

Jesus' ministry was characterised by a passionate attention to those that suffer. Broadly speaking, these were the poor and the sinners. The poor were either born into poverty or had become poor through misfortune. They had no way out of their poverty and were not part of acceptable society because they were unclean and generally uneducated. They were at the mercy of others. Remember now that in Jesus' day it was believed that people were poor because God had rejected them and people were wealthy because God had approved of them. A religious leader who blessed the poor with special attention was therefore viewed suspiciously because it seemed that he was going against God's judgement.

---

[1] The contents of chapters 7 to 13 were truths that were brought home to me after reading Albert Nolan's excellent *Jesus before Christianity*. Although I have personally done a lot of new work on these themes and have also used other resources in these chapters much of what is articulated is owed to the perspective and content of this book.

The sinners were social outcasts because of their professions: prostitutes, tax collectors, herdsman, robbers, gamblers, usurers. The poor and the outcasts are referred to in the gospels as the poor, the blind, the lame, the crippled, the lepers, the hungry, the miserable, sinners, prostitutes, tax collectors, demoniacs, the persecuted, the downtrodden, the captives, all who labour and are overburdened, the rabble who know nothing of the law, the crowds, the little ones, the least, the last, the lost sheep of the house of Israel. Jesus generally refers to them as poor or little ones.[2]

Remarkably, Jesus became an outcast himself! Associating with the unclean made you unclean, associating with the outcasts made you an outcast.[3] Jesus therefore became an outcast by choice! Why would he do such a remarkable thing? The answer is one word: compassion!

JESUS WAS MOVED BY COMPASSION
Jesus' compassion - personally and deeply moved

When we use the word 'compassion', we must understand it as Jesus lived it. Jesus was personally and deeply moved to act in a loving way to those who suffered. There was nothing mechanical, functional or legalistic about his loving deeds (i.e. he was not doing it because it was a commandment). His loving deeds were a direct result of his heart genuinely going out to those who suffer. Jesus was deeply moved to act. This is made clear when we note the Greek verb *splagchnizomai,* which is translated into English as 'compassion'. This word literally means 'to be moved as to one's bowels' and the root of the word is the same as the word for bowels. This word makes clear that Jesus was personally and deeply moved by people's needs and plight. Jesus was completely in touch with how love is something that arises from his intestines, bowels, entrails and heart. In modern terms we speak of a 'gut reaction'.

Jesus was deeply aware of his connection with people around him. Remember how the Genesis Creation story shows that we were created for unity with each other as humans. Jesus was deeply in touch with this unity, this solidarity, and so feels the suffering of others very personally and deeply. Jesus knew that we are all one flesh and one family.

In the following verses Jesus' compassion is referred to:

---

[2] Mark 1.23, 32-34, 40; 2.3, 15, 17; 3.1; 9.17-18, 42; 12.40, 42;
Luke 4.18; 5.1; 6.20-21; 7.34, 37, 39; 10.21; 11.46; 14.13, 21; 15.1-2; 18.10, 13, 22;
Matthew 5.10-12; 8.28; 9.10, 14; 10.3, 15, 42; 11.28; 15.24; 19.30; 20.16; 21.31-32; 25.40, 45;
John 7.49; 9.1-2, 8, 34

[3] Chapter 3 of Albert Nolan's *Jesus before Christianity* gives an excellent insight into the reasons why these were outcasts in society and why those associating with them became outcasts.

When he saw the crowds, he had compassion for them, because they were harassed and helpless, like sheep without a Shepherd. (Matthew 9.36) Moved with compassion, Jesus touched their eyes. Immediately they regained their sight and followed him. (Matthew 20.34)

The following are more references to Jesus' compassion: Matthew 14.14; Mark 1.41; 6.34; 8.2; 9.21-22; Luke 7.13. Even where the word is not used we see throughout the gospels that Jesus felt unrestrained compassion for those who suffer.

Compassion makes you the hero in his stories

In the following stories Jesus emphasizes the compassion (pity) of one of the characters who is clearly presented as the hero of the story. In Matthew 18.23-35 Jesus tells the story of the compassionate king who forgives a slave's debt. Note verse 27 *'And out of pity for him, the lord of that slave released him and forgave him the debt.'*

In Luke 10.25-37 Jesus tells the story of the good Samaritan. Note verse 33, *'But a Samaritan while traveling came near him; and when he saw him, he was moved with pity.'*

In Luke 15.11-32 Jesus tells the story of the Prodigal Son. Note verse 20: *'So he set off and went to his father. But while he was still far off, his father saw him and was filled with compassion; he ran and put his arms around him and kissed him.'*

The compassion of God has come to us!

There are 78 references to compassion in the Old Testament and almost all of them refer to God as compassionate. These are mostly the writings of the prophets in which the compassion of God is proclaimed as the core identity of God. The Psalms sing often of God as compassionate. In the Old Testament there is almost no reference to a person being compassionate. Then something remarkable happens as we go into the New Testament where for the first time a person, Jesus, is referred to as compassionate. In this we see something important – Jesus had the remarkable effect on people that they were left with the clear impression that the compassion of God had come to them in him!

More than that, the ministry of Jesus drew attention to the quality of compassion as the central quality of God. Until Jesus' ministry the image of God that was dominant in the Jewish faith was the image of purity. God's holiness was a Being of Pure Separateness. The Old Testament had spoken and sung of God's compassion, but it had not affected the consciousness of a Jew much at all. Pursuing purity was seen as the way to honour God. But in Jesus, God was experienced as coming 'up close and personal', bringing healing and wholeness, offering friendship and hospitality, as love and kindness – in a word 'compassionate'. This felt like good news, and that is exactly what they called it (*Gospel* means 'good news').[4]

In Matthew 9.11-13 when Jesus is challenged for eating with sinners and other outcasts, he responds, *'Those who are well have no need of a physician, but those who are sick Go and learn what this means, "I desire compassion, not sacrifice." For I have come to call not the righteous but sinners.'*

In God's special coming to humanity in Jesus the focus is on oppressed peoples. God comes to an oppressed people and pays particular attention to those oppressed amongst the oppressed. The earliest followers of Jesus were oppressed people. The Jesus movement began as a movement among the oppressed. This observation is not just of historical interest – as if to say 'Oh, isn't that curious!' It is important for us to see that God's intention was and is liberation from oppression and good news for the poor.

A Christianity that is indifferent to the quest for liberation is in defiance of Jesus. A Christianity that is unmoved by the plight of suffering people is in defiance of Jesus. A Christianity that oppresses people is in defiance of Jesus.

Your compassion is a sign that you are part of the Shepherd's flock

There should therefore be no doubt that compassion for those who suffer needs to be a characteristic of every follower of Jesus. God's Spirit can fill me to such an extent that love can become part of my body too, that I too will be moved by

---

[4] The following references are some of the most important stories, sayings and pictures that Jesus used to share the God-image of compassion (I have only drawn the selection from Luke's Gospel): Luke 10.25-37; 13.18-19; 14.15-24; 15.1-32; 18.9-14; 16.19-31.

my insides to show love to those who suffer. To live with compassion makes it clear that you are a life-giving part of Jesus' flock.

One of the most serious dynamics in society is the way in which compassion is reduced to our only being moved by the suffering of our nearest and dearest friends and family. When someone close to us loses their job, or gets cancer, or is hijacked or is T-boned by a drunk driver, then we feel the full gut-wrenching, heartbreaking experience of compassion. But for most of the rest of suffering in society we are indifferent, unmoved and hardened. This dynamic is happening within most people most of the time and is something that has been described by Pope Francis in *Evangelii Gaudium* as 'the globalisation of indifference'.

It is clear that we need to follow Jesus as he leads us to attend to people who suffer and are in need. Jesus' compassion for those who suffer is so strong that we will meet him in the encounter with suffering people. It is not that the suffering person becomes Jesus – or even that the encounter with the suffering person will necessarily be pleasant or rewarding. Rather we will be practising God's love and so will find our own inner life awakened to true love, compassion and empathy.

This is certainly part of being 'born again' in the truest sense of the phrase. God's love will be born again within hearts that had become indifferent. God's love would have awoken us because we decided, at long last, to listen to the cries of the oppressed. As we opened up our ears, heart and gut to these cries of suffering our inner life softened and became responsive. We knew again what it means to be a fully human child of God.

Christian spirituality always includes loving action for those in need. True Christian spirituality is never a menu of spiritual disciplines that are divorced from compassion for those in need. Because Jesus made the suffering ones central, his true followers do so too.

As a young married couple, Angela and I were blessed with a very special series of experiences that all started with her responding to the move of compassion within. She had been deeply and personally moved by a 14-year-old who played the role of 'man of the house' in a township shack in Rini, Grahamstown. Once a month Sipho[5] met my wife Angela when he would escort his mother to fetch her social grant at the Cape Provincial Administration where Angela worked as a social worker. His mother was blind and badly deformed by leprosy. Sipho's sister suffered from severe schizophrenia. The care, maturity and discipline with which he lived were deeply impressive. Angela and I built up a relationship with him and soon discovered that he had potential as an artist. As we sought to support him so others cooperated with

---

[5] Name has been changed.

the efforts – which enabled years of art lessons, a place at Rhodes University to study Fine Art and support for his efforts to establish himself as a professional artist. This has been a treasured relationship for the three of us – one in which we have all received so much. The great lesson it taught me was that personal contact with a suffering person is what awakens compassion and that acting on that inner impulse is often followed by some really special miracles and relationships.

You and I need to reflect on whether we view being a disciple of Jesus as a journey of compassion or of purity. Do we teach our children more often about compassion or purity? For many of us the God image of purity was passed on to us by our parents – 'God is watching what you do and even what you think! Be careful.' It is time for us to be personally and deeply moved to love and to pass this spirit on to our children.

I am deeply challenged by the realisation that Jesus predicted that in a society struggling with high crime rates, compassion would become very difficult (note though that the crime situation is not allowed as an excuse): *'And because of the increase of lawlessness, the love of many will grow cold. But the one who endures to the end will be saved.'* (Matthew 24.12-13)

JESUS INSPIRED POWERFUL FAITH
A catchy faith!

Faith was something people caught from Jesus. Those who had contact with Jesus, spoke to him, watched him minister and go about life, in most instances experienced faith coming to life within themselves. Sometimes this happened with only a small amount of contact. People 'caught' faith from Jesus like catching an infection – except this was a healing and life-giving infection!

It seems that Jesus was at times pleasantly surprised at how catchy his faith was. Matthew records Jesus' amazement at the centurion who had so confidently appealed to Jesus' authority to heal: *When Jesus heard him, he was amazed and said to those who followed him, 'Truly I tell you, in no one in Israel have I found such faith.'* (Matthew 8.10)

You can sense how the woman with haemorrhages had caught this faith: *… for she said to herself, 'If I only touch his cloak, I will be made well.'* (Matthew 9.21)

How was it that Jesus had this effect on people? It was Jesus' own faith, his own lifestyle and convictions, which awakened faith in those who encountered him. Confidence is infectious. A courageously lived faithful life has a big impact on those who see it.

What Jesus Practised

Jesus' ministry was a ministry of awakening faith – people started to have faith in God as a result of this ministry. Specifically they came to have faith in God's power to act. They came to believe in God's reign and in Jesus himself as the special agent of that reign. Faith can therefore be seen as a gift people received from Jesus. By this I mean that contact with Jesus caused faith to be born within a person. Or to put it another way, Jesus inspired people to have real faith.

A uniquely powerful faith

The faith that people caught from Jesus was of a very powerful kind. This is part of the reason why Jesus did emphasise the importance of faith.[6] Jesus believed that this faith was the only power that could heal and save the world. It was the power he offered people to fix the mess they and the world were in.

Faith, for Jesus, is a force which once captured, can achieve what would seem impossible, and indeed would be impossible without faith. Once this faith is captured then it becomes the power of God to act. Faith is the true conviction that God is good and that good will triumph over evil. When a

---

[6] It is interesting to note that there are only three references to Faith in the Old Testament, but 30 in the Gospels and a further 160 in the rest of the New Testament.

person embraced this type of faith with their heart, soul, mind and strength then good did triumph in their lives.

To make this clear we must realise that the opposite of faith is fatalism. Fatalism is the belief of most of the people most of the time. It is evidenced in statements like: 'You can't change the world', 'Just accept reality', 'Nothing can be done about it', 'There is no hope', 'Don't try and change things', 'People can't change'. Do these statements sound familiar? It is very difficult for God to work through people with such attitudes and beliefs. Jesus set about setting people free from fatalism by awakening them to faith.

Jesus put a lot of effort into inspiring people to believe in God's ability to accomplish what would seem impossible. In the following passage the metaphor used is of an event that truly seems impossible, namely casting a mountain into the sea. (This is most likely a metaphor about the downfall of political and religious powers. These powers would have seemed immovable at the time – like mountains.):

> *Jesus answered them, 'Have faith in God. Truly I tell you, if you say to this mountain, "Be taken up and thrown into the sea," and if you do not doubt in your heart, but believe that what you say will come to pass, it will be done for you. So I tell you, whatever you ask for in prayer, believe that you have received it, and it will be yours.'* (Mark 11.21-24)

The power of faith lies not in the conviction but in the truth of the conviction. Faith derives its power from the truth of what is believed. The power of faith is the power of truth. Faith in God is to believe that God is good and that goodness will triumph over evil, that goodness is stronger than evil, that truth is stronger than falsehood, and that God will triumph over Satan. This belief is true for indeed there is a power for good in the world that is irresistible and that will win the war with evil. Nolan brings the point home with this great statement, 'Anyone who thinks that evil will have the last word or that good and evil have a fifty-fifty chance is an atheist.'[7]

Note the confidence that is possible when faith has captured a person's heart and mind:

> *And just then some people were carrying a paralyzed man lying on a bed. When Jesus saw their faith, he said to the paralytic, 'Take heart, son; your sins are forgiven.'* (Matthew 9.2)

---

[7] Albert Nolan, *Jesus Before Christianity*, p. 85.

Then Jesus answered her, 'Woman, great is your faith! Let it be done for you as you wish.' And her daughter was healed instantly. (Matthew 15.28)

Jesus said to him, 'Go; your faith has made you well.' Immediately he regained his sight and followed him on the way. (Mark 10.52)

The effect of this was astonishing. Incredible things happened in and through people once faith had set their minds and hearts ablaze. We see that faith released a power within people that was beyond them. There were many times that Jesus said to a person who had been healed, *'your faith has healed you'.*[8] People's lives were changed; they left sinful ways and followed Jesus. People gave their material goods and money away. People risked danger for the sake of Jesus. People were prepared to be poor and outcasts for the sake of Jesus and the love he invited them to share. A whole new way of life was embraced by those who placed their faith in Jesus.

After Jesus' ascension his disciples continued to be confident in what Jesus could do. One example is when Peter and John put their faith in Jesus to heal a lame beggar. The religious leaders arrested Peter and John and in the trial were greatly impressed by the boldness of their faith: *Now when they saw the boldness of Peter and John and realized that they were uneducated and ordinary men, they were amazed and recognized them as companions of Jesus.* (Acts 4.13)

Your faith in Jesus is a sign that you are part of the Shepherd's flock

We must be in no doubt that being a Christian today includes living with faith as a way of life, rather than resigning oneself to the world as it is. Fatalism in all its disguises must be resisted. The Kingdom grows as people live out their faith in Jesus. To live with faith shows that a real encounter with Jesus has taken place, for faith is always a gift that will remain from that encounter. Faith shows that we remain as part of his flock and as useful agents of God in this world.

We talk so often about putting our faith in Jesus that we forget that it all started with Jesus putting faith in certain people before they put faith in him. This is seen in the call of the disciples in the Gospels where Jesus starts his ministry with putting faith in the qualities of those fishermen, tax collector and others. Their response is to leave everything behind and follow Jesus so that they can discover what this man of God has seen in them! They want to actualise the potential Jesus has seen in them. They intuit that it is life-fulfilling

---

[8] See the following references for more instances of Jesus referring to a healing faith: Matthew 8.13; 9.27-30; 15.28; Mark 5.34-36; Luke 17.19.

for them to discover and live what Jesus sees in them. Jesus' faith in them awoke their faith in him. Do you sense the faith Jesus has in you?

I will unpack more about faith in a chapter 15 when we focus on your personal relationship with Jesus. There I will talk about faith as a five-step dance.

ACCEPTED BY JESUS!
A new start

People who encountered Jesus received two gifts from him. The first was the gift of faith mentioned in the previous section. The second was his way of accepting people as they were, even in their sinfulness, which essentially meant that a person received the gift of a new start to their lives.

Jesus' association with outcasts (poor, sinners, etc) was done in a particularly intimate way – he shared a meal with them.[9] In the culture of the day, a meal was an intimate form of association and friendship and was never shared with someone you did not approve of or who was in a class lower than yours. In this way people experienced Jesus' grace and forgiveness. Jesus' practice was to constantly accept people and in so doing build community across the divisions that sin causes. (Remember what we learnt in the third chapter – that sin divides.)

Grace is the freedom to have a conversation with the one I have wronged. Jesus' practice embodied this core meaning of grace. As we know, Jesus represented God to those around him in both his position as rabbi and sage in the community and in his own unique understanding of his identity as being one with the Father.

Jesus' sharing of meals with these outcasts caused a scandal because it meant that he approved of them and accepted them. The statement that he was *a friend of tax collectors and sinners* was intended as an insult at Jesus for this practice of meal sharing.

Albert Nolan tenderly describes the impact these fellowship meals had on the participants:

> It would be impossible to overestimate the impact these meals must have had upon the poor and the sinners. By accepting them as friends and equals Jesus had taken away their shame, humiliation and guilt.

---

[9] See Luke 15.1-2; Mark 2.15 and parallels; Luke 7.34-50; 11.37; 14.1; 14.12-13; 19.1-10. See Genesis 26.27-30 as a good example of the practice of sharing a meal with someone being a demonstration of being at peace with them.

By showing them they mattered to Him as people He gave them a sense of dignity and released them from their captivity. The physical contact which He must have had with them when reclining at table (see John 13.25) and which He obviously never dreamed of disallowing (Luke 7.38-39) must have made them feel clean and acceptable. Moreover, because Jesus was looked upon as a man of God and a prophet, they would have interpreted His gesture of friendship as God's approval of them. They were now acceptable to God. Their sinfulness, ignorance and uncleanness had been overlooked and was no longer being held against them.[10]

The New Start is the result of forgiveness

In those days sickness was seen as a consequence of sin. Jesus' healings were therefore seen as, amongst other things, a consequence of forgiveness. Although Jesus does not always view sickness as a consequence of sin, he does take the opportunity to offer everyone the grace of forgiveness. This comes out powerfully in the event of the healing of the paralysed man in Jesus' home town of Capernaum. Note here how Jesus does not seek for details about sin, rather he accepts the man, forgives and gives a new start:

> *When he returned to Capernaum after some days, it was reported that he was at home ... Then some people came, bringing to him a paralyzed man, carried by four of them ... When Jesus saw their faith, he said to the paralytic, 'Son, your sins are forgiven.' Now some of the scribes were sitting there, questioning in their hearts, 'Why does this fellow speak in this way? It is blasphemy! Who can forgive sins but God alone?'... But so that you may know that the Son of Man has authority on earth to forgive sins – he said to the paralytic – 'I say to you, stand up, take your mat and go to your home.' And he stood up, and immediately took the mat and went out before all of them; so that they were all amazed and glorified God, saying, 'We have never seen anything like this!'* (Selected verses from Mark 2.1-12)

It was Jesus' faith in the Father's unconditional forgiveness for all that triggered this same faith to be awoken in others too. That new faith set people free from their past and set them on a path of wholeness. They were given a new start to their lives, fresh in the awareness of God's love and acceptance of them.

---

[10] Albert Nolan, *Jesus before Christianity*, p. 39.

The potential for a new start as a result of forgiveness (which is expressed by Jesus as an acceptance of the person regardless of past sins) comes out powerfully in Jesus' encounter with a woman who is brought to him after she had been caught in the act of adultery.

> *Early in the morning he came again to the temple. All the people came to him and he sat down and began to teach them. The scribes and the Pharisees brought a woman who had been caught in adultery... When they kept on questioning him, he straightened up and said to them, 'Let anyone among you who is without sin be the first to throw a stone at her.'... Jesus straightened up and said to her, 'Woman, where are they? Has no one condemned you?' She said, 'No one, sir.' And Jesus said, 'Neither do I condemn you. Go your way, and from now on do not sin again.'* (Selected verses from John 8.2-11)

It is very precious to be given a new start to life, especially if that new start contains an awareness of God's love and acceptance. This is beautifully portrayed in the event found in Luke 7.36-50 where a woman publicly anoints Jesus' feet with ointment and tears. She does this in response to Jesus' generous acceptance of her which gave her a new start to life. His host inwardly mocks the naïveté of Jesus, to which Jesus responds:

> *'I tell you, her sins, which were many, have been forgiven; hence she has shown great love. But the one to whom little is forgiven, loves little.' Then he said to her, 'Your sins are forgiven.' But those who were at the table with him began to say among themselves, 'Who is this who even forgives sins?' And he said to the woman, 'Your faith has saved you; go in peace.'*

Accepting your forgiveness is a sign that you are part of the Shepherd's flock

The most incredible moment of Jesus' forgiving love is his prayer from the cross, *'Father, forgive them; for they do not know what they are doing.'* (Luke 23.34) In this moment he gives all humanity the chance of a new start.

Hear the Good News for yourself: the you that you struggle to forgive is already forgiven. His graciousness includes you and he wants you to know that. Receive this gracious gift and embrace a new start to your life!

Jesus also taught what he practised and I will unpack some of what he said about forgiveness in the section dealing with Jesus' teachings.

AN OVERFLOW OF JOY

Let us remember Jesus set out to heal and save the world. Everything he did was out of his compassion for suffering people. His two key 'gifts' to people were faith and a new start with God. This was the foundation on which he could teach them the way of God's reign. The three dynamics of compassion, faith and a new start summarise the impact of Jesus' ministry. These three dynamics of course overlap completely with the abiding 'faith, hope and love' that Paul speaks of in 1 Corinthians 13.13.

The result of Jesus' compassion, faith and forgiveness was an irrepressible joy in the lives of those who allowed themselves to be changed by him. This joy is evident in those who were healed and forgiven as well as in Jesus' fellowship meals and festive celebrations. Jesus himself was clearly a remarkably cheerful person whose disposition and teaching caused people to let go of their worries and fears. He made the reason for joy clear by telling the stories of the lost sheep, coin and son (all in Luke 15) which highlight God's love for the lost and that when a person returns to God's love a party is necessary! Jesus also famously encouraged his followers to 'abide' in him (stay connected like a branch to a vine) so that amongst other things: *'my joy may be in you, and that your joy may be complete.'* (John 15.11)

Missing Jesus?

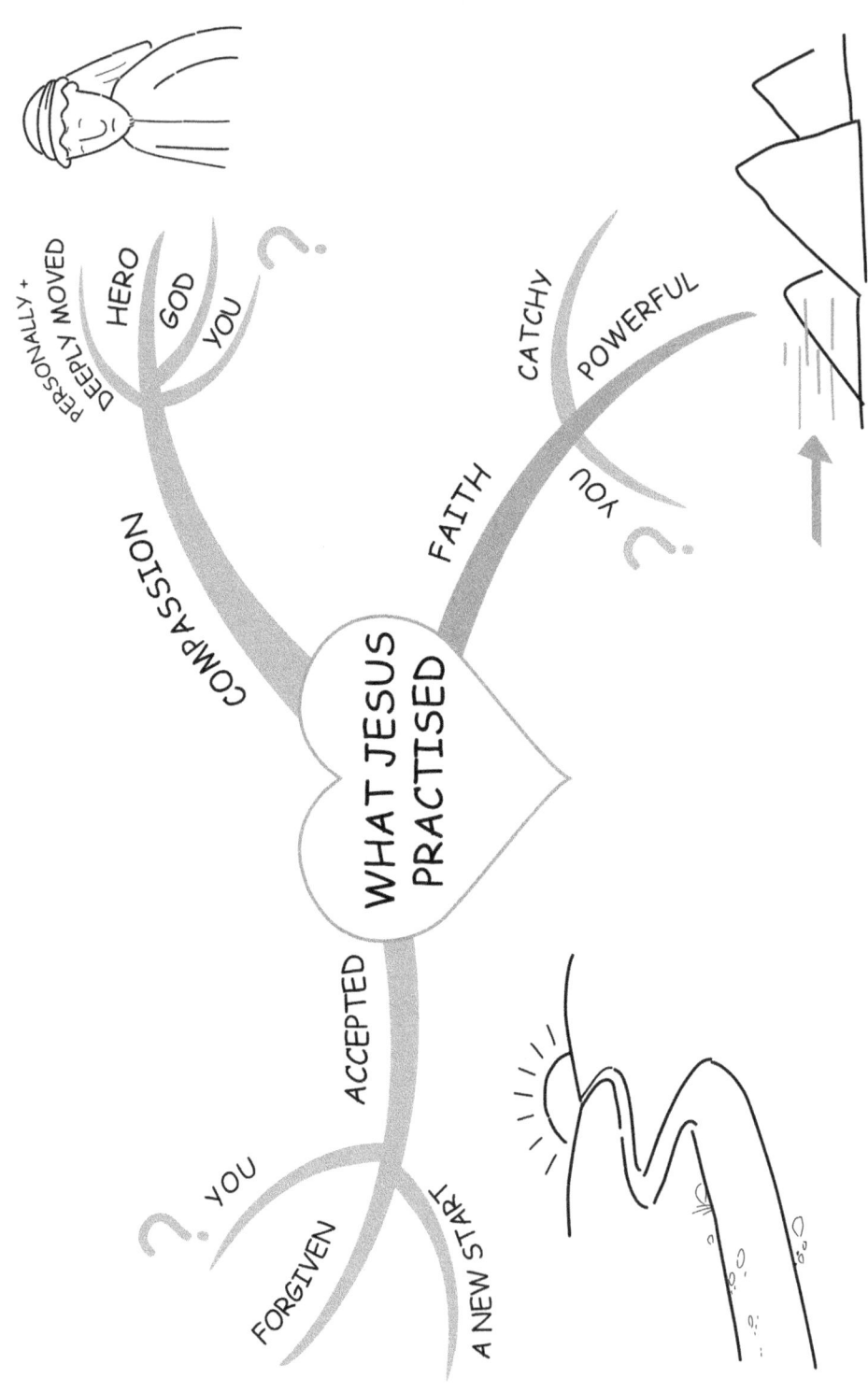

162

SUGGESTIONS FOR DISCUSSION, REVISION, REFLECTION AND APPLICATION

(These questions are intended for group work, but can easily be adapted for personal use.)

1. What is the most important message to you in this chapter? (Remember to also make a note of this on your 'God spoke to me' page.)
2. Icebreaker question: Of all the places you have lived/visited, which was the one you liked the best? (The question must be answered quickly. As a group, do not spend longer than 5 minutes in total on this question.)
3. Read Matthew 9.9-13 and answer the following questions:
   a. Why do you think Matthew responded so immediately to the call of Jesus?
   b. How did sinners experience Jesus then? How did Jesus relate to them?
   c. How do sinners experience Christians today? How do we relate to them?
   d. What did Jesus do to be experienced as a compassionate person? Try and make a list.
4. Below are a variety of suggestions and questions to aid your appreciation of this chapter. Do not attempt to do all of them! Choose those that are most appropriate to your unique situation and/or group. The questions are designed to help variously with revision, understanding, appreciation, reflection or application of the content.
   a. What caused the followers of Jesus to describe him as compassionate? Was it the things he did? Was it the way he looked at people? Try and picture his ministry in your mind.
   b. How do we become compassionate/remain compassionate in a society that struggles with a high crime rate? What practices might help us?
   c. Which suffering person/group does Jesus want you to love in a personal way? What are you going to do about this? It would be ideal at this point to make your intentions clear to the group. Invite them to hold you accountable to these over the coming weeks.
   d. What impact would faith have on your life if you woke up tomorrow morning with double the faith you have now?

e. Respond to Albert Nolan's statement, 'Anyone who thinks that evil will have the last word or that good and evil have a fifty-fifty chance is an atheist.' Do you like this statement? Why/why not?
f. Respond to the statement, 'The you that you struggle to forgive is already forgiven.' Does this help? Does this console you? Why/why not?
g. Do you see Jesus as a joyful person? Discuss your varying answers.

GOD SPOKE TO ME ...

8

THE KINGDOM HAS COME!
JESUS TEACHES KINGDOM CONSCIOUSNESS

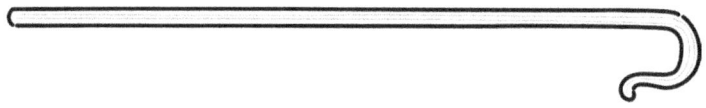

*Every day Jesus was teaching in the temple ...
all the people were spellbound by what they heard.*
(Luke 19.47-48)

As part of the research I did for this guidebook I sat down and read through the Gospels according to Matthew, Mark, Luke and John. As I journeyed through this delightful task an often neglected but major facet of Jesus' life became very clear to me – Jesus was a teacher.

Throughout his ministry Jesus did a lot of teaching about what it meant to live according to God's reign. There was a lot of deep content to his teaching. His teaching was clearly aimed at getting the listeners to grasp that living according to God's reign was different from the way in which they had lived until then. Repentance of a previous way of life, and turning to God and his way was the keynote of Jesus' teaching. Jesus also made it clear that responding faithfully to his teaching was a matter of life and death.

Matthew, Mark and Luke – all three record that at Jesus' transfiguration a voice from the cloud declared about Jesus *'Listen to Him!'* The impact on the reader is meant to be 'God wants me to listen to the teachings of Jesus!' (See Matthew 17.1-8, Mark 9.2-8 and Luke 9.28-36 for accounts of the transfiguration.)

Chapter 1 of this guidebook made it clear that Jesus' teachings are neither understood nor followed by many modern Christians. The words of Jesus at the end of the Sermon on the Mount highlight how important it is to take his teachings seriously:

> 'Not everyone who says to me, "Lord, Lord," will enter the kingdom of heaven, but only the one who does the will of my Father in heaven. ... Everyone then who hears these words of mine and acts on them will be like a wise man who built his house on rock... And everyone who hears these words of mine and does not act on them will be like a foolish man who built his house on sand. The rain fell, and the floods came, and the winds blew and beat against that house, and it fell — and great was its fall!' Now when Jesus had finished saying these things, the crowds were astounded at his teaching, for he taught them as one having authority, and not as their scribes. (Matthew 7.21-29)

Add to this the very last verse of Matthew's Gospel and one is left in no doubt about the ultimate importance of Jesus' teachings: Jesus instructs the disciples to go into the world and make disciples of all nations *'teaching them to obey everything that I have commanded you.'* (Matthew 28.20)

JESUS ANNOUNCED GOD'S REIGN ON EARTH: AN OVERVIEW OF JESUS' KINGDOM CONSCIOUSNESS TEACHING
From beginning to end

From the very beginning of his ministry to the very end, the theme of the Kingdom of God was the essential message of Jesus' ministry. Jesus opened his public ministry with the words, *'The time is fulfilled, and the kingdom of God has come near; repent, and believe in the good news.'* (Mark 1.15). He ends his ministry as king of his kingdom and declares, *'All authority in heaven and on earth has been given to me.'* (Matthew 28.18). In between the beginning and the end, Jesus continuously teaches on the theme of the Kingdom of God (The term 'Kingdom of Heaven' that Matthew often uses is completely synonymous with the term 'Kingdom of God'.) Impressively there are about 150 references to the Kingdom of God or Kingdom of Heaven in the Gospels!

Before sharing some of Jesus' actual teachings on the Kingdom of God I would like to give an overview of those teachings.

Coming to terms with some terms

The term 'Reign of God' is a very helpful term to use in our unpacking of Jesus' teachings on the Kingdom. The term, 'Reign of God', is slightly truer to the original meaning of the Greek term for 'Kingdom of God', *'Basileia tou Theou'* which refers to God's reign as extending over the entire universe and as present in the lives of those who bow to that reign. *Basileia* refers to both kingship (the power and the rule of the king) and kingdom (the domain, the territory). The 'Reign of God' is the extent of God's effective will. With the term 'Reign of God' one is able to access the reality that God reigns on earth wherever people seek his will. In so doing his reign surpasses the reign of any earthly ruler. The word *'basileia'* is probably derived from the Greek word for 'base' or 'foundation'. A synonym for 'Kingdom of God' could therefore also be 'The world-wide foundation of God'.

The term 'Kingdom of God' referred to the Jewish expectation of the reign of God on earth after the arrival of the Messiah. Jesus' announcement that the Kingdom of God is near (at hand), is astonishing. He is saying, 'The Reign of God has arrived and you are invited to change your life according to that great news.' When Jesus spoke of the Kingdom of God his language was charged with urgent political, religious, social, economic and cultural electricity. Our terms for the Kingdom of God must therefore try and capture the vitality and significance that the term 'Kingdom' had in Jesus' day. To help us we could use modern terms like 'The Global super-power of God', or 'The Global revolution of God'.

Jesus made it clear that God's reign in our lives is more important than any other kingdom (country, empire, allegiance) we may belong to. It is very important that we don't have an 'other-worldly' idea about God's reign. It is something that has started in this world and it is our calling to live according to that reign. Living according to God's reign has spiritual, social, political, relational and cognitive implications.

Jesus has an intense stand-off with Pilate about the Kingdom in John 18:

Jesus answered, 'My kingdom is not from this world. If my kingdom were from this world, my followers would be fighting to keep me from being handed over to the Jews. But as it is, my kingdom is not from here.' Pilate asked him, 'So you are a king?' Jesus answered, 'You say that I am a king. For this I was born, and for this I came into the world, to testify to the truth. Everyone who belongs to the truth listens to my voice.'

This passage has often been lost in translation and misunderstood to be saying 'My Kingdom is not of this world.' That has given the impression that Jesus' Kingdom is other-worldly, or that it doesn't apply to living life in this world. But note above that the NRSV has correctly translated the meaning of the original languages. Jesus is talking about the origin of his Kingdom, he is talking about where it comes from, and asserting that his empire is not from a world's power but from God. This standoff is clearly a contest between two rival agents of two rival empires. Both empires make a difference to everyday life on earth. Jesus represents God's purposes and Pilate represents Rome's purposes.

The terms 'King', 'Son of God', 'Saviour' and 'Shepherd' are all titles that were applied to Jesus by himself and by his disciples. But all these terms were also applied to the Roman Emperor by the doctrines of the Empire! With these very similar terms, used for two different emperors, who were contemporaries but who represented very different visions for society, Jesus and the disciples are forcing us to compare, contrast and choose between rival empires. The two empires have vastly different missions in the world. The two empires have a very different influence on people's lives and on society.

This blatant contrasting of the two empires was so helpful then because the foundational and pervasive presence of the Roman Empire made it difficult for people to envision a different way of living in the world.

A faithful reading of the Gospels today must therefore include a reflection on empire as we experience it today and how Jesus is in contest with its power and values. Read the gospels well to see more clearly the contours of the contrast between the Kingdom of God and the dominating empires of today, and also the rivalry of their values.[1]

The great value of the term 'Kingdom Consciousness Movement'

It is also valuable to say that Jesus set about establishing a 'Kingdom Consciousness Movement'. A Consciousness Movement is a movement in which the people embrace a new consciousness for their lives. They have realised that the consciousness with which they live is not life-giving enough and that it is healthier and more appropriate to live with a new consciousness. The shift to a new consciousness is normally led by a leader or leaders of the movement.

To help you see the value of my suggestion here I will draw attention to two powerful consciousness movements and their positive impact on people's lives. In both instances appreciate how powerful it is when a person changes

---

[1] If you are interested in reading more on these themes then I suggest Professor Warren Carter's two books: *The Roman Empire and the New Testament: An Essential Guide*, Abingdon, 2006, and *John and Empire: Initial Explorations*, Continuum Books, 2008.

the consciousness with which they live – when they think about life in a new and better way.

The first example is the incredibly important Black Consciousness Movement (BCM) led by Steve Biko and others. The genius of the BCM was to see that liberation for black people needed to include a psychological liberation, a liberation from inferiority consciousness, as well as socio-economic and political liberation. The BCM's success reveals the potency of a consciousness movement. The BCM in its broadest sense continues to be an important and necessary movement for building positive and assertive outlooks on life and context.[2]

The second example is the 'Twelve step programme' in which an addict adopts a new set of guiding principles for their life. Essential to this programme is that the addict shifts their consciousness to admit that they are an addict and to view themselves, for the rest of their lives, as a recovering addict. This programme continues to be the most successful method for an addict to live a new and sober life. The programme was developed by Bill Wilson and Dr Robert Holbrook Smith in 1935 and was immediately successful and became transformative throughout the world when they published *Alcoholics Anonymous: The Story of How More Than One Hundred Men Have Recovered from Alcoholism* in 1939. The power of the new consciousness proposed in this programme has been helpful to all people struggling with any form of addiction and compulsions.

I am convinced that it is enormously helpful for us to appreciate Jesus as a founder and leader of the Kingdom Consciousness Movement. I believe this perspective will help us to unlock and appreciate the lasting impact of Jesus' teachings and ministry. It is clear that Jesus wanted people to live with a new consciousness. He deeply desired that people would live conscious that the long-awaited Kingdom of God had begun in his ministry. He wanted them to shift from a consciousness of waiting for God's intervention into a consciousness that the intervention had now taken place, that God's reign had begun and that

---

[2] My choice of the phrase 'Kingdom Consciousness Movement' is not meant to detract from BCM at all. It is interesting for me to read Steve Biko embracing our relationship with God as a person's greatest allegiance. In *I Write What I Like* he says, 'Freedom is the ability to define oneself with one's possibilities held back not by the power of other people over one but only by one's relationship to God and to natural surroundings.' (Biko, Steve; *I Write What I Like*, p. 101.) I would like to go even further and point out how Steve Biko had much to say about the way in which Christianity should be better harnessed to inform consciousness of black people. Amongst his challenges to the church are: 'Try being true to Jesus' radical ministry', 'redefine the message of the Bible to make it relevant to struggling masses', 'make the Bible relevant to black people to keep them going on their long journey to freedom', 'deal with the spiritual poverty of black people'. This is all quoted in Tinyiko Maluleke's excellent chapter 'May the *Black God Stand, Please! Biko's Challenge to Religion*', in A. Mngxitama, A. Alexander, N.C. Gibson (eds), *Biko Lives! Contemporary Black History*.

they needed to re-orientate their lives to this new reality.

Once this new identity of living in God's reign was embraced, Jesus then inspired the individual to become an active agent of change in his or her locality. Kingdom Consciousness gives each person an exciting sense that they are God's person in and for the world.

Jesus' focus was not only on the individual but also on creating a united group based on this new identity. This identity also included a special emphasis on the precious value of each person regardless of status and encouraged people to hold their heads up high in defiance rather than surrender to oppressors.

The Reign of God, as Jesus proclaimed it, is a term that encompasses a new way of thinking and a new way of behaving. It is a new way of thinking in that it is a new consciousness, a new way of thinking about life, self, God, others and creation. It is also a new way of behaving in that it is a new way of acting and reacting. It is the way of radical love. Jesus still draws us to his way through the continued impact of his being and through our putting his teachings into practice. We grow through a continual cognitive and behavioural response to Jesus.

The reign of God is a truth that can only be known to the degree that we get involved with it – otherwise it remains a theory in a book. The Reign of God must be embodied to be experienced as real. Jesus' proclamation of the reign of God opens up for each person an entry point into something so large that a truly meaningful life is found in abandoning oneself to it. Meaning in life is experienced when you involve yourself in something more important than yourself, when you find your place in a larger scheme. This too is part of Kingdom Consciousness. Involve yourself fully in this opening Jesus gives you!

It is important to appreciate that Kingdom Consciousness is the true power of a Christian in any era. Many have grown weary of the institutional focus of the church and are turning away from her. The church should however realise that she fulfils her identity as the Bride of Christ when her members live with a radical Kingdom Consciousness.[3]

Jesus' teachings were always very real and practical and related to the problems of their day. In this way people were empowered to discover solutions to problems that they faced and so Jesus provided them with hope. These solutions were often embraced as a group and so a new sense of humanity also emerged in the Kingdom Consciousness Movement.

Jesus' preaching and teaching about the Reign of God were almost entirely in immediate and relational terms. We are called to immediately change our consciousness. We are called to live now according to God's reign that has begun. We are invited to relate to people and all of life now in a way that honours God's reign. We are called to work out, now, in our current context, what it means that God's reign has begun here and now. This is summed up in the Lord's Prayer where Jesus teaches us to pray, *Your kingdom come. Your will be done, on earth as it is in heaven.* (Matthew 6.10)

Part of the essence of Jesus' teaching and preaching on the Reign of God is the awareness that evil's reign in this world had now been replaced by God's reign and that Jesus was inviting people to choose the side of ultimate victory. Jesus also emphasised that God's reign was a new way of seeing the world. Choosing sides and seeing the world in a new way is what the call to repentance is all about.

Repentance is the English translation of the Greek word *metanoia* which means 'turning around' and 'change of mind'. Turning around, of course, changes your view. You can stand in the same spot and look north and then look south and you will see two completely different views. The Reign of God

---

[3] In this regard I have always enjoyed the following words of Richard Halverson: 'Christianity began as a relationship with the living Christ and one another. It then went to Greece where it became a philosophy, then to Rome where it became an institution, then to Europe where it became a culture and then to America where it became an enterprise.'

does mean that we have a completely different view of life. Another way to say it is that a change in consciousness is the deepest meaning of a 'change of mind'. In Jesus' world view 'heaven' is a new way of seeing life.[4]

Jesus' Kingdom teachings have the intention of changing the norms and conventions we live with. He does this by pointing to a usual norm of living and then he presents a Kingdom way as a more life-giving way. This intention motivates most of his teachings and is very clear in places like the Sermon on the Mount. It's easy to notice when Jesus says, *'You have heard that it was said … but I say to you'* but is not limited to those teachings. An example is Jesus' teaching against the world's norm of retaliation. Retaliation, getting even, compensation, reparation and being penalised are all norms and conventions in society. Jesus inspires us to rather find ways to respond to evil with goodness, grace, kindness and generosity. Look at Matthew 5.38-42 and Luke 6.27-36 for two more references.

Kingdom Consciousness is a communal consciousness, not an individual consciousness. We misunderstand many of Jesus' teachings, and much of the Bible, when we seek them to have meaning that relates to our lives as a separate reality from other people and society at large. Jesus' teachings are addressed to people and how they, together, think. It may be helpful to think here of the Black Consciousness Movement again. Just as BCM taught black people to appreciate black identity within the black community, so we should learn to appreciate Kingdom identity within a Kingdom community.

A number of Jesus' teachings make the point that God's reign is revealed by the way in which we face times of testing. A time of testing knocks us out of a comfort zone and exposes how dependent we are on those comforts. If we remain faithful to the values of the Kingdom in that time of testing, rather than betray the Kingdom for the sake of the comforts, then God's reign is seen to be firmly established in our lives. This has a way of growing the influence and extent of God's reign in society. See passages such as Matthew 24.36 – 25.13 and note the repeated refrain *'Keep awake therefore, for you do not know on what day your Lord is coming.'* This phrase refers to the unexpected nature of times of testing and how our discipleship is tested in those times – Jesus expects us to be

---

[4] The book of Revelation gives us insight into how the Kingdom of Heaven is prevailing over the Kingdom of this world. Revelation is clear that this is reality as it is now. The vision of Revelation takes evil and its role seriously, but also gives us insight into God's Reign thus stimulating a strong Kingdom Consciousness. One is left in no doubt that God reigns and that his kingdom has started. This is beautifully presented in many scenes, one of which is after the blowing of the seventh trumpet when loud voices in heaven are heard singing *'The kingdom of the world has become the kingdom of our Lord and of his Messiah, and he will reign forever and ever.'* Then the twenty-four elders who sit on their thrones before God fell on their faces and worshipped God, singing, *'We give you thanks, Lord God Almighty, who are and who were, for you have taken your great power and begun to reign.'* (Revelation 11.15-16)

able to stand up for him when those unexpected times of testing come.

As you go through the teaching of the Kingdom Consciousness Movement notice how the idea of the Reign of God is something so big that it includes all the aspects of your life. You can get involved with the sure knowledge that you are surrendering yourself to something that pulls you in the direction of life rather than nothingness, meaninglessness or destruction.

In this section I have given an overview of Jesus' teaching of the Kingdom Consciousness Movement.[5] This will help you to appreciate the next few sections of this chapter where I give you some of the recorded words of Jesus. The overview I have just shared will also help you to relate to the next four chapters which deal with the specific values of the Kingdom Consciousness Movement.

ALLOW GOD TO BE GOD

God's reign is honoured wherever God is allowed to be God – wherever God is given the highest priority and allegiance. God's reign is honoured where we submit to God's will. I need to admit that if I do not submit to God's will then I have not allowed God to be my god, rather I have made him less than God and more of an advisor. This comes through in the following of Jesus' teachings:

Some of Jesus' most difficult and demanding sayings about the Reign of God are those which call us to be prepared to sacrifice for him and his reign: *'Whoever loves father or mother more than me is not worthy of me; and whoever loves son or daughter more than me is not worthy of me; and whoever does not take up the cross and follow me is not worthy of me. Those who find their life will lose it, and those who lose their life for my sake will find it.'* (Matthew 10.37-39. Luke 14.25-26 records a similar saying but in even more demanding and troubling language. A deep and detailed study of the Luke 14 passage mentioned here reveals that Jesus is not teaching us to hate our families – he is only asserting that our love for him be greater.[6])

Essentially, Jesus is unreservedly challenging us to allow God to be God and is remarkably placing himself in the position of God. Whatever or whoever gets my highest and ultimate loyalty is my god.

Jesus often emphasised the need to submit to God's reign and bear fruit: *'Therefore I tell you, the kingdom of God will be taken away from you and given to a people that produces the fruits of the kingdom.'* (Matthew 21.43)

---

[5] In these 'Kingdom Consciousness' chapters I do not pay attention to Jesus' teachings on the following important themes because I cover them in other parts of the guidebook: Jesus' teaching about himself; Jesus' teaching about his relationship with the Father; Jesus' teaching about the Holy Spirit.

[6] Read Matthew 15.3-9 to see Jesus exposing the godlessness of neglecting our responsibilities to families.

Here, Jesus went so far as to say that his own family are those who do the will of God: *'Who is my mother, and who are my brothers?' And pointing to his disciples, he said, 'Here are my mother and my brothers! For whoever does the will of my Father in heaven is my brother and sister and mother.'* (Matthew 12.48-50. See also Matthew 7.21)

We must not think of God's reign as a strange insertion into this world, for this world belongs to God. This is made clear in the parable of the weeds sown by an enemy at night after the owner had sown good seed. The owner allows the two to grow together. After telling this parable the disciples ask him to explain, which he does:

> *He answered, 'The one who sows the good seed is the Son of Man; the field is the world, and the good seed are the children of the kingdom; the weeds are the children of the evil one, and the enemy who sowed them is the devil; the harvest is the end of the age, and the reapers are angels. Just as the weeds are collected and burned up with fire, so will it be at the end of the age. The Son of Man will send his angels, and they will collect out of his kingdom all causes of sin and all evildoers, and they will throw them into the furnace of fire, where there will be weeping and gnashing of teeth. Then the righteous will shine like the sun in the kingdom of their Father. Let anyone with ears listen!'* (See Matthew 13.24-30, 36-43)

Although we are invited to enter God's reign by choice, we must realise that God, being God, cannot be avoided through our refusal to choose. All are judged:

> *'Again, the kingdom of heaven is like a net that was thrown into the sea and caught fish of every kind; when it was full, they drew it ashore, sat down, and put the good into baskets but threw out the bad. So it will be at the end of the age. The angels will come out and separate the evil from the righteous and throw them into the furnace of fire, where there will be weeping and gnashing of teeth.'* (Matthew 13.44-50)

THE PRIORITY OF THE KINGDOM OF GOD

In the following teachings and sayings of Jesus it is impressed upon us that Jesus saw it as His primary priority to teach the good news of the Kingdom:

At daybreak he departed and went into a deserted place. And the crowds were looking for him; and when they reached him, they wanted to prevent him from leaving them. But he said to them, 'I must proclaim the good news of the kingdom of God to the other cities also; for I was sent for this purpose.' So he continued proclaiming the message in the synagogues of Judea. (Luke 4.42-44. See also Matthew 9.35; Matthew 10.5-8; Matthew 16.16-19; Matthew 24.14; Luke 12.32)

THE DYNAMICS OF GOD'S REIGN

As part of his teaching on the Reign of God Jesus gives us insight into how God's reign works. Generally Jesus taught this in the captivating metaphors of simple parables in which we gain insight into the essential dynamic forces of God's reign in this world. Jesus as a teacher is able to dance between different metaphors, similes and images and so give us an empowering and encouraging kaleidoscope of insight into how God's reign works.

The well known parable of the Sower shows us that we need to offer God the fertile soil of our heads, hearts and hands to be part of his Kingdom:

'Hear then the parable of the sower. When anyone hears the word of the kingdom and does not understand it, the evil one comes and snatches away what is sown in the heart; this is what was sown on the path. As for what was sown on rocky ground, this is the one who hears the word and immediately receives it with joy; yet such a person has no root, but endures only for a while, and when trouble or persecution arises on account of the word, that person immediately falls away. As for what was sown among thorns, this is the one who hears the word, but the cares of the world and the lure of wealth choke the word, and it yields nothing. But as for what was sown on good soil, this is the one who hears the word and understands it, who indeed bears fruit and yields, in one case a hundredfold, in another sixty, and in another thirty.' (Matthew 13.18-23)

In many ways Jesus stimulates us to appreciate the power of the apparent small things of this world, and in so doing have faith in the vulnerable ways of God's reign:

He put before them another parable: 'The kingdom of heaven is like a mustard seed that someone took and sowed in his field; it is the smallest of all the seeds, but when it has grown it is the greatest of shrubs and becomes a tree, so that the birds of the air come and make nests in its branches.' He told them another parable: 'The kingdom of heaven is like yeast that a woman took and mixed in with three measures of flour until all of it was leavened.' (Matthew 13.31-33)

Jesus lays a strong emphasis on the small and hidden place of the heart (which in the understanding then was the place of the will). Jesus understood that a person would only truly be obedient if that person's heart was surrendered to God. When a person surrendered themselves to God then God would be at liberty to change their will and would be able to write his will on their hearts. This very important point will help you the reader to avoid falling into the long debate about whether the Kingdom of God is an inner reality or an outer reality in the world. It is both – it is firstly an inner reality of God's reign in the person's heart, then it is an outer reality as that person is faithful to God in the world. It is not either/or; it is both/and. Remember that Jesus is not just interested in us doing good things – he is interested in us becoming good. We will only truly do good consistently and with integrity when we are actually good within ourselves. Notice this theme in the following passages:

> 'Either make the tree good, and its fruit good; or make the tree bad, and its fruit bad; for the tree is known by its fruit. You brood of vipers! How can you speak good things, when you are evil? For out of the abundance of the heart the mouth speaks. The good person brings good things out of a good treasure, and the evil person brings evil things out of an evil treasure.' (Matthew 12.33–35).

> He said to him, 'You shall love the Lord your God with all your heart, and with all your soul, and with all your mind.' This is the greatest and first commandment. (Matthew 22.36–38).

> 'For where your treasure is, there your heart will be also.' (Matthew 6.20–21).

See the following references for more of Jesus' teachings on this theme: Matthew 5.8; 5.28; 15.7-9; Luke 8.11-15; 17.20-21.

One often has the sense that Jesus is turning the world upside down because he blesses and affirms what is frequently marginalised. Jesus is actually turning the world right side up and promises the blessing and presence of God for all who quest for him and his will:

> 'Blessed are the poor in spirit, for theirs is the kingdom of heaven. Blessed are those who mourn, for they will be comforted. Blessed are the meek, for they will inherit the earth.

> Blessed are those who hunger and thirst for righteousness, for they will be filled. Blessed are the merciful, for they will receive mercy. Blessed are the pure in heart, for they will see God. Blessed are the peacemakers, for they will be called children of God. Blessed are those who are persecuted for righteousness' sake, for theirs is the kingdom of heaven.' (Matthew 5.3-10)

Jesus asserts that the quest for God and his will needs to be the first priority of any person's life. All other good things will fall into place if they make the Kingdom their priority: 'But strive first for the kingdom of God and his righteousness, and all these things will be given to you as well.' (Matthew 6.33)

The ultimate value of God's reign in our lives and world is found in these words that have become standard metaphors in the English language: '*The kingdom of heaven is like treasure hidden in a field, which someone found and hid; then in his joy he goes and sells all that he has and buys that field. Again, the kingdom of heaven is like a merchant in search of fine pearls; on finding one pearl of great value, he went and sold all that he had and bought it.'* (Matthew 13.44-46)

To enter into the Kingdom needs a death to worldly values and a re-birth into God's Kingdom: *Jesus answered him, 'Very truly, I tell you, no one can see the kingdom of God without being born from above.'* (John 3.3)

ABUNDANT LIFE

Jesus often refers to God's reign as giving a person abundant life. The term 'life' is an important concept in Jesus' teachings. Sometimes he uses just the word 'life', other times it is the term 'eternal life' and at other times 'abundant life'. All of these terms refer to the same concept.

Essentially the concept is that a person who lives with Kingdom Consciousness will experience life as it is meant to be, life in all its fullness, abundant life. They will actualise their potential. They will fulfil their purpose in life. They will experience life as good. They will be free from that which diminishes, traps and dissipates life. They will live for that which has real value. This is life that begins the moment a person enters into Kingdom Consciousness and continues into eternity in God's presence.

The term 'eternal life' is the English translation of *zoe aionios*, which is literally 'the life of the coming ages'. It includes the idea of endless life, but is actually about the life in the age (aeon) that the Messiah inaugurates. John says that *zoe aionios* is the present possession of those who believe in Jesus. 'Eternal life' or 'abundant life' is the term, particularly in John's Gospel, for the age of God's reign, which had broken into the current age.

Jesus clearly saw 'eternal life' as a quality of life that became part of the experience of those who followed him. It is important to see that Jesus did not think of eternal life as something that started once a person died. Nor was eternal life merely about an infinite length of life. No, it was about the special quality of a full life lived in intimate relationship with God.

Jesus made it clear that you had to follow him and join the Kingdom Consciousness Movement if you wanted to experience eternal life. The following passages make this clear:

Then someone came to him and said, 'Teacher, what good deed must I do to have eternal life?' And he said to him, 'Why do you ask me about what is good? There is only one who is good. If you wish to enter into life, keep the commandments.' He said to him, 'Which ones?' And Jesus said, 'You shall not murder; You shall not commit adultery; You shall not steal; You shall not bear false witness; Honor your father and mother; also, You shall love your neighbor as yourself.' The young man said to him, 'I have kept all these; what do I still lack?' Jesus said to him, 'If you wish to be perfect, go, sell your possessions, and give the money to the poor, and you will have treasure in heaven; then come, follow me.' (Matthew 19.16-21)

Kingdom Consciousness clearly has a life-giving effect. In this passage Jesus describes how we come to have a spring of abundant life in our being:

Jesus said to her, 'Everyone who drinks of this water will be thirsty again, but those who drink of the water that I will give them will never be thirsty. The water that I will give will become in them a spring of water gushing up to eternal life.' (John 4.13-14)

'I came that they may have life, and have it abundantly.' (John 10.10)

The following passages are more of Jesus' teachings about how eternal life is experienced by those who believe and follow Him – John 3.14-16; 5.21-24, 6.25-40, 10.27-28; 11.25-27; 12.44-50, 14.6; 17.1-26; 20.31.

The parable of the prodigal son highlights how a living person was actually dead spiritually, but then came back to life. For Jesus it is clearly important to be spiritually alive in this life (see Luke 15.22-32).

Jesus believes that our choices define who we are and whose we are. He believes that we reveal our values and beliefs through our choices and decisions. He made it clear that there are real dangers to getting caught up with the lure of fallen worldly pleasures and pursuits. The pursuit of these pleasures and goals is a destructive, dissipating and diminishing path. It is a path that may be described as 'death' rather than 'life'. Jesus was deeply concerned that people understand that it is necessary that they make a decision for or against the Kingdom. They needed to see that a choice to surrender to God is necessary if they were to be saved from the deadly clutches of the world. The next four chapters of this guidebook unpack in detail the values of the world and the values of the Kingdom.

It is important to appreciate that in Jesus' day the values of the world were determined in a foundational and ubiquitous way by the Roman Empire. The leaders of the Jewish temple and state had submitted themselves to Roman rule, with the result that everyday political, social, economic and religious life was formed and informed by the Roman Empire.⁷ Jesus' claims to have instituted God's Rule and of offering the benefits of that rule are made at the same time as Rome was proclaiming the benefits of its rule. We must appreciate that Jesus and the Gospel writers intentionally offer a myriad of claims to contest the purported benefits of Roman rule and the hierarchical and exploitative values of that rule.⁸

When Jesus says, *'The time is fulfilled, and the kingdom of God has come near; repent, and believe in the good news.'* (Mark 1.15) the Greek word used here for 'time' is *'kairos'*. *'Kairos'* is a special Greek word for time and carries the meaning of 'time to decide', 'opportunity', 'time filled with meaning', 'the time when things are brought to crisis' 'the decisive epoch waited for', 'opportune or seasonable time' and 'the right time'.⁹

---

⁷ The temple authorities had completely abandoned the Hebrew belief that God was their King. They had done this in order to win favour from Rome who would then give them permission to maintain the worship life of the temple. John's Gospel has evidence of their allegiance to the Emperor in John 19 when they are insisting that Pilate crucify Jesus, who they assert is against the Roman Empire: *From then on Pilate tried to release him, but the Jews cried out, 'If you release this man, you are no friend of the emperor. Everyone who claims to be a king sets himself against the emperor.' When Pilate heard these words, he brought Jesus outside and sat on the judge's bench at a place called The Stone Pavement, or in Hebrew, Gabbatha. Now it was the day of Preparation for the Passover; and it was about noon. He said to the Jews, 'Here is your King!' They cried out, 'Away with him! Away with him! Crucify him!' Pilate asked them, 'Shall I crucify your King?' The chief priests answered, 'We have no king but the emperor.' Then he handed him over to them to be crucified.*

⁸ If you are interested in reading more on these themes then I suggest Professor Warren Carter's two books: *The Roman Empire and the New Testament: An Essential Guide*, Abingdon, 2006. *John and Empire: Initial Explorations*, Continuum Books, 2008.

⁹ *Enhanced Strong's Lexicon*, J. Strong, Woodside Bible Fellowship, Ontario, 1996.

Here are some of his teachings about the choice between life and death. Here, and in other places, you see that Jesus does not encourage self-preservation! This really goes against what makes common sense to us. Jesus makes self-sacrifice rather than self-preservation into a Kingdom value:

'Enter through the narrow gate; for the gate is wide and the road is easy that leads to destruction, and there are many who take it. For the gate is narrow and the road is hard that leads to life, and there are few who find it.' (Matthew 7.13-14)

Then Jesus told his disciples, 'If any want to become my followers, let them deny themselves and take up their cross and follow me. For those who want to save their life will lose it, and those who lose their life for my sake will find it. For what will it profit them if they gain the whole world but forfeit their life? Or what will they give in return for their life?' (Matthew 16.24-26. See also 18.8-9)

YOUR KINGDOM CONSCIOUSNESS IS A SIGN THAT YOU ARE PART OF THE SHEPHERD'S FLOCK

Embracing a vital Kingdom Consciousness shows that I am close to Jesus the Shepherd. Perhaps the following metaphor can help. Think of the world as a ship that we all live on. The captain of the ship used to be Satan, but Jesus has taken the captaincy and control of the helm. Satan still lives on board even though he is in chains. Satan is free to influence as many as will listen. But Satan cannot take the helm. Satan cannot change the direction of the ship. Although God is not in control of everything that happens on the ship, he does determine the destiny. We each decide whether to listen to Jesus the legitimate captain or to Satan the deposed captain.

Many years ago I heard of the testimony of a young conscientious objector who faced a court in USSR because he refused to go into the army. The young man explained his allegiance to the Kingdom of God and how this meant that he refused to take up arms for the USSR. The judge was surprisingly quite sympathetic but in the end said to him that it would be acceptable to hold his beliefs if the Kingdom of God had actually come. The young Christian replied that the Kingdom of God had come and he was being true to it!

It is good to appreciate that the proclamation of God's reign arrived in Jesus and has fresh and unique significance in each generation and context. At present in Southern Africa there is a definite way in which announcing God's reign is linked with the need for justice – we are aware that God is calling afresh for good news for the poor and for liberation of the oppressed. We are missing Jesus if we do not respond to this call and its unique and fresh significance in our context. We need to join God and God's choices for justice. Kingdom Consciousness is therefore a revolutionary consciousness! The Kingdom Consciousness Movement is about engagement with the struggle for justice and the subversion of the current order until it conforms to norms of the Kingdom of God. Remember that the first good news was good news for the poor.

The Kingdom has come! Jesus teaches Kingdom Consciousness

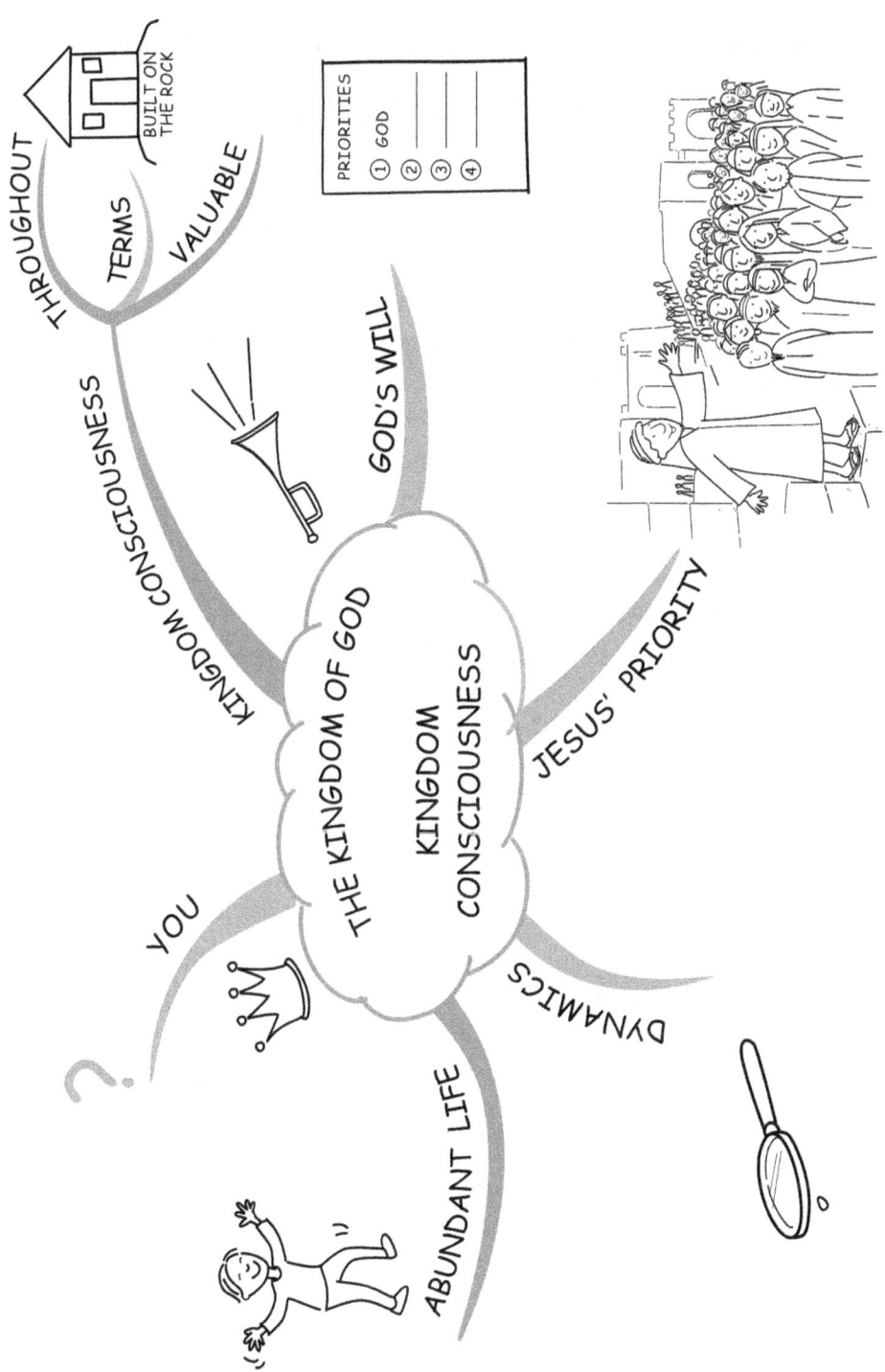

SUGGESTIONS FOR DISCUSSION, REVISION, REFLECTION AND APPLICATION

(These questions are intended for group work, but can easily be adapted for personal use.)

1. What is the most important message to you in this chapter? (Remember to also make a note of this on your 'God spoke to me' page.)
2. Icebreaker question: Who was your childhood hero? Why? (The question must be answered quickly. As a group, do not spend longer than 5 minutes in total on this question.)
3. Read Matthew 7.21-29 and answer the following questions:
   a. Verses 21-23 seem very definite. Why do you think Jesus was so uncompromising then?
   b. Who are people today who say 'Lord, Lord' but actually do not belong to Jesus?
   c. Is your house built on Jesus if you believe in Jesus? If not, what more is needed? Pay close attention to what Jesus says here.
   d. What do you think needs to change in your life in order to be more true to this teaching?
4. Below are a variety of suggestions and questions to aid your appreciation of this chapter. Do not attempt to do all of them! Choose those that are most appropriate to your unique situation and/or group. The questions are designed to help variously with revision, understanding, appreciation, reflection or application of the content.
   a. What do you find helpful about this perspective that Jesus' teachings on the Kingdom can best be understood as the formation of a 'Kingdom Consciousness Movement'?
   b. When we are honest we admit that we really do struggle to allow God to be God. By this we mean that we struggle to give God our highest and ultimate loyalty. Do you want to follow Jesus' teaching? What needs to change in your life for you to truly have God as your highest and truest devotion?
   c. Putting God first in our lives does mean that we have to put his Kingdom first. What one thing can you do to grow your submission to

God's reign?
d. What do you feel is most special about abundant life?
e. In what ways is a worldly sense of the good life different from Jesus' offering of abundant life? Try to list some of the differences.
f. Choose three aspects of a Kingdom Consciousness that you resolve to adopt. Share these with someone.

GOD SPOKE TO ME ...

9

JESUS VALUED SHARING AND NOT GREED

'Where your treasure is, there your heart will be also...
You cannot serve God and wealth' (Matthew 6.21 and 24c)

AN OVERVIEW OF JESUS' TEACHINGS ON MONEY AND POSSESSIONS

Jesus' teaching on money and possessions is generally regarded as the most difficult in the Gospels. Jesus taught us that the Reign of God is a situation where people do not hoard but rather share their surplus with those in need.

A society where we hoard, where some are poor, made poor, kept poor, and others have more than they need is, according to Jesus, part of the kingdom of Satan. The Kingdom of God is one structured on the value of sharing.

We see this Kingdom Consciousness embraced by Jesus who lived with a remarkable attractive largeness of Spirit. His personal style and teachings were characterised by a beautiful unrestricted generosity and abundance. His teachings pushed for a generosity in giving that some deemed to be unfair. He practised this generosity in giving of himself in abundant ways on a daily basis in the giving of his time and energy to those who needed him, especially those who needed him the most.

When he fed the multitudes at the Sea of Galilee there was more than enough for everyone and lots left over. In subtle ways this prefigured the sacrificial giving of his own life and how we would continue to be nourished by him as the 'bread of life'. He taught that people should give and not count the cost at all. He encouraged people to trust in God's generosity to care for their own needs.

The amount of teaching Jesus gave on the theme of money and possessions is staggering, and no other theme, except the Kingdom of God itself, receives greater attention. The impact that Kingdom Consciousness has on money and possessions was the dominant teaching theme of Jesus. One is left in no doubt that being a follower of Jesus has radical implications for our economic behaviour.[1]

LOAD SHEDDING[2]

Jesus viewed people's possessions as burdens and blockages to abundant living and so he encouraged people to shed these loads:

---

[1] Donald Kraybill's *Upside Down Kingdom*, chapters 5-7 are excellent reading on this theme.

[2] This title needs a brief explanation for non-South African readers. This title is a pun on the term that our electricity supplier has used since 2007 when our demand for electricity has been greater than their ability to supply. They shut down electric power to parts of the system to avoid the failure of the system. 'Load Shedding' is their term for this.

'Do not store up for yourselves treasures on earth, where moth and rust consume and where thieves break in and steal; but store up for yourselves treasures in heaven, where neither moth nor rust consumes and where thieves do not break in and steal. For where your treasure is, there your heart will be also.' (Matthew 6.19-21)

Zacchaeus stood there and said to the Lord, 'Look, half of my possessions, Lord, I will give to the poor; and if I have defrauded anyone of anything, I will pay back four times as much.' Then Jesus said to him, 'Today salvation has come to this house'. (Luke 19.8-9)

Matthew records in detail the occasion when Jesus condemned the scribes and the Pharisees for their lifestyles. Jesus is relentless in this attack on them and the overall impression we get is of the scribes and Pharisees living dark, burdened, trapped and sickly lives. Many in society would not have seen it this way. Many would have thought that the scribes and Pharisees had 'arrived' and were living the god-blessed good life. But Jesus scratches beneath the surface and exposes the sickly inner life, which is spilling out and spoiling other people's lives too. Here is some of the speech that relates to money and possessions:

Then Jesus said to the crowds and to his disciples, 'The scribes and the Pharisees sit on Moses' seat; therefore, do whatever they teach you and follow it; but do not do as they do, for they do not practice what they teach. They tie up heavy burdens, hard to bear, and lay them on the shoulders of others; but they themselves are unwilling to lift a finger to move them...

'But woe to you, scribes and Pharisees, hypocrites! For you lock people out of the kingdom of heaven. For you do not go in yourselves, and when others are going in, you stop them. Woe to you, scribes and Pharisees, hypocrites! For you cross sea and land to make a single convert, and you make the new convert twice as much a child of hell as yourselves...

'Woe to you, scribes and Pharisees, hypocrites! For you tithe mint, dill, and cummin, and have neglected the weightier matters of the law: justice and mercy and faith. It is these you ought to have practiced without neglecting the others. You blind guides! You strain out a gnat but swallow a camel! Woe to you, scribes and Pharisees, hypocrites! For you clean the outside of the cup and of the plate, but inside they are full of greed and self-indulgence. You blind Pharisee! First clean

the inside of the cup, so that the outside also may become clean. Woe to you, scribes and Pharisees, hypocrites! For you are like whitewashed tombs, which on the outside look beautiful, but inside they are full of the bones of the dead and of all kinds of filth. So you also on the outside look righteous to others, but inside you are full of hypocrisy and lawlessness.' (Matthew 23.1-28, selected verses)

FREEDOM!

Jesus taught that we can easily be possessed by our possessions. He helped us see that we can so easily lose our freedom for allowing God to be God in our lives. Our money and possessions quickly become the ruling factor in our decisions. Through our materialism we lose our identity as free agents to follow God and fulfil our human potential.

Jesus teaches about money and possessions because of what he wants for the individual, not because of what he wants from the individual. He is not teaching on these matters so that he can get money from people, but so that they can enjoy freedom and be able to understand what has true and lasting value.

The rich young ruler to whom Jesus said *'Go sell all that you have and give to the poor'* was not being offered poverty in place of riches, but rather freedom from captivity. For Jesus the opposite of rich is not poor, but free! Possessions held this man tightly in its grasp and he was unable to experience the abundant life he wanted whilst in this state. Note also that Jesus is inviting the young ruler to join the group of disciples that are following Jesus. All the disciples following Jesus had sold what they owned and were keeping a common purse from which to live. If the young ruler had joined this group he would not have been in an impoverished state by selling all that he had. His needs would have been met from a common purse. But his possessions kept him captive. Here is part of the reference:

As he was setting out on a journey, a man ran up and knelt before him, and asked him, 'Good Teacher, what must I do to inherit eternal life?'... Jesus, looking at him, loved him and said, 'You lack one thing; go, sell what you own, and give the money to the poor, and you will have treasure in heaven; then come, follow me.' When he heard this, he was shocked and went away grieving, for he had many possessions (Mark 10.17-22)

Jesus valued sharing and not greed

Note also in this above passage that the man is caught up in a quest for his own acceptability to God. The core question of life for him is private salvation. In response Jesus nudges him into the real world, the world where there is suffering and where God's people are called to live out their concern for such people. Jesus seeks to sow seeds of compassion in him.

Now take a look at these passages in which Jesus exposes the dangers of money and possessions:

> 'No one can serve two masters; for a slave will either hate the one and love the other, or be devoted to the one and despise the other. You cannot serve God and wealth.' (Matthew 6.24)

> 'And others are those sown among the thorns: these are the ones who hear the word, but the cares of the world, and the lure of wealth, and the desire for other things come in and choke the word, and it yields nothing.' (Mark 4.19)

Jesus is not shy to say that our money and possessions can prevent us from accepting kingdom consciousness:

> *'It is easier for a camel to go through the eye of a needle than for someone who is rich to enter the kingdom of God.'* (Mark 10.25)

Jesus made it clear that being a disciple meant leaving behind the hold money and possessions have on us:

> *'So therefore, none of you can become my disciple if you do not give up all your possessions.'* (Luke 14.33)

Jesus only once personally chose to refer to something as an abomination or detestable. The one instance is in Luke 16.15 and he is referring to greed, love of money and the prizing of money as an abomination (detestable). It is a strong word and appears in the Old Testament only 50 times. In the OT it is mostly used to condemn practices related to idolatry. Jesus' use of the word in relation to the love of money is clearly an indication of how strongly he felt about the matter and also how he viewed it as idolatrous:

> *'No slave can serve two masters; for a slave will either hate the one and love the other, or be devoted to the one and despise the other. You cannot serve God and wealth.' The Pharisees, who were lovers of money, heard all this, and they ridiculed him. So he said to them, 'You are those who justify yourselves in the sight of others; but God knows your hearts; for what is prized by human beings is an abomination in the sight of God.'* (Luke 16.13-15)[3]

Jesus' own difficulty with convincing people of these teachings led him to assert that some are so attached to their luxuries that even a visitation from the dead would not lead to repentance! Here is the parable:

> *'There was a rich man who was dressed in purple and fine linen and who feasted sumptuously every day. And at his gate lay a poor man named Lazarus, covered with sores, who longed to satisfy his hunger with what fell from the rich man's table; even the dogs would come and lick his sores. The poor man died and was carried away by the angels to be with Abraham. The rich man also died and was buried. In Hades, where he was being tormented, he looked up and saw Abraham far away with*

---

[3] The Greek word that is translated into English as abomination / detestable is *bdelugma* /**bdel**·oog·mah/. The only other time Jesus is recorded as using the word is when he is quoting someone else, namely Daniel's prophecy, which he quotes in Matthew 24.15 (and its parallel in Mark 13.14).

Lazarus by his side. He called out, "Father Abraham, have mercy on me, and send Lazarus to dip the tip of his finger in water and cool my tongue; for I am in agony in these flames." But Abraham said, "Child, remember that during your lifetime you received your good things, and Lazarus in like manner evil things; but now he is comforted here, and you are in agony. Besides all this, between you and us a great chasm has been fixed, so that those who might want to pass from here to you cannot do so, and no one can cross from there to us." He said, "Then, father, I beg you to send him to my father's house – for I have five brothers – that he may warn them, so that they will not also come into this place of torment." Abraham replied, "They have Moses and the prophets; they should listen to them." He said, "No, father Abraham; but if someone goes to them from the dead, they will repent." He said to him, "If they do not listen to Moses and the prophets, neither will they be convinced even if someone rises from the dead."' (Luke 16.19-31)

PRACTISE SHARING

Jesus taught that the core value in the realm of money and possessions in God's reign is the value of sharing. He exposed the fallen way of the world to be the practice of greed and hoarding. Here are some of his teachings:

'If anyone strikes you on the cheek, offer the other also; and from anyone who takes away your coat do not withhold even your shirt. Give to everyone who begs from you; and if anyone takes away your goods, do not ask for them again. Do to others as you would have them do to you… If you lend to those from whom you hope to receive, what credit is that to you? Even sinners lend to sinners, to receive as much again. But love your enemies, do good, and lend, expecting nothing in return. Your reward will be great, and you will be children of the Most High; for he is kind to the ungrateful and the wicked. Be merciful, just as your Father is merciful.' (Luke 6.29-36)

'But when you give a banquet, invite the poor, the crippled, the lame, and the blind. And you will be blessed, because they cannot repay you, for you will be repaid at the resurrection of the righteous.' (Luke 14.13-14)

It is essential to note the important role that sharing with those in need plays in the scene Jesus gives us of himself on the throne reviewing our lives:

> *'Then the king will say to those at his right hand, "Come, you that are blessed by my Father, inherit the kingdom prepared for you from the foundation of the world; for I was hungry and you gave me food, I was thirsty and you gave me something to drink, I was a stranger and you welcomed me, I was naked and you gave me clothing, I was sick and you took care of me, I was in prison and you visited me."…Truly I tell you, just as you did not do it to one of the least of these, you did not do it to me. And these will go away into eternal punishment, but the righteous into eternal life.'* (Selected verses from Matthew 25.34-46. We will come back again to this important scene later.)

In the parable of the workers and the hours Jesus says the Kingdom of Heaven is like a vineyard where no one has a claim to more money than others! He says that in the Kingdom of Heaven we are compassionate and generous to those who would have too little for their own provision:

> *'For the kingdom of heaven is like a landowner who went out early in the morning to hire laborers for his vineyard… When evening came, the owner of the vineyard said to his manager, "Call the laborers and give them their pay, beginning with the last and then going to the first." When those hired about five o'clock came, each of them received the usual daily wage. Now when the first came, they thought they would receive more; but each of them also received the usual daily wage. And when they received it, they grumbled against the landowner, saying, "These last worked only one hour, and you have made them equal to us who have borne the burden of the day and the scorching heat." But he replied to one of them, "Friend, I am doing you no wrong; did you not agree with me for the usual daily wage? Take what belongs to you and go; I choose to give to this last the same as I give to you. Am I not allowed to do what I choose with what belongs to me? Or are you envious because I am generous?"'* (Matthew 20.1-15)

This next famous event is as much a miracle of sharing as it is a miracle of multiplication. Note that Jesus challenges the disciples to share but they refuse. A little boy, with the remarkable confidence of youth, is the one who rises to Jesus' challenge. Jesus then shares this gift with everyone:

> *After this Jesus went to the other side of the Sea of Galilee, also called the Sea of Tiberias. A large crowd kept following him, because they saw the*

Jesus valued sharing and not greed

signs that he was doing for the sick. Jesus went up the mountain and sat down there with his disciples. Now the Passover, the festival of the Jews, was near. When he looked up and saw a large crowd coming toward him, Jesus said to Philip, 'Where are we to buy bread for these people to eat?' He said this to test him, for he himself knew what he was going to do. Philip answered him, 'Six months' wages would not buy enough bread for each of them to get a little.' One of his disciples, Andrew, Simon Peter's brother, said to him, 'There is a boy here who has five barley loaves and two fish. But what are they among so many people?' Jesus said, 'Make the people sit down.' Now there was a great deal of grass in the place; so they sat down, about five thousand in all. Then Jesus took the loaves, and when he had given thanks, he distributed them to those who were seated; so also the fish, as much as they wanted. When they were satisfied, he told his disciples, 'Gather up the fragments left over, so that nothing may be lost.' So they gathered them up, and from the fragments of the five barley loaves, left by those who had eaten, they filled twelve baskets. When the people saw the sign that he had done, they began to say, 'This is indeed the prophet who is to come into the world.' (John 6.1-14)

Jesus teaches that God will lead by example and share his Kingdom with the poor: *Then he looked up at his disciples and said: 'Blessed are you who are poor, for yours is the kingdom of God.'* (Luke 6.20). Also *'Do not be afraid, little flock, for it is your Father's good pleasure to give you the kingdom.'* (Luke 12.32)

It must also be understood that when Jesus is teaching about forgiveness of debts, he is speaking of forgiveness in all spheres of our lives (not just of debts). His primary way of communicating this was to speak of financial debt. This does mean that we are not at all justified for excluding financial debt from our understanding of these passages! Debt and the exploitation of debtors was a huge social problem in Jesus' day. An example of this is the Lord's Prayer: *And forgive us our debts, as we also have forgiven our debtors.* (Matthew 6.12)

Another example is the Parable of the unforgiving servant:

> *'For this reason the kingdom of heaven may be compared to a king who wished to settle accounts with his slaves. When he began the reckoning, one who owed him ten thousand talents was brought to him; and, as he could not pay, his lord ordered him to be sold, together with his wife and children and all his possessions, and payment to be made. So the slave fell on his knees before him, saying, "Have patience with me, and I will pay you everything." And out of pity for him, the lord of that slave released him and forgave him the debt. But that same slave, as he went out, came upon one of his fellow slaves who owed him a hundred denarii; and seizing him by the throat, he said, "Pay what you owe." Then his fellow slave fell down and pleaded with him, "Have patience with me, and I will pay you." But he refused; then he went and threw him into prison until he would pay the debt. When his fellow slaves saw what had happened, they were greatly distressed, and they went and reported to their lord all that had taken place. Then his lord summoned him and said to him, "You wicked slave! I forgave you all that debt because you pleaded with me. Should you not have had mercy on your fellow slave, as I had mercy on you?" And in anger his lord handed him over to be tortured until he would pay his entire debt. So my heavenly Father will also do to every one of you, if you do not forgive your brother or sister from your heart.'* (Matthew 18.23-35)

INVEST IN ABUNDANT LIFE

Jesus does encourage people to focus their energies on an investment that has better returns than an investment in possessions, namely an investment in an abundant and meaningful life found in a relationship with God.

Someone in the crowd said to him, 'Teacher, tell my brother to divide the family inheritance with me.' But he said to him, 'Friend, who set me to be a judge or arbitrator over you?' And he said to them, 'Take care! Be on your guard against all kinds of greed; for one's life does not consist in the abundance of possessions.' Then he told them a parable: 'The land of a rich man produced abundantly. And he thought to himself, "What should I do, for I have no place to store my crops?" Then he said, "I will do this: I will pull down my barns and build larger ones, and there I will store all my grain and my goods. And I will say to my soul, Soul, you have ample goods laid up for many years; relax, eat, drink, be merry." But God said to him, "You fool! This very night your life is being demanded of you. And the things you have prepared, whose will they be?" So it is with those who store up treasures for themselves but are not rich toward God.'
(Luke 12.13-21)

Here the emptiness of the investment in worldly luxury is exposed: *'But woe to you who are rich, for you have received your consolation. Woe to you who are full now, for you will be hungry.'* (Luke 6.24-25)

TOWARDS ECONOMIC SYSTEMS OF SHARING

Jesus did assess the economic systems of his day and teach people how to relate to them. Jesus did not propose a particular economic system, but rather a set of values by which to live in any economic system. History has of course shown that no economic system can be deified. All systems can be abused to the enrichment of some and the injustice of others. Theory shows that each economic system has merit, and practice shows that each economic system can be corrupted by greed. Jesus seems to me to indicate that any system needs the following values to be lived by those in the system.

'Give to God the things that are God's'

This is a very powerful statement! Everything belongs to God – therefore we are being taught that God must be allowed to be God in our lives. We are taught the primary importance of honouring God with all that we have. This means that we need to do God's will with everything that we have:

So they watched him and sent spies who pretended to be honest, in order to trap him by what he said, so as to hand him over to the jurisdiction and authority of the governor. So they asked him, 'Teacher, we know that

> you are right in what you say and teach, and you show deference to no one, but teach the way of God in accordance with truth. Is it lawful for us to pay taxes to the emperor, or not?' But he perceived their craftiness and said to them, 'Show me a denarius. Whose head and whose title does it bear?' They said, 'The emperor's.' He said to them, 'Then give to the emperor the things that are the emperor's, and to God the things that are God's.' And they were not able in the presence of the people to trap him by what he said; and being amazed by his answer, they became silent. (Luke 20.20-26)

'You have made it a den of robbers'

The activities at the temple in Jerusalem accounted for an estimated 90% of the economy of the city. The largest part of this activity centred on all the support services for the sacrificial system (obtaining animals, stabling animals, feeding animals, selling and re-selling animals, temple exchange rate to buy animals, etc.) This whole system had become corrupted by greed and so Jesus attacked it. It is not too difficult to imagine the temple and city authorities' anger at Jesus for attacking their economy! In this we see Jesus attacking the corruption of the system by greed, not the system itself:

> The Passover of the Jews was near, and Jesus went up to Jerusalem: Then he entered the temple and began to drive out those who were selling things there; and he said, 'It is written, "My house shall be a house of prayer"; but you have made it a den of robbers.' Every day he was teaching in the temple. The chief priests, the scribes, and the leaders of the people kept looking for a way to kill him; but they did not find anything they could do, for all the people were spellbound by what they heard. (Luke 19.45-48. See also John 2.13-17 for a more detailed account of this event.)

'Proclaim the year of the Lord's favour'

Jesus not only wanted individuals to start sharing, he also wanted the system of hoarding to be transformed! In this way Jesus does call for an economic system to embrace the values of sharing. Part of God's instructions to the covenant people was that they should obey a Jubilee year every 50 years. This was the 'year of the Lord's favour' in which land would be redistributed, debt cancelled and slaves freed. When God's reign began with the coming of the Messiah the Jubilee regulations would become permanent practice. Jesus declares in this sermon that he is the Messiah and the time has come for this new social structure!

> *When he came to Nazareth, where he had been brought up, he went to the synagogue on the Sabbath day, as was his custom. He stood up to read, and the scroll of the prophet Isaiah was given to him. He unrolled the scroll and found the place where it was written: 'The Spirit of the Lord is upon me, because he has anointed me to bring good news to the poor. He has sent me to proclaim release to the captives and recovery of sight to the blind, to let the oppressed go free, to proclaim the year of the Lord's favour.' And he rolled up the scroll, gave it back to the attendant, and sat down. The eyes of all in the synagogue were fixed on him. Then he began to say to them, 'Today this scripture has been fulfilled in your hearing.'* (Luke 4.16-21)

At the heart of this Jubilee year is the understanding that economic systems need to place human values at their centre rather than monetary values. The Jubilee year did this by making humans equal with each other every 50 years. It was a rudimentary way in which God was saying that economic systems must not exploit people. Can we develop economic systems that are not determined by the law of profit but rather by needs of humanity? This is Jesus' challenge to us.

It is vital that we appreciate that poverty has been caused by the current economic systems of our world. Leaders love to talk about the eradication of poverty – yet they mostly do this to gain favour. In their actions however they comply with the relentless gears of the socio-economic machine that increases the wealth and power of a few at the expense of the many. Poverty is not random, it is deeply systemic and intentional. It is intentional because it is necessary that the goods and pleasures be produced by labour that is as cheap and minimal as possible using resources that are as low-priced as possible.

Anglican Archbishop Njongonkulu Ndungane, who also served a prison term on Robben Island, has become an activist for debt relief for the poorest countries in the world. He highlights that this is essential if poor countries are to be released from their downward-spiralling poverty. He also points out that the wealth of northern hemisphere countries was in part gained by the poorer countries of the southern hemisphere: 'The northern hemisphere has a special responsibility. The prosperity of the countries of the developed world has not been earned by their citizens alone; most of it has been given to them by earlier generations; and much has been brought to them from their colonies and their relationships with poorer parts of the world, often from unequal and exploitative relationships. They have been given much. To whom much is given, from him, from her, much will be expected.'[4]

---

[4] Njongonkulu Ndungane, *A World with a Human Face: A Voice from Africa*, p. 56.

YOUR FREEDOM TO SHARE RATHER THAN HOARD IS A SIGN THAT YOU ARE PART OF THE SHEPHERD'S FLOCK

Jesus clearly wanted his followers to stand out as people who are free from the lure of wealth and are able to share. We each need to allow ourselves to be constantly challenged, exposed and transformed in this area of our lives. It is in our own interests, and the interests of society, that we resist the temptation to water down this message of Jesus.

I remember how when I fell in love with Angela we both were very happy to spend a lot of money on each other. We both changed from people who kept money for ourselves into people who were happy to spend on each other. Truly falling in love does bring about this change. Being in a love relationship with God would make this change too. When you fall in love both your heart and your wallet are touched. As a married couple we no longer speak of 'mine' and 'yours', but of 'ours'. It is good to nurture a sense of 'ours' with regard to money and possessions in your relationship with God too.

My colleague and friend, Mark Stephenson, once put it this way: 'If Jesus knocked on any church door today would he say "I know you love me, I hear it in the hymns you sing and in the wonderful ways you praise me, but what are you doing about poverty, unemployment, housing, health and education?"'

It is important to appreciate that the global forceful reality of consumerism is what breeds our greed. The global economy is dependent on humans (consumers) buying and consuming more and more goods and pleasures as time goes on. Consumerism is the force that exists to encourage and stimulate our ever-increasing desire for more 'stuff' – in other words consumerism breeds our greed. Consumerism is therefore a force that we face every day that is designed to undermine our virtues and encourage our vices. Consumerism motivates the vices of greed, hoarding, envy, covetousness, pleasure-seeking, and pride. Consumerism is therefore anti-Christian and anti-Kingdom Consciousness.

Greed, hoarding, envy, covetousness, pleasure-seeking and pride are all descriptions of the dynamics in an inner life of a person – dynamics of an inner life that is caught up in our own interests and concerns. Such an inner life does not have space for the needs of others, or any concerns for the poor. Such an inner life is too distracted by the interest in the next purchase or the next pleasure to really care about the brutal realities of poor and oppressed peoples. This is a dehumanised place to be and it would be good if we saw its dangers for what they are.

Essentially the call for us is to resist these forces that lead to indifference and respond by nurturing compassion (we reflected on this in chapter 7). Further we need to nurture a simple and prudent lifestyle that is not duped or tempted by consumerism. We should think often of consumerism when we pray, 'Lead us not into temptation'.

John Wesley (1703–1791) is one of the most incredible examples I know of a heart set free from bondage to possessions and money. When he was paid 30 pounds a year he needed 28 pounds for living expenses and gave 2 pounds away. When his income rose to 60 pounds he gave 32 pounds away and lived on 28 pounds! As his published works became popular his income increased to such an extent that he was able in a single year to give 1400 pounds away 'through his brethren the poor'. John Wesley was content with a simple lifestyle and this enabled him to be generous in his sharing. He did not follow the normal practice of increasing his living standard as his income increased. He was truly a free man who was able to be generous through his simple lifestyle.

I also love the story from the Middle Ages about an itinerant preaching friar who had long distances to travel between his preaching places. One day a wealthy merchant gave him a donkey on which to ride. It was with great pleasure that this preacher set out on his next journey. When he arrived at the church he tethered the animal outside. But throughout the service his attention was drawn to the donkey. Was it properly secured? Had he left it in a safe place? What if it got stolen? These worries nagged at him and distracted him. When the service finished he went to see if all was well with his donkey, and indeed all was well. But he knew that a new danger had entered upon his life. He untied the donkey, slapped it and drove it off. Then he said, 'God forbid that my soul should be tethered to a donkey!' We need to ponder this story and seek to be conscious about all the ways our soul is tethered to our money and possessions.

Are you completely free to give generously and sacrificially? If not, Jesus insists that you must release more and more of your money and possessions to the poor until you reach a place of freedom.

In 2005 the biggest anti-poverty movement came together under the banner of 'Make Poverty History'. I believe Jesus would say to us that we will not make poverty history until we deal with greed. He would propose the renaming of the campaign into 'Make Greed History'.

Jesus valued sharing and not greed

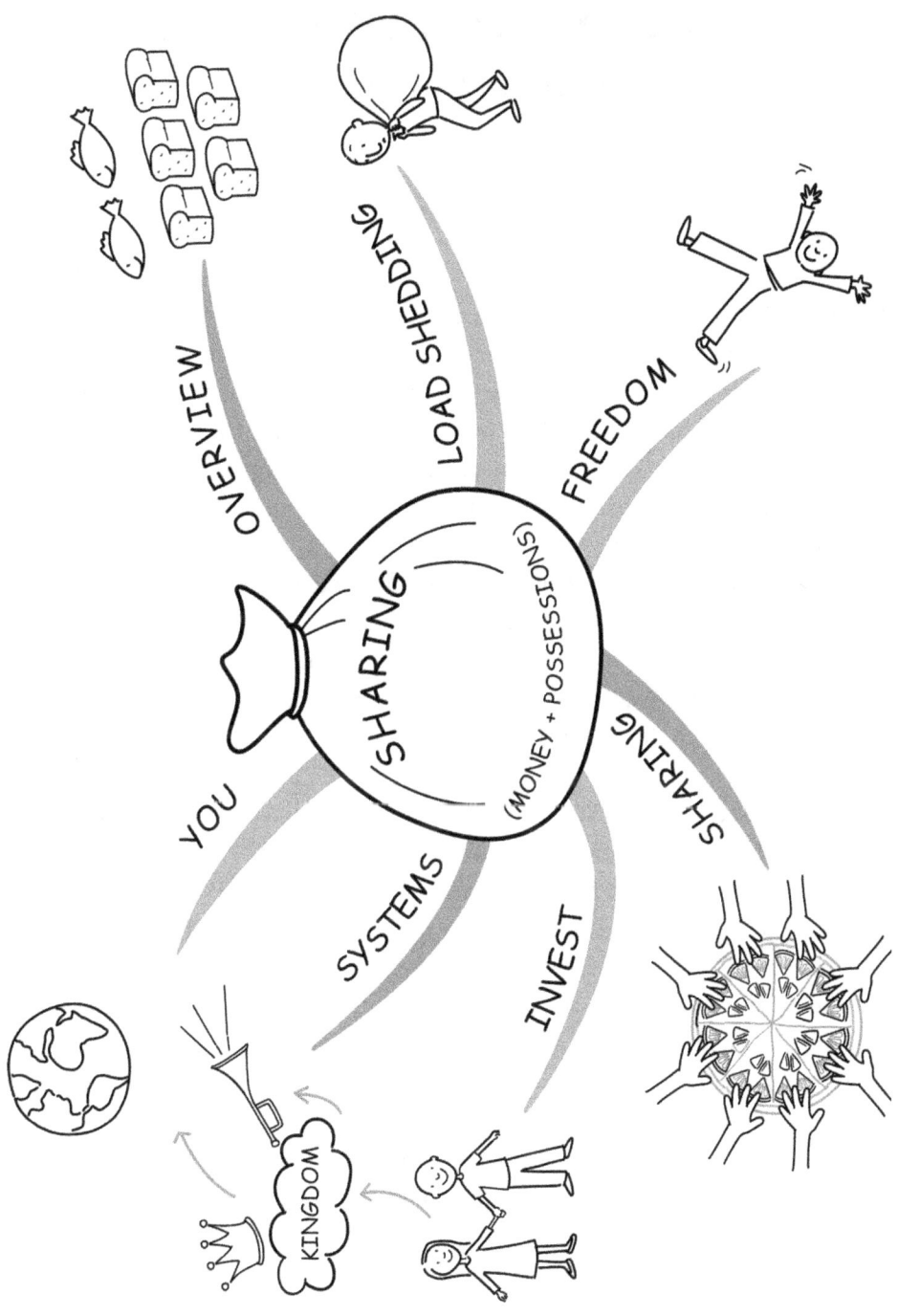

SUGGESTIONS FOR DISCUSSION, REVISION, REFLECTION AND APPLICATION

(These questions are intended for group work, but can easily be adapted for personal use.)

1. What is the most important message to you in this chapter? (Remember to also make a note of this on your 'God spoke to me' page.)
2. Icebreaker question: If you were sent to live on a space station for three months and only allowed to bring three personal items with you, what would they be? (The question must be answered quickly. As a group, do not spend longer than 5 minutes in total on this question.)
3. Read Mark 10.17-31
   a. What would you feel if you were that man and Jesus said this to you?
   b. Discuss verse 21. What does it all mean?
   c. Discuss verse 25. What does that saying mean?
   d. Discuss verse 27. How might God's presence and power help a person to share their money and possessions?
   e. Imagine you are a preacher who has been assigned this passage for a Sunday sermon. What is the good news proclamation in this passage? What would your three points be?
   f. What does this passage challenge in your life? Will you personally open yourself to the presence and power of God? How will you do this?
4. Below are a variety of suggestions and questions to aid your appreciation of this chapter. Do not attempt to do all of them! Choose those that are most appropriate to your unique situation and/or group. The questions are designed to help variously with revision, understanding, appreciation, reflection or application of the content.
   a. What did Jesus mean by the following statement, 'No one can serve two masters; for a slave will either hate the one and love the other, or be devoted to the one and despise the other. You cannot serve God and wealth.' (Matthew 6.24).
      i. Do Christians generally try and serve both?
      ii. What do you need to do to avoid serving God and wealth?

iii. Does this only apply to the rich?
  iv. How does wealth get in the way of serving God?
  v. Is money always bad?
b. Which part of this chapter did you experience as challenging? Enlightening?
c. Someone says to you that sharing wealth is just dumb. How would you try and explain the wisdom of Jesus' teaching about sharing?
d. How might our economic system be changed to honour Jesus' vision for society? Or is it the people in the system that need to be changed? Or both?
e. What can you do to be true to Jesus' call to be a sharing person? Make a list as a group.
f. What specific new activity is Jesus calling me to here? Share your answer/s with the group and invite them to hold you accountable in future meetings.

GOD SPOKE TO ME ...

10

JESUS VALUED PEOPLE AND NOT PRESTIGE

*'Do not judge by appearances,
but judge with right judgment.'*
(John 7.24)

AN OVERVIEW OF JESUS' TEACHING ABOUT HONOUR

Honour was the most prized dimension of existence for the culture of Jesus' day. Jesus gives the theme a lot of attention and affirms the importance of honour, but exposes how the cultural and religious practices of the day bred a false, destructive and divisive sense of honour. Jesus brought about a Kingdom Consciousness by essentially showing that in God's reign people are valued as people.

J.D.M. Derrett pointed out that, 'In the oriental (including the Mediterranean culture) world to this day prestige is more important than any other factor and people will commit suicide rather than forfeit it.'[1] That society was so structured that each person had a place on the ladder and was acutely aware of what their place was. Who was above them (and therefore better than them) and who was below them (and therefore not as good as them)? Status and prestige (as false expressions of honour) were based on external factors such as ancestry, wealth, authority, education, apparent (but not real) virtue, appearances and vocation.

---

[1] JDM Derrett, *Jesus' Audience*, Seabury Press, 1973, p. 40.

Essentially this was a culture that was maintained by some people being honoured and others being shamed. This system of honour and shame was based mostly on the external factors mentioned in the previous paragraph. Jesus believed this system to be evil and challenged it in many ways. He exposed the religious way in which this system was practised – honour given if you were seen to be pious, publicly religious, and 'moral' about one or two things which were usually not central issues.

You will see in the texts given that Jesus viewed his culture's infatuation with status and prestige as evil. Jesus dared to cast a vision of a society in which such external distinctions were meaningless and where people mattered as people. Jesus taught that in God's reign people are valued as people. People have value as children of God, which means that people have value inherent in themselves.

In Jesus' own dealings with people they sensed that they had value in and of themselves. Jesus' attitude to women and children flows from his insistence that they matter because they are people. Jesus frequently showed respect to 'sinners' publicly and even ate with them, which was a way of accepting them and being dismissive of the honour and shame system.

You will see in the texts that follow that Jesus wanted people to strip themselves of the false values of wealth and prestige and become real people. Jesus viewed this infatuation with prestige, status and class as the main cause of hypocrisy – people felt forced to be false in the public eye in order to be honoured. Jesus attached great value to the person who was genuine in their love for God and neighbour. Jesus exposed those who were only trying to give the impression of love for God and neighbour. In this way Jesus placed a great emphasis on characteristics like integrity and authenticity.

In many ways the foundation of a proper sense of honour is found in Jesus' teaching on the greatness of love. Love of God and love of neighbour certainly 'puts me in my place':

When the Pharisees heard that he had silenced the Sadducees, they gathered together, and one of them, a lawyer, asked him a question to test him. 'Teacher, which commandment in the law is the greatest?' He said to him, "'You shall love the Lord your God with all your heart, and with all your soul, and with all your mind." This is the greatest and first commandment. And a second is like it: "You shall love your neighbor as yourself." On these two commandments hang all the law and the prophets.' (Matthew 22.34-40)

It is this real love that moved Jesus to busy himself with healings and exorcisms for those in need rather than spend time trying to build a positive profile with the people in power. He would rather invest in those in desperate circumstances than respect the honour boundaries of his culture.

TRUE HONOUR

One of the great gifts of Jesus' teaching is that he succeeds in bringing about a society that gives honour to what is truly honourable. A worldly and fallen society gives honour to very superficial things. God's Reign is truly experienced in those people and parts of society that recognise the value of what is truly honourable.

Jesus highlights the importance of humility and to not trust in appearances but rather to live a genuine inner trust in God's grace. Jesus often warns against pretentiousness and all attempts to impress and find favour in the eyes of those watching us. Jesus often takes a particular stance against religious practices that are practised for the purpose of gaining prestige and status:

He also told this parable to some who trusted in themselves that they were righteous and regarded others with contempt: 'Two men went up to the temple to pray, one a Pharisee and the other a tax collector. The Pharisee, standing by himself, was praying thus, "God, I thank you that I am not like other people: thieves, rogues, adulterers, or even like this tax collector. I fast twice a week; I give a tenth of all my income." But the tax collector, standing far off, would not even look up to heaven, but was beating his breast and saying, "God, be merciful to me, a sinner!" I tell you, this man went down to his home justified rather than the other; for all who exalt themselves will be humbled, but all who humble themselves will be exalted.' (Luke 18.9-14)

'Beware of practicing your piety before others in order to be seen by them; for then you have no reward from your Father in heaven. So whenever you give alms, do not sound a trumpet before you, as the hypocrites do in the synagogues and in the streets, so that they may be praised by others. Truly I tell you, they have received their reward. But when you give alms, do not let your left hand know what your right hand is doing, so that your alms may be done in secret; and your Father who sees in secret will reward you. And whenever you pray, do not be like the hypocrites; for they love to stand and pray in the synagogues and at the street corners, so that they may be seen by others. Truly I tell you, they have received their reward. But whenever you pray, go into your room and shut the door and pray to your Father who is in secret; and your Father who sees in secret will reward you. When you are praying, do not heap up empty phrases as the Gentiles do; for they think that they will be heard because of their many words. Do not be like them, for your Father knows what you need before you ask him ...

'And whenever you fast, do not look dismal, like the hypocrites, for they disfigure their faces so as to show others that they are fasting. Truly I tell you, they have received their reward. But when you fast, put oil on your head and wash your face, so that your fasting may be seen not by others but by your Father who is in secret; and your Father who sees in secret will reward you.

'Do not store up for yourselves treasures on earth, where moth and rust consume and where thieves break in and steal; but store up for yourselves treasures in heaven, where neither moth nor rust consumes and where thieves do not break in and steal. For where your treasure is, there your heart will be also' (Matthew 6.1-21, selected verses)

In this next passage Jesus again emphasises humility and not exalting ourselves in front of others. However he does not want us to think that public actions of true good are to be avoided. In fact he encourages an act that would have been very public and scandalous in his day. The people Jesus teaches us to invite into our homes would have been outcasts in those days and our reputation would actually have been diminished in the community's eyes through this party he encourages us to host. The point is that such a public act of true good is something that is truly honourable:

> *When he noticed how the guests chose the places of honor, he told them a parable. 'When you are invited by someone to a wedding banquet, do not sit down at the place of honor, in case someone more distinguished than you has been invited by your host; and the host who invited both of you may come and say to you, "Give this person your place" and then in disgrace you would start to take the lowest place. But when you are invited, go and sit down at the lowest place, so that when your host comes, he may say to you, "Friend, move up higher"; then you will be honored in the presence of all who sit at the table with you. For all who exalt themselves will be humbled, and those who humble themselves will be exalted.'*
>
> *He said also to the one who had invited him, 'When you give a luncheon or a dinner, do not invite your friends or your brothers or your relatives or rich neighbors, in case they may invite you in return, and you would be repaid. But when you give a banquet, invite the poor, the crippled, the lame, and the blind. And you will be blessed, because they cannot repay you, for you will be repaid at the resurrection of the righteous.'* (Luke 14.7-14)

In the event of the woman caught in adultery, which we have referred to already, please note, in the context of this teaching theme, how Jesus took a lived example of fallen honour and shame and was able to assert where true honour is found. When Jesus was confronted by the scribes and Pharisees (those who used religion to shame others and honour themselves) with the dilemma of the woman caught in adultery, he masterfully levelled the playing field. To the scribes and Pharisees he said *'Let anyone among you who is without sin be the first to throw a stone at her.'* (John 8.7). Jesus succeeds in getting these self-righteous accusers to acknowledge that they are not what they seem, that they are also sinners, that they are hiding their own sin. Next we see, *When they heard it, they went away, one by one, beginning with the elders; and Jesus was left alone with the woman standing before him. Jesus straightened up and said to her, 'Woman, where are they? Has no one condemned you?' She said, 'No one, sir.' And Jesus said, 'Neither do I condemn you. Go your way, and from now on do not sin again.'* (John 8.9-11). Instead of shaming her Jesus opens the door to a new future for her, free from shame and free to do the right thing.

The whole theme of true honour emerges in this next passage in a special way. Here we see Jesus challenging those who honour God outwardly but who are inwardly mercenary toward people, even their own family:

> *'And why do you break the commandment of God for the sake of your tradition? For God said "Honour your father and your mother," and, "Whoever speaks evil of father or mother must surely die." But you say that whoever tells father or mother, "Whatever support you might have had from me is given to God," then that person need not honor the father. So, for the sake of your tradition, you make void the word of God. You hypocrites! Isaiah prophesied rightly about you when he said: "This people honours me with their lips, but their hearts are far from me; in vain do they worship me, teaching human precepts as doctrines".'* (Matthew 15.3-9.)[2]

Early in John's Gospel we see Jesus challenging people to only seek affirmation (glory) from God, not from humans: *'I do not accept glory from human beings… How can you believe when you accept glory from one another and do not seek the glory that comes from the one who alone is God?'* (John 5.41 and 44)

Later in the same book we hear John's own judgement of certain authorities who had come to believe in Jesus but had not been prepared to stand up for their beliefs: *'Nevertheless many, even of the authorities, believed in him. But because of the Pharisees they did not confess it, for fear that they would be put out of the synagogue; for they loved human glory more than the glory that comes from God.'* (John 12.41-43)

Lastly it is worth noting that Jesus had such an incredible reputation of humility and true honour that a hymn was written in the early church years about this. We are fortunate that this hymn has been preserved in Philippians 2.6-11. It has been preserved by Paul who quotes it in support of calling the early church to humility and looking to the interests of others rather than self. Here is the reference, including Paul's motivation:

---

[2] This passage needs to help us interpret the very difficult passage of Luke 14.26 *'Whoever comes to me and does not hate father and mother, wife and children, brothers and sisters, yes, and even life itself, cannot be my disciple.'* It would be an obvious mistake to think of Jesus encouraging us to hate.

Do nothing from selfish ambition or conceit, but in humility regard others as better than yourselves. Let each of you look not to your own interests, but to the interests of others. Let the same mind be in you that was in Christ Jesus, who, though he was in the form of God, did not regard equality with God as something to be exploited, but emptied himself, taking the form of a slave, being born in human likeness. And being found in human form, he humbled himself and became obedient to the point of death—even death on a cross. Therefore God also highly exalted him and gave him the name that is above every name, so that at the name of Jesus every knee should bend, in heaven and on earth and under the earth, and every tongue should confess that Jesus Christ is Lord, to the glory of God the Father.

VALUE PEOPLE AS PEOPLE

Jesus sought to warn people about the delusion of the world's infatuation with prestige and status. He also showed that people in positions of prestige and status are not actually better people than others, nor are they people of greater value. He sought to give insight into God's judgement on such matters:

'Blessed are you when people hate you, and when they exclude you, revile you, and defame you on account of the Son of Man. Rejoice in that day and leap for joy, for surely your reward is great in heaven; for that is what their ancestors did to the prophets.... Woe to you when all speak well of you, for that is what their ancestors did to the false prophets.' (Luke 6.22-26)

As he taught, he said, 'Beware of the scribes, who like to walk around in long robes, and to be greeted with respect in the marketplaces, and to have the best seats in the synagogues and places of honor at banquets! They devour widows' houses and for the sake of appearance say long prayers. They will receive the greater condemnation.' (Mark 12.38-40)

'Woe to you Pharisees! For you love to have the seat of honor in the synagogues and to be greeted with respect in the marketplaces. Woe to you! For you are like unmarked graves, and people walk over them without realizing it.' (Luke 11.43-44)

It is within this teaching theme of Jesus that we are best able to understand Jesus' conflict with the teachers of the law about their application of religious traditions. A religious tradition is something that you practise in order to honour God. But a religious tradition can actually violate the love of God and when that happens you need to practise the love of God instead of the tradition. What often happens in religious practice is that the fulfilling of a tradition makes me feel religious and presents me as religious to the world around me. This is when the practising of religion is more interested in prestige and appearances rather than the real love of God.

Jesus invested a lot of energy and courage in challenging this pretentiousness amongst religious people. Jesus asserted that the person in need mattered far more than the appearance of being godly (prestige). It's almost summed up in Jesus' statement *'Do not judge by appearances, but judge with right judgment.'* (John 7.24). We can be sure that this indictment applies to secular pretentiousness just as much as it does to religious. The Sabbath regulations were the site of most of these challenges from Jesus, but as you will see it applied to other traditions too.

The next three passages show Jesus' insistence on the value of a person, especially a person in need, above the religious observance of the Sabbath and the pretence that goes with that observance[3]:

> *Now he was teaching in one of the synagogues on the sabbath. And just then there appeared a woman with a spirit that had crippled her for eighteen years. She was bent over and was quite unable to stand up straight. When Jesus saw her, he called her over and said, 'Woman, you are set free from your ailment.' When he laid his hands on her, immediately she stood up straight and began praising God. But the leader*

---

[3] See also Mark 2.23-28, Mark 3.1-6, Luke 6.1-11, Luke 14.1-6, John 5.1-18 and the whole of John 9.

of the synagogue, indignant because Jesus had cured on the sabbath, kept saying to the crowd, 'There are six days on which work ought to be done; come on those days and be cured, and not on the sabbath day.' But the Lord answered him and said, 'You hypocrites! Does not each of you on the sabbath untie his ox or his donkey from the manger, and lead it away to give it water? And ought not this woman, a daughter of Abraham whom Satan bound for eighteen long years, be set free from this bondage on the sabbath day?' When he said this, all his opponents were put to shame; and the entire crowd was rejoicing at all the wonderful things that he was doing. (Luke 13.10-17)

He left that place and entered their synagogue; a man was there with a withered hand, and they asked him, 'Is it lawful to cure on the sabbath?' so that they might accuse him. He said to them, 'Suppose one of you has only one sheep and it falls into a pit on the sabbath; will you not lay hold of it and lift it out? How much more valuable is a human being than a sheep! So it is lawful to do good on the sabbath.' Then he said to the man, 'Stretch out your hand.' He stretched it out, and it was restored, as sound as the other. But the Pharisees went out and conspired against him, how to destroy him. (Matthew 12.9-14)

'Did not Moses give you the law? Yet none of you keeps the law. Why are you looking for an opportunity to kill me?' The crowd answered, 'You have a demon! Who is trying to kill you?' Jesus answered them, 'I performed one work, and all of you are astonished. Moses gave you circumcision (it is, of course, not from Moses, but from the patriarchs), and you circumcise a man on the sabbath. If a man receives circumcision on the sabbath in order that the law of Moses may not be broken, are you angry with me because I healed a man's whole body on the sabbath? Do not judge by appearances, but judge with right judgment.' (John 7.19-24)

Jesus' astute perception enabled him to see that people often misuse religious language to give a false and misleading boost to their prestige and respectability. He also believed that they do this so that they can manipulate people and he therefore taught that it was evil. This is part of the core reason for his teaching against swearing oaths – that it is a practice of appealing to divine realities to boost your prestige so that you can get your own way with people. Here is how Jesus put it:

'Again, you have heard that it was said to those of ancient times, "You shall not swear falsely, but carry out the vows you have made to the Lord." But I say to you, Do not swear at all, either by heaven, for it is the throne of God, or by the earth, for it is his footstool, or by Jerusalem, for it is the city of the great King. And do not swear by your head, for you cannot make one hair white or black. Let your word be "Yes, Yes" or "No, No"; anything more than this comes from the evil one.' (Matthew 5.33-37)

#LORDSMUSTFALL

This theme is unsettling for those in positions of power! Jesus shows that God's reign is a reality where there are no 'lords', especially no one to lord over another. Eventually God's reign will result in a flattening of all such social and political power structures.

Mary would have started such a # movement of #lordsmustfall. Even before Jesus' birth Mary realised that God in Jesus was opposing the world's infatuation with prestige: *'His mercy is for those who fear him from generation to generation He has shown strength with his arm; he has scattered the proud in the thoughts of their hearts. He has brought down the powerful from their thrones, and lifted up the lowly.'* (Luke 1.50-52)

In the previous chapter I referred to Jesus' long and detailed condemnation of the scribes and the Pharisees for their lifestyles. I want to share the parts of the speech that relate to the appearances of status, prestige and honour:

Then Jesus said to the crowds and to his disciples, 'The scribes and the Pharisees sit on Moses' seat; therefore, do whatever they teach you and follow it; but do not do as they do, for they do not practice what they teach. They tie up heavy burdens, hard to bear, and lay them on the shoulders of others; but they themselves are unwilling to lift a finger to move them. They do all their deeds to be seen by others; for they make their phylacteries broad and their fringes long. They love to have the place of honor at banquets and the best seats in the synagogues, and to be greeted with respect in the marketplaces, and to have people call them rabbi. But you are not to be called rabbi, for you have one teacher, and you are all students. And call no one your father on earth, for you have one Father—the one in heaven. Nor are you to be called instructors, for you have one instructor, the Messiah. The greatest among you will be your servant. All who exalt themselves will be humbled, and all who humble themselves will be exalted.' (Matthew 23.1-11)

A Kingdom Consciousness also results in a strong sense of my value as a person and how inappropriate it is to be subservient to those of higher status and prestige. A Kingdom person does not grovel, is not servile, does not abase oneself, does not suck up, curry favour, ingratiate or cozy up. Rather a Kingdom person is chin up and relates to all with a sense of equality and confidence. Jesus modelled this for us in his dealings with those who would have been considered his superiors – Chief Priests, Council, Temple leaders, Caiaphas the High Priest, Annas, Pontius Pilate, and Herod. Peter and John modelled this when they appeared before the rulers, elders, scribes, Annas, Caiaphas and others in the high-priestly family. Peter and John's boldness made the dignitaries aware that they were *companions of Jesus* (Acts 4.13).

In this next teaching Jesus empowers victims to assert this dignity in the face of injustice from people of status:

'You have heard that it was said, "An eye for an eye, and a tooth for a tooth." But now I tell you: do not take revenge on someone who wrongs you. If anyone slaps you on the right cheek, let him slap your left cheek too. And if someone takes you to court to sue you for your shirt, let him have your coat as well. And if one of the occupation troops forces you to carry his pack one kilometre, carry it two kilometres. When someone asks you for something, give it to him; when someone wants to borrow something, lend it to him.' (Matthew 5.38-42 Good News Bible translation.)

How should authority be viewed, then? What should those who are 'lords' do? Jesus taught that those in authority should use their position as servants. This theme is taught by Jesus in a few places. Here are two passages. The first follows on Jesus being asked to grant 'lordship' to two of the disciples:

> *So Jesus called them and said to them, 'You know that among the Gentiles those whom they recognize as their rulers lord it over them, and their great ones are tyrants over them. But it is not so among you; but whoever wishes to become great among you must be your servant, and whoever wishes to be first among you must be slave of all. For the Son of Man came not to be served but to serve, and to give his life a ransom for many.'* (Mark 10.42-45)

The second passage is in response to an argument amongst the disciples about greatness:

> *Then they came to Capernaum; and when he was in the house he asked them, 'What were you arguing about on the way?' But they were silent, for on the way they had argued with one another who was the greatest. He sat down, called the twelve, and said to them, 'Whoever wants to be first must be last of all and servant of all.'* (Mark 9.33-35)

WOMEN DISCIPLES

It was because people mattered as people that Jesus was well known for something that would have been remarkable in his day – his welcome and inclusion of women and children. There were many ways in which women were regarded as people of lesser value in Jesus' day. Women were excluded from public life; when in public they had to be completely covered and were to talk to no one; daughters were considered a source of cheap labour and profit; wives were virtually slaves to their husbands; they were forbidden to teach; their most important function was producing male babies.

Jesus did not abide by this religious and cultural devaluing of women. He allowed women to follow him in public; he spoke to them; he affirmed Mary of Bethany for not doing domestic chores and choosing the way that was reserved for men; women travelled with him; financial support was given by women; women were the first witnesses to the resurrection.

Luke records for us that women were amongst the disciples that followed Jesus. Jesus was probably the only rabbi of his time to have women disciples!

> *Soon afterwards he went on through cities and villages, proclaiming and bringing the good news of the kingdom of God. The twelve were with him, as well as some women who had been cured of evil spirits and infirmities: Mary, called Magdalene, from whom seven demons had gone out, and Joanna, the wife of Herod's steward Chuza, and Susanna, and many others, who provided for them out of their resources.* (Luke 8.1-3)

I say more on this elsewhere in this guidebook, but for now we must appreciate that women and children did not have anything counting in their favour in the prestige stakes. But for Jesus they are children of God, and so are welcome and in fact are especially welcome because they have been marginalized: *Jesus said, 'Let the little children come to me, and do not stop them; for it is to such as these that the kingdom of heaven belongs.'* (Matthew 19.14)

TO VALUE PEOPLE AS PEOPLE IS A SIGN THAT YOU ARE PART OF THE SHEPHERD'S FLOCK

Jesus' proclamation and ministry brings into being a special dynamic of God's Reign, namely the awareness of all people's equal value as God's children. To live out this ethic is a core part of Kingdom Consciousness.

There is enormous power that will be unlocked within us when we rebel against the way in which society dominates us or the way in which we lord our authority over others. Black Consciousness gave the gift to many of a personal sense of dignity to replace the sense of worthlessness. That message continues to be important for all, as Allan Boesak makes clear: 'We cannot speak a language of hope and resilience, of resistance and redemption, if we do not unlearn the language of imperial compliance: of domination and subjugation, of carelessness and indifference, of diplomatic evasion.'[4] Let us all embrace this new dignity in our land.

There is an invitation to us Christians in churches to go on a difficult journey. We are invited to review our relationships and structures and ask, 'to what extent do we truly value people rather than prestige?' Those of us in denominations with denominational newspapers will note that the vast majority of the photographs are of the Bishops. We can note how clerical dress becomes increasingly fancy and reveals our place on the ladder of prestige. We can also ask ourselves, 'how much of our time is dedicated to serving communities rather than to big events that display our strength?' We can reflect on the church as a sleeping giant capable of great service in society – waiting to be awoken from

---

[4] Allan Aubrey Boesak, *Pharaohs on Both Sides of the Blood-Red Waters: Prophetic Critique of Empire*, p. 81.

its dreams of prestige.

The concern and fear about what others think of us prevents us from being open and honest about who we really are and what we are struggling with. This is one of the main reasons that contributes to churches not being places where real transformation happens. We hide who we really are and pretend to be people who are better. In this way we evade transformation because we cannot 'come clean' about the real state of our lives out of fear of rejection and judgement. Churches are places where we are silent about our need for transformation and also silent about how little change does take place in people. But if we accepted Jesus' teaching here we would shrug off concerns about human approval, we would accept people for who they really are, and then this space of honesty and vulnerability would be a catalyst for real change.

There is another application of this teaching that finds itself on an almost opposite part of the spectrum – the practice of doing good in secrecy. It is important that there are good acts of service that we do without actually telling anyone that we have done so. The effect of this is that we do not have human approval, praise or affirmation as our reward for the good that was done.

I see part of this Kingdom Consciousness in the beautiful words of one of Africa's greatest middle distance runners and Olympic gold medalist, Noureddine Morceli, who said after winning Olympic gold, 'God teaches you to be dignified in defeat and modest in victory. The records and medals are wonderful, but they're mere trinkets in reality. They cannot feed all the people in the world who are hungry, clothe all those who are cold, comfort all those who are troubled, or bring peace to all those who are at war. This is a race we must all run together.'

Jesus valued people and not prestige

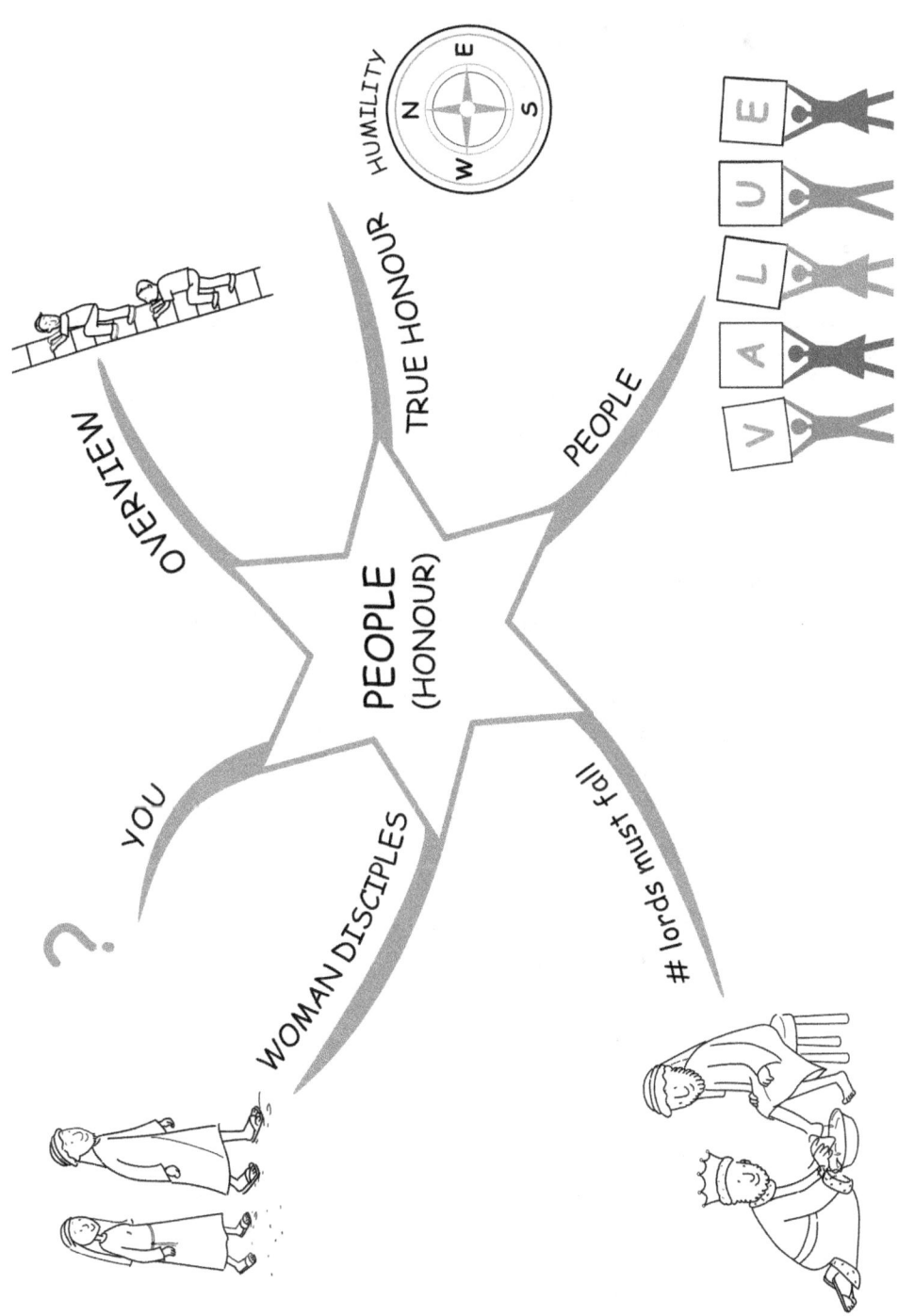

SUGGESTIONS FOR DISCUSSION, REVISION, REFLECTION AND APPLICATION

(These questions are intended for group work, but can easily be adapted for personal use.)

1. What is the most important message to you in this chapter? (Remember to also make a note of this on your 'God spoke to me' page.)
2. Icebreaker question: Who was your favourite music group in high school? (The question must be answered quickly. As a group, do not spend longer than 5 minutes in total on this question.)
3. Read Luke 14.7-14 and answer the following questions.
    a. Note that this is a wedding banquet story. It is good to remind yourself of the content of chapter 4.
    b. To some extent Jesus tells us something about God and his Kingdom when his parable speaks about the host of the banquet. What do we learn about God and his Kingdom?
    c. Why are prestige and status so important for us?
    d. What is wrong with claiming a place of honour for myself?
    e. What would be included in a godly pursuit of honour?
    f. What would be good ways for us to apply verses 12-14? Try and make a list.
4. Below are a variety of suggestions and questions to aid your appreciation of this chapter. Do not attempt to do all of them! Choose those that are most appropriate to your unique situation and/or group. The questions are designed to help variously with revision, understanding, appreciation, reflection or application of the content.
    a. What are symbols of status and prestige today?
    b. Is all status and prestige wrong?
    c. What does Jesus view as true honour? How did he personally live this?
    d. How can you personally value people as people? Does your congregation value people as people? Can you apply this at work?
    e. What progress has happened in the role of women in society? What progress still needs to happen?
    f. Who are marginalised people today?

g. Discuss how you as a group can begin to be more open, honest and vulnerable with each other. If you are not part of a small group, can you find someone with whom you can be open, honest and vulnerable as to the true state of your life and discipleship?
h. Will you accept the call to do good without anyone knowing it was you who did it? Will you do something in the next week or two?
i. What can you do to be true to Jesus' call to value people and not prestige? What can you do to treat all people with equal dignity, regardless of their status in society? What specific new activity is Jesus calling you to here? Share your answers with the group and invite them to hold you accountable in the coming weeks.

GOD SPOKE TO ME ...

11

LOVE STEPS ACROSS BOUNDARIES

'Truly I tell you, just as you did it to one of the least of these who are members of my family, you did it to me.... Truly I tell you, just as you did not do it to one of the least of these, you did not do it to me.'
(Matthew 25.40 and 45)

AN OVERVIEW OF JESUS' TEACHING ABOUT SOLIDARITY

In the society in which Jesus lived, the third most important concern, after prestige and wealth, was group solidarity. Strong group solidarity existed amongst those bound by flesh, blood, class, friendship and within the confines of an elitist sect (e.g. Essenes, Pharisees). Love and loyalty were strong within these groups. Although the Jewish people as a whole also had group solidarity, these smaller group solidarities were stronger.

Jesus opposed this exclusive form of love, teaching that love in the reign of God is an all-inclusive love of all people. It is vital that we grasp this way of understanding love in the Reign of God if we are to honour God's reign through our Kingdom Consciousness. Love in the Reign of God steps across all boundaries, it excludes no one and it embraces all. In the Kingdom Consciousness Movement we live with a sense of solidarity with all people and with an awareness of the need to honour those connections. In the Kingdom Consciousness Movement we do not separate life into 'us' and 'them'.

In Matthew 16.1-4 Jesus is asked for a sign to indicate that God is at work in him. Jesus opposes the request and says that the only sign they will get is the *'sign of Jonah'*. The most important feature of Jonah's life is not that he was swallowed by a whale, but that he was the prophet God used to bring the rebellious and pagan people of Nineveh to God. He had been swallowed by the whale because he did not have the compassion for the people of Nineveh that God had. The sign of Jonah is therefore about God's love functioning as a boundary-crossing love. Jesus was like Jonah crossing boundaries that a respectable Jew believed should not be crossed. The sign of Jonah is the ministry that shows that God's love is for all.

Jesus' own boundary-crossing love is seen in his friendliness to a number of people and groups who were regarded as 'outsiders' in his day. Amongst these were the 'poor' who were deemed to be outside of God's provision because of their sin. The 'sinners' were also a group that Jesus befriended. These were social outcasts because of their professions (prostitutes, tax collectors, herdsman, robbers, gamblers and usurers, to name some examples).

As shown in the previous chapter, Jesus also crossed the boundary separating women from men. Those who observed Jesus and all who were blessed by his attention, became aware that he ignored the divisions that society had created and that his sense of solidarity was all-inclusive.

Jesus prayed that all who believed in him would be a united body showing the world that the love he taught is a love that steps across boundaries:

> *'I ask not only on behalf of these, but also on behalf of those who will believe in me through their word, that they may all be one. As you, Father, are in me and I am in you, may they also be in us, so that the world may believe that you have sent me. The glory that you have given*

me I have given them, so that they may be one, as we are one, I in them and you in me, that they may become completely one, so that the world may know that you have sent me and have loved them even as you have loved me.' (John 17.20-23)

SUFFERING PEOPLE BECOME A PRIORITY

God's all-inclusive love is love that prioritises the needs of those who are suffering in some way, or are in particular need. So although God's love is for all people, there is a prioritisation in this love. It would be good for us to understand this well. This does not make God's love selective (which would seem the opposite of all-inclusive) because it is actually the nature of love to rush toward need. I once heard Trevor Hudson tell the story of a mother who had five children and was asked by a psychologist which of her children she loved the most! This was of course a very unfair question, but he insisted on asking it and getting an answer. The mother repeatedly said that she loved them all equally. Eventually, after his persistent repetition of the question, she refined her answer to say, 'When one child is hurting or suffering or sad or lonely or struggling, then I am particularly moved by that one in my heart, but otherwise I love them all the same.' This is a good way to understand God's love for all, prioritising those in need.

As a human Jesus was an incredible incarnation of this love of God. He too would courageously and passionately attend to those who were in need in some way – especially those who were rejected by religious leaders and teachers.

This theme is presented very forcefully by Jesus in some of his best known teachings. We see this in Jesus' description of 'Judgement day' of Matthew 25. (Interestingly the word 'judgement day' does not appear in this teaching – but most of our Bibles have added that heading to the passage.) Jesus describes a scene in which he is on the throne and dividing the caring from the uncaring. In this teaching Jesus picks up on the normal understanding of solidarity that the Jewish culture lived with, namely that a deed, good or bad, done to one member of the family was done to all members of the family. Jesus then taught that this perspective should be extended to any person who was in need:

'When the Son of Man comes in his glory, and all the angels with him, then he will sit on the throne of his glory. All the nations will be gathered before him, and he will separate people one from another as a shepherd separates the sheep from the goats, and he will put the sheep at his right hand and the goats at the left. Then the king will say to those at his right

> hand, "Come, you that are blessed by my Father, inherit the kingdom prepared for you from the foundation of the world; for I was hungry and you gave me food, I was thirsty and you gave me something to drink, I was a stranger and you welcomed me, I was naked and you gave me clothing, I was sick and you took care of me, I was in prison and you visited me." Then the righteous will answer him, "Lord, when was it that we saw you hungry and gave you food, or thirsty and gave you something to drink? And when was it that we saw you a stranger and welcomed you, or naked and gave you clothing? And when was it that we saw you sick or in prison and visited you?" And the king will answer them, "Truly I tell you, just as you did it to one of the least of these who are members of my family you did it to me." Then he will say to those at his left hand, "You that are accursed, depart from me into the eternal fire prepared for the devil and his angels; for I was hungry and you gave me no food, I was thirsty and you gave me nothing to drink, I was a stranger and you did not welcome me, naked and you did not give me clothing, sick and in prison and you did not visit me." Then they also will answer, "Lord, when was it that we saw you hungry or thirsty or a stranger or naked or sick or in prison, and did not take care of you?" Then he will answer them, "Truly I tell you, just as you did not do it to one of the least of these, you did not do it to me." And these will go away into eternal punishment, but the righteous into eternal life.' (Matthew 25.31-46)

Another of Jesus' famous teachings on this theme is the parable of the 'Good Samaritan'. Jesus tells this parable after a lawyer recites the commandment to love your neighbour as yourself and then asks the question, 'Who is my neighbour?' Essentially this is a question about group solidarity. In the story we discover that those in need are our neighbour and that we are a neighbour to them when we help them:

> Just then a lawyer stood up to test Jesus. 'Teacher,' he said, 'what must I do to inherit eternal life?' He said to him, 'What is written in the law? What do you read there?' He answered, 'You shall love the Lord your God with all your heart, and with all your soul, and with all your strength, and with all your mind; and your neighbour as yourself.' And he said to him, 'You have given the right answer; do this, and you will live.'
>
> But wanting to justify himself, he asked Jesus, 'And who is my neighbour?' Jesus replied, 'A man was going down from Jerusalem to Jericho, and fell into the hands of robbers, who stripped him, beat him,

and went away, leaving him half dead. Now by chance a priest was going down that road; and when he saw him, he passed by on the other side. So likewise a Levite, when he came to the place and saw him, passed by on the other side. But a Samaritan while traveling came near him; and when he saw him, he was moved with pity. He went to him and bandaged his wounds, having poured oil and wine on them. Then he put him on his own animal, brought him to an inn, and took care of him. The next day he took out two denarii, gave them to the innkeeper, and said, "Take care of him; and when I come back, I will repay you whatever more you spend." 'Which of these three, do you think, was a neighbour to the man who fell into the hands of the robbers?' He said, "The one who showed him mercy." Jesus said to him, 'Go and do likewise.' (Luke 10.25-37)

Who is my neighbour?

Jesus' opposition to Scribes, Pharisees and Sadducees was not a sign that he didn't love them – rather it was a sign that he did love them. If he had not spent time with them, argued with them or eaten with them then that would have meant that his love did not extend to them. His opposition to them was a necessary part of his love for the downtrodden. His love for the suffering ones needed to include coming to their defence against those who caused much of their suffering. Because the love he brought was God's love, Jesus obviously also had an agenda to get the religious leaders to practise this love. They were, after all, the official representatives of God and Jesus wanted to get them to properly embrace the nature of God's love.

Jesus' passion for suffering people is not only a passion for those who are suffering physically but also for those who are 'lost' spiritually. This emerges powerfully in a set of teachings on his love for the 'lost'. Jesus shares this teaching in response to being criticised for his friendship and fraternising with sinners. Jesus tells three parables, namely the Lost Sheep, the Lost Coin and the Lost Son, all of which are found in Luke 15. Here is an account of the first of those stories:

Now all the tax collectors and sinners were coming near to listen to him. And the Pharisees and the scribes were grumbling and saying, 'This fellow welcomes sinners and eats with them.' So he told them this parable: 'Which one of you, having a hundred sheep and losing one of them, does not leave the ninety-nine in the wilderness and go after the one that is lost until he finds it? When he has found it, he lays it on his shoulders and rejoices. And when he comes home, he calls together his friends and neighbors, saying to them, "Rejoice with me, for I have found my sheep that was lost." Just so, I tell you, there will be more joy in heaven over one sinner who repents than over ninety-nine righteous persons who need no repentance.' (Luke 15.1-7)

Jesus had another very powerful and evocative way of demonstrating God's all-inclusive love. We find this in his welcoming tax collectors into the Kingdom and eating with them and even inviting them to follow him as disciples (Mark 2.14-15; Luke 19.2; Mathew 11.19; Luke 7.34). In this practice Jesus is being most radical in stepping across boundaries because everyone despised the tax collectors. The tax collectors were detested by the non-elite Galileans who were Jesus' primary audience and amongst whom Jesus was very popular. The tax collectors were also hated by the aristocratic Jewish leadership who Jesus often opposed and who were essentially against Jesus. Jesus demonstrates to both friend and foe just how inclusive the Kingdom is.

It is with this specific value in mind that we may best understand the apparently difficult words of Jesus in which he seems to call us to hate our father and mothers. This is not Jesus' intention in this teaching at all. Essentially he is asserting that our family solidarity must be transcended in order to be true to a greater solidarity in God's reign: *Now large crowds were traveling with him; and he turned and said to them, 'Whoever comes to me and does not hate father and mother, wife and children, brothers and sisters, yes, and even life itself, cannot be my disciple.'*[1] (Luke 14.25-26)

The power of Jesus' teaching is that he shows that this love that steps across boundaries is not a passive love. It is not merely an attitude of saying 'I love all people'. The nature of this love is that it makes reaching out to lost, suffering and alienated people a priority in our lives.

ENEMY LOVING

Jesus taught that every boundary, even the boundary between enemies, must be overcome by love. Enemies are the ultimate 'them' in the us/them divide and so Jesus really drives the point home that love in God's Kingdom is not hemmed in by any boundaries. The love that Jesus calls us to is *agape*, which is unconditional and sacrificial love. *Agape* is a word that is often used to describe God's love. *Agape* is the highest form of love and is what Jesus expects from us.

The Jews hated the Gentiles and regarded them as the enemy, referring to them as 'pagan dogs'. Jesus made it clear that Gentiles were included in the reach of God's love and this was a factor that evoked a lot of resistance to Jesus by the religious authorities. In Jesus' first sermon recorded in Luke 4 the hearers were at first impressed with Jesus, but this quickly turned to anger when he went on to speak of the Gentiles receiving the Gospel too. Clearly Jesus was teaching that the Reign of God which the Messiah inaugurated was for all people, Jew and Gentile:

> *All spoke well of him and were amazed at the gracious words that came from his mouth. … And he said, 'Truly I tell you, no prophet is accepted in the prophet's hometown. But the truth is, there were many widows in Israel in the time of Elijah, when the heaven was shut up three years and six months, and there was a severe famine over all the land; yet Elijah was sent to none of them except to a widow at Zarephath in Sidon. There were also many lepers in Israel in the time of the prophet Elisha, and none of them was cleansed except Naaman the Syrian.' When they heard this, all in the synagogue were filled with rage. They got up, drove him out of the town, and led him to the brow of the hill on which their town was built, so that they might hurl him off the cliff. But he passed through the midst of them and went on his way.* (Selected verses from Luke 4.22-30)

---

[1] *The Holy Bible: New Revised Standard Version*, 1996, c1989 (Luke 14.25-26). Thomas Nelson: Nashville.

In this next passage we hear Jesus plainly calling for love of enemies:

> 'You have heard that it was said, "You shall love your neighbour and hate your enemy." But I say to you, Love your enemies and pray for those who persecute you, so that you may be children of your Father in heaven; for he makes his sun rise on the evil and on the good, and sends rain on the righteous and on the unrighteous. For if you love those who love you, what reward do you have? Do not even the tax collectors do the same? And if you greet only your brothers and sisters what more are you doing than others? Do not even the Gentiles do the same? Be perfect, therefore, as your heavenly Father is perfect.' (Matthew 5.43-48. See also Luke 6.27-31)

John's Gospel gives us insight into a beautiful effect of Jesus' boundary-crossing love when he practised profound solidarity with a Samaritan woman. Samaritans were another set of enemies to the Jews in Jesus' day:

> *So he came to a Samaritan city called Sychar,... A Samaritan woman came to draw water, and Jesus said to her, 'Give me a drink.' (His disciples had gone to the city to buy food.) The Samaritan woman said to him, 'How is it that you, a Jew, ask a drink of me, a woman of Samaria?' (Jews do not share things in common with Samaritans.)... Just then his disciples came. They were astonished that he was speaking with a woman, but no one said, 'What do you want?' or, 'Why are you speaking with her?' Then the woman left her water jar and went back to the city. She said to the people, 'Come and see a man who told me everything I have ever done! He cannot be the Messiah, can he?' They left the city and were on their way to him. Many Samaritans from that city believed in him because of the woman's testimony, 'He told me everything I have ever*

done.' So when the Samaritans came to him, they asked him to stay with them; and he stayed there two days. And many more believed because of his word. They said to the woman, 'It is no longer because of what you said that we believe, for we have heard for ourselves, and we know that this is truly the Savior of the world.' (John 4.4-42 selected verses)

When you look up this passage above please note that between verses 21 to 24 there is a discussion about which is the correct mountain to worship on. Jesus is saying that his coming brings an end to some places on a map being more important than other places on a map. This has great significance for us because Christians often get caught up with a nationalism that puts their own side of the border as a priority over someone from somewhere else. When we think this way we are not thinking with a Kingdom Consciousness. In the community of the Kingdom geographical boundaries are crossed by disciples who see that we are all family.

TO PRACTISE A LOVE THAT STEPS ACROSS BOUNDARIES IS A SIGN THAT YOU ARE PART OF THE SHEPHERD'S FLOCK

In chapter 3 we saw how sin divides us in the four relationships of life. Since then we have seen how Jesus has come as a challenge to that divisive effect of sin as he has brought into being the Reign of God and with it the Kingdom Consciousness that love must step across boundaries. This love is a transformative love for 'Love unites, and by uniting, transforms all that it unites' (as my Professor, Brian Gaybba, phrased it).

The African notion of *Ubuntu* highlights that our African worldview is more inclined to a communal consciousness than other worldviews may be. *Ubuntu* in its essence is aware that a person is only a person through other people. In this insightful notion my personhood is defined by my relationships with other people. Who I am, is defined by how I relate to others. This is truly profound and highlights a really helpful African communitarian philosophy.

Ubuntu really offers fertile soil from which to embrace Jesus' communitarian view as described in this and other chapters. *Ubuntu* was really the spirituality that made the choices for reconciliation in South Africa possible at the Kempton Park CODESA negotiations and in the achievements of the Truth and Reconciliation Commission[2]. *Ubuntu* is such a powerful notion, pregnant with many Kingdom possibilities, that it is worth recording these beautiful words from Allan Boesak that describe what has already been achieved by *Ubuntu*:

---

[2] This reality is convincingly described throughout Allan Boesak's *Pharaohs on Both Sides of the Blood-Red Waters: Prophetic Critique of Empire*, see especially chapter 4.

We set aside justifiable victor's justice, did not claim the power of well-deserved victim's justice, but chose for the vulnerability of survivor's justice.... We called all South Africans survivors: we all survived this horror called apartheid. And at the deepest heart of that lies Ubuntu: the understanding that my humanity is inextricably bound with your humanity; that I am only what I am when you are what you are meant to be; that in hurting or despising or dehumanizing me you are hurting, despising and dehumanizing yourself; that in my embracing and forgiving you I restore your humanity and mine and restore the community that was lost because of what you have done. This is a generosity of spirit that is stunning in its depth and its width. This is a spirituality that has far-reaching and radical political implications.[3]

Ubuntu is of course still trapped somewhat by the African cultural perspective. At present two examples are worth mentioning – the African hierarchical worldview and also the view of the roles of women. *Ubuntu* does not necessarily fully reach out across such boundaries that are culturally determined. This is where Jesus' values can be embraced and can elevate *Ubuntu* into a uniquely powerful Kingdom dynamic here in Southern Africa.

Dr Teddy Sakupapa asserts that *Ubuntu* is best viewed as a notion that is not unalterable but can develop and grow. He says, 'I consider Ubuntu a living tradition that is constantly reinvented owing to cultural dynamism, and ... is infused with Christian and human rights discourses.' He goes on to suggest 'a view of the church as an ubuntu community. This implies an ecclesiology of inclusion .... The community called Ubuntu (ecclesiology) derives its existence from Jesus, the ideal expression of Ubuntu whose Ubuntu is continually expressed in the church through the Holy Spirit.... Ubuntu may be appropriated in ecclesiology since it resonates with the broad outlines of the doctrine of God as the divine community... the unity and interaction within the community called Ubuntu entails participation and solidarity.'[4] This solidarity needs to be particularly attentive to those who suffer, those on the margins, those disempowered, those oppressed, the victims.

Jesus' call to solidarity with those who suffer is a truth that beckons all who would be true disciples during times of injustice, exploitation and corruption. This call was really put into words very well in the 1986 Belhar confession of the Uniting Reformed Church of Southern Africa. Here is article 4 of that confession:

---

[3] *Pharaohs on Both Sides of the Blood-Red Waters*, p. 24-25.

[4] Teddy C. Sakupapa, 'Ecumenical Ecclesiology in the African Context: Towards a View of the Church as *Ubuntu*', *Scriptura*, Volume 117, Number 1, June 2018, p. 9-11.

> We believe that God has revealed Godself as the One who wishes to bring about justice and true peace on earth; that in a world full of injustice and enmity God is in a special way the God of the destitute, the poor and the wronged and that God calls the church to follow in this; that God brings justice to the oppressed and gives bread to the hungry; that God frees the prisoners and restores sight to the blind; that God supports the downtrodden, protects the strangers, helps orphans and widows and blocks the path of the ungodly; that for God pure and undefiled religion is to visit the orphans and the widows in their suffering; that God wishes to teach the people of God to do what is good and to seek the right; that the church must therefore stand by people in any form of suffering and need, which implies, among other things, that the church must witness against and strive against any form of injustice, so that justice may roll down like waters, and righteousness like an ever-flowing stream; that the church, belonging to God, should stand where God stands, namely against injustice and with the wronged; that in following Christ the Church must witness against all the powerful and privileged who selfishly seek their own interests and thus control and harm others. Therefore, we reject any ideology which would legitimate forms of injustice and any doctrine which is unwilling to resist such an ideology in the name of the gospel.[5]

What has been said so far highlights that compassion for suffering people and enemies is the only way to concretely demonstrate that God's all-inclusive love has taken root in our lives. Commenting on the parable of the Good Samaritan, Albert Nolan brings this point home for us with the following important words, 'If we allow the parable to move us, if we allow the parable to release those deeper emotions which we have been taught to fear, we shall never again have to ask who our neighbour might be or what love might mean. We shall go and do likewise in the teeth of whatever barriers. Only compassion can teach a man what solidarity with his fellowman means.'[6]

Dr. Sakupapa emphasises this when he sums up saying, 'The church as an Ubuntu community and in that regard, a moral community, participates in the struggles for peace and justice in the world. The church as Ubuntu community stands in solidarity with the world.'[7]

In a very real way it is important for us to appreciate that our relationships

---

[5] Accessed from https://kerkargief.co.za/doks/bely/CF_Belhar.pdf on 3rd December 2018.
[6] Albert Nolan, *Jesus before Christianity*, p. 67.
[7] 'Ecumenical Ecclesiology in the African Context', p. 12.

with suffering people reveal the real nature of our relationship with Jesus. Every day we meet Jesus in these people. Every day our faith in Jesus is tested. Do we love him through loving these people? Do we reject him through rejecting these people? Do we really behave like disciples?

Sin blinds us to the demands of love. The Scribes, Pharisees and Sadducees were people who were blinded to the demands of love. Jesus tried to open their eyes, but they were so blind that they chose to execute him. Sin's blinding effect leads to Jesus' crucifixion! Let us realise then that our blindness to the demands of love today is our participation in the sin that killed Jesus.

This blindness has had many tragic results in history, as I indicated in chapter 1. Satirists like John Cleese are able to quickly expose the stupidity of some of the church's history. I once attended a live show in which he imagined two priests talking to each other during Christianity's inquisition in the 15th Century. These two priests were watching all the bonfires in which heretics were being burnt and justified their actions by saying, 'they deserve to be burnt because they have not accepted our interpretation of the Gospel of Love!'

It is however wonderful to reflect on the progressive boundaries that were overcome by Jesus and his faithful followers as recorded in the New Testament:

- Jesus' ministry – society's outcasts, marginalised, suffering ones, enemies and Gentiles are shown God's love[8]. Then,
- Pentecost – Jews from many lands hear and receive the Gospel. Then,
- Philip's ministry to Samaritans (Samaritans were half-caste Jews and were hated by Jews) and to an Ethiopian eunuch. Then,
- Cornelius invites Peter to minister to him – the first recorded instance, after the ascension, of Jesus' followers ministering to a gentile. Cornelius was sympathetic to Jewish faith. Then,
- Ministry to Gentiles at Antioch – Jewish Christians on their own initiative preach the Gospel to Gentiles.
- God's love in Jesus is now extended to *all nations* and *all people* in those nations.

---

[8] The following are some examples of Jesus' ministry to Gentiles: Jesus ministered to the centurion (Matthew 8.5-15 and parallels); the Canaanite woman whose faith surprised and impressed him in the Pagan district of Tyre and Sidon (Matthew 15.21-28); the demoniac at Gerasenes (Luke 8.26-39 and parallels), note that in Mark and Luke's version of this story the healed man is instructed by Jesus to remain in his home in Gentile territory and proclaim the Gospel to them. It must also be remembered that Galilee was a very mixed race territory since it had been part of the old Northern Kingdom that had been emptied of most Jews and filled with Assyrian placements in 722 BC. Jesus therefore grew up in a mixed-race context and did much of his ministry in that context. There were instances where Jesus said to His disciples 'Go nowhere among the Gentiles, and enter no town of the Samaritans, but go rather to the lost sheep of the house of Israel.' (Matthew 10.5-6). This was a matter of strategy due to time pressures related to their training, not a matter of exclusion of Gentiles or Samaritans from the Gospel.

Since then faithful followers of Jesus the Shepherd have honoured his reign by stepping across the barriers of slavery; barriers between roles, status and rights of men and women; and barriers between the status and rights of black and white people. Currently the church is overcoming the barriers that once rejected people of same-sex orientation.

This radical inclusiveness of the Gospel was a great aid to the growth of the church in the first 400 years. Two key elements of this inclusiveness have been noted by researches. The first is the impact of the inclusion of women. Women who became Christian taught the faith to their children and so their children became Christian too. The second is the behaviour of Christians during contagious epidemics that swept across areas where the church had taken root. Christians persevered with caring for sick people at great personal cost. This made a very powerfully positive impression on populations.

This whole theme of love for suffering people was profoundly brought to the world's attention in the 20th Century by the German Lutheran pastor and theologian Dietrich Bonhoeffer during Adolf Hitler's genocidal reign. Bonhoeffer knew that Christians had to practise a boundary-crossing solidarity and defend and protect Jews. He made it clear that coming to the aid of Jews in their crisis was an essential part of Christianity's witness in Germany. In 1935 he said, 'Only those who cry out for the Jews may also sing Gregorian chants.'[9] Bonhoeffer made it clear that a Christian's worship only had integrity if their lives honoured God's reign. This saying became the motto of all those who understood the task of the church as not in looking out for herself and reproducing herself but in defending the weak. Bonhoeffer was arrested for

---

[9] Quote taken from Afterword of *Life Together*, p. 125. Note that Gregorian chanting was a common form of worship in the Lutheran church at the time.

his role in helping Jews escape Germany and whilst in prison he was linked to the plot to assassinate Hitler. He was executed by special order of Hitler in the closing days of the Second World War.

This love that steps across boundaries is at the heart of the Christian faith and without it Christianity is not worthy of its name.

Love steps across boundaries

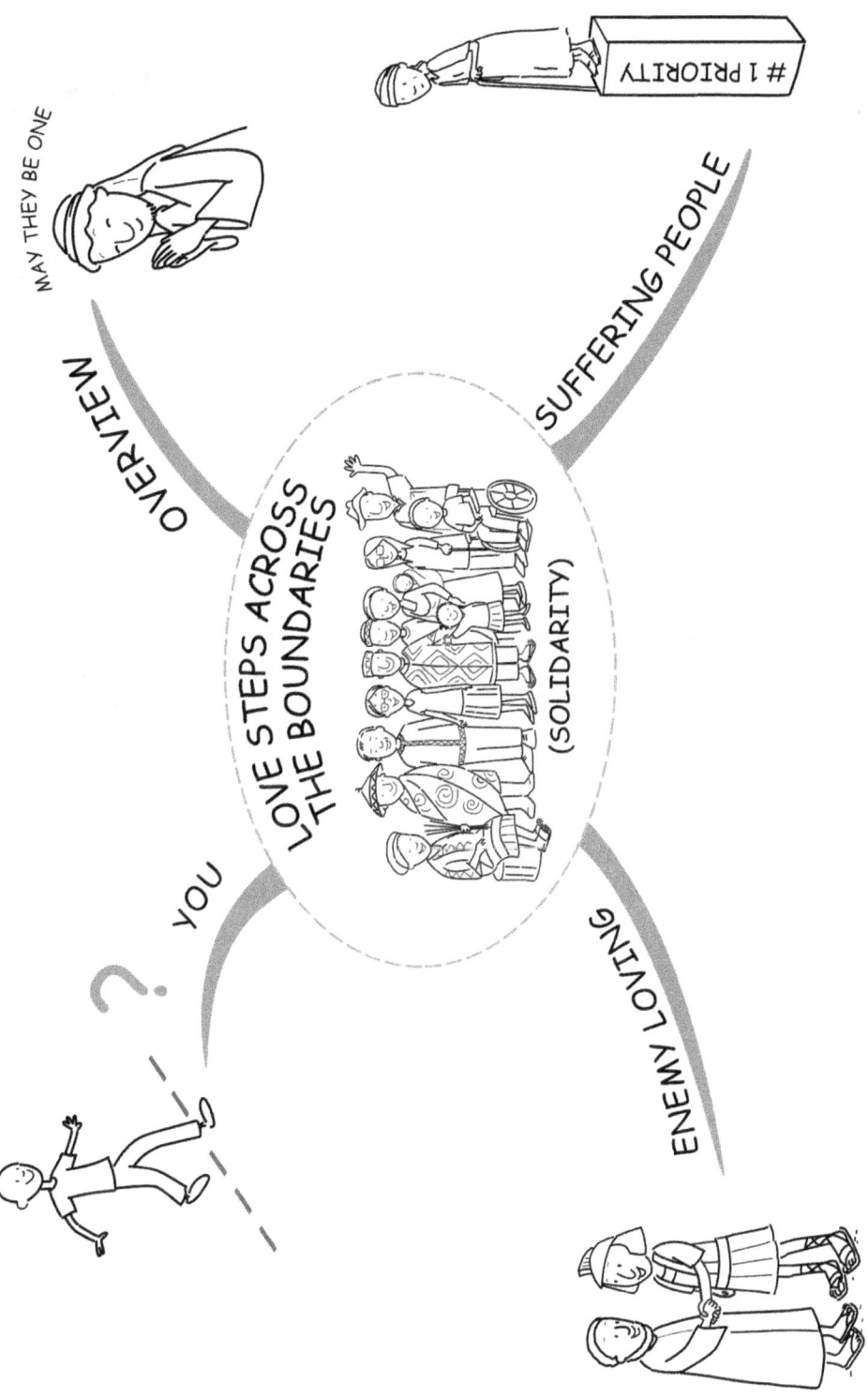

SUGGESTIONS FOR DISCUSSION, REVISION, REFLECTION AND APPLICATION

(These questions are intended for group work, but can easily be adapted for personal use.)

1. What is the most important message to you in this chapter? (Remember to also make a note of this on your 'God spoke to me' page.)
2. Icebreaker question: What is the weirdest thing you have ever eaten? (The question must be answered quickly. As a group, do not spend longer than 5 minutes in total on this question.)
3. Read Luke 10.25-37 and answer the following questions:
   a. This is one of a number of instances in Jesus' ministry where he was asked about private salvation (*'What must I do to inherit eternal life?'*). Have you noticed how Jesus' answer pushes the questioner out of their privatised faith? What do you think this says to your own view of inheriting 'eternal life'?
   b. It seems that the lawyer in this story knew the answer. Why did he not put it into practice?
   c. What makes it difficult for you to put your faith into practice?
   d. What behaviour was Jesus hoping for in the lawyer? In others who also heard him tell the story? In those who heard the early preachers tell the story (oral tradition)? In you reading the story today?
   e. Have you ever been a 'good Samaritan'? Share the story.
   f. Has anyone ever been a 'good Samaritan' to you? Share the story.
4. Below are a variety of suggestions and questions to aid your appreciation of this chapter. Do not attempt to do all of them! Choose those that are most appropriate to your unique situation and/or group. The questions are designed to help variously with revision, understanding, appreciation, reflection or application of the content.
   a. Who is my neighbour? Try and answer this personally.
   b. Which suffering people should today become a priority? Try and make a list. Who do you know belongs to that list? Can you list their names? Can you be a neighbour to anyone on that list?
   c. Respond to the statement, *'South Africa has enough economic problems*

of its own and should therefore not accept refugees into our land.' What would Jesus say? Which of Jesus' teachings are relevant here?

d. Who do you think is your enemy? Or who has declared you their enemy? What do you feel about Jesus' teaching about your relations with that person? If you want to follow Jesus in this matter – what could you do?

e. In the section 'To practise a love that steps across boundaries is a sign that you are part of the Shepherd's flock.' I have given a simple account of the progressive boundaries that were overcome by Jesus and his faithful followers during New Testament times. If you were to continue that simple history from then until the present day, what would you view as the most important boundaries that have been overcome? What current boundaries is the church struggling with?

f. Discuss how *Ubuntu* can help us in this journey of stepping across boundaries. Discuss how *Ubuntu* itself needs to evolve to be faithful to Kingdom Consciousness.

g. What boundaries does your love need to cross if you are to become obedient to Jesus' call to love your neighbour? What are you going to do about this? Invite the group to hold you accountable to your answer.

GOD SPOKE TO ME ...

12

LOVING SERVICE IS THE MOST POWERFUL FORCE IN THE WORLD

*'You also ought to wash one another's feet.
For I have set you an example, that you
also should do as I have done to you.'*
(John 13.14-15)

AN OVERVIEW OF JESUS' TEACHING ABOUT POWER

The issue of power is an important matter. Jesus dealt with the matter of power both in the world (kingdom of Satan) and in God's Kingdom. The issue of power and the structures of power (who has power over whom and who can decide what for whom) is what we today call politics. The exercise of power in the two kingdoms is completely different. In the kingdoms of this world, or the reign of Satan, power is found in domination. In the Reign of God power is found in service. Jesus believes that loving service is the most powerful force in the world.

Jesus is teaching that power in the Reign of God has got nothing to do with domination and oppression; rather it is the power of love and service. A Kingdom Consciousness believes that true power lies in loving service, even though the power of domination may seem stronger from a worldly perspective.

Jesus teaches that those in authority should use their positions and the structures that are at their disposal for love and service in society. Jesus used his own authority to serve those in need, to serve his disciples and even to serve the integrity of the Jewish faith. Eventually this culminates in Jesus giving his own life as an act of service.

THE PRIORITY AND THE POWER OF LOVING SERVICE

In this passage we hear Jesus' call to loving service as core to Kingdom Consciousness and Practice:

> 'But it is not so among you; but whoever wishes to become great among you must be your servant, and whoever wishes to be first among you must be slave of all.' (Mark 10.43-44)

Jesus made it clear that love is the way of God and therefore also the power of God in this world:

> 'If you love those who love you, what credit is that to you? For even sinners love those who love them. If you do good to those who do good to you, what credit is that to you? For even sinners do the same. If you lend to those from whom you hope to receive, what credit is that to you? Even

sinners lend to sinners, to receive as much again. But love your enemies, do good, and lend, expecting nothing in return. Your reward will be great, and you will be children of the Most High; for he is kind to the ungrateful and the wicked. Be merciful, just as your Father is merciful.' (Luke 6.32-36)

It is this aspect of Jesus' teaching that is also part of his extended and intense criticism of the scribes and Pharisees in Matthew 23.1-12. Although we have looked at that passage earlier I encourage you to read it again and see now how Jesus warns people against following the example of the scribes and Pharisees because they do not have servant hearts, nor are they caring, compassionate or humble. Jesus teaches that a loving servant heart is an essential quality in the Kingdom Consciousness Movement.

Jesus encourages acts of loving service by affirming them:

While he was at Bethany in the house of Simon the leper, as he sat at the table, a woman came with an alabaster jar of very costly ointment of nard, and she broke open the jar and poured the ointment on his head. But some were there who said to one another in anger, 'Why was the ointment wasted in this way? For this ointment could have been sold for more than three hundred denarii, and the money given to the poor.' And they scolded her. But Jesus said, 'Let her alone; why do you trouble her? She has performed a good service for me. For you always have the poor with you, and you can show kindness to them whenever you wish; but you will not always have me. She has done what she could; she has anointed my body beforehand for its burial. Truly I tell you, wherever the good news is proclaimed in the whole world, what she has done will be told in remembrance of her.' (Mark 14.3-9)

JESUS' PRACTICE OF LOVING SERVICE

Jesus led by example in practising acts of loving service:

Now before the festival of the Passover, Jesus knew that his hour had come to depart from this world and go to the Father. Having loved his own who were in the world, he loved them to the end. The devil had already put it into the heart of Judas son of Simon Iscariot to betray him. And during supper Jesus, knowing that the Father had given all things into his hands, and that he had come from God and was going to God, got up from the table, took off his outer robe, and tied a towel around himself.

Then he poured water into a basin and began to wash the disciples' feet and to wipe them with the towel that was tied around him... After he had washed their feet, had put on his robe, and had returned to the table, he said to them, 'Do you know what I have done to you? You call me Teacher and Lord—and you are right, for that is what I am. So if I, your Lord and Teacher, have washed your feet, you also ought to wash one another's feet. For I have set you an example, that you also should do as I have done to you.' (John 13.1-15, selected verses)

Jesus himself had so much faith in loving service that he remained faithful to this activity even after it brought intense opposition from religious leaders. Eventually Jesus was killed due to his refusal to back down on the work of God's love. In a very real way Jesus died because of love.

It is also true that Jesus viewed his death as an act of loving service offered to the world. Jesus' service to the poor, sick, sinners, scribes, Pharisees, disciples and everyone else, was the service of awakening faith in the reign of God. When this brought him deadly opposition he was faced with the option to hide, or water down his ministry. Jesus then made the decision that he could serve the world better by dying for it than by staying alive!

Jesus decided that his death, as a result of his faithfulness to the Kingdom, could awaken faith in God's reign amongst many people. Jesus therefore offered his life as an act of service to the entire world, hoping that it would awaken faith in God's reign. Now we know that for 2 000 years, billions of people across the world have accepted God's reign in their lives as a result of this act of loving service. When you and I reflect on the results of this great act of loving service then we are left in no doubt that this is the most powerful force in the world. It is the power of God!

FORGIVENESS AS THE PRACTICE OF LOVING SERVICE

It is in the light of this teaching theme that we can most insightfully focus on Jesus' teachings on forgiveness. Jesus clearly taught forgiveness as a core value in the Kingdom Consciousness Movement. At its heart, forgiveness is an act of profound service to those who wrong us. It is an act that gives the person a new start in their relationship with you. It is an act that shows that you have not set up a boundary wall separating you from the person who has wronged you.

At its deepest level, forgiveness is an act that trusts love to be the most powerful force in the world. Forgiveness keeps the door open for God's love to heal and transform us and those who have wronged us. Forgiveness believes that love must have the last word.

Jesus' teaching on forgiveness is perhaps summed up in the 'Lord's Prayer', where we are taught to pray: *And forgive us our debts, as we also have forgiven our debtors* (Matthew 6.12). Jesus knew that we needed to receive forgiveness from God and that we needed to forgive those who had wronged us. The reference to debt is appropriate because to forgive someone who has wronged you is to say to them 'you don't owe me anything' and 'I'm not expecting anything from you'.

Remember how in Matthew 18.21-35 Jesus emphasised generosity in forgiveness in the parable of the servant who would not forgive the debt owing to him even though he himself had been released from debt. For more references to Jesus' teaching on forgiveness see Matthew 6.14-15, Mark 11.25 and Luke 17.3-4.

In our review of Jesus' ministry in chapter seven we saw that Jesus was radically committed to the good news that we have all been given a new and fresh start in the forgiveness and love of God. Jesus knew that hope for society lay in our generosity in forgiveness and love towards each other. Just as the forgiveness and generosity in God's love had transformed our relationship with God so that same forgiveness and generosity would transform life on earth if we practised it.

Does this mean that we tolerate or justify evil? No, not at all. An approach of love and forgiveness was for Jesus, and will be for us too, the only way to open up the possibility of a new start in the wrongdoer. The deep truth is that the wrongdoer is also made in the image of God and their greatest need is to make a new, more authentic, start to their life. Our refusal to forgive such people will only trap them in their unauthentic behaviour. Forgiveness and love are our way of counting on God to dissolve the roots of evil.

Forgiveness is healing and liberating for the person doing the forgiving too. A lack of forgiveness can eat away at my own being and even come to dominate the mood of my life. I have always loved the words of David Benner, 'To forgive is to set a prisoner free and to discover that the prisoner is me'. Forgiveness is a vital grace in our relationship with ourselves and with those who have wronged us.

This is part of the radical core of the Kingdom of God and is often mocked as being weak or foolish, but 1 Corinthians 1.25 reminds us of the opposite – *For God's foolishness is wiser than human wisdom, and God's weakness is stronger than human strength.*

NON-VIOLENCE

Jesus was very clear about turning his back on violence. He viewed it as a power of this world (Satan) that had nothing to do with God's reign. The temptation to be a Messiah who used violence was a very real and strong temptation, but one that Jesus refused to bow to.

Reflect on the following of Jesus' sayings:

> 'Blessed are the peacemakers, for they will be called children of God.' (Matthew 5.9)

> 'You have heard that it was said to those of ancient times, "You shall not murder"; and "whoever murders shall be liable to judgment." But I say to you that if you are angry with a brother or sister, you will be liable to judgment; and if you insult a brother or sister, you will be liable to the council; and if you say, "You fool," you will be liable to the hell of fire. So when you are offering your gift at the altar, if you remember that your brother or sister has something against you, leave your gift there before the altar and go; first be reconciled to your brother or sister, and then come and offer your gift.' (Matthew 5.21-24)

Jesus answered:
> 'My kingdom is not from this world. If my kingdom were from this world,

my followers would be fighting to keep me from being handed over to the Jews. But as it is, my kingdom is not from here.' (John 18.36-37).

Obviously Jesus' teaching in Matthew 5.38-42, where he encourages turning the other cheek and carrying the pack an extra mile, is a teaching that supports non-violent resistance to evil.

Then Jesus said to him:

'Put your sword back into its place; for all who take the sword will perish by the sword.' (Matthew 26.52) [1]

You and I cannot be faithful Jesus followers without letting go of our desire to control and dominate, which is our trust in the power of this world. This must be replaced by the practice of loving service, which is the power of God to act in us and through us. We are invited to let go of our love of power and rather embrace the power of love.[2]

Loving service may seem little compared to domination and violence, but Jesus imaginatively helps us to see its power in these parables where Kingdom love is seen to work like a mustard seed and yeast. Loving service may seem small and vulnerable, but it ends up blessing an exceptional number, like a mustard seed becoming a tree giving homes to many birds. Loving service may seem impotent but it has exceptional powers of transformation, like yeast has in dough:

He put before them another parable: 'The kingdom of heaven is like a mustard seed that someone took and sowed in his field; it is the smallest of all the seeds, but when it has grown it is the greatest of shrubs and becomes a tree, so that the birds of the air come and make nests in its

---

[1] There are one or two sayings of Jesus and instances in his life that have been used by some to justify violence, gun ownership, armed resistance, war, etc. The foundations of their arguments are weak because they read the passages out of context and do not attempt to be faithful to the whole of Jesus' revelation. Matthew 10.34 *'Do not think that I have come to bring peace to the earth; I have not come to bring peace, but a sword.'* When read in the context of what Jesus is saying it is clear that the 'sword' is one that his followers will suffer, not one that they may use against others. Note also that the fact that a disciple (maybe more than one) had a sword and once used it does not mean that he was complying with Jesus' will in doing so – in fact Jesus scolded him and healed the person injured by the blow. Kraybill's book, *Upside down Kingdom*, chapter 2, details Jesus' refusal to use violence. It is also important to remember that in scripture Jesus and his followers often refer to the Word of God as a 'sword' with which to fight the enemy.

[2] It is important to appreciate that in the book of Revelation there is a strong call for Christians to abstain from violence. There are scenes of swords being used to conquer, but this is always a metaphor for the Word of God. When the awful influence of the Beast is described, the following message to abstain from violence and to rather endure and be faithful is given to the reader: *Let anyone who has an ear listen: If you are to be taken captive, into captivity you go; if you kill with the sword, with the sword you must be killed. Here is a call for the endurance and faith of the saints.* (Revelation 13.9-10. The middle part clearly picks up on Jesus' well-known saying of Matthew 26.52.)

branches.' He told them another parable: 'The kingdom of heaven is like yeast that a woman took and mixed in with three measures of flour until all of it was leavened.' (Matthew 13.31-33; parallels in Mark 4.30-32 and Luke 13.18-19)

TO RELY ON LOVING SERVICE AS GOD'S POWER IS A SIGN THAT YOU ARE PART OF THE SHEPHERD'S FLOCK

It was at a funeral of a man that I dearly respected that I first heard these words, words quoted by his daughter during her tribute to him: 'Love is the law of life. We live that we may learn to love. We love that we may learn to live. No other lesson is required of us.'[3] That sentence powerfully and inspirationally sums up the pursuit of those who faithfully follow Jesus the Shepherd. These words in the heart of this wonderful Christian man had certainly defined him – he was a teacher who remained committed to teaching for many years after retirement. In fact he was teaching up until the day he was taken into hospital for his cancer, a mere few months before he passed away!

Loving service is
long lasting legacy

---

[3] He loved these words and lived by them. They are from *The Book of Mirdad* by Lebanese author Mikha'il Na'ima.

Love needs to be practised – it is not just a warm fuzzy attitude in the heart of a person of faith. John Wesley referred to faith alone without love and works of mercy as the grand pest of Christianity!

Think of what can be done through genuine love in the world. Compare the power of the most powerful nation in the world to the power of loving service. Which has the power to feed the hungry, heal the sick, clothe the naked, comfort the lonely, give drink to the thirsty and bring *shalom*[4] to this world? Only those with love in their heart will make any progress on these fronts. The power of the world in and of itself will do nothing. Any secular or religious organisation that makes progress with these matters is doing so because there are people committed to loving service in them. Clearly loving service is the most powerful force in the world! Only loving service has the power to fix the world's problems.

Look deeply and see that we in South Africa have witnessed that the spiritual power of the quest for justice through the people of this land has been successful even when challenged by a well-resourced, highly trained and motivated army. Allan Boesak points out that: 'South Africa gave so much hope to the world, not because we fought a successful revolution. The armed struggle waged by the liberation movements never really made a dent in white South Africa's military supremacy, and it is high time we stop pretending that it did. We did so because we brought apartheid to its knees through our persistent struggle, our willingness to sacrifice, and the extraordinary moral courage of our people. What captivated the world during all those years was not our military successes, but our spiritual strength.'[5]

We need to learn well from this excellent heritage as we continue to follow Jesus who leads us in the powerful path of sacrificial love. On Maundy Thursday we sang the hymn 'When my love to Christ grows weak'. Singing the hymn is a profound journey of being personally impacted by Jesus' courageous faith and love expressed in the giving of his life. I was particularly inspired by how the powerful poetry of the last verse summed up this important dimension of Jesus' life and our call to practise loving service too: 'Then to life I turn again, Learning all the worth of pain, Learning all the might that lies in a full self-sacrifice'.

The transformation in society that Jesus enables is essentially the result of a transformed heart and mind. That transformation will lead to the bringing of justice and all else that the Kingdom means. Africa has multiple examples

---

[4] *Shalom* is the Hebrew word for 'Peace'. It refers to a situation of justice in which there is no conflict and no need for conflict.

[5] Allan Boesak, *The Tenderness of Conscience: African Renaissance and the Spirituality of Politics*, p. 70.

of the replacement of colonial rule by black African dictators and oppressors. In this it is clear that Jesus has not had his way in the transformation of those societies – for in Jesus' way the new leader would know that true power is in loving service. The heart of a leader is a vitally important place!

Desmond Tutu was blunt about this matter when he reflected on oppressive regimes in Africa: 'For we must confess, sadly and humbly, that Africa has one of the worst records of violations of human rights. Africa has a spate of military dictatorships. In many places, all that has changed for the people who suffer is the complexion of the oppressor. In colonial times the oppressor was of a different complexion. Sadly today the complexion of the oppressor is the same as the complexion of the oppressed.'[6] Please God, may we come to a point at which every leader in every sphere of life has discovered the beauty, grace and power of loving service!

Now we are called to go further in this matter of loving service than we have gone before. Loving service for those who suffer will often cause us to suffer in turn! Questing for justice will sometimes bring suffering at the hands of those who are ruthless in upholding their power and privilege. There is moreover an emotional burden when exposing oneself to raw suffering, hardship, deprivation and desperation that can be quite traumatic. The needs of the needy are a bottomless pit of requests. This is all part of loving service that is prepared to suffer in order that a situation of suffering may be transformed by Jesus' Kingdom. May we have the grace to go this far in the matter of loving service. This is part of following Jesus who took up his cross and called us to do the same.

---

[6] Desmond Tutu, *Rainbow People of God: South Africa's Victory over Apartheid*, p. 154.

Missing Jesus?

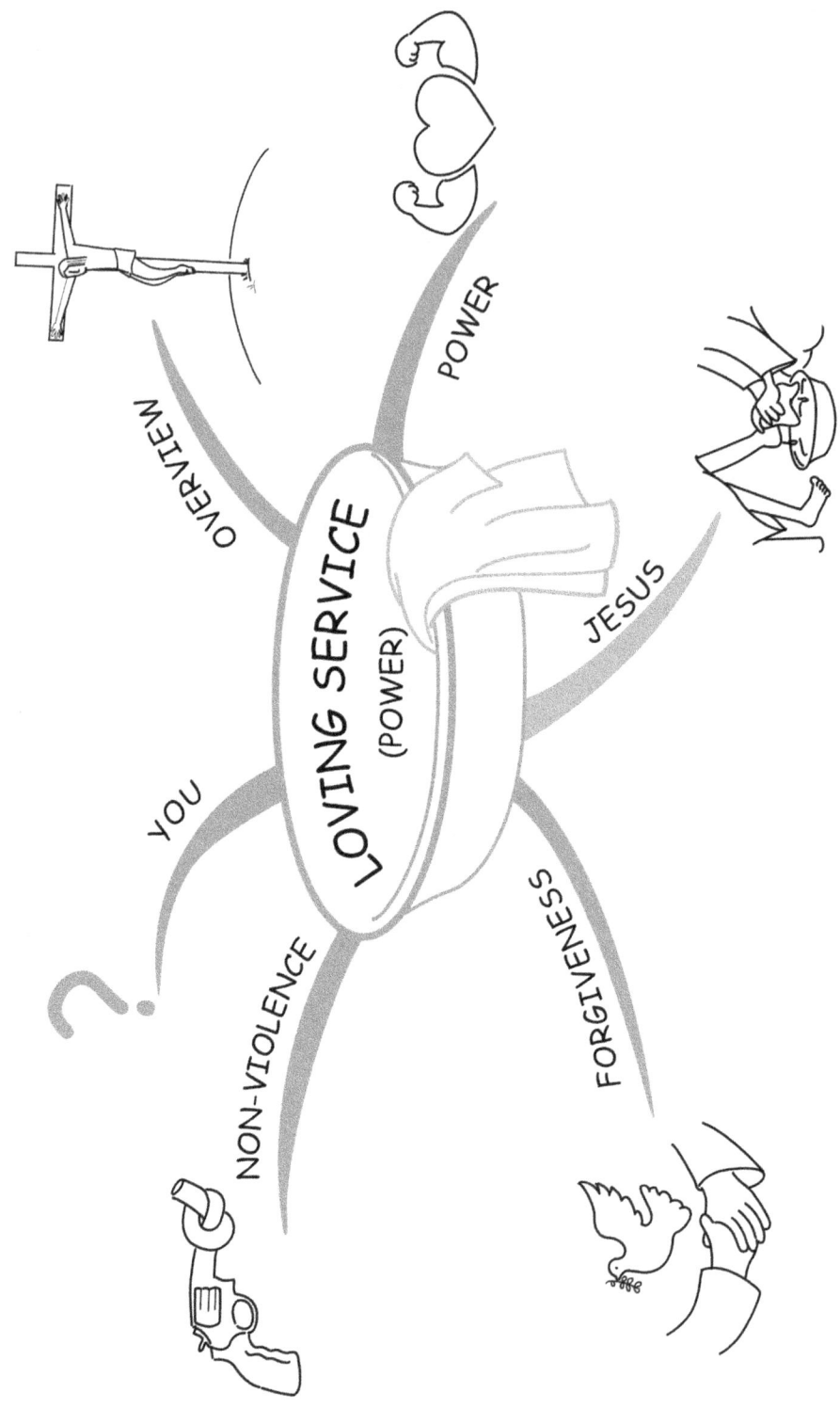

256

SUGGESTIONS FOR DISCUSSION, REVISION, REFLECTION AND APPLICATION

(These questions are intended for group work, but can easily be adapted for personal use.)

1. What is the most important message to you in this chapter? (Remember to also make a note of this on your 'God spoke to me' page.)
2. Icebreaker question: Do you have any hidden talents? (The question must be answered quickly. As a group, do not spend longer than 5 minutes in total on this question.)
3. Read John 13.1-15 and answer the following questions:
   a. What does this passage tell us about the kind of person Jesus was?
   b. Imagine being there as one of the people whose feet get washed! What are your thoughts and feelings when he is about to start on your feet (and you are watching him wash the feet of the person next to you)? How dirty are your feet? Imagine they are very dirty and Jesus is giving them a good clean – what are you thinking and feeling? Now he is finished and has moved to the next person – reflect on what he has done for you. What does this mean about his relationship with you? What does this mean about your relationship with him?
   c. Read verses 14-15. This is the core of the life application Jesus longs for, for his followers. With what kind of spirit does such a person live? What kind of person is always ready to serve?
   d. Can you see the two types of power at odds with each other in this scene? On the one hand Judas and the political machinations; on the other Jesus and the power of loving service? Describe situations of similar power dynamics today.
   e. What kinds of acts of service are similar to washing feet today?
4. Below are a variety of suggestions and questions to aid your appreciation of this chapter. Do not attempt to do all of them! Choose those that are most appropriate to your unique situation and/or group. The questions are designed to help variously with revision, understanding, appreciation, reflection or application of the content.
   a. Where do you get power from? What empowers you? What gives you

influence? What disempowers you? Who has power over you? Who is influential in your life?

b. How much confidence do you have in the power of loving service? How much are you prepared to risk for this?

c. What makes loving service powerful?

d. Who could benefit from your forgiveness? Are you willing to forgive and let love have the last word?

e. Jesus refuses to use violence and teaches followers to also be non-violent. How can we apply this? What are the difficulties and complexities in applying this?

f. What is your response to the call, 'We are invited to let go of our love of power and rather embrace the power of love'? In what areas of your life are you specifically challenged here?

g. Is there some act of loving service you feel called to? Perhaps commit to it and ask the group to hold you accountable.

GOD SPOKE TO ME ...

13

HOPE OF THE WORLD
THE 'ALREADY' AND 'NOT YET' REALITY OF GOD'S REIGN

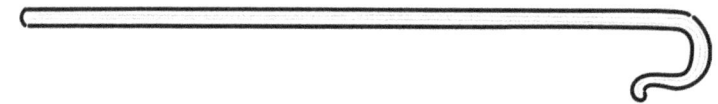

'I watched Satan fall from heaven like a flash of lightning.'
(Luke 10.18)

In this chapter we conclude the focus on Jesus' Kingdom teachings and the Kingdom Consciousness that this calls for, by drawing together some important threads that are relevant to all of the values of his reign.

JESUS AS BATTLE LEADER OF THE KINGDOM

The vital reality that Jesus impresses upon us is that a new consciousness is necessary because a new reality has come into being. God's reign has begun in a decisive way and people are invited by Jesus to change their thinking to appreciate this. This new reality has begun through the life and ministry of Jesus. Jesus is the One who is battling successfully against Satan and thereby bringing about a new world in which we can live. Jesus is battle leader of the Kingdom of God against the Kingdom of Satan.

It is Jesus' coming that has inaugurated the reign of God. It is in Jesus' faithfulness that evil is vanquished on earth and God's reign launched. It is in Jesus' power that the tide turns and God's victory spreads like yeast in the dough. It is in Jesus' teachings that we come to grasp the values and core dynamics of this Reign of God. The important awareness here is that Jesus is the leader in this movement that honours God's reign. You don't need to wait for another leader; Jesus has come and is available to lead you. No other leader will have the astounding credentials that Jesus has. Already in Jesus' day he was recognised as the long-awaited good king. This whole theme comes to an astounding climax when Jesus says: *'All authority in heaven and on earth has been given to me. Go therefore and make disciples of all nations, baptizing them in the name of the Father and of the Son and of the Holy Spirit, and teaching them to obey everything that I have commanded you. And remember, I am with you always, to the end of the age.'* (Matthew 28.18-20)

In this next piece Jesus likens himself to a robber! At the end of this encounter Jesus essentially says that just as a robber needs to tie up the owner of the house before he can plunder the house, so he has tied up Satan and is plundering where Satan used to have power. This is a very important description of how the Reign of God has started with Jesus' coming because it required Jesus to come and overpower Satan:

> *Then they brought to him a demoniac who was blind and mute; and he cured him, so that the one who had been mute could speak and see. All the crowds were amazed and said, 'Can this be the Son of David?' But when the Pharisees heard it, they said, 'It is only by Beelzebul, the ruler of the demons, that this fellow casts out the demons.' He knew what they were thinking and said to them, 'Every kingdom divided against itself is laid waste, and no city or house divided against itself will stand. If Satan casts out Satan, he is divided against himself; how then will his kingdom stand? If I cast out demons by Beelzebul, by whom do your own exorcists cast them out? Therefore they will be your judges. But if it is by the Spirit of God that I cast out demons, then the kingdom of God has come to you. Or how can one enter a strong man's house and plunder his property, without first tying up the strong man? Then indeed the house can be plundered.'* (Matthew 12.22-29)

This proclamation leads us to understand that in the battle with evil, Jesus and his Kingdom are on the offensive. Sometimes we feel besieged by evil, but the truth is that evil is besieged by Jesus! Following Jesus closely means being on the offensive against Satan; it means asserting Jesus' values in places where Satan's values are present; it means asserting Jesus' power where Satan's is being used. It means taking territory from Satan and redeeming lives and communities trapped by him. When we do this we can have the faith that even if victory for Jesus does not seem immediately evident we are on the winning side and that over time Jesus will triumph.

The disciples were delighted to learn that following Jesus included following him into battle against Satan. In Luke 10 we see that Jesus sends out 70 disciples in pairs to heal the sick and to proclaim that the Kingdom of God has come. When these 70 disciples return we read that they excitedly share with Jesus that demons had surrendered to them:

The seventy returned with joy, saying, 'Lord, in your name even the demons submit to us!' He said to them, 'I watched Satan fall from heaven like a flash of lightning. See, I have given you authority to tread on snakes and scorpions, and over all the power of the enemy; and nothing will hurt you. Nevertheless, do not rejoice at this, that the spirits submit to you, but rejoice that your names are written in heaven.' (Luke 10.17-20)

Evil is a constant reality in this world and we must see that Jesus leads us into battle against evil. This battle continues today and our following of Jesus must include following Him into battle against evil. It is important though that we appreciate that in Jesus and his ways are found the victory over evil. We cannot use the means and tactics of Satan's ways to battle against Satan. Jesus continues to lead as the book of Revelation also makes clear: *Then I saw heaven opened, and there was a white horse! Its rider is called Faithful and True, and in righteousness he judges and makes war.* (Revelation 19.11). To the extent that we follow Jesus and his ways (the faithful, true and right ways, says Revelation 19.11), to that extent we can meet evil with a battle song of triumph.

Luke's Gospel highlights that Jesus' ministry of ushering in God's reign was an experience of liberation for downtrodden and suffering people:

He unrolled the scroll and found the place where it was written: 'The Spirit of the Lord is upon me, because he has anointed me to bring good news to the poor. He has sent me to proclaim release to the captives and recovery of sight to the blind, to let the oppressed go free, to proclaim the year of the Lord's favour.' And he rolled up the scroll, gave it back to the attendant, and sat down. The eyes of all in the synagogue were fixed on him. Then he began to say to them, 'Today this scripture has been fulfilled in your hearing.' All spoke well of him and were amazed at the gracious words that came from his mouth. They said, 'Is not this Joseph's son?' (Luke 4.17-22)

Why the theme of liberation? As Jesus understood it, Satan ruled the world. Jesus' ministry was therefore a ministry of setting people free from Satan's rule and the effects of his rule, enabling them to live according to God's rule, which had now begun. Jesus' preaching was part of his liberating ministry. He exposed the values of Satan's rule and proclaimed the values of God's reign. Helping you understand those values is a major purpose of this guidebook.

Jesus was clear that the fight against oppression is a fight against evil. He knew that people were not randomly in desperate circumstances – they were desperately in need because of the forces of evil.

The passage from Isaiah that Jesus chose to read expresses God's abiding will that poverty, captivity and oppression must be overcome. On one of the darkest days of South Africa's history Desmond Tutu also chose this passage of Isaiah 61.1-4 and made this message clear so that there would be no doubt as to the eternal rightness of the struggle for justice:

> Yes, the God Jesus came to proclaim was no neutral sitter on the fence. He took the side of the oppressed, the poor, the exploited, not because they were holier or morally better than their oppressors. No, he was on their side simply and solely because they were oppressed. Yes, this was the good news Jesus came to proclaim – that God was the liberator, the

one who set free the oppressed and the poor and the exploited. He set them free from all that would make them less than he wanted them to be, fully human persons as free as Jesus Christ showed himself to be. And so all the mighty works which Jesus performed, healing the sick, opening the eyes of the blind, forgiving the sins of all sinners, were to set them free so that they could enjoy the glorious liberty of the children of God.[1]

These words were preached on 25th September 1977, at Steve Biko's funeral. He went on to highlight that Jesus was also executed as a result of his ministry against the forces of evil – but that evil could not have the final word because God will not be overcome and thwarted. God will have the final word on what he has stated and started.

The following passages from John's Gospel all point to a similar conclusion, namely, God's reign has come to us in Jesus of Nazareth. He is the one through whom God's presence is real in our lives (which is what Kingdom Consciousness is all about): *'I am the light of the world. Whoever follows me will never walk in darkness but will have the light of life.'* (John 8.12. See also John 4.26; 6.35; 10.36; 8.58-59; 10.7-18; 15.1.)

THE KINGDOM IS 'ALREADY' AND 'NOT YET'

There is an 'already' and a 'not yet' dimension to the reign of God. Jesus ushered in the reign of God – that is the 'already' dimension. But only in the consummation of all things, after the second coming of Jesus, will the reign of God be fully established – that is the 'not yet' dimension.

Jesus' promise of God's reign still to be fully achieved ideally has the effect of motivating us to work towards their achievement. God's promises to us are always meant to be things we work towards, never something we wait lazily for.

The theology of the end times is called 'eschatology'. We say that Jesus practised and taught an inaugurated eschatology. By this term we understand that for Jesus the Kingdom was inaugurated in his ministry and that this would culminate in the fulfilment of the Kingdom in the end times. This is also known as 'realised eschatology'.

Unfortunately the 'not yet' dimension of the Reign of God affects some Christians negatively and they lose faith and commitment. The remedy for this is to ensure that you don't lose sight of all the signs that God's reign has begun. This is what Jesus told John the baptiser to do when the latter's imprisonment

---

[1] Desmond Tutu, *Rainbow People of God: South Africa's victory over apartheid*, p. 18.

was causing him to doubt Jesus as the bringer of God's reign. You can find this event recorded in Luke 7.18-35, but here are a few of the verses:

> *So John summoned two of his disciples and sent them to the Lord to ask, 'Are you the one who is to come, or are we to wait for another?' When the men had come to him, they said, 'John the Baptist has sent us to you to ask, "Are you the one who is to come, or are we to wait for another?"' Jesus had just then cured many people of diseases, plagues, and evil spirits, and had given sight to many who were blind. And he answered them, 'Go and tell John what you have seen and heard: the blind receive their sight, the lame walk, the lepers are cleansed, the deaf hear, the dead are raised, the poor have good news brought to them. And blessed is anyone who takes no offense at me.'*

To have met Jesus was to have met someone who kept prompting people to be more alert and watchful. Many of Jesus' teachings and stories are designed to get people to be vigilant about what is going on around them, and to be watchful for signs and ready for action. Jesus insists on this because the Kingdom has come and people need to be alert enough to see this and to participate in the opportunities that arise. Jesus' references to being ready for the Son of Man are best understood as teaching us to be constantly vigilant for how opportunities to honour Jesus are hidden in the daily challenges of our lives. These teachings are best understood in an 'already and not yet' frame of reference – Jesus is already present, therefore let us be alert as to how to serve his kingdom. Also, Jesus is working towards the full establishment of his reign on earth, therefore let us be alert to how this develops. This theme fills a lot of Jesus' teaching, but I share one section of this teaching with you now: *Therefore you also must be ready, for the Son of Man is coming at an unexpected hour. Who then is the faithful and wise slave, whom his master has put in charge of his household, to give the other slaves their allowance of food at the proper time? Blessed is that slave whom his master will find at work when he arrives. Truly I tell you, he will put that one in charge of all his possessions.* (Matthew 24.44-47. You will get the full impact of this teaching if you read the whole section, namely Matthew 24.36-25.13)

The Reign of God is a possibility whose time has come. It is present as a prospect and possibility in every situation you face. It is present as new life in every context. The reign of God is history-making as it nudges events, through specific choices, to reflect God's purpose for life. The Reign of God is found in all the progress toward goodness, truth and love that is made in the world. The Reign of God has already begun on earth and we are involved with the historical progress towards fulfilment of that Reign. It is profoundly life-giving for each person to grasp their capacity for enabling God's Kingdom to come on earth as it is in heaven. Each person in their sphere of influence can contribute to this progress, in their homes and in their chosen careers and places of work and in the communities in which they live.

Jesus viewed the suffering that is involved with faithfulness to the Kingdom as the *'birth pangs'* (Matthew 24.8, Mark 13.8 and John 16.19-24). This is a powerful paradigm shift! We are invited to view the suffering of discipleship in the same way as a mother views labour pain – a necessary experience to bring life into the world.

When a person chooses for the Kingdom then the 'not yet' dimension of the Kingdom grows as an 'already' dimension in their lives. The future then has a positive impact on the present and choosing for the Kingdom shows that you are fulfilling your purpose in the present.

All our efforts in faithfulness to Jesus' teachings, and through the work of his Spirit, will only bring about the Kingdom in a penultimate way. The ultimate coming of the Kingdom will be what Jesus accomplishes by his own strength and love and in his time and wisdom. But it is clear that we are part of his plan! Jesus is relying on our efforts, even though they can only produce a penultimate realisation of the Kingdom. Jesus is of course personally involved in what we are doing in faithfulness to him. Our willing partnership is an important sign of the times that his Kingdom has come and is on its way to its final culmination.

Our efforts against injustice and evil will not fully realise the Kingdom, but faithfulness to the Kingdom will bring justice and real goodness to this world. We will discover that our efforts against injustice and evil have been all about preparing the way for the full coming and reign of Jesus. We will discover that our witnessing and working for the Kingdom have been 'making the crooked paths straight' in preparation for the coming of the Lord. (See Luke 3.4-6).N.T. Wright has a helpful analogy that I would like to share with you:

> Rather, think of it like this. Jesus is the medical genius who discovered penicillin; we are doctors, ourselves being cured by the medicine, now applying it to those who need it. Jesus is the musical genius who wrote the greatest oratorio of all time; we are the musicians, captivated by his composition ourselves, who now perform it before a world full of muzak and cacophony. The Kingdom did indeed come with Jesus; but it will fully come when the world is healed, when the whole creation finally joins in the song. But it must be Jesus' medicine; it must be Jesus' music.[2]

---

[2] T. Wright, *The Lord and His Prayer*, p. 30.

God's complete unopposed reign is still to come and will be God's accomplishment. Hope is experienced when we live with a daily faith in what God is doing in this world and what we can do for God. This is not a life of wishful sky-gazing, but a life that is true to God's reign. Love is the driving force of the Kingdom Consciousness Movement, just as it was the driving force of Jesus' life. Paul highlights these three characteristics often, the best known occasion being 1 Corinthians 13.13 *'And now faith, hope, and love abide, these three; and the greatest of these is love.'*

THE FOUR RELATIONSHIPS OF LIFE IN THE REIGN OF GOD

In his teaching Jesus is bringing into being an existence of friendship with God, myself, fellow human beings and the environment. The reign of God is that reality where this four-fold friendship exists. Those who live with a Kingdom Consciousness experience God's reign in their lives and in their world. I am true to the Reign of God when I am true to this four-fold friendship. Disciples of Jesus are those who strive for this friendship in the four relationships of life.

This friendship that is love, and is achieved through love, cannot be spoken of in an exaggerated way. Being a Christian does not mean that we become 15% more loving, as if to say that our relationships with other people merely improve. Rather, it means that we are accepting reconciliation in all the relationships of life, and will seek to be true to that reconciled state. Being a Christian puts us into a whole new paradigm of relationships! This new paradigm of reconciliation does not just improve our relationships, it transforms them. Remember Jesus' own passionate prayer before dying is built on the sure knowledge that God's plan for humanity is no less than unity between humanity, Father, Son and Spirit! Jesus prays that we '... *may all be one. As you, Father, are in me and I am in you, may they also be in us, so that the world may believe that you have sent me.*' (John 17.21)

Allow me to make a specific comment on our relationship with our environment now. It has become clear that the current generations have a divine calling on our lives. We need to change the way in which humans live on the planet. The current lifestyle and ways of supporting the lifestyle have brought the environment to the point of collapse. Time is running out fast and if we do not make the changes then future generations will live on an inhospitable planet (and most will not live). Human population will be reduced by natural disaster, disease and competing for resources. In the language of chess, we are in 'check'. If we don't make the right moves the game will be over. It is our responsibility to make the change, turn the tide. Future generations will either be grateful for our courage and tenacity to make the changes that were needed, or they will blame us for not fulfilling this clear divine calling upon us. Jesus' words to us are: *'Hypocrites! You can look at the earth and the sky and predict the weather; why, then, don't you know the meaning of this present time?'* (Luke 12.56)

WHAT DOES 'CHRIST' MEAN?

Every Christian refers to Jesus as the 'Christ'. *Christos* is the Greek word for Messiah – the hoped-for saviour of the Jewish people. What does it mean when we as Gentiles acknowledge Jesus as the Messiah? I believe it means that we celebrate Jesus as the hope of the world. This means that when we invite him into our lives we must change to be conformed to the hope that he offers the world. By accepting him as Messiah we know that he is not just a personal saviour, it means that we know that he is society's saviour too. This is why it is absolutely essential that we take Jesus' teachings on the Reign of God seriously. We must understand them, know them and live them. As Soren Kierkegaard has said, 'Jesus wants followers, not admirers!'

As disciples we will need to show that Jesus' Kingdom way and Kingdom principles give us needed direction in societal problems that didn't even exist in Jesus' day. I am thinking here of the population explosion crisis as probably the most serious, awkward, perplexing, challenging, complicated and awful crisis we face. At the time of Jesus there were an approximate 300 million people in the whole world, compared to the 2017 figure of 7.6 billion. It took the world a few hundred thousand years to reach the population figure of 1 billion, which it did in 1800 AD. By 1930 we reached 2 billion, and less than 100 years later we are fast approaching 8 billion. The crisis is an awful vicious circle of poverty because poverty leads to parents having more children, and then those larger families lead to increased poverty.[3] The bottom line is that we have to find a solution to the problem of poverty. This will require us to apply our best minds, our best co-operation globally, and a full reliance on the Holy Spirit to transform our ways of unsustainable and unjust living.

Jesus' Kingdom values can certainly be likened to the constellation in the night sky by which sailors plotted their course – Jesus' Kingdom values give us the direction we need, they show us where society's solutions are found, if followed they will stop us getting caught on the reef that is now so close. These modern crises that dehumanise so many people and cause so much misery are deep sins, sins which grieve God deeply, sins for which we all need to take responsibility.

Christians who follow Jesus in this way are a minority. They are a remnant, seeking to be truly faithful in today's upside-down world. Please do not underestimate the power of a faithful minority. It continually sows seeds of doubt in the minds of the majority ('maybe they are right', 'they have something I don't have'). This does eventually turn the tide to the right way of living.

This powerful call is summed up in a commissioning moment at the end of the Emmaus week-end experience. The leader says to each pilgrim, 'Christ is counting on you', to which the pilgrim responds, 'And I am counting on him'.

---

[3] Carl Sagan, in *Billions and Billions: Thoughts on Life and Death at the Brink of the Millennium*, wrote: 'There is a well-documented correlation between poverty and high birth rates. In little countries and big countries, capitalist countries and communist countries, Catholic countries and Moslem countries, Western countries and Eastern countries – in almost all these cases, exponential population growth slows down or stops when grinding poverty disappears. This is called demographic transition. It is in the urgent long-term interest of the human species that every place on Earth achieves this demographic transition. This is why helping other countries become self-sufficient is not only elementary human decency, but is also in the interest of those richer nations able to help. One of the central issues in the world population crisis is poverty.' I found this quote in Ian McCallum's *Ecological Intelligence*, Fulcrum Publishing, Cape Town, 2008, p. 227.

THE COST OF DISCIPLESHIP

Following Jesus as the Good Shepherd is a costly choice – this is the true meaning of taking up our cross. In Luke 9.23-26 we read these words, *Then he said to them all, 'If any want to become my followers, let them deny themselves and take up their cross daily and follow me. For those who want to save their life will lose it, and those who lose their life for my sake will save it. What does it profit them if they gain the whole world, but lose or forfeit themselves? Those who are ashamed of me and of my words, of them the Son of Man will be ashamed when he comes in his glory and the glory of the Father and of the holy angels.'*

These chapters on the Kingdom Consciousness Movement have highlighted how God's reign, come in Jesus, is so different from Satan's reign (this world). If I choose to be a disciple of Jesus it will cost me my place in this world, but I gain a place in God's reign. It is worth the cost!

It is clear that the choice to be a disciple of Jesus should include me in the fight against the evil of injustice and oppression. This will put me up against those people and their systems that are determined to cling to their power and privilege and will be ruthless in their defence of what they have and what they still want to gain. Jesus was clear about the cost of discipleship and warned his disciples about the coming persecutions that work for the Kingdom would bring: false accusations, floggings, imprisonment, death threats and betrayal. Jesus was clear that work for the Kingdom was worth even the ultimate sacrifice. Jesus and his disciples had found that the Kingdom was of such a great value and was abundant with so much life, love and hope that it was worth dying for. Their death would seed the growth of the Kingdom and a harvest of the spread of that life, love and hope. Can we be disciples like that?

MEMORISING JESUS' MINISTRY

It is very important that each Christian be able to clearly understand and remember an outline of the teachings of Jesus. It is knowledge that we should have at the tip of our tongue. Your life can be set on the right track by memorising and applying the essence of Jesus' teachings.

Remember, Jesus said that the one who hears his teachings and acts on them is like the wise man who built his house on the rock. Jesus also asserted that those who live by the spirit of his teachings are sheep who have stayed with the shepherd and are part of abundant life forever. To this end I offer the following summary of Jesus' practice and teachings (chapters 6 to 12 of this guidebook) and include a mnemonic of the word VALUE:

In his life and practice Jesus was moved by **Compassion** in all that he did.

He gave two important gifts, **Faith and Forgiveness.**

In his teachings Jesus made God's reign actual through awakening people to Kingdom Consciousness by teaching the *values* of God's reign:

Victory	The reign of God has begun. Are you on the side of victory?
Assets	Sharing of assets is valued rather than greed.
Level	People are valued regardless of their level in society.
Us/them	Love must step across society's boundaries between people.
Energy	Love is the Godly energy and power to save the world.

YOUR KINGDOM LIFESTYLE IS A SIGN THAT YOU ARE PART OF THE SHEPHERD'S FLOCK

Each Christian needs to realise that if they want to be Christlike then they need to like what Christ liked.

The theme throughout this guidebook is: 'Understanding, experiencing and participating in the life that Jesus offers the world'. There is an important link between learning and living, between understanding and participating, between knowledge and practice. Many years ago I came across these words, 'You cannot understand God until you have obeyed Him. The only part of God that you understand is the part that you have obeyed!'[4] The following words of Oswald Chambers make the same point:

> All God's revelations are sealed to us until they are opened to us by obedience. You will never get them open by philosophy or thinking. Immediately you obey, a flash of light comes. Let God's truth work in you by soaking in it, not by worrying into it. Obey God in the thing He is at present showing you, and instantly the next thing is opened up. We read tomes on the work of the Holy Spirit when… five minutes of drastic obedience would make things clear as a sunbeam. We say, 'I suppose I shall understand these things some day.' You can understand them now: it is not study that does it, but obedience. The tiniest fragment of obedience, and heaven opens up and the profoundest truths of God are yours straight away. God will never reveal more truth about Himself till you obey what you know already.[5]

One of the excellent decisions that was made in our transition to the 'new South Africa' was to make a choice for reconciliation rather than a continuation of conflict. Unfortunately our society and so many individuals in our society did not take the next step that true Christian reconciliation required, namely the transformation of our relationships with each other. Those relationships were meant to become characterised by restitution, dignity, equity and justice. The fault here is threefold. Firstly our political and business leaders have not transformed the way in which our economy works so as to benefit social transformation. Secondly, too many privileged individuals who could have personally embraced an ethic of sharing, caring and upliftment of people they know have rather opted for self-protection and profiteering. Thirdly, political and business leaders have stuffed themselves on the multiple opportunities for self-enrichment that have come their way. The result of all of this is that our society has become awfully economically divided and has become a tinderbox of social upheaval.

I hope that this guidebook has made it clear that we followed Jesus' way in choosing reconciliation for our county. I also hope that it is clear that Jesus' values of sharing rather than greed, of people rather than prestige, of a boundary-crossing love and of servanthood combine to bring a Christian to be the kind of person who remains on the journey of reconciliation and all that it means.

---

[4] Source unknown, though it has the ring of Oswald Chambers.
[5] Retrieved from https://utmost.org/classic/whereby-shall-i-know-classic/ on 7/12/2018.

Our choice for reconciliation in South Africa is being blamed for giving too few gains to the need for economic transformation. This is a mistake. It is quite possible that even fewer gains would have been made in a continued situation of conflict. The disciple of Jesus however is led to make sure that reconciliation is not a kind of piety that ignores issues of justice. Disciples of Jesus need to personally involve themselves in transformation in the relationships within their field of influence. If a disciple is in a leadership position in politics or business then that disciple has the enormous privilege of being able to bless many people.

There are many who feel that they cannot make a difference to the problems in society. They forget that because of our inter-connectedness every action we take does have an impact on those around us. Sometimes the impact is small, sometimes it is big. Quantum physics has enabled us to see that the flutter of a butterfly wing in one part of the planet can potentially cause a cyclone in another.[6] Jesus taught about the power in the mustard seed to be a home for many birds. The radiating ripples on a pond when a pebble has been dropped into it display how our actions too radiate out and touch those around us. John Wesley had a lovely proverb, 'God is so great, that He communicates greatness to the least thing that is done for His service.'

There is a powerful story that has become precious to us in South Africa about how the lives of many people in our nation and even the world were changed for the better by the simple act of a white priest lifting his hat in courtesy to a black woman in the 1940s. The man was Rev. Trevor Huddleston, who was a priest in Sophiatown. The woman was Aletta Tutu and standing next to her was her nine-year-old son, Desmond. Desmond Tutu, who like Huddleston became an archbishop, has often said that that moment changed his life in the way it made him aware of God's Kingdom. He saw a lived example of the truth that God's Kingdom people have a way of relating to each other that is different to the way of the world. That moment became one of the seeds that produced the fruit that Desmond Tutu has been for us in South Africa and the world.

---

[6] Quantum physics is so deeply aware of inter-connectedness that it asserts that in investigating the causes of a cyclone you need to factor in the butterfly wings beating on the other side of the world!

SUGGESTIONS FOR DISCUSSION, REVISION, REFLECTION AND APPLICATION

(These questions are intended for group work, but can easily be adapted for personal use.)

1. What is the most important message to you in this chapter? (Remember to also make a note of this on your 'God spoke to me' page.)
2. Icebreaker question: What do you have no talent for? (The question must be answered quickly. As a group, do not spend longer than 5 minutes in total on this question.)
3. Read Luke 4.16-22 and answer the following questions:
    a. What kinds of things were Jewish people looking forward to when they read this passage from Isaiah?
    b. Discuss the meaning of each of the phrases in Isaiah's prophesy. What do these promises tell us about God's intentions in relation to people?
    c. Try and imagine the impact of Jesus, a new rabbi with a real gravitas, saying that in their hearing the scripture of Isaiah has been fulfilled! What were the feelings? Thoughts?
    d. How does the ascended Jesus attempt to fulfil this prophesy today? Or, did the prophesy only apply to Jesus of Nazareth's earthly ministry?
    e. What can a passage about the fulfilment of this prophesy mean for us today? What are our thoughts? Feelings?
    f. In what way can we participate in Jesus' desire to fulfil this passage now?
4. Below are a variety of suggestions and questions to aid your appreciation of this chapter. Do not attempt to do all of them! Choose those that are most appropriate to your unique situation and/or group. The questions are designed to help variously with revision, understanding, appreciation, reflection or application of the content.
    a. Do you really believe that God's reign has begun? What difference should such a belief make to your life?
    b. Do you properly understand the 'already and not yet' theology? Discuss any struggles you have.
    c. What would you want to say to someone who says 'Be realistic! The Kingdom of God has not yet begun.'

d. How do you respond to Kierkegaard's belief that 'Jesus wants followers, not admirers'?
   i. Does this disturb you? Explain?
   ii. Does this inspire you? Why?
e. What is the most difficult price for you to pay to be a follower of Jesus?
f. In the light of the discussions and reflections so far, respond to the statement, 'Do what you can, with what you've got, where you are' (Theodore Roosevelt). Does this challenge you to 'do what you can'? What specific activities are you challenged to do? Invite the members of the group to hold you accountable to doing these activities.
g. Take time to memorise the section entitled 'Memorising Jesus' ministry'. Test each other's ability to recall and explain the overall content of Jesus' ministry.

GOD SPOKE TO ME ...

14

JESUS' DEATH AND RESURRECTION

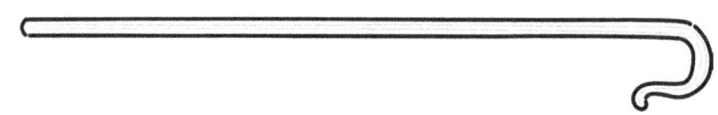

For in him all the fullness of God was pleased to dwell, and through him God was pleased to reconcile to himself all things, whether on earth or in heaven, by making peace through the blood of his cross. (Colossians 1.19-20)

We have been deeply blessed in our journey through these chapters in which we have unpacked the practice and teachings of Jesus' ministry. What a special journey it has been!

The religious authorities became increasingly opposed to Jesus and so he faced a growing threat. It is very important for us to understand how Jesus responded to this threat and why he responded in the way he did. The significance of his death is found in this.

JESUS' DEATH – SEALING GOD'S FRIENDSHIP WITH HUMANITY

'Jesus died for my sins' is an expression of mere sentiment for many Christians. The sense for them is that Jesus' death was about them and for them as individuals. This has the very unfortunate effect of taking Jesus' death out of its original context and making it a personal matter. Jesus' death does have personal significance for everyone but it is essential for us to appreciate the actual meaning of his death when it happened, if we are to appreciate its full and eternal meaning. Its meaning *in time* is linked with its meaning *for all time*. Its meaning in the context then is linked with its meaning for other contexts.

The expression, 'Jesus died for my sins', often betrays that we have missed the all-inclusive Kingdom ministry of Jesus and what immediately preceded his crucifixion. 'Jesus died for *my* sins' is most likely an expression of someone who has skipped over what happened then and has made Jesus' death only relevant to their life now – even though they are talking about what happened then, namely Jesus' death by crucifixion. This section is dedicated to helping you to see Jesus' death in context.

The reality of friendship (communion, union, reconciliation) with God that Jesus established in his birth and ministry is not a theological interpretation of Jesus' ministry that was noticed after the event. On the contrary, the religious authorities noticed it as it was happening and opposed it in increasingly determined ways. The religious leaders noticed Jesus' own friendship with sinners and how he offered God's friendship to them and they were appalled and judged it to be blasphemy.

Jesus was not left to carry on his ministry unhindered but faced increasingly hostile opposition. His response to this opposition was crucial, for it would either make or break the friendship that he had established. If Jesus turned his back on the sinners then the friendship he had established would be broken. If Jesus persisted in his friendship, even at the cost of his life, then that friendship would be sealed.

Let us first understand the religious opposition to Jesus that was mainly led by the Pharisees and Scribes.[1] The core of their objection was that Jesus accepted sinners as his friends, that he did this in God's name and that he claimed to have a special relationship with God. This meant that he believed that God accepted them in this way too. Jesus was asserting himself as a friend of God and a friend of sinners. For the religious rulers of the day the two could not go together; a friend of God would have to be an enemy of sinners. Their expectation was that the Messiah would destroy God's enemies and reward the righteous. The Pharisees expected that they would be amongst those rewarded. Instead Jesus befriended sinners, proclaimed God's forgiveness upon them and offered them the blessings of God's Kingdom. Jesus was also judged to have an impious attitude toward the law. These were the combined reasons for the religious leaders judging Jesus to be a blasphemer. The religious penalty for blasphemy was death.

Secondly, let us understand the political opposition to Jesus that was led by the Sadducees, Chief Priests, Herodians and officials of the Roman Empire. Jesus' acceptance of the Messiah status and title also meant that he was a political threat in the Roman Empire. Jesus proclaimed a Kingdom in which Yahweh ruled. Roman rulers did not hesitate to execute opponents of their rule. Jesus also posed a political threat to the religious leaders who benefited politically from Roman rule. This was mainly the High Priest and his extended family (they were appointed by Rome) and the Sadducees (who were the ruling upper class and benefited from the status quo). It is this political coalition that is referred to as 'The Jews'[2] in John's Gospel. Rome expected the religious rulers to 'keep the peace' amongst Jewish devotees if they wished to continue to have religious freedom at the temple. The stir that Jesus had created, especially at the temple, caused a significant political problem for the Jewish religious leaders.

This opposition to Jesus became so fierce that death was inevitable if he continued with his ministry. For Jesus this meant making a choice, to either die for God's love for all humanity, or compromise this love and save his own life. Jesus' response was to be faithful to his love, God's love, for all. He chose to be faithful and bear the consequences of that faithfulness. Jesus chose to continue

---

[1] These Pharisees and Scribes would have mainly belonged to the 'House of Shammai', who was an influential conservative, exclusivist and strict religious scholar of the time.

[2] John 9.22 *(The blind man's) parents said this because they were afraid of the Jews; for the Jews had already agreed that anyone who confessed Jesus to be the Messiah would be put out of the synagogue.* Here are ordinary Jews afraid of 'the Jews' who clearly are a group in authority at the synagogue. See also John 7.13, 19.38 and 20.19 for other references to Jews fearing 'the Jews'. Therefore when we read that 'the Jews' called for the execution of Jesus we must not think of all Jews, or even a majority of Jews, demanding Jesus' death, but rather realise that a small ruling elite are being referred to.

with his ministry of love expressed in his friendships, teaching and healings, in spite of opposition. Someone coined a phrase that sums up Jesus' attitude towards his opponents – *'You can take my life but you can't take my love!'* Nothing could cause him to let go or betray his love, God's love, for people. Jesus came to view his inevitable death as the price he had to pay for his love of humanity.

E. Stanley Jones, speaking of Jesus' execution on the cross, writes, 'It was not an accidental, marginal type of happening; it grew out of the nature of the facts. It had to happen. For it is a law of life that where love meets sin in the loved one, at the junction of that sin and that love, a cross of pain is set up.'[3]

We have seen how Jesus' birth and ministry re-established unity, community and friendship between God and humanity. Because Jesus died rather than betray this friendship, he succeeded in sealing it forever. By laying down his life he succeeded in blazing a trail of reconciliation between God and humanity, a trail that all people of all times could benefit from.

It may be helpful to see the effects of Jesus' birth, ministry and death in the light of the metaphor of trail blazing. I have had the privilege of building a path up Houw Hoek peak in the Overberg with a retired Baptist pastor, Gerald McCann. We started by attaching flags to the vegetation along the route of the intended path. This was followed with a special herbicide spray that is used to kill the vegetation in a strip about 25 cm wide. We then had to spend many hours over many months with spades and picks to remove the vegetation from that strip. Once this was done, the path had been truly blazed and could be easily followed. It was wonderful to then take family and friends up this towering peak through the particularly abundant fynbos of that area. Jesus' birth could be likened to flagging the route, his ministry and death could be likened to making the path clear for all to follow. A pathway between God and humanity has been opened up by Jesus for all to walk on.

Jesus took the burden sinful human beings imposed on him, died under that burden, and never broke community with us. The burden placed on him by sinful rulers was the excruciating and sadistic death by crucifixion. Jesus accepted that burden. The only way to avoid the burden would have been to capitulate to the demands of the religious and political rulers. Jesus chose rather to honour the love bond between God and humanity. Jesus gives his life as the price he has to pay for this love bond. Jesus gives his life to protect the forgiveness that God has offered humanity in his birth and ministry. Jesus chose to honour the reality of God's reign which was the re-established friendship between people and God.

---

[3] E. Stanley Jones, *Abundant Living*, Hodder and Stoughton, p. 369.

Because Jesus never broke community with us, that community between God and humanity is sealed forever. The saving significance of Jesus' death is that he endured it as the price for being true to his love for sinful humanity. He died in order to preserve the unity with sinful humanity that he established with his incarnation and lived out in his life. His death therefore saved that unity forever.

Jesus' death on the cross is not his defeat at all. His death on the cross is his victory! He has reached the finish line with complete faithfulness, having established and preserved unity with God as a reality available to all. The cross is the victory of God's love for humanity. This is a very special victory over the forces of evil and sin that separate us from God. If Jesus had betrayed his love for humanity then the threat of crucifixion would have been victorious. But because he does not recoil in the face of the threat, he is victorious.

We are saved by the fact that Jesus' love was not defeated. We are saved by the fact that he endured death as a price he had to pay for his love of sinful humanity. Jesus' death therefore seals humanity's friendship with God that was re-established in his birth and deepened in his ministry.[4]

---

[4] Please look at the following texts that present these dynamics surrounding Jesus' death: Mark 3.1-6; Luke 20.9-19; Matthew 11.19; Matthew 13.57; Luke 13.33; John 10.30-38; John 14.9; John 5.18; Mark 8.29-30; Mark 2.6-7; John 9.29; John 1.46-51; John 6.15; Luke 19.38-40; Luke 16.14; Matthew 20.16; Matthew 12.1-14; John 11.45-57; Mark 10.45; Matthew 20.28; John 12.23-31.

THE RESURRECTION – DEMONSTRATION OF THE FRIENDSHIP IN THE FOUR RELATIONSHIPS OF LIFE[5]

In chapter 12 we saw how Jesus taught that loving service is the most powerful force in the world. In the previous section we saw that Jesus gave his life as an act of loving service. Jesus lovingly gave his life in the face of hate from his opponents. He had acquired the force to commit that supreme act through many accumulated acts of loving service during his lifetime. His ability to love so powerfully came from the empowering effects of his daily acts of loving service.

Because of the real power of loving service, a beautiful discovery is made on the third day after his death. The followers of Jesus discover that the force of Jesus' love is so strong that not even death could maintain a hold on him. A loving life rose victorious over a hateful execution. Like a buried seed sprouting to life, Jesus burst forth very much alive from the tomb. The followers of Jesus found him absent from the tomb and then encountered him alive and well and ministering again!

It has become clear that Jesus died in order to preserve and seal the bond of unity between God and humanity that he had re-established in his birth and ministry. You should remember that sin's nature is to divide, and destroy that which it divides. The execution of Jesus was therefore sin's final attempt to divide and destroy the love bond between God and humanity that Jesus had re-established. Fortunately for us it failed because of Jesus' powerful love.

One could think of a number of factors that make Jesus' death a victory rather than a defeat. Firstly, evil failed because Jesus died rather than betray the love bond. Evil is only victorious over good when it succeeds in getting the good person to do evil. If the good person remains good and is even prepared to die rather than do evil, then the good person is victorious over evil. Evil could only have been victorious if Jesus had turned from love, or been unprepared to pay the price for love, or if he had betrayed his love for humanity. Jesus' faithfulness ensured that division does not come into the love bond.

Secondly, evil failed because Jesus comes back from death to this world that had rejected him in such an ultimate way. That return was a great act of forgiveness, and therefore an act of love, and therefore a demonstration that the love was not defeated in death. It demonstrates that love is more powerful than hate.

Thirdly, Jesus' resurrection proves sin's arrogance wrong. Sin thought that it could hold Jesus, the author of life, in death's clutches, but was proved radically wrong by the resurrection.

---

[5] Please look at the following texts that present these aspects of Jesus' resurrection: Matthew 28; Mark 16; Luke 24; John 20-21.

The resurrection is therefore a glorious demonstration to the whole world that sin has no power to break the love bond of friendship between God and humanity!

Jesus' ministry during his resurrection appearances powerfully demonstrated the victorious nature of the re-established friendship in the other three relationships of life too:

- ***Friendship with self*** – Jesus' ministry during that time furthered the work of enabling people to be set free from sin and allow all their faculties to be pressed into the service of love (e.g. Peter's reinstatement in John 21.15-19).
- ***Friendship between people*** – Jesus' commissioning of his followers furthered the work of uniting them to be a community of people serving God's loving purposes in this world (e.g. Matthew 28.16-20; Mark 16.15-18; Luke 24.44-49; John 20.21-23; Acts 1.8).
- ***Friendship with the environment*** – The fact that Jesus did have a body after his resurrection,[6] that he was not just a soul or spirit, is a remarkable message about the value of the human body. Appreciate that Jesus in his resurrection takes on created form again. If matter (creation) was not important then Jesus would have appeared in a non-material way. In this incarnated state after the resurrection Jesus is showing a profound oneness with creation. He is showing that God has not turned his back on the created world even though it has rebelled. He is showing that we should not turn our back on the created world. He did not turn his back on creation and nor should we. Jesus returned as a friend to his body. He shows the importance of our own friendship with our body, creation and environment.

This really does lead us to believe that God does not want to destroy his creation, in spite of humanity's sinfulness. God's desire is for creation's original purpose to be fulfilled. Jesus' resurrection affirms the value of all creation. This sends a clear message to humanity to value and care for all creation, and to live in such a way as to ensure its healthy future.

Later in this chapter and in the chapters on the Holy Spirit I will say more about the resurrection life that we may all enjoy because of what Jesus has done. The term 'resurrection life' is a favourite term of the Apostle Paul to describe the Christian life. Jesus' resurrection completes his work of making reconciliation a reality in the four relationships of life. This state of reconciliation is available

---

[6] Jesus' resurrected body was a body that was not bound by time and space, but was a body nonetheless. It is believed that our resurrected bodies will be the same kind of bodies. I believe that those who die united to Christ by the Holy Spirit will receive this resurrected body at their death.

to all. Those who enjoy the resurrection life enjoy friendship in the four relationships of life.

The resurrection life is the life of the fullness of salvation. Through relationship with Jesus a human life may be transformed completely by the Spirit of Love. It is a life in which there is no obstacle to union with God, others, self or environment. It is the life that is meant to be the ultimate reality for every human being!

FURTHER EFFECTS OF JESUS' RESURRECTION ON THE WORLD TODAY

> *We know that all things work together for good for those who love God, who are called according to his purpose.* (Romans 8.28)

It is very empowering for Christians to realise that the power of Jesus' resurrection continues in the world today. Ever since his resurrection there is a power active in the world which, if participated in, will bring good from bad, love from hate, victory from failure, strength and insights from adversity, endurance from trials, a new life after the collapse of the old, wholeness after illness and life after death.

Jesus' resurrection power means that death, and the forces of death, need not have the last word. Until the second coming and the final culmination of all things, bad things will still happen to us all, but the resurrection power says that good can come from bad. In fact Jesus' resurrection empowers us to fight the bad in the world.

A faithful act done as a disciple of Jesus is significant even if it is done in the face of enormous odds or evil. God's resurrection power can bring fruit from every seed sown. As my late friend Sello Pelesane said, 'If God be God, his love cannot fail.'[7]

The power of God that was evidenced in Jesus' birth, ministry, death and resurrection is clearly more powerful than the forces of evil. The resurrection therefore assures us that victory ultimately belongs to God. The decisive battle was won by Jesus and it is only a matter of time before evil will be completely vanquished.

> *For we know that if the earthly tent we live in is destroyed, we have a building from God, a house not made with hands, eternal in the heavens.*
> (2 Corinthians 5.1)

The resurrection of Jesus also means that I may look forward to death as a new personal beginning for my life. Scripture teaches me that there is a blessed life for God's children beyond this life. Death really is the end of one chapter of my life and the beginning of another chapter. I personally live on after my body has died; I live on in God's presence, in a dwelling he has prepared for me, with a resurrected body that he has given me. This is wonderful news for all of us, but particularly meaningful for those who suffer so much in this life.[8]

> *'Look at my hands and my feet; see that it is I myself. Touch me and see; for a ghost does not have flesh and bones as you see that I have.'* (Luke 24.39)

There was something definitely bodily about Jesus after the resurrection: Jesus was not a ghost (Luke 24.37); he could be touched (Luke 24.39; John 20.27); he could eat (Luke 24.42-43; John 21.13-15). His body was however different from what it had been before his resurrection. The Gospels tell us that Jesus went through walls and locked doors (John 20.26); he disappeared at will (Luke 24.31); he was able to now be with his disciples everywhere and at all times (Matthew 28.20); he was only seen or recognised when he allowed it to happen (Luke 24.31; John 20.15-16; Mark 16.12; John 21.12).

---

[7] This was the theme of his Easter Weekend programme in the year 2004.

[8] 2 Corinthians 5.1-10 and 1 Corinthians 15.35-58 are special passages to read in helping us grasp life after death and the resurrection of our own bodies.

What the records show us is that the resurrected Jesus was human, but now with a transformed human body. The ascension of Jesus brought an end to his appearances but he continues to have this transformed human body, now in heaven. This means that Jesus did not, after his death and resurrection, simply 'go back to being God' – no, he is risen as a human being and as such is forever part of the Trinity. Jesus, the man with human and divine natures, is part of God and part of this world forever!

BE FAITHFUL TO THE GOD REVEALED IN JESUS

We have been on a detailed journey together of appreciating the meaning and significance of Jesus' birth, ministry, death and resurrection. This journey has occupied us for most of this guidebook and I hope you have found it inspirational, informative and transformative.

I invite you now to step back from the detail and think about the overall understanding you have of God and also of why Jesus died. People have many different ideas on these two important matters. You and I need to make up our own minds. I hope to be helpful to you by offering you a way of filtering good ideas from less good ideas.

Seeing the melody

When I was a child one of my favourite imagination games was to be a conductor – perhaps you enjoyed this too. I would use a chopstick and imitate the gesticulations of the conductor of a mighty orchestra performing a dramatic overture, something like Tchaikovsky's 1812, the one with the cannon blasts. At that age I loved the sense of the conductor's power, this man who could make music just by waving his arms.

I'm also amazed by the genius of the composer – a genius that is at once both intimate and expansive. The composer carries in her mind and heart the full expanse of the sound she seeks to produce. But she's also able to zoom in and write each note for each instrument. The composer knows each part intimately and carries the hope that if each part is fulfilled at the right time then the mystery of her composition will be revealed. The composer is the genius who is the source of it all. Surely we know what the composer is like from the composition, for it is a loving act of creative self-expression. It is clear to see how the composer's art is so similar to the work of our Creator God and that creation is a testimony to God's intimate and expansive genius.

Now that I'm grown up I still enjoy imitating conductors. Most recently a performance of Karl Jenkins' *The Armed Man: A Mass for Peace*, under the baton of Alexander Fokkens, left me spellbound. Our daughter was in the choir, so we purchased the video recording and I have been able to watch the performance a few times.

What impresses me powerfully now is the way in which the conductor embodies the drama, mood and meaning of the music being performed. Through his facial expressions, posture, arm movements and gestures he becomes the bodily expression of the music. As the score changes so his dramatic personification changes, helping the choir and orchestra to perform with one voice. It's so impressive to see him succeed in each moment to be the sum of all the parts of the performance – to represent in his body the moment by moment meaning of the whole. In his dramatic way the conductor says it all, enabling each part of the orchestra and choir to do what it needs to do with just the right timing, volume, mood and meaning.

The audience sees very little of what the conductor is doing because his back is turned to them – even though his goal is to please the audience. But on the video of my daughter's concert I can watch him, moment by moment. A curl of his mouth, a hunch of his shoulders, a swing of his arm, a rise on his toes or a flick of his fingers – all draw forth the magical music.

And gratitude! At times his face winks with gratitude for the performers, a face that no doubt launches their thousand efforts. When it's all over he gently blows them a kiss whilst the air sparkles with the not yet expressed delight in a powerful composition performed with passion and skill. As the conductor turns to the audience, the spell on us is broken and we leap to our feet in noisy gratitude.

Each time I witness such a performance I am deeply moved by crosscurrents of emotion and meaning that surge up in my being and splash down my cheeks. Then all of a sudden I sense a deeper meaning, no doubt there all the time, awaiting recognition – that Jesus was like a conductor who impressively embodied the great meaning of life. This was Jesus' great achievement and this is what I love so much about him.

In Jesus I have a conductor who gives dramatic and visible expression to the meaning of life. I love to see the way he gave daily bodily expression to love, beauty, truth, faith, compassion and so much more. In his daily decisions, routines, disciplines, reactions, gestures, teachings, deeds and so much more he embodied the perfect expression of the Creator's will and character. Jesus comes closer than anyone ever has or ever will to personify the sum of all parts of life. The great melody of life seems to be visible in his living of it. Indeed Jesus says it all, enabling me to play my small part of the 'all' as I seek to follow him faithfully.

Jesus as the revelation of God

The first writers to reflect on the meaning and significance of Jesus' birth, ministry, death and resurrection were convinced that the Jesus event should change the way we look at life. In other words they completely adopted a Kingdom Consciousness. In this Kingdom Consciousness they saw that Jesus established the Kingdom and achieved reconciliation in the four relationships of life. They also believed that Jesus revealed the nature of God to us.

This world-changing perspective is presented in very beautiful ways by the New Testament writers. Let me share a few of the passages with you:

Ephesians 1.3-10: *Blessed be the God and Father of our Lord Jesus Christ, who has blessed us in Christ with every spiritual blessing in the heavenly places... In him we have redemption through his blood, the forgiveness of our trespasses, according to the riches of his grace that he lavished on us. With all wisdom and insight he has made known to us the mystery of his will, according to his good pleasure that he set forth in Christ, as a plan for the fullness of time, to gather up all things in him, things in heaven and things on earth.*

Hebrews 1.1-4: *Long ago God spoke to our ancestors in many and various ways by the prophets, but in these last days he has spoken to us by a Son, whom he appointed heir of all things, through whom he also created the worlds. He is the reflection of God's glory and the exact imprint of God's very being, and he sustains all things by his powerful word. When he had made purification for sins, he sat down at the right hand of the Majesty on high, having become as much superior to angels as the name he has inherited is more excellent than theirs.*

Colossians 1.17-20: *He is the image of the invisible God, the firstborn of all creation; for in him all things in heaven and on earth were created, things visible and invisible, whether thrones or dominions or rulers or powers—all things have been created through him and for him. He himself is before all things, and in him all things hold together. He is the head of the body, the church; he is the beginning, the firstborn from the dead, so that he might come to have first place in everything. For in him all the fullness of God was pleased to dwell, and through him God was pleased to reconcile to himself all things, whether on earth or in heaven, by making peace through the blood of his cross.*

> John 1.14-18: *And the Word became flesh and lived among us, and we have seen his glory, the glory as of a father's only son, full of grace and truth. (John testified to him and cried out, 'This was he of whom I said, "He who comes after me ranks ahead of me because he was before me."') From his fullness we have all received, grace upon grace. The law indeed was given through Moses; grace and truth came through Jesus Christ. No one has ever seen God. It is God the only Son, who is close to the Father's heart, who has made him known.'*

> 2 Corinthians 3.14-16 *describes how only in turning to Jesus is the veil of misunderstanding removed when reading scripture. But their minds were hardened. Indeed, to this very day, when they hear the reading of the old covenant, that same veil is still there, since only in Christ is it set aside. Indeed, to this very day whenever Moses is read, a veil lies over their minds; but when one turns to the Lord, the veil is removed.*

Simply put: Jesus the Christ reveals God, God's will and fulfils God's will. Jesus is God come to us. Jesus is God's action in the world. Jesus is God's response to sin, evil and death in the world. As Christians we are followers of Christ, we are those who have faith in him. This means that he determines our understanding of God and God's will.

Reading scripture with Jesus as the lens

This guidebook has enabled us to understand Jesus and his witness. It is clear that Jesus reveals to us a God of love and compassion. It is also clear that God is prepared to suffer personally for the love that he has for humanity. He always resisted the temptation to retaliate, injure or even curse a person. Jesus' own suffering is not punishment for sin; rather it is the consequence of remaining loving in a sinful world. William Barclay puts it this way: 'the Cross was a window in time allowing us to see the suffering love which is eternally in the heart of God'.[9] It is precisely through this loving gift of his life that Jesus conquers sin, evil and death in the world.

On this important theme of Jesus revealing God to us, Carlo Carretto wrote these powerful words:

> That God is beautiful is no secret. It is written on every flower, on the sea and on the mountains. That God is immense is no secret. All

---

[9] William Barclay, in *Acts of the Apostles*, p. 27, is commenting on Peter's sermon on Pentecost. It is important to note that this theme, of the love of God shown in Jesus, is central to all of the sermons of the early church, found in sermons of Acts.

you have to do is look at the universe ... What is the secret? Here it is: God is a crucified God. God is the God who allows Himself to be defeated; God is the God who has revealed Himself in the poor. God is the God who has washed my feet; God is Jesus of Nazareth. We are not accustomed to a God like this.

This has a few implications that are essential for 'finding the Shepherd we lost'. Every revelation, including the Bible, should be understood through Jesus, who is himself the mystery of God's will revealed. Jesus becomes the lens of the spectacles we use to understand God and scripture.

Practically this means that when we read the Bible we allow the revelation of Jesus to be the criterion and filter for everything we read. If something is contradictory to Jesus' revelation then we cannot allow it to have equal authority in our lives or to replace what we know about God from Jesus. Contradictory messages need to be somehow interpreted through what we have come to understand from Jesus.

I should never hold onto a belief that is contrary to the revelation of Jesus, even if I can find scriptural support for my belief. I should never believe something about God that cannot be consistent with the God revealed in Jesus.

Would Jesus kill a person? Would Jesus require the death of a person for any purpose? Would Jesus kill millions of people? Would Jesus give a person a disease? Would Jesus cripple a person? Does Jesus seek revenge? His birth, ministry, death and resurrection together chorus NO. Rather, they sing the sacrificial song of a God of love who would suffer rather than cause suffering, be harmed rather than cause harm.

IDEAS OF THE ATONEMENT

'Ideas of the atonement' refers to the ideas, doctrines, theories, themes and motifs that Christians have about how we are reconciled to God through Jesus. Your own idea of the atonement will have an impact on every aspect of your relationship with Jesus and of the living of your life. It is one of those ideas that we carry that will give a certain flavour to everything else in our lives. I invite you to spend the next few minutes thinking about your view of the atonement and to particularly think about it in the light of all that Jesus reveals to us about God.

I believe that it should be beyond dispute that our idea of the atonement should be as faithful as possible to the essential meaning and drama of Jesus' historical birth, ministry, death and resurrection.

To help you in your thinking I offer you very simple summaries of the main ideas of the atonement. The ideas here are the four main ways in which Christians have understood the saving work of Jesus' death. The view you hold will fit under the umbrella of one of these views. It might not fit exactly, but these four descriptions should help you see where your idea of the atonement fits within the theology of Christianity.[10] I believe this theme is so important that I have developed it more fully in an essay that interested readers will find at the end of the book (see Appendix 1).

Classic Idea

God created humanity to enjoy life in all its fullness and to experience a good relationship with God, other people, all creation and ourselves. God is determined to fulfil this intention in spite of sin and evil that have robbed humanity of it. God's love and power will not be thwarted. So God comes to us in Jesus who is full of the love and power of God and he personally has victory over sin, evil and death. Jesus gives his Spirit to us so that the battle against sin, evil and death may continue until its final culmination, which will be the

---

[10] These ideas have variations in the way in which they are described by different theological perspectives. There is no doubt however that they can be grouped and summarised as I have done.

Jesus' death and resurrection

full establishment of God's reign. Jesus' resurrection is a manifestation of this decisive victory over the powers of evil that was won on the cross. Those who place their faith in Jesus receive this reconciliation from God and are released from the hold of sin, death and evil.

This is called the 'Classic Idea' because it is the standard idea of the New Testament, the early church and the church of the Patristic period. In fact this idea was the favoured idea for the whole Christian world for the first thousand years of Christianity.[11]

---

[11] The New Testament is a continuous description of this theme. It is best to just open your New Testament and read and notice it. If you would like to be pointed to specific places you could look for example at: Matthew 12.22-30; Luke 10.17-20; Mark 15.39; John 16.25-33; Acts 2.22-41; Acts 13.16-39; Romans 6.1-11; Romans 8.1-4; Romans 8.31-39; 2 Timothy 1.8-14; 1 John 5.1-12; 1 Corinthians 15; Colossians 2.15; Revelation 17.14; Revelation 19.11-21.

Penal Substitution idea

God loves us so much that he sent his Son to be the sinless human and then be executed as the sacrifice for our sins. In this way God has paid the price for our forgiveness and we may escape the punishment due to us. Through receiving Jesus into my life I receive the forgiveness of sins because he has paid the price for me.

The foundational paradigm for this Penal Substitution idea is found in the Old Testament sacrificial system in which prescribed sacrifices are made by people to God to give God the honour that is due to him. There are seeds of the idea in the New Testament although it is not nearly as pervasive there as the Classic Idea.[12] This idea has dominated Western Christianity's view of the atonement since the 11th Century.

---

[12] The main New Testament passages believed to share this motif are: 2 Corinthians 5.21; 1 Peter 2.24; Galatians 3.13; Colossians 2.14 and Romans 3.24-26. These passages do not all necessarily need the Penal Substitution idea for them to make sense. For example, the very next verse after Colossians 2.14, namely verse 15, is a concise description of Jesus' victory over earthly and spiritual evil powers and is thus a testimony to the pervasive scriptural witness to what became the Classic Idea.

Ransom

Humanity is held captive by the devil because of our sin and God wants to free us. Jesus is given to the devil, in his death, as a ransom price to set us free. However Jesus rose from the dead and thereby escaped from the devil. In this way the devil lost both humanity and his ransom price. Through this ransom we are released from servitude to the law and from sin and we now belong to God.

The idea of ransom has its foundation in both Old and New Testament metaphors of God at work to save humanity and make us his own people again.[13]

Subjective idea

The problem with sin is that it diminishes the abundant life God desires for us. So Jesus comes to lead us into that abundant life of joy. God has sent his Son to demonstrate God's love, to be an example of how to live and to lead us out of our ignorance. Jesus does this by being a teacher and by being the supreme example of an abundant loving life. In this way Jesus saves us through the effect he has on us. When we look at the cross and see God's incredible love for us

---

[13] See Matthew 20.28, Mark 10.45, 1 Timothy 2.6.

we are drawn into a relationship with God. Our response to Jesus leads to our sins being forgiven and us being reconciled to God. Jesus' death is a seal on his teaching and the supreme example of the love of God. Jesus' death saves us through the influence it has on us.

This Subjective idea was developed in the 11th Century in opposition to the Penal Substitution idea, but it only gained popularity during the Enlightenment of the 18th and 19th Century.

Which idea of the Atonement is more faithful to the God revealed in Jesus?

How do you think you are reconciled to God by Jesus? Your answer will be aligned to one of the ideas of the atonement I have described above. Although all of these ideas have a Biblical foundation I invite you to make the following question the core question for your own review of your view: 'Which idea of the Atonement is more faithful to the God revealed in Jesus?'

All of the views have value and all of them are in some way part of our understanding of the meaning of Jesus' saving work. This guidebook is closely aligned to the Classic Idea of the atonement. In other words, I believe that the Classic Idea is more faithful to the meaning and drama of Jesus' birth, ministry, death and resurrection. Please read Appendix 1 for a more detailed assessment of each of the views.

DEVELOPING YOUR PICTURE OF GOD – THE FIRST THREE MONTHS OF A LIFE-LONG JOURNEY

Essentially I have been saying that Jesus is our picture of God. It is important for each follower of Jesus to ensure that they keep working on their picture of God and that their picture of God be in tune with the revelation of God in Jesus. This is an essential part of staying close to Jesus our Shepherd.

Our picture of God will inform what kind of a Christian we are. If we have a Christ-like picture of God then we will become Christ-like. If we have an inaccurate picture of God, then we will miss the mark in our Christian witness.

Trevor Hudson highlights some of the commonly held views of God together with the usual negative consequences of those views:

> Those who view God as an impersonal force tend towards a cold and vague relationship with Him. Those who see God as a heavenly tyrant, intent upon hammering anyone who wanders outside His laws, seldom abandon themselves with joy to the purposes of His kingdom. Those who imagine God to be a scrupulous book-keeper, determined to maintain up-to-date accounts of every personal sin and shortcoming, rarely acknowledge their inner contradictions and struggles in His presence. Those who regard God as a divine candy-machine (just say a prayer and you can get what you want) inevitably end up in disillusionment.[14]

We all have pictures of God that are to varying degrees not in keeping with his self-disclosure in Jesus. Re-drawing our picture is part of our journey as disciples. This is essentially not a theological exercise but the development of your personal relationship with Jesus.

It has become clear in this guidebook that the Gospels were written so that you can get to know Jesus well. Here is a suggestion that can help you to appreciate this purpose of the Gospels: for the next three months, set time aside each day to read a portion from Matthew, Mark, Luke or John. Journey through your chosen gospel from beginning to end, perhaps reading no more than about ten verses a day. As you read, be conscientious about keeping company with Jesus and getting to know him. Try to understand his feelings, his teachings and his power; why he does what he does, why he responds the way he does to people and situations. Try and work out Jesus' own logic and intuitions. Get to know his insights and priorities. Observe his values and motives. Think about

---

[14] *Signposts to Spirituality*, p. 21.

what all this means to you in your life. This exercise is suggested in Trevor Hudson's book, *Signposts to Spirituality*. He tells us what will be the effect of this exercise: 'As we follow Jesus through the pages of the Gospels we are reminded of what God is like and how we can live in partnership with Him. Upon this memory the Holy Spirit acts, causing Jesus to become for us a living presence and making us mindful of His wishes for our daily lives.'[15]

This is such a precious exercise that I encourage you to do it at least once a year, using a different Gospel each time.

You will be transformed by the picture

I remember when our son, Luke, started to play a new piece of music on the piano. He was about 12 at the time. I love listening to our children practise musical instruments in the home because I love the sound of live music, even if the tune is still being learned. I was in my study working as I listened to him repeatedly try the new piece of music, but as much as he practised I could not hear the tune. A few days later he was practising again and I could still not detect the tune. The same happened a few days later. Perplexed, I walked past the piano to see what piece it was – to my surprise it was 'The Can-Can'! His playing in no way resembled that familiar tune.

Being transformed into the likeness of Jesus the Christ is similar to that. We need to spend a lot of time going over the 'musical score' (the Gospels) before the 'tune' of Jesus emerges in our own lives. Practising for the tune involves studying, meditating, praying, understanding, obedience and then reflection on that obedient action.

Eventually it becomes clear to ourselves and those around us that Jesus has taken real shape in our lives and that he really is the giver of abundant life for ourselves and our world. Then others are attracted to dance with us as disciples of Jesus, just as I was moved to dance when Luke finally made the piano sing the fun tune of 'The Can-Can'!

---

[15] *Signposts to Spirituality*, p. 36.

JESUS' BIRTH, LIFE, MINISTRY, DEATH AND RESURRECTION IN A NUTSHELL

The birth, life, ministry, death and resurrection of Jesus continue to have a profound effect on life. What he achieved then was an achievement for all time. When Jesus was *born* God became physically part of humanity's world and in so doing overcame the division between God and humanity that had begun with sin. In his *ministry* Jesus re-established friendship in the four relationships of life, showing and teaching the way of love and obedience. In his *death* Jesus sealed the love bonds established in his birth and ministry through dying rather than betraying them. In his *resurrection* Jesus demonstrated the victorious nature of the re-established friendship. In his resurrection Jesus is transformed, thereby enabling him and his love to be part of humanity's world forever. His resurrection ushers in the start of the transformation of all humans who place their faith in him. The remainder of this guidebook will help you to experience this life-giving transformation that Jesus has made possible.

Sometimes Jesus' victory over the forces of evil can seem very distant when we are struggling for justice against oversized forces of greed and exploitation. In that situation we feel defeated, despairing and desperately alone. Perhaps it is good to remember Jesus' words to his disciples when they returned from their first foray of growing the Kingdom. They returned confident – unlike the situation I am reflecting on – but Jesus' words to them are good news to us in our despair: *'I watched Satan fall from heaven like a flash of lightning.'* (Luke 10.18)

Satan is a conquered reality and we will know victory in our struggles. As Allan Boesak says of these words of Jesus: 'They are rooted in the promises of of God and the Lordship of Christ over every single inch of life, including our struggles for dignity and justice… They hold out the inextinguishable hope for a people in struggle whose faith is fundamental to that struggle.'[16]

Earlier I have said that Kingdom Consciousness is a revolutionary consciousness – and it applies here again when we see that part of the Kingdom Consciousness Movement is to work for the downfall of evil. Those who join the struggle for justice with this intention are watered from a life-giving well within them that is far more sustaining than motivations of hatred, heroism or ideology. This is the essence of resurrection faith.

---

[16] Allan Boesak, *Pharaohs on Both Sides of the Blood-Red Waters: Prophetic Critique of Empire*, pp. 8-9.

Jesus' death and resurrection

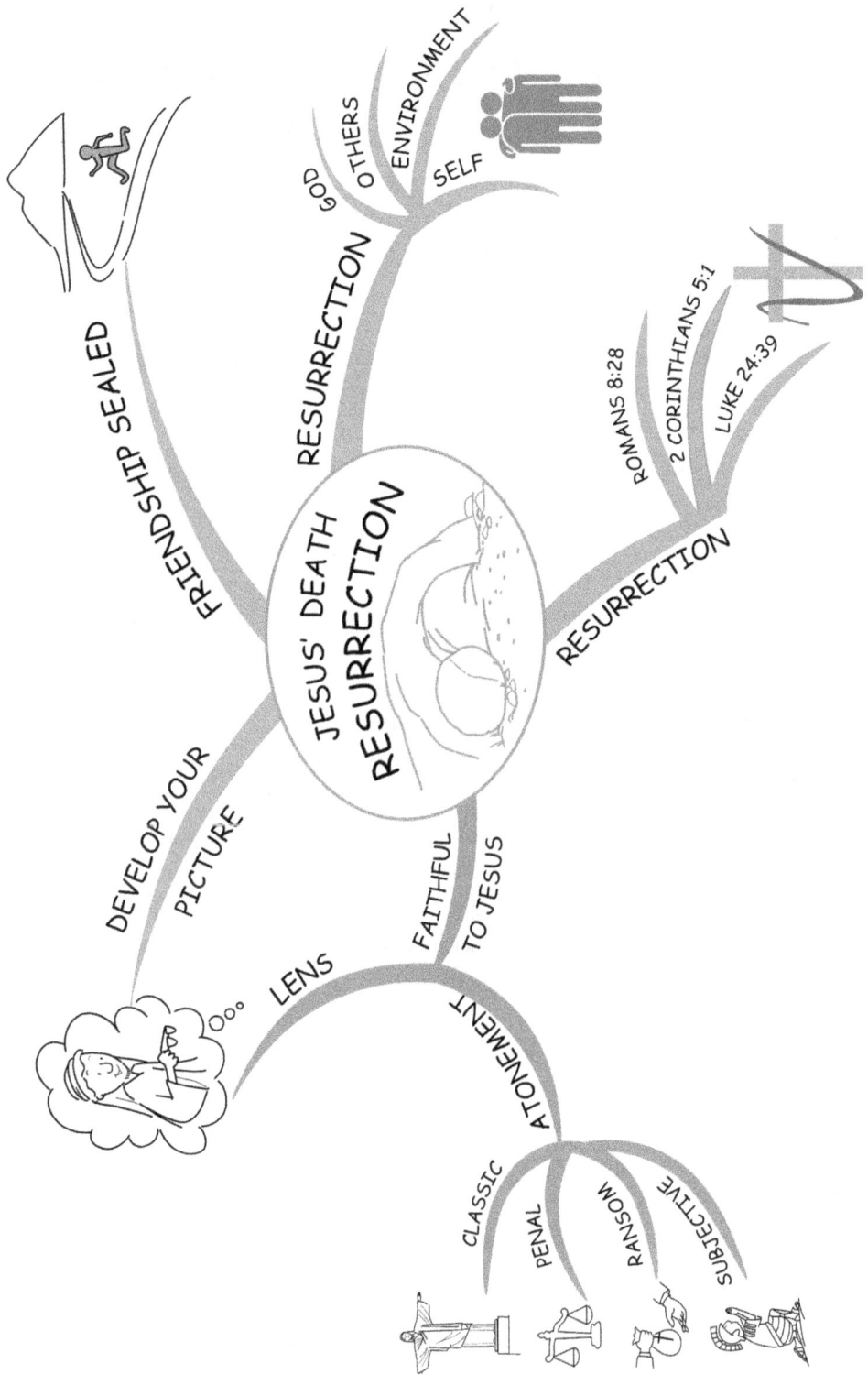

SUGGESTIONS FOR DISCUSSION, REVISION, REFLECTION AND APPLICATION

(These questions are intended for group work, but can easily be adapted for personal use.)

1. What is the most important message to you in this chapter? (Remember to also make a note of this on your 'God spoke to me' page.)
2. Icebreaker question: What would you do in life if you knew you could not fail? (The question must be answered quickly. As a group, do not spend longer than 5 minutes in total on this question.)
3. Read Luke 20.9-19 and answer the following questions:
   a. This passage helps us understand why Jesus was killed. What explanation does this passage give? Can you explain it in your own words?
   b. How is this different from your usual view?
   c. What does this passage tell us about God?
   d. What would have been an honouring response from the tenants? How could this same God-honouring response have been given to Jesus? What would be a God-honouring response today?
4. Below are a variety of suggestions and questions to aid your appreciation of this chapter. Do not attempt to do all of them! Choose those that are most appropriate to your unique situation and/or group. The questions are designed to help variously with revision, understanding, appreciation, reflection or application of the content.
   a. What does Jesus' death mean to you? Has this meaning changed over time? Answer these questions from a personal perspective.
   b. What do Christians lose out on if they only focus on Jesus' death?
   c. How are we saved by Jesus' death? What are the effects of Jesus' death?
   d. How are we saved by Jesus' resurrection? What are the effects of Jesus' resurrection?
   e. What should you do about the belief that in Jesus you are reconciled to God? Should you tell others the good news that in Jesus they too, may be reconciled to God?
   f. What should you do about the belief that in Jesus you are reconciled to other people? How should this affect your relationships? What should

you do about the people from whom you are alienated?

g. What should you do about the belief that in Jesus you are reconciled to your environment? What service should we as Christians offer our environment (remember that this is both natural and human-made environment)? What specific service could you offer?

h. What should you do about the belief that in Jesus you are reconciled to yourself? What changes does this realisation make to your life? How can you make the most of this particular aspect of reconciliation?

i. In the section 'Jesus as the revelation of God' I have included the classic passages of scripture in which writers articulate the philosophy-shaping impact of Jesus as the revelation of God. Which one of these passages would you chose as a personal favourite? Why that one? Perhaps you could memorise it and place it somewhere prominent.

j. What beliefs do people have about God that are not consistent with the revelation of God in Jesus? Try and make a list of some of them. Which one is the most serious in your view?

k. In what ways has Jesus changed your picture of God? For which change are you particularly grateful?

l. If you were not aware of the existence of divergent atonement theories, what were your first thoughts on reading about them here?

m. Which is the atonement theory that is closest to your own current idea?

n. What do you think is the value in each theory of the atonement? What do you think are the problems in each theory?

o. Which theory of the atonement is, in your view, closest to the God revealed in Jesus?

p. Are you willing to review and perhaps change your idea of atonement? If yes, how would you do this?

q. In the section 'Developing your picture of God' I suggest a Bible reading project. Have you familiarised yourself with the suggestion? If you are drawn to follow the suggestion, then tell someone when you plan to start.

MISSING JESUS?

GOD SPOKE TO ME ...

PART 3

FINDING THE SHEPHERD

15

ENTRUSTING YOURSELF TO THE SHEPHERD

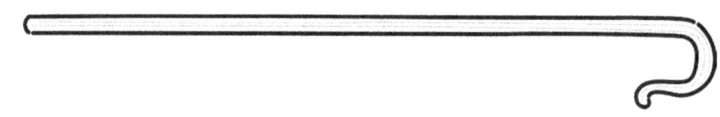

'For you were going astray like sheep, but now you have returned to the shepherd and guardian of your souls.'
(1 Peter 2.25)

It was at an evening service, many years ago, that I became convinced that I had to accept Jesus as my Lord and Saviour. I don't remember the sermon or what we sang – in fact I don't think anything in the service was designed to draw any of the congregation into making commitments that evening. I was a teenager who had been going to church for years already – and now this overwhelming conviction had filled my heart and mind. I remember going home and kneeling at my bed in my room and praying a prayer in which I made it clear that I was entrusting my life and soul to Jesus.

Many years have passed since that moment and in those years I have at times strayed far from Jesus and at other times enjoyed a very close relationship. One thing is clear to me – that entrusting our lives to Jesus is not a 'once off' decision, but part of the dynamic of a lifelong journey.

Now the focus of this guidebook moves into the realm of our response to Jesus. I have described how we were created for community in the four relationships of life and that Jesus has won for us a state in which that community can be experienced. We want to personally experience what Jesus has made available. We want to experience a real friendship with God, others, our environment and ourselves. The reality of community becomes a subjective life experience for you through your faith in Jesus. You need to entrust yourself to him as your Shepherd if you are to experience the blessings of his flock.

JESUS, THE GRACIOUS, GENEROUS AND GOOD SHEPHERD

I have written earlier in this guidebook about the reality of how we each need people to follow and how we may even follow people without actually having consciously chosen them as leaders. I remember, as a high school pupil, following the world view of a teacher with whom I also did a lot of trail hiking. He introduced me to the importance and practice of critical thinking. This was a very useful life lesson to learn. I remember when I was a young adult having an older friend who led me astray to do stupid, reckless and destructive things with him. He was not a good influence on my life and I came close to doing some deadly things with him.

Choosing good and life-giving leaders is one of the most important decisions in life. The most important metaphor for leadership in the Bible is that of the Shepherd. Leaders are shepherds of the people. The New Testament invites us to entrust ourselves to Jesus as a leader by describing him as a Good Shepherd. Because of who Jesus is, choosing him as your ultimate leader is the most important decision of your life. This means that Jesus is not just someone to get to know, worship or believe in, but someone to follow.

Choosing Jesus as our ultimate leader also gives us criteria for other leaders whom we will look up to and emulate, learn from and follow. Followers of Jesus make great leaders.

Those who choose Jesus as their leader and entrust their lives to him will receive this state of community as a gift from him. This is what it means to be 'saved' or 'justified'. In the beginning of the guidebook I showed that sin results in alienation. Those who receive Jesus as the Good Shepherd of their life are forgiven the results of their sin and then know this reconciliation. This is the extent of the forgiveness of our sins. Everything that we have done to separate ourselves from God is forgiven! I am 'justified', which means that I am treated 'just-as-if-I'd' never sinned. We are 'just' in the sense of being in a correct, or right, relationship with God. This is offered to us as a free gift of God's grace. It is through the work of the Holy Spirit that we are saved and justified.[1]

An analogy is found in everyday shopping. When you reach the till to pay for your goods the teller scans the barcode which is linked to the computer programmed with that item's information. Imagine you took a bottle of Grape Juice and filled it with Coca-Cola. When you scanned the bottle of Coca-Cola it would read 'Grape Juice' even though the contents were Coca-Cola. In the same way, Jesus as our Shepherd makes us part of the 'righteous' even though a lot of personal transformation needs to happen for us to live up to that description. We have complete access to unity in the four relationships of life even though we have not done anything to deserve it.[2]

Although I have given this guidebook the subtitle 'Finding the Shepherd we lost' the deeper truth is that when we eventually entrust ourselves to Jesus as Shepherd we are doing so because he has been seeking us by his Spirit and has done all things necessary for us to experience full community with him. When we find the Shepherd we lost we discover that what has happened is that we have been found by him. Any awareness of being lost, any desire for growth, any quest for truth, any dissatisfaction with current discipleship and any awareness that one may be missing the full influence of Jesus – this is all given to us by the Holy Spirit. Any finding, any discovery, any answers, any understanding, any growth, and any transformation – this too is given to us

---

[1] The role of the Holy Spirit in our lives will be unpacked in detail in the next chapters. For now, read the following important passages that relate to being saved and justified: John 3.5; Romans 3.21-31; Romans 5; Romans 6.3-4; Colossians 1.13; Ephesians 2.1-20 and 1 John 3.14.

[2] This analogy is used by Dallas Willard in *The Divine Conspiracy*, p. 43f. He discusses both the power and danger of this analogy.

by the Holy Spirit. This guidebook celebrates that the journey of finding the Shepherd we lost is really a journey of being recovered by the Good Shepherd who is always seeking the lost sheep.

OUR LOSTNESS EXPOSED

I have referred to how our awareness of being lost is the work of the Shepherd too. Although we are saved by the whole of Jesus' life and ministry, not just his death, it is however, the scene of Jesus suffering an agonising death on the cross that wakes me up most dramatically to the love of God. It is a very real personal experience. I am overwhelmed by God's very real love for humanity, as I stand at the foot of the cross and see Jesus wracked with pain, taking his last breath, with words of forgiveness on his lips: *'Father, forgive them; for they do not know what they are doing.'* (Luke 23.34). I realise that it is the greatest foolishness to stay away from God's love for me; I must come home to God.

When I look at Jesus on the cross the true state of my own life is exposed to myself. It is as if God presses the 'pause' button and everything that makes up my life, the way I am living my life, is caught in a freeze frame. I am stopped by Jesus of Nazareth on the cross. The scene of him on the cross, and the scene of my life, come face to face.

The real state of my life is exposed to me. I am created to be sinless and loving and when I stand before the crucified Jesus and see what it really means to be sinless and loving I am exposed as having fallen far short of what God created me to be. Such an encounter, between my life now and Jesus on the cross, has an enormous impact on me.

Every single person in this world has their sin exposed in the presence of the crucified Jesus! All lack of love, hard-heartedness, selfishness, unkindness. All wasting away of life in meaninglessness, pettiness. All our longings, some of which are intense, for things that are of no good value. Our ignoring of vulnerable ones, lonely ones, hurting ones. Any tolerance of injustice or exploitation or corruption. All infatuation with prestige, status, popularity. Any greed, hoarding. All reliance on violence, force, weaponry. Any bitterness, resentment, grudges. Any abuse of people or substances. All unbelief in God. Any doubt in our ability to serve him. Our independence from God, our pride and self-importance and the anger, hatred, malice, revenge, envy and jealousy that flows from self-importance.

This encounter with Jesus of Nazareth on the cross is a sobering encounter for all – even for those who have been on a long journey of discipleship. Every single person who pauses to see the cross as the culmination of Jesus' ministry is exposed in their state of lostness (or whatever part of our life is still lost is exposed). Whenever we stand before the cross on which Jesus of Nazareth hangs we experience a moment of judgement, a moment when our relationship to life is exposed to ourselves and to God. The present state of our existence is revealed in its true state.

This exposure is a gift of grace – for there is time for repentance. This judgement is an act of love – for it opens our eyes to the truth. Without this exposure we continue blind to our fallen state, unaware of our lostness.

How do we respond to Jesus? How do we change the direction of our lives and turn to him? How do we let him change us? How do we follow him? How do we receive all this love that he offers? How do we let him be our saviour? How do we entrust ourselves to this Good Shepherd? How do we accept him and his offer of salvation?

The answer to all of this is faith. I accept, I respond, I follow, I open myself, I entrust through faith in Jesus.

ENTRUSTING YOURSELF TO THE SHEPHERD – FAITH AS A FIVE-STEP DANCE

Faith in Jesus is a response to Jesus that involves five essential steps.

One of the steps is *faith as conviction*. One of the important effects that Jesus had on people was that he was able to awaken in them a strong faith in God's ability to triumph over evil, sickness and difficulties. This was faith functioning as a very powerful conviction. This was faith in the sense of being convinced and confident and fully awakened to God's power. The Gospels are full of references to Jesus emphasising the importance of such faith.[3] This faith was so powerful that God's triumph over evil, sickness and difficulties was experienced by those who held it.

We are invited to place that faith (conviction, sureness) in Jesus as the One through whom good will triumph over evil and God's reign will be established. We are invited to a confident conviction that Jesus is the best leader to follow.

Many people, including many Christians, oppose certain movements in society with the words, 'Don't be idealistic, be realistic!' But what does it mean to be realistic? For a Christian it should mean being true to the reality that Jesus established in this world – the reality of reconciliation in the four relationships of life.

Our calling, as followers of Jesus, is to live true to reconciliation in the four relationships of life. Martin Luther King Jr. in his acceptance speech of the Nobel Peace Prize in 1964, said: 'I refuse to accept the idea that the "isness" of man's present nature makes him morally incapable of reaching up for the eternal "oughtness" that forever confronts him.'

The opposite of faith as conviction is fatalism. Fatalism believes that 'you can't change the world'; 'nothing can be done about it'; or 'you must accept reality', etc. Fatalism does not believe in the power of God to effect change. Faith as conviction however believes in God's ability to effect change and enables God to work that change in me and through me.

The opposite of faith as conviction is also dull belief. Dull belief is seen in all Christians who believe in God but it makes no difference to their lives and therefore these Christians are not characterised by any distinctiveness of the Jesus way. They are dull and bland, there is no Jesus flavour to them. Dull belief makes the Christian life a very peripheral matter and of no consequence to the real world of human action. Dull belief is the very opposite of a Kingdom Consciousness.

Another of the steps is *faith as belief*. We are invited to believe in Jesus as the One in whom the fullness of God was pleased to dwell (Colossians 1.19). We are invited to believe in Jesus as the One through whom we may experience access to community in the four relationships of life. We are invited to believe in Jesus as the One through whom we may experience new and abundant life (John 10.10).

Such faith in Jesus is essential for us to experience these truths and dyna-

---

[3] Over and over again Jesus says to a person who has been cured, 'Your faith has healed you.' – Mark 5.34 and parallels; Mark 10.52 and parallels; Matthew 9.28-29; Luke 17.19; Mark 5.36 and parallels; Matthew 8.13; Matthew 15.28. For other references on Jesus' emphasising the power of faith see Matthew 21.22; Mark 9.23; Matthew 17.20; Mark 11.23-24; Matthew 14.28-31; Matthew 17.19-20; Mark 6.5-6.

mics in our own lives. Jesus openly encouraged people to believe in him: *'Do not let your hearts be troubled. Believe in God, believe also in me.'* (John 14.1).

A moment later Jesus says, in John 14.6: *'I am the way, and the truth, and the life. No one comes to the Father except through me.'*

Peter, in 1 Peter 2.6, declares that Jesus is the cornerstone who is *'chosen and precious; and whoever believes in Him will not be put to shame'*. John 2.11 and 20.30-31 tells us that Jesus' deeds were signs that led to belief in Jesus.

Faith as belief may be seen as the cognitive dimension of faith. Chapter 4 showed that such faith is an inspiring and reasonable faith, not a dramatic leap into the dark.

Faith as belief needs to include a journey of abandoning belief in the world's beliefs (values, principles) and embracing the beliefs (values, principles) that Jesus taught. These teachings of Jesus were presented in chapters 7 to 13. Believing in Jesus must include a belief in the things that he taught. Too many Christians believe in Jesus in name only and overlook most of his principles (values, beliefs). It is my assertion that such Christians are missing Jesus in their lives.

Faith as belief is a quest of the mind – a quest for making sense of the world. Faith as belief is about facing all the big questions of life. It is, as the old definition of theology goes, faith seeking understanding. It is the journey of facing the tough questions and questing courageously for answers. It is the journey of letting go of half-truths and gaining fuller truths.

Faith as belief is certainly about growing up and letting go of a god who was the fulfilment of my fantasies and infantile projections. Faith as belief is about fully facing our disappointments and disillusionment with how our beliefs in God have not lived up to earlier expectations. If we persist in this honest way we will reach the grander and more beautiful landscapes of deeper and fuller truth.

The quest of faith as belief never finds the burly messenger carrying incontestable proof about God. Rather it is a journey into a landscape where there is the discovery of meaning in a relationship with God who is then known and deeply loved. At this life-giving stream, surrounded by majestic peaks of meaning, we know ourselves for what we truly are – a child and able partner with God in the ongoing loving purpose of creation.

The opposite of faith as belief is not doubt but misbelief or unbelief. Faith as belief is a journey in which we grow in our appreciation of who Jesus is and what he calls us to believe in. It is a journey towards truer beliefs. It is a journey towards our greater purchase in who Jesus is for us and for the world.

Another of the steps is *faith as repentance*. In Matthew and Mark's Gospels the first sermon Jesus gives is an urgent demand to repent. The first word in John the baptiser's first sermon was 'repent' and the first sermon ever preached on the day the church was formed culminated in the word 'repent'! Clearly it is an essential part of our relationship with God.[4]

Repentance has very little to do with remorse. Remorse means being sorry for my sin, and is quite useless unless it is accompanied by a turning from, repenting of, my sin. Essentially, this is turning away from that which alienates me from God, my fellow human, my environment, myself. In this step, my old self dies, so that Jesus may start a new life in me. It would be good to go back to Chapter 3 to recall in greater detail what sin is.

When Jesus told people to repent, he said that the reason was because the Kingdom of God had come near. Jesus is saying, 'In the light of recent developments you need to re-think the direction of your life.'

If I offered someone a lift to Johannesburg from Cape Town and I took the N2 highway they would say to me 'you are on the wrong road, turn around'. I may reply, 'I am sorry I am on the wrong road' – that would be remorse, but if I continued driving eastwards on the N2 my remorse would be worthless. I need to turn the car around and get onto the correct road. Turning the car around is what repentance is all about. In fact, the word 'repentance' is the English translation of the Greek word *metanoia,* which partly means 'turning around' and 'changing one's mind'.

---

[4] Mark 1.14-15; Matthew 4.17; Matthew 3.2; Luke 3.3; Acts 2.38.

Psalm 119.59 sums up what repentance is all about: *I have taken stock of my ways: and have turned back my feet to your commands.* It's all about taking stock of my life and turning back to God and his ways.

Jesus' gruesome but loving death on the cross awakens us to our sin and the need for repentance. In Jesus' love we see how far we have fallen short in being loving. We also see what destructiveness sin causes when left to continue. In the previous section I referred to how our sin is exposed to ourselves by Jesus on the cross. Faith as repentance is all about turning from that which is exposed. Jesus on the cross causes us to take stock of our lives and turn back to God.

To repent is to rethink everything in your life in the light of Jesus, to look at your relationships, your politics, your lifestyle – everything – in the light of all that he stands for. To repent is not a single moment but is a journey in which you are open to the possibility that everything may change over time. To repent involves a deep awareness that you may be wrong about many things and that you are willing to realign yourself with Jesus.

Faith as repentance is that moment when you get up, leave your sin behind, and follow Jesus. This is what Matthew did when Jesus called him (Matthew 9.9). Matthew turned from his old life, in order to accept, with both hands, the new life being offered by Jesus.

Faith as repentance is best understood within an understanding of grace. I like to define grace as the freedom to have a conversation with the one I have wronged. Repentance is the gift to turn to God in prayer and have a conversation with him about what I have done wrong. The word 'conversation' is a good word because it helps to move me away from a paradigm in which I see my sins as a list and that I need to name the sins on that list to have them forgiven. Often this 'debit and credit' paradigm does not help me transform because it doesn't get under the surface of the sin and engage honestly with what is going on. A conversation will enable me to talk honestly about what happened, why I think it happened, and so on. This will be true confession. In the conversation I will also be attentive to what God has to reveal to me by his Spirit. Grace makes such true repentance possible.

The opposite of faith as repentance is not doubt but arrogance. It is the arrogance of presumption that we do not need to change. It is the blindness of arrogance about the stumbling blocks that must be removed for Jesus to work in our lives. Faith functioning as repentance is really a journey of surrender to Jesus.

Another of the steps is *faith as obedience*. This is faith as an act of the will. In this step we show that our will is converted too. In this step we commit ourselves to God for the direction of our life. In this step we show our loyalty to Jesus. This step is all about building our life, lifestyle, values, actions, and priorities in line with Jesus as our shepherd leader. In this step especially faith is seen to be a verb rather than a noun.

Jesus as the Shepherd teacher is clear that his teachings are not just suggestions or ideas to think about but rather truths that need to be put into practice. This is implied in all of his teaching, but is forcefully impressed upon the listeners at the end of the great Sermon on the Mount:

> *'Everyone then who hears these words of mine and acts on them will be like a wise man who built his house on rock ... And everyone who hears these words of mine and does not act on them will be like a foolish man who built his house on sand.'* (Matthew 7.24-26)

In Paul's writings faith and obedience are so closely linked that he speaks of the 'obedience of faith' (see for example Romans 1.5 and Romans 16.26). Scripture presumes that faith in Jesus includes loyalty to Jesus and all that Jesus taught. The New Testament book of James is also well known for teaching a faith that must be lived out in obedient works. The whole book is excellent to read but I encourage you to at least read James 2.14-26.

Faith as obedience is about building a life of community with God, my fellow humans, myself, and my environment. Faith as obedience means trusting Jesus as the person on whom to build my life.

Remember that the truth Jesus lived is that God is love. Faith as obedience means living the truth, which therefore means living to love. This is why the New Testament teaches that only those who love can say they know God:

> *Those who say, 'I love God,' and hate their brothers or sisters, are liars; for those who do not love a brother or sister whom they have seen, cannot love God whom they have not seen. The commandment we have from him is this: those who love God must love their brothers and sisters also.* (1 John 4.20-21)

In our consumerist society, Jesus is too often seen as a commodity to add to my life. This is where Jesus is offered as the one who will ensure that you do not go to hell when you die. The person thinks: 'I better get Jesus so that I am insured against hell.' Jesus is then an insurance policy which you purchase, but then put away without him actually making any difference to the way you live your life. That is to have a dead faith.

Repentance and obedience are closely related. Faith as repentance is the turning point that puts me on the road Jesus is leading as the Shepherd. Faith as obedience is the daily act of following Jesus. This distinction between repentance and obedience is quite neatly seen when you think of Matthew the tax collector who left his tax booth when Jesus called him (that is repentance), and then followed Jesus for the rest of his life (that is obedience). As Soren Kierkegaard said: 'Jesus wants followers, not admirers.'

True faith is not the absence of doubt but the presence of action! The opposite of faith as obedience is not doubt but rebellion. The opposite of faith as obedience is disloyalty. Discipleship is a pilgrimage of trust that is lived out in daily obedience.

Another of the steps is *faith as trust.* In this step we entrust our lives into God's hands. It is a step of trust, surrender, entrusting, and leads to intimacy with God. Paul writes tenderly of faith as trust when he writes to Timothy saying:

> *I am reminded of your sincere faith, a faith that lived first in your grandmother Lois and your mother Eunice and now, I am sure, lives in you… For this gospel I was appointed a herald and an apostle and a teacher, and for this reason I suffer as I do. But I am not ashamed, for I*

> *know the one in whom I have put my trust, and I am sure that he is able to guard until that day what I have entrusted to him.* (Selected verses from 2 Timothy 1.5-12)

Here faith is to decide to trust God's grace. It is to trust God for forgiveness and for new life. Here faith is to entrust oneself to God because we are now aware that on our own we are not realising our potential. Here faith trusts God's grace that offers us life as a child of God in which we realise our potential. Faith is to trust this gracious offer and the power of God to give us new life.

Jesus encourages faith as trust when he teaches us to not worry about our provisions but rather to trust God. See Matthew 12.22-31 for this reassuring teaching.

Faith as trust is often expressed in the daily spiritual disciplines of prayer and scripture reading. In these, and in all the spiritual disciplines, there is the awareness that on my own power I will slip back into inauthentic existence, but through the spiritual disciplines I receive power from God to live authentically as a child of God.

Faith as trust is the faith journey that goes much deeper than belonging to a religious group or believing in a set of intellectual truths. Faith as trust is a journey that holds on to the ways of Jesus when other ways might seem wiser or more expedient. Faith as trust is the journey of commitment to love and grace, which is the power of the cross, even when this way seems weak and foolish.

Faith as trust is also about being willing to risk for the sake of Jesus and his Kingdom. This is an essential element of faith because progress will not be made until we are prepared to step out of our anxious hesitation and entrust our lives and our service to God. William James put it this way:

> So far as man stands for anything and is productive or originative at all, his entire vital function may be said to deal with maybes. Not a victory is gained, not a deed of faithfulness or courage is done, except upon a maybe; not a service, not a sally of generosity, not a scientific exploration or experiment or textbook, that may not be a mistake. It is only by risking our person from one hour to another that we live at all.[5]

---

[5] William James, *The Will to Believe*, 1897, p. 59 (recorded in Interpreters Bible, volume 8, p. 489).

The opposite of faith as trust is therefore self-sufficiency – to believe that we do not need God's power or grace in our lives.

You would have noticed that throughout this section I have included comments on what the opposite and fallen orientation of one's being is when compared to faith. In this I have challenged the idea that the opposite of faith is doubt. Often the path of faith includes doubt, but still believes, carries conviction, repents, obeys and trusts. The point is that faith is not dependent on certainty or proof. Faith is a life-enhancing orientation of one's being to God, regardless of any doubts or lack of proof.

An acronym to help you remember the five elements of a life of faith could be CBROT (Conviction, Belief, Repentance, Obedience, Trust), said phonetically as 'see brother for tea'.[6]

TO DRAW THESE THOUGHTS TOGETHER

These five steps of faith are obviously ongoing, continuous and interrelated. They are all equally important. Together they make my faith in Jesus full and alive. These steps are best understood as five steps in a dance. It is a unified and distinctive dance that has five steps. If you leave one of the steps out you cannot do the dance properly. As soon as you have finished doing the five steps you do them again. Keep dancing!

---

[6] My thanks to Maurice Adams for this acronym.

There are obviously overlapping areas in defining these five steps of faith, for each step is not completely distinguished or separate from another step. Really I have described them as steps, but they can also be described as dimensions or aspects of faith. Essentially the differences between the steps are nuanced, yet it is very important to appreciate the different dynamics and dimensions that make faith full and alive.

It is important to understand that we do not earn salvation through placing faith in God. Salvation is God's gift to us through Jesus. Faith opens us to receive the gift. Without these steps of faith we are not able to receive or unpack the gift of salvation offered by God in Jesus. This whole transaction is soaked in the grace of God – God's grace offered to us in Jesus and God's grace at work in us by his Spirit awakening faith. Paul is eager for us to appreciate this in Ephesians:

You were dead through the trespasses and sins in which you once lived, following the course of this world, following the ruler of the power of the air, the spirit that is now at work among those who are disobedient. All of us once lived among them in the passions of our flesh, following the desires of flesh and senses, and we were by nature children of wrath, like everyone else. But God, who is rich in mercy, out of the great love with which he loved us even when we were dead through our trespasses, made us alive together with Christ—by grace you have been saved—and raised us up with him and seated us with him in the heavenly places in Christ Jesus, so that in the ages to come he might show the immeasurable riches of his grace in kindness toward us in Christ Jesus. For by grace you have been saved through faith, and this is not your own doing; it is the gift of God— not the result of works, so that no one may boast. For we are what he has made us, created in Christ Jesus for good works, which God prepared beforehand to be our way of life. (Ephesians 2.1-10).

Imagine a boy playing with his dad in the garden and how the son delights to climb up onto a jungle gym and jump off it into his father's arms. Each time he jumps the father catches him. The son has got faith in the father and so is able to do something slightly dangerous. Who gets the credit for the son's faith? The father, of course, who is reliable and faithful. The son's faith is a gift to the son from the father who is faithful. It is similar with our relationship with God – our faith is not something we have 'done', it is not a work that earns salvation, it is a gift that enables us to trust God.

Some people struggle intensely to live with a faith that is confident and fully surrendered and trust filled. John Wesley was famously someone who struggled in this way but emerged from the struggle with a blazing faith. I would like to recount some of what he described of this struggle and its empowering conclusion. What is described here is a journey of about three and a half years of intense questing, from 1735 to 1738:

> Many comforters assured me that I had faith. As a Wesley, I was supposed to have faith. I was an ordained minister from a family of ministers… I preached on faith to the faculty and students at St. Mary's Church, Oxford. But I did not have the faith which I wanted and knew that I needed. This faith by the power of the Holy Spirit would come to me later. Then I would be able to lead many into the same powerful spiritual experience… The faith that I wanted was a sure trust and confidence in God. I wanted to experience forgiveness from my sins and a oneness with God through the work of Jesus… I wanted a faith which no one can have without knowing he has it… In my discussions with Peter Bohler, I was amazed by his accounts of a living faith. He insisted that the fruits of holiness and happiness were part of such a faith… On my next visit with Peter I agreed that faith is a sure trust and confidence which man has in God, that through the merits of Christ his sins are forgiven, and he is reconciled to God… What I could not understand was what he spoke of as an instantaneous work. I could not understand how this faith could be given in a moment. How could one be turned from sin and misery into righteousness and joy in the Holy Spirit instantaneously? I returned to the Scriptures to search this point again. I particularly studied the Acts of the Apostles. To my utter astonishment, I found scarcely any instances of conversions except of the instantaneous kind… Peter brought me Christians who testified God had changed them in a moment. In a moment, they said, God had given them a living faith in Jesus. That faith transferred them from darkness into light, out of sin and fear into holiness and happiness… I had continued to seek this faith, though with some strange indifference, dullness, and coldness until May 24. In the evening of that day, I went very unwillingly to a prayer meeting in Aldersgate Street. About 8.45, I was listening to a reading of Luther's preface to the Epistle to the Romans. While he was describing the change which God works in the heart through faith in Christ, I felt my heart strangely warmed. I felt that I did trust in Christ, Christ alone, for salvation. An assurance was

given me that He had taken away my sins, even mine, and saved me from the law of sin and death.[7]

From that moment John Wesley's ministry became incredibly powerful and fruitful. He led a revival movement in the United Kingdom, which gave birth to the Methodist Church and a further 35 denominations and also sparked many charismatic renewal groups. The important element of the testimony for us is to see how faith is a gift from God by his Spirit. Some struggle intensely before receiving this breakthrough in their being. We all need to be open to the way in which the Holy Spirit can awaken our beings to this flood of light, consolation and power. This quest for faith is an act of faith which leads to a great gift of faith from the Holy Spirit.

Also, faith is not an act that takes place once for all, but issues in the life of faith – a journey in which we steadily orientate ourselves to the grace and power of God and all that that makes possible in our lives.

Learning and living these five dance steps is a journey of a lifetime. That journey begins with that simple, yet vital and life-changing moment of accepting Jesus into your life. Revelation 3.20 *'Listen, I am standing at the door, knocking; if you hear my voice and open the door, I will come in to you and eat with you, and you with Me.'* If you have not yet taken a step of placing your faith in Jesus then I encourage you to do so today.

If you would like to receive Jesus into your life then I encourage you to pray this prayer, either in these words, or in similar words of your own:

> Dear Jesus, I hear you knocking at the door of my life to come in and be my Lord and Saviour.
> I now open the door and invite you in.
> Please forgive me for my sins that separate me from you.
> I want to be in a good relationship with you.
> I trust you now.
> Through you Lord Jesus I want to die to sin and be born again to a new life with you.
> I pray this prayer in the powerful name of Jesus, Amen

SHEPHERD'S JOY!

After telling the story of the lost sheep, Jesus said *'Just so, I tell you, there will be*

---

[7] *The Holy Spirit and Power*, pp. 1-9. This book is a paraphrase of John Wesley's sermons on the Holy Spirit by Clare Weakley.

more joy in heaven over one sinner who repents than over ninety-nine righteous persons who need no repentance.' (Luke 15.7) I like that – I have this image in my mind of all the angels in heaven stopping their work to have a party when you or I turn to Jesus. Rightfully so, because Jesus is the hope of the world, and that hope becomes more of a reality with each person that commits their life to him.

Another thought excites me: Each time a person places their faith in Jesus they mark up another failure for the religious and political rulers who had arranged for Jesus' execution. These rulers had hoped to put an end to Jesus' loving ministry through killing him. What happened is that their killing of Jesus had the opposite effect – the cross brought home to people then, and to people today, the extent of God's love. Instead of Jesus' death ending his loving ministry it has multiplied it.

Jesus' death is like a seed that has fallen to the ground, died, and now continues to produce a harvest[8].

---

[8] Speaking of his death, Jesus in fact said *'Unless a grain of wheat falls into the earth and dies, it remains but a single grain; but if it dies, it bears much fruit.'* John 12.24

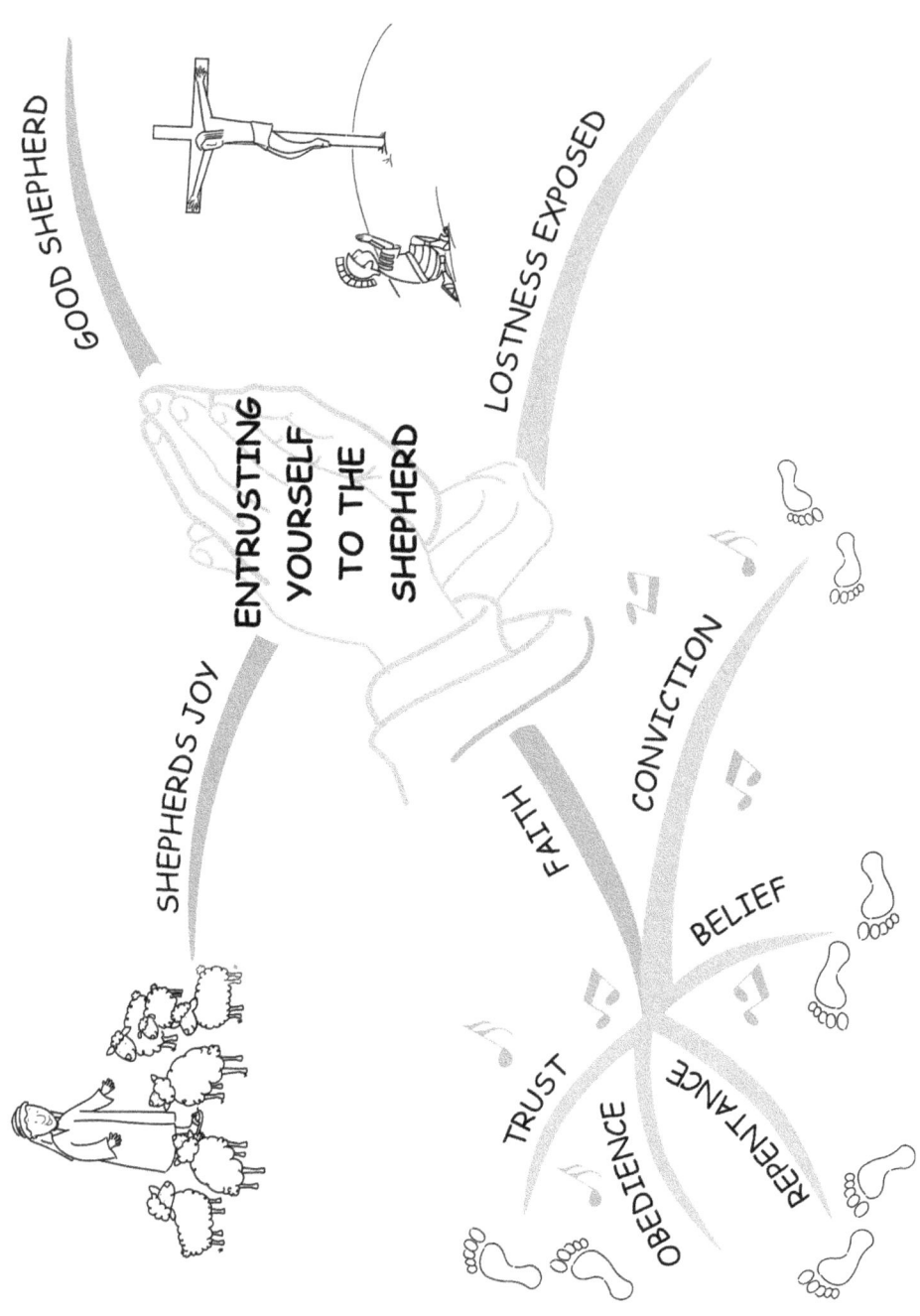

SUGGESTIONS FOR DISCUSSION, REVISION, REFLECTION AND APPLICATION

(These questions are intended for group work, but can easily be adapted for personal use.)

1. What is the most important message to you in this chapter? (Remember to also make a note of this on your 'God spoke to me' page.)
2. Icebreaker question: What would you do if you did not have to work? (The question must be answered quickly. As a group, do not spend longer than 5 minutes in total on this question.)
3. Read Ephesians 2.1-10 and answer the following questions:
   a. What does this passage tell us about grace?
   b. What does this passage tell us about the role of faith in salvation?
   c. What does this passage tell us about the role of works in salvation? What is a correct understanding of the role of works in the living of our lives?
4. Below are a variety of suggestions and questions to aid your appreciation of this chapter. Do not attempt to do all of them! Choose those that are most appropriate to your unique situation and/or group. The questions are designed to help variously with revision, understanding, appreciation, reflection or application of the content.
   a. If you have accepted Jesus as your Lord and Saviour then spend time remembering the moment you made that decision clear to Jesus. Tell the group about that moment. Also describe the build-up to making the decision.
   b. What has changed in your life since you decided to follow Jesus? Share your answer with the group.
   c. What do you receive from Jesus when you place your faith in Him? Try and relate your answers to the four relationships of life.
   d. What does it mean to say – 'I have been saved by Jesus.' Or 'Jesus is my saviour'?
   e. If we are part of the Shepherd's flock is it because we found the Shepherd we lost, or is it because we were found by the Shepherd? In which way are both senses true?

f. What particular aspects of your own lostness have been exposed by Jesus?
g. What are the five steps in the faith dance? Describe them briefly in your own words.
h. Read through each of the steps of faith carefully. Which step represents a strength in your relationship with God? Which step represents a weakness? Can your strength help your weakness? What else can help your weakness? Take a decision that will lead to growth and share the decision with someone.
i. How is faith a gift?
j. Can you relate to John Wesley's struggle with faith? What can you learn from his struggle?

Some important matters to reflect on in the coming week:
a. If you have not specifically made it known to Jesus that you receive him into your life then pray the prayer in the section 'To draw these thoughts together'. If you do this then please share the decision with someone.
b. What changes would you like God to make to your life? Pray for these changes.
c. What changes has God made to your life? Give thanks to God for these changes.
d. In this chapter I propose that we are very clear that we see ourselves as followers of Jesus. What further change would it make to your life to be more intentional and thorough about following Jesus? Make a list of some of the aspects and number them from most radical change to least radical change. Choose one to put into effect this week. Ask the group to hold you accountable.

GOD SPOKE TO ME ...

16

WHO IS THE HOLY SPIRIT?

JESUS CONTINUES HIS MISSION!

> *While staying with them, he ordered them not to leave Jerusalem, but to wait there for the promise of the Father. 'This', he said, 'is what you have heard from me; for John baptized with water, but you will be baptized with the Holy Spirit not many days from now ... But you will receive power when the Holy Spirit has come upon you; and you will be my witnesses in Jerusalem, in all Judea and Samaria, and to the ends of the earth.'* (Acts 1.4-8, selected verses)

For a change I was not the preacher, I was sitting with the congregation listening to the guest preacher. After his sermon he prayed the simple words, *'Come Holy Spirit'* and then again *'Come Holy Spirit'* and in that moment we as a congregation were awash with the gentle presence of the Holy Spirit, a presence who was experienced as a cloud of peace giving us a profound sense of God's loving closeness. A few minutes later Paul Cameron, the preacher, invited any who would want to be prayed for to go into the chapel after the service. A large group of about 40 people went for prayer and that time was also blessed by a remarkable sense of God's closeness, this time as a profound sense of his presence as Healer. The prayer prayed for each person was the simple faith-filled invitation *'Come Holy Spirit'* and in each instance a deep and tender experience of God was experienced. Many experienced healing and hope, relief and recovery. Transformation and blessing characterised that day at church. The prayers for healing continued for over three hours!

These experiences associated with the prayerful invocation *'Come Holy Spirit'* reveal to us that God is experienced in very real ways in our lives by his Spirit. It discloses to us that God's presence is made real by his Spirit. The Spirit's work is to make noticeable the presence and the power of God in our lives.

This chapter in our journey explores the work of the Holy Spirit. It is a chapter that unpacks the ways in which Jesus continues to be with us, leading us and being life for us.[1]

JESUS CONTINUES HIS MISSION!

Jesus' resurrection appearances continued for forty days and it should be of no surprise that his focus was on nurturing Kingdom Consciousness: *After his suffering he presented himself alive to them by many convincing proofs, appearing to them during forty days and speaking about the kingdom of God.* (Acts 1.3)

---

[1] If you are journeying through this guidebook as part of a congregational course then these chapters on the Holy Spirit will take place on a 'Holy Spirit Retreat' and will be followed by a time of individual reflection and corporate prayer. See 'How to use the book' and the website www.missingjesus.net for more information on this.

This forty days ended in a moment which we call the 'Ascension' – a moment when Jesus of Nazareth's ministry in his own body came to an end. I phrase this moment in that slightly awkward way because it would be wrong to say that 'Jesus' ministry came to an end', for we know that it has continued. It would also be wrong to say that his 'bodily ministry came to an end', for we have become his body. These are the important realities that are revealed in this chapter.

How would Jesus continue his mission after his own bodily presence came to an end? The answer is that he would give us his own Spirit and so continue his work through our own lives and through the corporate life of the church that was to form.

Jesus had promised to give his Spirit in a number of instances during his ministry. John gives us a very detailed and intimate description of one of those instances:

> 'And I will ask the Father, and he will give you another Advocate [can also be translated as 'Helper'] to be with you forever. This is the Spirit of truth, whom the world cannot receive, because it neither sees him nor knows him. You know him, because he abides with you, and he will be in you.' 'I will not leave you orphaned; I am coming to you. In a little while the world will no longer see me, but you will see me; because I live, you also will live. On that day you will know that I am in my Father, and you in me, and I in you…' 'Those who love me will keep my word, and my Father will love them, and we will come to them and make our home with them…' 'I have said these things to you while I am still with you. But the Advocate, the Holy Spirit, whom the Father will send in my name, will teach you everything, and remind you of all that I have said to you… And now I have told you this before it occurs, so that when it does occur, you may believe.' (John 14.16-29, selected verses)

So Jesus promises to be with us forever through the Spirit who will be given to us. This Spirit is described as a helper (an advocate) and as God's Spirit (Holy Spirit). We will unpack this more a little later.

It is important to note that all the writers who describe Jesus' Ascension highlight Jesus' assurance to his disciples that he would continue to be with them through his Spirit and that they would continue his work in the power his Spirit gave them. Luke, the author of 'Acts', describes:

> While staying with them, he ordered them not to leave Jerusalem, but to wait there for the promise of the Father. 'This', he said, 'is what you have

> *heard from me; for John baptized with water, but you will be baptized with the Holy Spirit not many days from now .. But you will receive power when the Holy Spirit has come upon you; and you will be my witnesses in Jerusalem, in all Judea and Samaria, and to the ends of the earth.' When he had said this, as they were watching, he was lifted up, and a cloud took him out of their sight.* (Acts 1.4-9, selected verses)

Matthew describes: *Now the eleven disciples went to Galilee, to the mountain to which Jesus had directed them. When they saw him, they worshipped him; but some doubted. And Jesus came and said to them, 'All authority in heaven and on earth has been given to me. Go therefore and make disciples of all nations, baptizing them in the name of the Father and of the Son and of the Holy Spirit, and teaching them to obey everything that I have commanded you. And remember, I am with you always, to the end of the age.'* (Matthew 28.16-20)

And Mark gives the simplest description, yet does not leave out this important dimension: *So then the Lord Jesus, after he had spoken to them, was taken up into heaven and sat down at the right hand of God. And they went out and proclaimed the good news everywhere, while the Lord worked with them and confirmed the message by the signs that accompanied it.* (Mark 16.19-20)

The presence of Jesus by his Spirit is experienced in an endlessly wide variety of ways – normal everyday experiences and extraordinary occurrences, subtle and dramatic, personal and social, encouraging and empowering, humbling and exalting, giving gifts and nurturing fruit.

The first very dramatic event was so remarkable and so soon after Jesus' ascension that it has come to be seen as the moment when the Spirit was poured out on all disciples. It happened at the Jewish festival of Pentecost, which is 50 days after Passover, and thus only 10 days after Jesus' ascension. In this record of some of what happened note that Jesus' Spirit is experienced in a dramatic way but also note that Peter assures all who turn to Jesus that they will, on that very day, also experience Jesus' Spirit:

> *When the day of Pentecost had come, they were all together in one place. And suddenly from heaven there came a sound like the rush of a violent wind, and it filled the entire house where they were sitting. Divided tongues, as of fire, appeared among them, and a tongue rested on each of them. All of them were filled with the Holy Spirit and began to speak in other languages, as the Spirit gave them ability...But Peter, standing with the eleven, raised his voice and addressed them, 'Men of Judea and all who live in Jerusalem, let this be known to you, and listen*

to what I say. Indeed, these are not drunk, as you suppose, for it is only nine o'clock in the morning...You that are Israelites, listen to what I have to say: Jesus of Nazareth, a man attested to you by God with deeds of power, wonders, and signs that God did through him among you, as you yourselves know— this man, handed over to you according to the definite plan and foreknowledge of God, you crucified and killed by the hands of those outside the law. But God raised him up, having freed him from death, because it was impossible for him to be held in its power...This Jesus God raised up, and of that all of us are witnesses. Being therefore exalted at the right hand of God, and having received from the Father the promise of the Holy Spirit, he has poured out this that you both see and hear...' Now when they heard this, they were cut to the heart and said to Peter and to the other apostles, 'Brothers, what should we do?' Peter said to them, 'Repent, and be baptized every one of you in the name of Jesus Christ so that your sins may be forgiven; and you will receive the gift of the Holy Spirit. For the promise is for you, for your children, and for all who are far away, everyone whom the Lord our God calls to him.'... And day by day the Lord added to their number those who were being saved. (Acts 2.1-47, selected verses)

So, Jesus' work continues in this world by his Spirit, especially through those who are disciples, who follow Jesus closely and are attentive to his Spirit. In this guidebook's journey the vitally important point we are focusing on now is that Jesus desires greatly to give us his Spirit so that he may personally empower us to follow him and make his good news known in word and deed.

Following Jesus is not easy, nor is it for the faint-hearted, and so we have a great need for Jesus' power and light. Allow me to unpack some of the dimensions of this ongoing work of Jesus.

THE HOLY SPIRIT AND THE TRINITY

The next paragraphs explain the essentially important identity and mission of the Holy Spirit. Many Christians have views of the role of the Holy Spirit that are inconsistent with our foundational understanding of who and what the Spirit is. These paragraphs lay down the basis of Biblical and theological understanding and experiencing the Holy Spirit.

Let us begin our journey into understanding and experiencing the Holy Spirit with an appreciation of the name 'Spirit'. Do this by getting into the shoes of a Hebrew who views a name as something that tells you about the person. The Hebrew also has such a deep respect for God that they will not say the name *Yahweh*. *Ruach*, the word translated into English as *Spirit*, means 'wind' and 'air', more specifically the power present in them. *Ruach* is a feminine noun in Hebrew. Wind and air were things you could not control, but which rather controlled you, and on which life was dependent. The idea being conveyed is of God's active and powerful presence.[2] The title 'Holy' was given in late Old Testament times as a roundabout way of saying 'Yahweh's Spirit'. The title *Holy Spirit* is common throughout the New Testament.

The Holy Spirit continues today to be an experience of God's active and powerful presence. The Holy Spirit makes Kingdom action possible. This is possibly the most important thing to appreciate about the work of the Holy Spirit. Alan Walker has a simple and evocative way of making this point: 'The meaning of the doctrine of the Holy Spirit is, God is where the action is. The doctrine of the Holy Spirit declares that God belongs to the living present, the passing moment – now. God is wrapped up in deeds. He is a dynamic presence in the world in human experience…Where is God? God is most seen in His mighty acts. He appears in events… He is the happening God.'[3]

---

[2] For a few references in the Old Testament see: Judges 14.6; 1 Kings 18.12; Judges 3.10; Judges 6.34; 1 Samuel 10.5-13; 1 Samuel 16.13.

[3] *Breakthrough – Rediscovering the Holy Spirit*, p. 9. Dr Alan Walker was superintendent of Central Methodist Mission in Sydney – Australia's largest and oldest Methodist Church. He was one of the only internationally regarded evangelists who visited to challenge apartheid and the government during a preaching tour of South Africa. He founded *Life Line* which was brought to South Africa by Peter Storey after Peter had spent time with Alan in Sydney.

Ruach

Who or what is the Holy Spirit?

One cannot seek to understand the Holy Spirit's identity without also understanding the identity of the Father and the Son because the identities of each of the Divine Persons of the Trinity are deeply linked (they are one). Remember that at the beginning of Chapter 2 when we explored the Trinity we learned that the Spirit's identity is the Love-bond. We appreciate therefore that the Spirit's love is expressed through the *bonding* character of love.

Who or what is the Holy Spirit for us? Scripture and the experience of the church are clear that the Holy Spirit is both a person (who is the Holy Spirit?) and a force (what is the Holy Spirit?). This is not a contradiction but a help in understanding the Holy Spirit's identity: The Holy Spirit is both the presence and power of God with us. The Holy Spirit is the way in which the Creator and the risen Christ and their power are present to us.

An overview of all of the New Testament books that speak of the Spirit in the life of the first believers shows that the Spirit is the agent of God's activity (answering the 'what' question). Also, the Spirit is experienced as a person who sees, searches, knows, teaches, dwells, cries out, leads, bears witness, desires, intercedes, helps, strengthens, grieves, etc. (answering the 'who' question).

The link between the Spirit's identity in the Trinity and the Spirit's role in our lives becomes clearer now. Brian Gaybba puts it this way: 'The Spirit is a Person whose identity is to be the means whereby God and Christ are present to each other and to us.'[4] The Spirit therefore is also the love binding us to the Father and the Son.

This then leads us into the understanding of the mission of the Spirit. Brian Gaybba astutely develops the thought for us by stating, 'The Spirit's mission is to be the love that unites and, by uniting, transforms all it unites.'[5] This simple statement should be appreciated in a very broad and inclusive way. This statement captures the purpose and method of the work of the Holy Spirit. In these chapters on the Holy Spirit you will see how the Holy Spirit is at work to help us experience the unity that Jesus has made possible. In the beginning of this guidebook I highlighted how sin divides, and by dividing, destroys all that it divides. These chapters will illuminate the ways in which the Spirit is God's loving presence and power who transforms all who are united in the Spirit's love.

---

[4] *The Spirit of Love*, p. 138.
[5] *The Spirit of Love*, p. 141.

The link between Jesus and the Spirit

We noted earlier that it is the Spirit's identity to be the way in which we experience the presence and power of the Father and the Son. This is however something that is often ignored or overlooked in modern Christianity, with sometimes tragic results. People do things, that they believe the Holy Spirit led them to do, which are a clear violation of Jesus' character (and therefore the Father's character too).

It is important to focus on the close link between Jesus and the Spirit. We must realise that the Holy Spirit will only reveal the Father and Son's truth, will only seek to unite us to their truth. Any revelation that is claimed to be of the Spirit but is contrary to the revealed will of the Father in Jesus must be rejected, for the Holy Spirit will not lead us in any other direction.

This connection between Jesus and the Spirit is evident in the following[6]:

Firstly, Jesus is given the Spirit of God after a long absence of the Spirit's presence with anyone. In fact no other person in the Bible was filled by the Spirit of God as much as Jesus was. Some references worth looking at are: Matthew 1.20; Mark 1.9-11 and parallels; Matthew 4.1-11 and parallels; Matthew 12.28; Luke 10.21; 1 Corinthians 15.45.

Secondly, the death and resurrection of Jesus was a pre-condition for the outpouring of the Holy Spirit. This point was made clear by Jesus in John 7.39 and John 16.7. The Holy Spirit is the Spirit of the crucified and raised Jesus. The Spirit is the spirit of the whole of Jesus' ministry as it was lived by him – his life, ministry, death and resurrection – all of which gives identity to the person and character of the Holy Spirit. Therefore it is only after the resurrection that Jesus breathes the spirit onto the disciples.

Thirdly, the Holy Spirit is the way in which the risen Jesus is actively present in the midst of his people. Please note that the Spirit does not replace Jesus because he is absent, it is Jesus' Spirit who is with his followers. Jesus is personally present with us by his Spirit. (Note how this underlines Jesus' divinity – God's Spirit is now Jesus' Spirit). Following Jesus is therefore not about following a leader from whom I am separated by 2000 years and thousands of kilometres; no, it is about following one who lives within me, and makes his wisdom and help known to me. For references see Matthew 28.20; John 14.15-18; 14.25-27; 16.7-11; 16.13-15; Romans 8.9.

Fourthly, Jesus is the one who is shown as the giver of the Holy Spirit. For references see John 14.26, John 20.22; 1 Corinthians 15.45.

The history of Christianity is far too cluttered with desperately sad events

---

[6] Here I am summarising Gaybba's presentation of these truths in *The Spirit of Love*, pp.18-25.

where people have done things that the 'Holy Spirit' led them to do, but which were in clear violation of the revelation of God in Jesus of Nazareth. It is an awful irony that people have justified their rebellion against Jesus on the leading of his Spirit! Chapter 1 highlighted some of these dreadful realities of missing Jesus.

The 'facelessness' of the Spirit

The truth that this section has underlined, namely that the Spirit's identity is to be the way in which the Father and the Son are present to us, leads us to understand the 'facelessness' of the Spirit. It is impossible to distinguish a personality of the Spirit apart from the Father and the Son. The Spirit does not have a third face in the Trinity, but is rather identified by being the way in which the Father and Son's love is present to us.

THE LIFESAVING STATION PARABLE

The following parable helps us to reflect on how much we allow Jesus' mission to continue through us by his Spirit. Our failings will reveal some of the places that Jesus is missing in our lives as Christians and church:

> On a dangerous sea coast where shipwrecks often occur, there was once a crude little life-saving station. The building was just a hut, and there was only one boat, but the few devoted members kept a constant watch over the sea, and with no thought for themselves, went out day and night tirelessly searching for the lost. Some of those who were saved and various others in the surrounding area wanted to become associated with the station and gave of their time and money and effort for the support of its work. New boats were bought and new crews trained. The little life-saving station grew.
>
> Some of the members of the life-saving station were unhappy that the building was so crude and poorly equipped. They felt that a more comfortable place should be provided as the first refuge of those saved from the sea. They replaced the emergency cots with beds and put better furniture in the enlarged building.
>
> Now the life-saving station became a popular gathering place for its members, and they decorated it beautifully because they used it as a sort of club. Fewer members were now interested in going to sea on life-saving missions, so they hired lifeboat crews to do this work. The life-saving motif still prevailed in the club's decorations, and there was

a liturgical life-boat in the room where the club's initiations were held. About this time a large ship was wrecked off the coast, and the hired crews brought in boat loads of cold, wet and half-drowned people. They were dirty and sick. The beautiful new club was in chaos. So the property committee immediately had a shower house built outside the club where future victims of shipwrecks could be cleaned up before coming inside.

At the next meeting, there was a split among the club membership. Most of the members wanted to stop the club's life-saving activities as being unpleasant and a hindrance to the normal social life of the club. Some members insisted upon life-saving as their primary purpose and pointed out that they were still called a life-saving station. But they were finally voted down and told that if they wanted to save the lives of all the various kinds of people who were shipwrecked in those waters, they could begin their own life-saving station. So they did.

As the years went by, the new station experienced the same changes that had occurred in the old. It evolved into a club, and yet another life-saving station was founded. History continued to repeat itself, and if you visit that sea coast today, you will find a number of exclusive clubs along that shore. Shipwrecks are frequent in those waters, but most of the people drown.[7]

Jesus' Spirit is given that we may continue his mission of sharing good news for the poor, release for the captives, opening the eyes of blindness and liberation for the oppressed. Can you and I ask ourselves – am I relying on the Spirit to help me to do this? Or is my life in the church very distant from these missional goals? Have I become distant from what Christianity is meant to be focused on? Is the congregation I am part of focused on these missional goals?

---

[7] This parable was written in 1953 by the Rev. Dr Theodore O. Wedel. I accessed this copy of it from http://loosecanon.georgiaepiscopal.org/?p=457 on 10/1/2018.

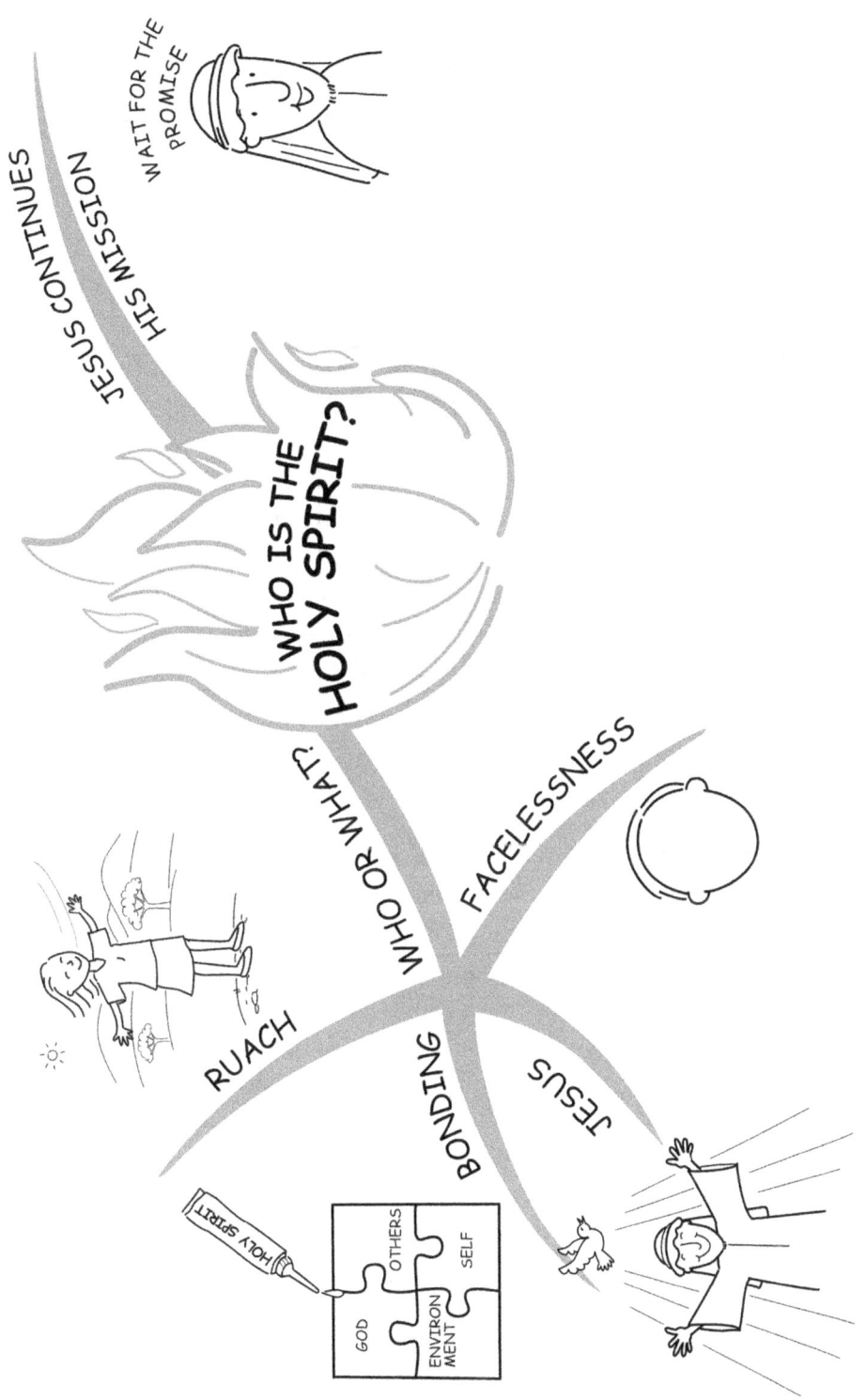

SUGGESTIONS FOR DISCUSSION, REVISION, REFLECTION AND APPLICATION

(These questions are intended for group work, but can easily be adapted for personal use.)

1. What is the most important message to you in this chapter? (Remember to also make a note of this on your 'God spoke to me' page.)
2. Icebreaker question (just for fun and to continue the journey of getting to know each other): Ask the group to quickly answer these questions – Would you rather: Visit the doctor or the dentist? Watch TV or listen to music? Have a beach holiday or a mountain holiday? Be invisible or be able to read minds? Be the most popular or the smartest person you know? Always be cold or always be hot? Be stranded on a deserted island alone or with someone you don't like? (These questions must be answered quickly. As a group, do not spend longer than 5 minutes in total on these icebreaker questions.)
3. Read John 14.15-29 and answer the following questions:
    a. Choose a verse or phrase that seems to resonate deeply with you. Spend time reflecting on these words. What is attracting you to the words? What need is being met for you? What call is perhaps emerging? In what area of your life are you being challenged? Share the verse or phrase with the others.
    b. Notice the union between God the Father and Himself that Jesus describes. As a group make sure that you have noticed all these descriptions. Help each other in this. Are there fresh insights for you here? Are you learning something that you did not know?
    c. Notice how we as disciples are promised a special closeness and union with God and Jesus. As a group make sure that you have noticed all these descriptions. Help each other in this. Are there fresh insights for you here? Are you learning something that you did not know?
    d. In what ways does this passage help us to understand the Spirit's role in continuing the mission of Jesus? What activities of the Spirit are described that help us to be disciples?
    e. Think of an instance when you have experienced this activity of the

Spirit. Perhaps share this event with the group.
- f. What does this passage say about the importance of Jesus' teachings?
- g. Discuss peace (verse 27). What does it mean to have peace in troubled times? How does Jesus give us peace? What makes for peace? Is peace nurtured and cultivated in our relationship with Jesus? If so, what are best practices?
- h. How is Jesus' giving of gifts different from how the world gives? (verse 27)
- i. Now that you have received the promise afresh of the Holy Spirit as your helper (advocate), is there a challenge that you will meet that prior to now you had not felt up to?

4. Below are a variety of suggestions and questions to aid your appreciation of this chapter. Do not attempt to do all of them! Choose those that are most appropriate to your unique situation and/or group. The questions are designed to help variously with revision, understanding, appreciation, reflection or application of the content.
   - a. What has been your most significant experience of the Holy Spirit? As you remember it, what can you learn from that experience that will help you to experience God's Spirit more often?
   - b. Think about the disciples of the early church who discovered that Jesus was continuing his ministry in and through them. This would have filled them with awe and excitement. What do you think was the most adventurous aspect of this ministry?
   - c. Think about the way in which you speak of God's Spirit? Do you mostly refer to the Spirit as a force or a person? Why? What is your experience of God's Spirit as a force? What is your experience of God's Spirit as a person?
   - d. Someone comes to you and asks: 'Who or what is the Holy Spirit?' What will you say?
   - e. How closely are Jesus and the Holy Spirit related for you? Has your view changed in any way since studying this chapter? In what ways has it changed?
   - f. What do you understand by the 'facelessness' of the Holy Spirit? Give an example.
   - g. 'The Spirit's mission is to be the love that unites and, by uniting, transforms all it unites.' Discuss all the ways in which this phrase relates to the content of this guidebook.
   - h. Is there any of the theology of this chapter that you do not understand? Try and get clarity in your group discussion.

i. Discuss your responses to the parable of the lifesaving station. Also, what changes are you prompted to make to your life as a result of this parable? Also, what should your church stop doing – and what should it start doing?

GOD SPOKE TO ME ...

17

THE HOLY SPIRIT IN MY RELATIONSHIP WITH GOD AND THE COMMUNITY

This Spirit he poured out on us richly through Jesus Christ our Saviour, so that, having been justified by his grace, we might become heirs according to the hope of eternal life.
(Titus 3.6 & 7)

There is a story that I read in one of Trevor Hudson's books that I have enjoyed telling for nearly 15 years:

> When electricity first became available to farmers living in the northern parts of England, there were varied responses. Some property owners refused to have powerlines on their land. They preferred kerosene lamps and lanterns to all the marvellous benefits of electricity. What intrigued me when I heard these stories, however, was the response of one elderly woman. She used the electricity, but each month when the meter was read, the amount she owed was very small. The local municipality installed another meter, but with much the same results. It was only later in conversation with her that the secret came out: 'Electricity is really wonderful,' the lady said to the municipal official, 'and I use it every night. When it gets dark I switch on the lights, find my matches, light my candle and then switch the lights off again!'[1]

---

[1] Trevor Hudson with Morton Kelsey, *Journey of the Spirit – Devotions for the Spiritual Seeker*, p. 21.

There are so many Christians who are like that lady – they have not entrusted themselves to the Holy Spirit, who is the power and presence of Jesus with us. This is also a kind of missing Jesus. They responded to God's grace offered in Jesus but yet have gone on to ignore Jesus and his Spirit. There are those for whom being a Christian has the absolute minimum of meaning. The Holy Spirit can be likened to the high-voltage electricity of life and it is available to all so that we may live abundant lives as disciples. Many chose to rather live on their own strength and their own resources and their own wisdom and their own willpower.

In this and the next chapter I will carefully share as much as I can, within the confines of a guidebook, about the transformative and dynamic difference that the Holy Spirit is able to effect for those who entrust themselves to him.

INTRODUCTION

We have seen how Jesus' birth, ministry, death and resurrection establish a unity in the four relationships of life. The role of the Holy Spirit is to accomplish within me what Jesus established in the world. I use the word 'accomplished' frequently in this section in order to convey the truth that the Holy Spirit makes real for you and me the new reality that Jesus established. The Holy Spirit enables me to share in the results of Jesus' birth, ministry, death and resurrection. The Holy Spirit enables me to experience this reconciliation in the four relationships of life that was established by Jesus' birth, ministry, death and resurrection. The idea I am following here is captured in Titus 3.6 & 7: *This Spirit he poured out on us richly through Jesus Christ our Saviour, so that, having been justified by his grace, we might become heirs according to the hope of eternal life.*

The Spirit enables me to inherit that which Jesus makes available. I am an heir to what Jesus established! The Holy Spirit accomplishes in me what Jesus established in the world. This is all part of what is meant by the statement: 'The Spirit's mission is to be the love that unites and, by uniting, transforms all it unites.'[2]

The Christian life is therefore fundamentally lived in the Spirit of Jesus and by the Spirit of Jesus. We can only be a real follower of Jesus when we are filled with his Spirit and live in and by his Spirit. This includes walking in the Spirit, being led by the Spirit and sowing to the Spirit.

There seems to me to be a problem with those who speak of the Holy Spirit in a very theological and almost academic and even liturgical way. Some do not

---

[2] *The Spirit of Love*, p. 141.

speak about the Holy Spirit at all. These seem to be missing out on the Holy Spirit as a dynamically experienced reality. For these there seems to be the kind of distance between them and the Spirit as there is between a reader and an exciting novel – all the action is being experienced by someone else.

There also seems to me to be a problem with those whose Christian experience is all about the 'wow' of the Holy Spirit. For them it is essential that they continually experience God in dynamic and fresh ways. Not all intense and exciting experiences are from God and nor do they all serve his Kingdom. A Christian should have discernment about this.

My prayer is that this chapter will be of great help to all who read it – for those who see themselves in the Christians of the above two paragraphs, and for those who are somewhere in-between.

THE HOLY SPIRIT ACCOMPLISHES MY UNITY WITH GOD

The unity with God that God created humanity to enjoy, but which was destroyed through sin, was re-established by Jesus in his birth and deepened in his ministry, sealed in his death and demonstrated in the resurrection and is now *accomplished* for each person who receives God's Spirit.

The Holy Spirit always makes the first move

The Holy Spirit begins work on drawing us to God long before we are conscious of this movement in our lives. I know of no Christian who could say that they entered into a relationship with God through their own efforts. Even when people do go through lengthy quests to find a god worth putting faith in, they eventually realise that their very thirst for God was the work of the Holy Spirit awakening them to the 'more' of life.

So the Holy Spirit's work of calling us, wooing us, attracting us, loving us and intriguing us into a relationship with God is something that is his work throughout our lifetimes and begins long before we decide to enter into a relationship with God.

When I grow up ...

When I look back on my life it always amazes me to reflect on how early on in my childhood God called me into ministry. Equally amazing is that God had become so real to me before that, meeting a great need that I had for a father after my mother and father had divorced due to his alcoholism and reckless behaviour. My mother and father divorced when I was four and we moved to East London. In our new home without my father I was desperately unhappy at first. During this time God's eye was upon my need and at that very young age made himself known to me as Father. This was so tangible that I instinctively put a chair in my room on which God would sit when I prayed! Within the next few years I also became aware of a call to full-time ministry as the vocation of my life. This call was so clear from such a young age that I recorded it at the age of nine in a 'When I grow up' essay that we had to write for school. Here is the actual essay that I wrote:

> What I want to be
> I want to be a Minerster or a teecher I want to be a Minersrer because He is Holly. I want to be a teecher because he can get the Scooll holidays. Now I am finished my story cold What I want to be.
>
> John W.
> Tr c

Of course this story is filled with all the naiveté, imagination, insecurities, desires and desperation of myself as a child. But that does not diminish the value of the events. God's Spirit had started to save me and lead me into a life of meaning and value. That is a journey that has continued throughout my life and those beginnings were never found to be mere wishful thinking but rather were the start of discovering the meaning and the 'more' of life through a relationship with God.

So the Holy Spirit is able to work with any person, in any part of the world, at any stage of their life – always for the purpose of lovingly caring for them and drawing them into a relationship with God.

The essence of eternal life

According to Jesus, 'eternal life' is exactly this experience of deep union between a person and God. After speaking a lot about the Holy Spirit in John 16, Jesus speaks of the result of the Holy Spirit's work by describing it as eternal life. He actually says that eternal life and this relationship of oneness with God are the same thing: *And eternal life means knowing you, the only true God, and knowing Jesus Christ, whom you sent.* (John 17.3 – Good News Translation). I call this the forgotten definition of eternal life.

Overwhelmingly personal

What is particularly special is that this relationship with God has an overwhelmingly personal quality to it. This is quite remarkable because in no other religion is this phenomenon so strong.

We enjoy this type of relationship with God thanks to the work of the Holy Spirit in our lives. As Paul says, it is the Holy Spirit who gives us *...a spirit of adoption. When we cry, 'Abba! Father!' it is that very Spirit bearing witness with our spirit that we are children of God, and if children, then heirs, heirs of God and joint heirs with Christ.* (Romans 8.15-17. Do not miss how this passage also speaks of the very important theme of us as heirs of what Jesus has established.)

For a Christian God is not only 'the God of our Fathers' that we have the privilege to worship, nor is God only the great 'Ground of our being' to whom we must orientate ourselves, nor is God only the obvious Creator who must be honoured. God is all of this and many more noble descriptions – but there is still more – and that more is the precious personal and intimate relationship that is an exquisite dimension given to us by the Holy Spirit. For us God is '*Abba*' with whom we each have a personal relationship.

It was Jesus who first invited people into such a relationship with God by telling them to say '*Abba*' when they pray (see Luke 11.2). *Abba* was the intimate word Jesus would have used as a child when he addressed his own father, Joseph. Jesus was the first Jewish rabbi to address God with this beautiful word and to teach his followers to do the same. The Holy Spirit continues this ministry of Jesus by helping each Christian to be blessed by a special sense of being God's child. The precious realisation here is that the Holy Spirit is enabling us to share in a similar relationship with God the Father as Jesus enjoyed! The Holy Spirit just needs to be given space in our hearts and minds for this.[3]

---

[3] The point of Jesus' use of the term *Abba* is that it is an intimate term for a warm loving relationship. The point is not to assert God as masculine. God does not have gender. Gender terms are metaphors. Even *Abba* is a metaphor. Feminine and motherly metaphors are also applied to God in the Bible. Always remember that God transcends personal and human metaphors. Also, the sad reality of many people having had destructive and hurtful experiences from fathers and men does not devalue Jesus' use of the term. We all need healing relationships of love and the Holy Spirit's work of giving us a relationship with God as a good '*Abba*' has enormous power to heal us even of horrible past experiences with men and fathers.

Trevor Hudson gives us a special insight into some of what this personal relationship means to us when he puts into words the types of things the Holy Spirit says to us: 'You are Abba's beloved. You are loved, accepted and forgiven. You belong to the family of God. You have complete access into the presence of God. You don't have to send in anyone else with your requests. You do not have to pretend to be what you are not. You can come as you are because you are dealing with someone who loves you very much.'[4]

You are now a temple!

God's Spirit so accomplishes my unity with God that I may have the great honour of being called a temple of the Holy Spirit: *Do you not know that you are God's temple and that God's Spirit dwells in you? (1 Corinthians 3.16. See also 1 Corinthians 6.19; Ephesians 2.22; John 14.16).*

Similarly the Holy Spirit unites me to Jesus so closely that he is described as living in me:

Galatians 2.19-20: *'I have been crucified with Christ; and it is no longer I who live, but it is Christ who lives in me',* and 2 Corinthians 13.5 *'Examine yourselves to see whether you are living in the faith. Test*

---

[4] *Holy Spirit Here and Now*, p. 113f.

yourselves. Do you not realize that Jesus Christ is in you?' and John 14.23: *Jesus answered him, 'Those who love me will keep my word, and my Father will love them, and we will come to them and make our home with them'* and then later in John 17.23 Jesus refers to his relationship with disciples as *'I in them'*.

Imagine a great cathedral that gives a distinct sense of God's presence as you walk into its cool sanctuary. It has been a place of worship for so long that the space is truly set apart for holiness. If Paul were writing today he would say: *'Do you not know that you are God's cathedral and that God's Spirit dwells in you?'*

Some hope-filled affirmations

The presence of God's Spirit within me is a constant assurance of salvation and of being united to God: *By this we know that we abide in him and he in us, because he has given us of his Spirit.* (1 John 4.13; see also 1 John 3.24).

Romans 8.26-27 gives us the beautiful reminder that my unity with God is even maintained by God's Spirit when I am too weak to do so myself: *Likewise the Spirit helps us in our weakness; for we do not know how to pray as we ought, but that very Spirit intercedes with sighs too deep for words. And God, who searches the heart, knows what is the mind of the Spirit, because the Spirit intercedes for the saints according to the will of God.*

The gift of God's Spirit to us is also a down-payment or guarantee that the unity we enjoy now with God will be fully accomplished after our death. A few verses from 2 Corinthians 5.1-5 are worth printing here: *For we know that if the earthly tent we live in is destroyed, we have a building from God, a house not made with hands, eternal in the heavens. For in this tent we groan, longing to be clothed with our heavenly dwelling ... He who has prepared us for this very thing is God, who has given us the Spirit as a guarantee.* (See also Ephesians 1.13-14; Romans 6.23; 1 Corinthians 15.55; 1 Corinthians 15.39-44; Romans 8.11)

Opening our ears

The Holy Spirit does not only help us to hear these tender affirmations but also helps us to hear God calling us to obey, surrender and learn when we read our Bibles. The Holy Spirit not only enables us to feel loved by God in a personal way but also helps us to hear God speak into our lives.

There are many ways in which God speaks to us, but the Bible is certainly the most important place and it is here that we experience part of the Holy Spirit's most important work in our lives. Through this work of the Holy Spirit the Bible is not an end in itself but a means to actually getting to know God, his Kingdom, his story in this world and then how I fit into that story. The Holy Spirit makes us conscious of these realities so that when I read the Bible I am on the look-out for how I can get to know God better, understand the dynamics of his Kingdom more fully, appreciate what God is doing in the world and become inspired about how my story can fit with God's story in the world. When I am reading a passage in the Bible the Holy Spirit will make certain parts stand out for me and will help me to see and hear God as I reflect and pray on what has been revealed to me.

The real experience of the actual relationship with God

I hope that part of the impression you are receiving is that the presence of God in our lives is experienced by his Spirit. This experience of God's presence is an essential aspect of our union with God. Our relationship with God is not merely our approving nod to the belief in the existence of God.

The simple prayer *'Come Holy Spirit'* referred to at the beginning of the first chapter on the Holy Spirit is our way of inviting the Holy Spirit to give us a sense of God's presence. Christians have prayed this prayer since the beginning of the church and often the invitation is said or sung liturgically in the Latin of 2000 years ago, *'Veni Sancte Spiritus'*.

When space is given for welcoming the Spirit and the invitation is made then the experience that follows is often an experience of God's loving closeness and accompanying experiences of peace, calmness, and kindness. The presence of the Spirit may result in emotions and bodily experiences too – sensation of heat, shaking, relief, release, tears, even laughter (which is part of the relief and release for some people). It is always a refreshing experience.

Paul Cameron describes his own experience of the Holy Spirit in the following words:

> I have journeyed with the presence of the Holy Spirit since 1994. Before I pray for healing for others, I always invite the presence of the Spirit. Almost always the Spirit brings a peace or calmness on a person. Often you can see this on their whole bodies, the absolute relief as the Spirit brings His tranquil presence. Sometimes the peace is so intense, people cannot believe what is happening! I have seen people weep in His presence, as He gently surfaces hurt. Most Sundays as I minister in different churches, and we pray for His presence, the mighty Godhead, the source of all, through Spirit come ordinary, often broken people and He showers them with His love and presence. Each encounter

appears to be different, often tailor-made to a person's needs. This gentle, mysterious presence always brings healing and restoration.[5]

THE HOLY SPIRIT ACCOMPLISHES COMMUNITY LIFE AMONGST PEOPLE

The unity between people that God created for us to enjoy, but which was destroyed through sin, was re-established by Jesus in his ministry, sealed in his death and demonstrated in the resurrection and is now *accomplished* by the Holy Spirit in the formation of the church which is the visible expression of community amongst people that God created us to enjoy.

Community is essential

This guidebook has reflected at length on divisions between people and what Jesus has done to overcome those divisions. So it is clear to us that a person who is following Jesus closely is someone who practises inclusion and community building. However in practice this is something many Christ followers struggle with. Differences between races, classes, cultures, nationalities, tribes, languages, philosophical persuasions, sexual orientation and other identifiers can be very high walls between people and cause real struggles in building a local community of unity. A core work of the Holy Spirit is to help us overcome these struggles and to particularly overcome these struggles through the community life of the church.

In a wonderful blend of truth and memorable phrasing someone said, 'The greatest sign of the Gospel is not what happens in someone but between people.' I like that!

It's always been a struggle for some people

It is worthwhile noting that the Apostle Peter struggled intensely with the inclusion of Gentiles in the early church. The Holy Spirit did not leave him in a narrow prejudiced place but enabled him to accept those he formally had found unacceptable and to include those he had proudly believed must be shunned.

The first moment was very dramatic and made the circle of who was included much larger than it had previously been. This first moment is the outpouring of the Holy Spirit in Jerusalem during the days when Jews from many lands had gathered for the festival of Pentecost.[6] In this moment Peter

---

[5] *Kingdom, Discipleship and Holistic Healing*, 2017 self-published booklet, p. 24. See www.paulcameron.org.za.

[6] Pentecost is the Greek name for a festival of gratitude for the first fruits (early harvest). It was more generally referred to as the 'Feast of Weeks' (Hebrew *Shavuot*). See Exodus 23.14-17; 34.18-24; Deuteronomy 16.16; 2 Chronicles 8.13. It was an obligatory observance for Jewish people.

and the disciples preach in languages they could not normally speak. Through insight given by the Spirit Peter immediately understands that the prophesy is being fulfilled – that a time has now come when God's Spirit is not limited to certain individuals (mostly mature men) for certain tasks, but that God's Spirit is now poured out on all believers. Peter proclaims this insight in his sermon which can be read in Acts 2.14-36. Here is a portion of it:

> *But Peter, standing with the eleven, raised his voice and addressed them, 'Men of Judea and all who live in Jerusalem, let this be known to you, and listen to what I say. Indeed, these are not drunk, as you suppose, for it is only nine o'clock in the morning. No, this is what was spoken through the prophet Joel: In the last days it will be, God declares, that I will pour out my Spirit upon all flesh, and your sons and your daughters shall prophesy, and your young men shall see visions, and your old men shall dream dreams. Even upon my slaves, both men and women, in those days I will pour out my Spirit; and they shall prophesy'.* ('All flesh' in Joel's passage refers to all races, viz. believers of all races)

At this stage Peter did not imagine that Gentiles would be included in the group of followers of Jesus. With firmness the Holy Spirit helped Peter overcome that deep conviction. Quite remarkably the Holy Spirit sends a Gentile man by the name of Cornelius, a centurion of the Italian cohort, to meet with Peter. Peter however would never think of meeting with a Gentile centurion, so the Holy Spirit first appears to Peter and firmly convinces him that he must not regard Cornelius as rejected by God because God's church must now include him. In the vision Peter is ordered to eat reptiles and other animals forbidden for a Jew, with the words *'What God has made clean, you must not call profane.'* (Acts 10.15). Like a good Jew Peter refuses, but the vision is repeated three times and Peter eventually gets the point. Peter does obey this prejudice-shattering vision and goes to meet Cornelius. To make matters more difficult for Peter, Cornelius is not alone but has called together a whole crowd of relatives and friends, but Peter is allowing himself to be led by the Spirit and says to them: *'You yourselves know that it is unlawful for a Jew to associate with or to visit a Gentile; but God has shown me that I should not call anyone profane or unclean.'* (Acts 10.28)

On that remarkable day the whole crowd not only become believers in Jesus, but also get filled with the Holy Spirit and speak in tongues and then are baptised with water. Peter ends up staying with this huge group of Gentiles for a number of days and they become good friends. The circle of Peter's world has grown enormously!

The body of Christ

I hope the character and originating role of the Holy Spirit is clear to you. It is the Holy Spirit who creates this very special community of unity amongst diverse peoples. This community is the church. The church is by definition a community of unity. The Holy Spirit creates the church and community at the same time. The church and a community of unity are meant to be synonymous, for both are the visible result of the Spirit's activity in the world.[7]

Through the work of the Holy Spirit my body, along with all believers' bodies, becomes the body of Christ because the same Spirit that gave Jesus his resurrected body now lives in us and unites us to each other and empowers us to historically represent and be Christ in the world.[8]

Saved for community

Unlike Peter, Paul had not found it so difficult to include Gentiles as part of God's people. For Paul, salvation is entered into individually rather than ethnically or nationally as in the old covenant. That which is entered into is a community of the new and final people of God. So although we are saved individually, we are saved for community, and that community is the beginning of the ultimate destiny of all God's people.

The Holy Spirit continues this work in both subtle and dramatic ways in our lives. The Holy Spirit is at work in our lives all the time to widen our circle. The Holy Spirit will prompt me to get to know a new person, to listen to their story and even become a friend. The Holy Spirit will humble me so that I can listen to those I never had time to listen to before. The Holy Spirit will soften my judgementalism and give me a larger awareness of God's world. The Holy Spirit will pause me in my knee-jerk rejections to different viewpoints long enough to begin to hear where they are coming from. The Holy Spirit will awaken in me an enjoyment of the others' culture, mannerisms, personality or interests. The Holy Spirit will enable me to forgive or ask for forgiveness. The Holy Spirit will help us make the most of new and different people that come into our lives from time to time (the Holy Spirit may have brought them into our lives just as he brought Cornelius and Peter together). The Holy Spirit will grow my compassion for those who suffer and will draw me to spend time with them, to learn from them and to develop solidarity with them. Further, God's Spirit can fill me to such an extent that love can become part of my body too, that I

---

[7] The New Testament testifies that the Holy Spirit was a key source for the unity that was so important to the early church. The Holy Spirit was present to enable the early church to reflect the community of unity that God wanted them to be. See Ephesians 2.18; 4.3-4; 1 Corinthians 12.9-13; Acts 2.44-47; 4.32-35.

[8] See 1 Corinthians 12.12-27; 6.15; 10.16; Colossians 1.18; Ephesians 1.23.

too will be moved from my heart and gut to show love to those who suffer. The Holy Spirit will even enable me to be secure enough to let go of privileges so that genuine unity can be achieved with someone outside of my place in society.

Not restricted to the church

It is edifying to appreciate that the Holy Spirit is doing this work of building community outside of the church too. The Spirit is the Spirit of Love and as such is at work wherever love is at work, even if no Christian title is accepted by those doing the work.

The Holy Spirit can be at work in people of other faiths too. The church is the visible result of the Spirit's work and therefore it should be obvious that the Spirit is at work outside of that visible result too. This is to say that the Spirit is at work in people's lives, drawing them into the church before they enter the church; the Spirit is at work developing communities of unity outside of the church; the Spirit is at work bringing healing outside of the Christian ministry of healing; the Spirit's work is not limited to the entity of 'church' just as God makes the sun to warm and the rain to water all of his creation.[9]

A truly charismatic moment

One morning in 1995 I was privileged to be part of a truly charismatic service – so named even though no one was speaking in tongues or being 'slain' in the Spirit. At the beginning of that year I had become the minister of Sea Point Methodist Church in Cape Town. This congregation offered three services a Sunday, two in English and one in isiXhosa. The amaXhosa congregation had become part of Sea Point Methodist in the 1960s after being forcibly removed by the state from their church in District Six. It was good that Sea Point had given 'them' a home, but the problem was that it had remained an 'us' and 'them' relationship for 30 years. Even the District had assigned a separate minister from Langa to be the minister of the Xhosa congregation at Sea Point – but Bishop James Gribble changed this arrangement with my appointment in 1995 and had assigned me to be the minister of all Sea Point Methodists' congregations.

To my great discomfort I discovered that the English and Xhosa congregations had never worshipped together in all those 30 years. So in that first year

---

[9] This theme is clearly presented in Brian Gaybba's *The Spirit of Love*, pp. 171ff. I particularly like the following lines: 'To believe that the Church is the sacrament of a unity that stretches beyond its borders is to believe that the Church is the visible structured embodiment of a larger reality. This larger reality is the unity, in Love, of a wide variety of people… We can and should look for signs of the Spirit's saving activity beyond the strict borders of the Church.'

and within the context of the recently birthed 'new South Africa' we held our first combined service. In this sense the service was truly 'charismatic' in that the Holy Spirit was uniting those who had been divided. We sang each other's hymns, enjoyed each other's liturgy and some even danced.

At the end of my sermon I gave an altar call inviting for confession and forgiveness between the members of the congregation. The Spirit moved very deeply and most of the congregation came to the front and gathered at the communion rail and shared in public acts of confession and reconciliation – kneeling, praying, hugging, smiling and crying. It was the beginning of regular combined services and also of our own 'Truth and Reconciliation' process that we shared in a small group setting.

THIS LASTS FOREVER!

As we end this chapter it is worth reflecting that community is the one reality that will last from history into eternity. Community was, is and will always be what God is achieving. Our participation now in appreciating and building that community are activities that have forever benefits! That gives those efforts great worth.

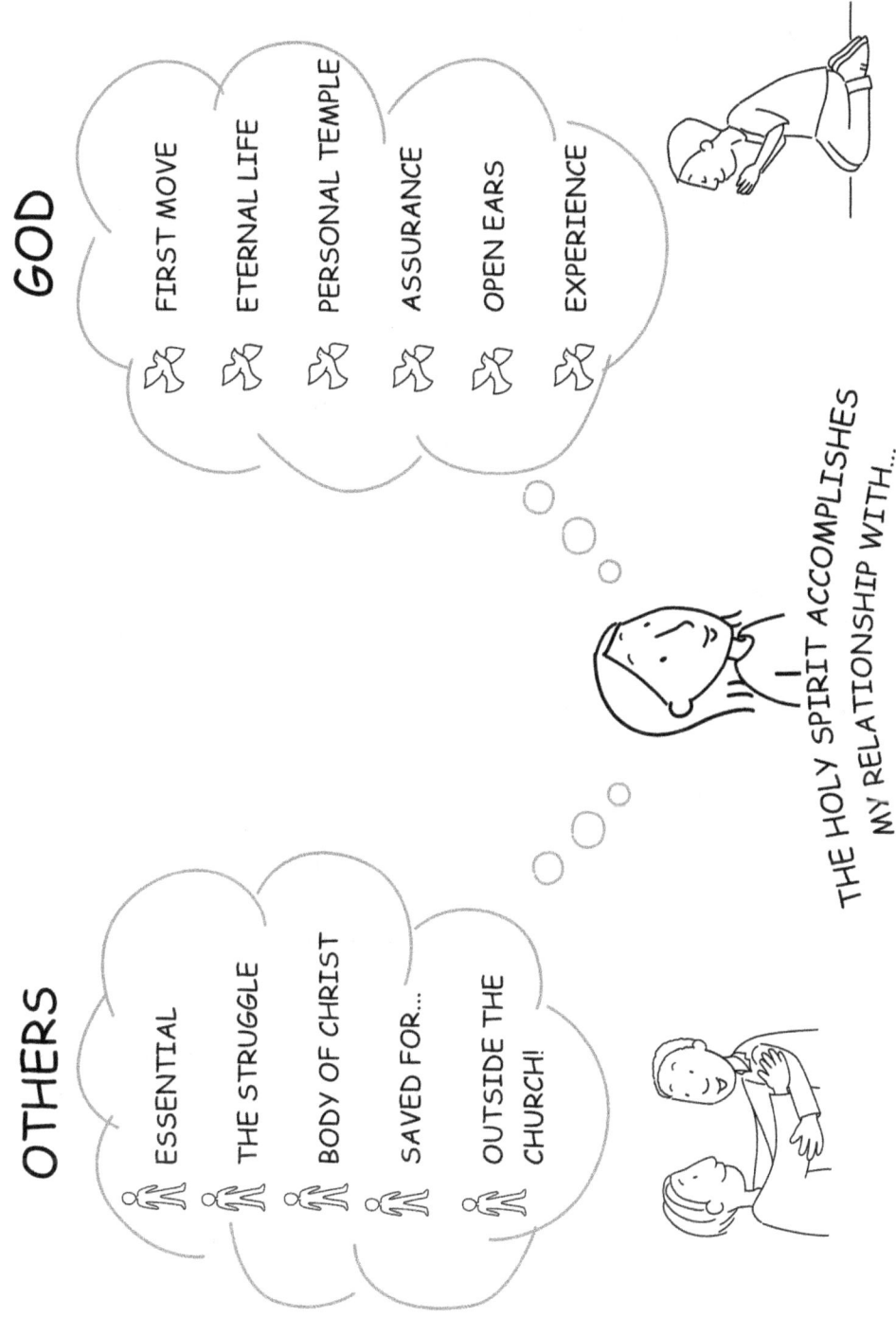

SUGGESTIONS FOR DISCUSSION, REVISION, REFLECTION AND APPLICATION

(These questions are intended for group work, but can easily be adapted for personal use.)

1. What is the most important message to you in this chapter? (Remember to also make a note of this on your 'God spoke to me' page.)
2. Icebreaker question: What book have you read lately that you would recommend? (The question must be answered quickly. As a group, do not spend longer than 5 minutes in total on this question.)
3. Read Romans 8.12-17 and answer the following questions:
   a. Read this passage carefully and note all the ways in which the Spirit gives us a special and real relationship with God.
   b. Discuss the impact this teaching had on gentiles who had been in pagan religions before putting faith in Jesus.
   c. What does this passage say about God?
   d. What does this passage say about us?
   e. What is your favourite line in this passage?
4. Below are a variety of suggestions and questions to aid your appreciation of this chapter. Do not attempt to do all of them! Choose those that are most appropriate to your unique situation and/or group. The questions are designed to help variously with revision, understanding, appreciation, reflection or application of the content.
5. General
   a. Who was the first person who really impressed you as filled with God's Spirit? What was it about the person that gave you this impression? How old were you?
   b. How much does the meaning of the opening story about electricity in England apply to you?
   c. Discuss any problems you may have in understanding the concept of the Spirit 'accomplishing' what Jesus has 'established'.
6. The Holy Spirit accomplishes my unity with God.
   a. What is the most important message to you in this section? If you are in a group gathering then pair up with a person sitting next to you and

give 5 minutes to share this with each other. (Remember to also make a note of this on your 'God spoke to me' page.)
   b. What has been for you the most precious experience of a personal relationship with God? Try and describe it. Has it been a relationship with God as Father (or Mother)? Or, has it been more a relationship with Jesus? Or both equally? When you speak to God, are you speaking to the Father or to Jesus? When God speaks to you – is it Jesus or the Father speaking?
   c. Do you struggle to enjoy a personal intimate relationship with God? Do you know why? Will you please talk to Jesus about this.
   d. What effect, if any, does it have on you to be referred to as 'God's cathedral'? Do people get a sense of the Spirit within you? Do you have a sense of the Spirit within you?
   e. Have you ever been unable to pray and have asked the Spirit to pray on your behalf?
   f. Do you hear God speak to you when you read Scripture? What might help you to experience it as a time of communion in your relationship with God?
   g. Think about areas of distance in your relationship with God? Pray to the Spirit for the grace to experience intimacy in these areas.
   h. Would you take the simple prayer: *'Come Holy Spirit'* and make it more part of your daily life? And when you are praying for others too?
7. The Holy Spirit accomplishes community life amongst people.
   a. What is the most important message to you in this section? If you are in a group gathering then pair up with a person sitting next to you and give 5 minutes to share this with each other. (Remember to also make a note of this on your 'God spoke to me' page.)
   b. Did you follow well the Holy Spirit's work in Peter's life to bring him to accept those he had formerly found to be unacceptable? If you were a Jew in Peter's shoes, which aspect would you have found most difficult?
   c. To what extent is love of neighbour a duty for you – or to what extent has the Holy Spirit made it part of who you are?
   d. Respond to this statement, 'The most segregated day of the week in South Africa is a Sunday. On this day people who work together, and even live in the same suburbs, go to their own racially and culturally segregated churches.'
      i. How true is this generally? How true is this of your congregation?
      ii. Is this a problem?
      iii. Is this segregation only along racial and cultural lines? Who else is

excluded from church? Who else doesn't feel welcome in church?
    iv. What are the blessings of diversity in a congregation? What do you personally enjoy about people different from you?
    v. Should anything be done about all these divisions? If so, discuss some things your congregation could do.
    vi. Think about what you could do to be part of the solution.

e. Share one example from your own life where the Holy Spirit has enabled you to build friendship with someone you had previously excluded.

f. What are the subtle ways you experience the Holy Spirit at work to help you widen the circle?

g. How can we be more responsive to the Holy Spirit's move to build community amongst people previously divided?

h. Identify a few places in society where the Holy Spirit is building community outside of the church? What is bringing these people together? How should the church respond? Can we learn from these movements?

GOD SPOKE TO ME ...

18

THE HOLY SPIRIT IN MY RELATIONSHIP WITH MY ENVIRONMENT AND MYSELF

For we are what he has made us, created in Christ Jesus for good works, which God prepared beforehand to be our way of life. (Ephesians 2.10)

THE HOLY SPIRIT ACCOMPLISHES A LIFE-GIVING RELATIONSHIP WITH MY ENVIRONMENT

We were created to live in harmony with our environment and to mould our environment into a testimony to love. (Remember that environment refers to both the natural and human-made environment.) This relationship was destroyed in the fall, but in his ministry Jesus pioneered the way of relating to the environment so that it enjoys and reflects the love of God. He sealed this with his death and demonstrated it in his resurrection. Jesus' Spirit is given to the world, but particularly to believers in the church, to empower us to *accomplish* this mission and bring about a harmony between us and our environment, resulting in the transformation of the environment.

Brother Sun and Sister Moon

God's Spirit that so wonderfully creates community for me with himself, other people and myself enables me to be someone who creates community with my environment. The Holy Spirit will grow in me a love and appreciation for creation which will be like God's own love for his Creation. By the work of the Holy Spirit I will be a good caretaker, steward, protector and defender of creation.

I will be saved from regarding creation as an object separate from myself. I will appreciate our vital connection with creation and our dependence on it. The Holy Spirit will lead me on a path until I eventually am able to relate to creation as family. St Francis of Assisi reached this place and by the Spirit of God penned 'The Canticle of the Creatures' in which he refers to the Sun as 'Sir Brother' and he refers to the earth as 'Sister Mother'. He also refers to wind and fire as 'brother', and the moon, stars and water as 'sister':

> Most High, all-powerful, good Lord,
> Yours are the praises, the glory, and the honor, and all blessing,
> To You alone, Most High, do they belong,
> and no human is worthy to mention Your name.
> Praised be You, my Lord, with all Your creatures,
> especially Sir Brother Sun,
> Who is the day and through whom You give us light.
> And he is beautiful and radiant with great splendor;
> and bears a likeness of You, Most High One.
> Praised be You, my Lord, through Sister Moon and the stars,
> in heaven You formed them clear and precious and beautiful.
> Praised be You, my Lord, through Brother Wind,
> and through the air, cloudy and serene, and every kind of weather,
> through whom You give sustenance to Your creatures.
> Praised be You, my Lord, through Sister Water,
> who is very useful and humble and precious and chaste.
> Praised be You, my Lord, through Brother Fire,
> through whom You light the night,
> and he is beautiful and playful and robust and strong.
> Praised be You, my Lord, through our Sister Mother Earth,
> who sustains and governs us,
> and who produces various fruit with colored flowers and herbs.[1]

---

[1] This is the first part of the canticle written by St Francis in 1225. This translation was taken from the website 'Custodia Terrae Sanctae', http://www.custodia.org/default.asp?id=1454 (accessed 09/22/2017).

Creation as a wild womb

God's Spirit also has a long history of leading God's chosen agents into the fierce landscape of wilderness areas in order to particularly refine them. There is a way in which creation is God's ally in softening, overwhelming and inspiring us.[2] I like to refer to creation as a 'wild womb'. God uses creation as a womb in which to birth individuals as faithful servants.

Our task is to build environments of hospitality

Our environment also consists of the human-made context of our lives. This human-made environment affects every moment of our lives, determining for example whether I have employment, whether that employment is able to

---

[2] Here are a few examples of the Spirit's extreme use of the fierce landscape of wilderness areas to refine God's agents: Jacob (especially Genesis 28.10-17 and Genesis 32.22-32), Moses (especially Exodus 3 and the giving of the law in Exodus 19-20), Elijah (especially 1 Kings 19.4-18), John the Baptiser lived in the wilderness, and Jesus spent 40 days in the wilderness (Matthew 4.1-11; Luke 4.1-13).

provide for the needs of my family, my access to services like education and healthcare, my access to resources like a library and internet, social freedoms and restrictions, the quality of the air I breathe, the price I pay for goods, and the crime levels of my city and suburb. In this the Holy Spirit will work towards love being reflected in the human-made context, making it a context of hospitality in which people can feel loved and at peace.

In small and sometimes big ways I help form this environment within which we live. I need to take this influence very seriously and use it to bring about improvements to society that are in keeping with God's will and reign. The values of the Kingdom Consciousness Movement as Jesus taught are values that are meant to be reflected in the structures of society. To be specific, society needs to reflect the value of sharing rather than greed, the value of people rather than prestige, the upliftment of the vulnerable and the marginalised, the value of service rather than domination.[3] This is at the heart of discipleship for a follower of Jesus and any progress in establishing these values in society will result in every person in that society living in a context that is good for them and is a blessing to them. In this way some of the blessings of the Kingdom are passed on to all in society. Jesus is truly life and hope for the world – even for those who do not know him, or who belong to other faiths. A true saviour of the world is a saviour who can be a blessing to absolutely everyone.

This arena of discipleship can be very difficult, demanding and dangerous in that one is involved in the power struggles of society and therefore up against very real opposition and enemies. It can also be complicated and difficult to analyse a situation and choose appropriate and strategic action and partners with which to work. It is the world of politics and economics. It is the world of political parties, NGOs, NPOs, trade unions, 'watchdog' organisations and civil society in general. It is the world of business ethics. It is the world of power struggles within organisations. It is clearly a world in which I need divine help!

Herein we come to a very important aspect of the work of the Holy Spirit – the Holy Spirit empowers, inspires and enlightens me in this discipleship. The Holy Spirit will give me the courage, resolve, persistence, patience, endurance, conviction and influence that I need in this work. The Holy Spirit will also lead me to good allies, teachers, books, people and organisations that will be helpful, informative and inspirational. The Holy Spirit will help me to be wise and discerning in response to all the influences that make this realm so complicated. The Holy Spirit will help me to connect Jesus' teachings to the social challenges. The Holy Spirit will help me to hear God's word and call,

---

[3] These themes are unpacked in detail in Kingdom Consciousness chapters of this guidebook, especially chapters 6-13.

despite the cacophony that accompanies society's power struggles.

An amazing dimension of this realm of the work of the Holy Spirit is that it is evidence of how God's Spirit has been, and continues to be, at work amongst people who are not Christians. All progress towards a just society is ultimately work that the Holy Spirit is bringing about in this world. The Holy Spirit has been poured out on the whole world to unite the environment with God which obviously includes the transformation of that environment. The environment is being transformed by love – and the source of love is the Spirit of Love.[4]

The church should lead the way

The above paragraph should not in any way diminish conviction that the church exists to be Jesus' body in today's world. The Holy Spirit's mission in the world is meant to be seen to be most clearly effective in the church.

Just as the relationship to his context was core to Jesus' Kingdom ministry, so is the relationship to context core to the Kingdom ministry of the church. The church has come into existence in response to Jesus' life and mission and to continue that life and mission. The church is called to clearly be the city on the hill shining with the light of Kingdom values.

Where necessary the church must be prepared to join the power struggles of society so that progress can be made on these fronts. The church should not seek to keep a safe distance from immersing herself in these struggles, even for the sake of avoiding conflict within herself, but should always remember that our loyalty is to the Kingdom. Poverty in the world is the most awful dehumanising reality and the church really needs to stand firmly with the poor and against injustice, for it is injustice that causes poverty. In these ways evangelism not only points to Jesus as God's love come to us, but also shows that it is God's will that love should become a historical reality in this world.

The pace is slow but God will bring it to fulfilment

The Spirit is at work to keep the world moving in the direction of improvement, progress, justice, peace and ultimately wholeness. It is a work that has begun and will reach fulfilment through the Spirit of God. All sinful aspects of the world will be transformed by the work of the Spirit.

---

[4] 'The very nature of the Spirit's role therefore is a social one, to build up society. From this it follows that to work for just social structures is to seek to give visible expression to the Spirit's work in the world… The implication of the above is that salvation history, the history of the Spirit's work in the world, is a dimension of all world history… Whatever 'secular' activity down the ages was devoted to creating just structures, and to enabling human beings to experience unity in love, can be seen as part of salvation history.' Brian Gaybba, *The Spirit of Love*, pp. 263-265.

As Christians we humbly accept that all human participation in the transformation of the world will not be enough to bring it to full restoration. The Holy Spirit who evokes our involvement in society's transformation will bring about the conclusion of what God has begun. We acknowledge that the pace of transformation is as slow as the tortoise.

Don't try this on your own

Surprisingly, just before he ascended, Jesus told the disciples to not carry on with the ministry they had started together! This is certainly not what we would have expected his parting instruction to be. He tells them rather to wait for the gift of the Holy Spirit and that they should not attempt ministry until that gift has arrived. We find this instruction in Acts 1.4-8

> *While staying with them, he ordered them not to leave Jerusalem, but to wait there for the promise of the Father. 'This,' he said, 'is what you have heard from me; for John baptized with water, but you will be baptized with the Holy Spirit not many days from now... But you will receive power when the Holy Spirit has come upon you; and you will be my witnesses in Jerusalem, in all Judea and Samaria, and to the ends of the earth.'*

The profound realisation for them then and us today is that witnessing, in word and deed, to our environment is not something we should attempt without the empowerment and enlightenment of the Holy Spirit. The Holy Spirit is Jesus' own Spirit and so those first disciples were hearing from Jesus that they would not only be witnessing based on their memory of their experiences with him, but that he would actually be with them personally as they go out to continue his mission.

In a vital way this is our experience too – the Holy Spirit makes our relationship with Jesus genuine so that our witnessing is from a first-hand perspective of personal encounter and experience rather than merely information about Jesus. Through the work of the Holy Spirit the revelation of Jesus becomes assimilated into our lives; we become disciples before we make disciples. Through the work of the Holy Spirit Jesus' teachings and ministry become internalised so that when we witness, it is experienced as powerful rather than empty religious chatter. Most importantly the Holy Spirit creates, grows and nurtures real love within us so that we are inspired, motivated and empowered to do genuinely loving deeds. All ministry of the church is really love made visible.[5]

Not only is the Holy Spirit at work within us when we witness, but is also at work within those who are listening or watching. This is dramatically demonstrated in the Pentecost event of Acts 2, but continues to be the experience of those who witness in word and deed. This does not always translate into immediate success, but the Holy Spirit is tirelessly at work within those who receive the witness so that what you have sown can help draw them towards the light of Jesus.

The gift of ears!

There is another very important way in which we need to rely on the Holy Spirit to help us in our witnessing, especially our speaking about Jesus. Like all communication, witnessing is meant to include listening as much as speaking. Most of us fail to attend properly to listening well to those with whom we are communicating. So we need to rely on the Holy Spirit to prompt us to make time for listening and in the listening to really hear what the person is revealing about themselves and where they are at. The Holy Spirit has already been at work in their life and our first task in witnessing may be to simply help them to see this. We can only do this if we make it a priority to listen to them with care and empathy. Trevor Hudson says this in a way that is profound, humorous and captivating: 'We do not only need the Holy Spirit's gift of tongues. We also need the Holy Spirit to give us the gift of ears!'[6]

Sharing grace not judgement

Further, it is very important to note that when Jesus breathes his Spirit onto the disciples in John 20.19-23, he simultaneously gives them the ministry of forgiveness. We must wake up and hear Jesus call on us to go out into the world

---

[5] See also Matthew 28.19-20; John 20.21-23; Acts 4.8; 6.10; 10.19, 44; 1 Corinthians 12.3.

[6] *Holy Spirit Here and Now*, p. 133.

in a gracious way that shares God's forgiveness. Unfortunately, Christians are often better known for their judgemental ways than their grace.

The blessing of unique gifts for service from the Spirit

The Holy Spirit ensures that there is specific giftedness amongst disciples. What the Spirit of Love is doing here is taking the whole of any person who is open to the Spirit and is harnessing their giftedness (talents, powers and abilities) to be used for loving service in the life of the church. The Holy Spirit may also give further gifts. Some of these gifts are quite ordinary and others are extraordinary, but all are equally important and intended to be used in loving service in the life of the church. A typical list of these gifts follows a little later in this section, but you will notice that all of them are aspects of human giftedness that are found inside and outside of the church.[7]

The Holy Spirit awakens new and existing giftedness in a person and uses it in the outward living of our faith. Some of this giftedness is already present in the person when they became a Christian but had not been used to serve God's purposes. In these instances the Holy Spirit's vital work is to take these gifts and harness them for loving service. Further, the Holy Spirit may give new gifts to a person which are needed because of the role in the Kingdom they need to play.

When reading 1 Corinthians 12-14 one realises that the Spirit of Love is a great force who takes these gifts and enables them to deepen the faith and love of the church. Paul shows that there are certain ecstatic phenomena that serve no loving purpose and are therefore not the sign of the Holy Spirit's activity (see also Romans 12). Let me give a quick example: A person normally has about three to five prominent or manifest gifts, so let us say the person in our example has the gift mix of tongues, helps and prophesy: the gift of tongues deepens their relationship with God, the gift of helps gives practical expression to their love of neighbour, the gift of prophesy enables them to speak truth to power in the environment. Do you note how each gift deepens faith and love?

The following is a list of the spiritual gifts that are found in scripture: Artistic Creativity, Craftsmanship, Giving, Hospitality, Knowledge, Mercy, Music, Organisation, Voluntary Poverty, Wisdom, Apostle, Counselling, Evangelism, Helps, Leadership, Missionary, Service, Shepherding, Singleness,

---

[7] In his encyclopaedic book on the Holy Spirit Brian Gaybba points out that: 'In the opinion of several authors, it is quite likely that even extraordinary phenomena like glossolalia or miracles of healing have their origin in natural human powers which scientific research does not yet fully understand sufficiently.' (*The Spirit of Love*, p. 219). William J. Samarin has studied the speaking in tongues (glossolalia) phenomenon in great depth in *Tongues of Men and Angels. The Religious Language of Pentecostalism*. Macmillan, New York, 1972. In his research he found glossolalia in various religious and non-religious settings (p. 149). His study also noted the many benefits of the practice of speaking in tongues.

Teaching, Deliverance, Discernment, Faith, Healing, Interpretation, Miracles, Prayer, Prophecy, Suffering and Tongues.[8] It is very important to understand that it is not possible to arrive at a definitive list of the gifts of the Holy Spirit. The Holy Spirit's empowering work cannot be limited to a list. It is also very important to appreciate that all followers of Jesus need to rely on his Spirit to ensure that their giftedness is used in service of the Kingdom. Without this reliance on the Spirit a gift may be used in egotistical and destructive ways.

It is important for you to be blessed by the realisation that the Holy Spirit wants to empower you for service (or to awaken the latent empowerment within you). Pray to the Holy Spirit that he will give you a willing servant heart and the gifts necessary for the service you do. John Wimber found that 'the gifts are not only given to mature people, but are given to willing people.'[9]

The ministry of healing

Jesus emphasised the ministry of healing and it was an aspect of his ministry that attracted a lot of attention. Jesus continues to desire to bring healing and wholeness to people, now through the empowerment of his Spirit.

The book of Acts records the disciples' healing ministry. In Acts 3 we read of Peter and John healing a lame man and how this event attracted a lot of interest, both in favour and against the healing (which is the same kind of response Jesus received in his healing ministry). Some of the other examples of healing in the disciples' early ministry were Acts 5.12-16, Acts 9.32-34 and 9.36-41, where the healing ministry of the Apostles, and especially Peter, is emphasised and how people in great numbers were attracted to this ministry. In Acts 8.4-8 we read of Philip's healing and exorcism ministry. In Acts 14.8-18 we read an account of Paul's healing ministry, which interestingly highlights how these events stir up faith in God, even though the pagan crowds at first proclaimed Paul and Barnabas to be the gods Hermes and Zeus respectively! Further events in Paul's healing ministry are recorded in Acts 19.11-12, 20.7-12, 28.1-10. In all instances the healing ministry is a clear effect of Jesus' reign being experienced in those situations. Healing happens because the Kingdom of God is a realm of wholeness.

These acts of Jesus by his Spirit that have been recorded in the book of Acts continue today. I have seen this in my own ministry and also through the healing ministry of the congregation I currently serve. In this work we have learned much from Paul Cameron. I love the down-to-earth way in which he

---

[8] This list is unpacked in detail in Christian Schwarz, *The Three Colours of Ministry*, NCD Discipleship Resources, 2001.

[9] John Wimber, *Power Evangelism*, p. 144.

describes his entry into and practice of the healing ministry and his conviction that all disciples can practise it:

Many years ago in my own life, after six years of study and four years as a pastor, I theoretically believed these Kingdom truths (about healing), but I had never practised them. I had no idea how to. At an Alpha conference back in 1994, these truths became a reality for me. As a result I sensed a call to be involved in healing. Now, twenty-two years on, after a long journey with my own healing and the healing ministry in general, I see God heal regularly, the promise of the kingdom fulfilled in people's lives. Our Kingdom healing inheritance often takes time to be fully comprehended and gently applied. But we can learn how to 'do healing', just as we can be taught how to evangelise, or to apply our faith in our daily lives.[10]

How does God guide us by his Spirit?

In closing this section I turn to the Holy Spirit's role in making decisions. This may seem a peripheral matter to end this important unit but it is not at all. We define ourselves by the decisions we make! Life is about choices and the things

---

[10] *Kingdom, Discipleship and Holistic Healing*, p. 10. See www.paulcameron.org.za. Paul was the guest minister I referred to at the beginning of the first chapter on the Holy Spirit.

we choose define who we are and what is important to us.

We need to learn a respect and sensitivity to the Holy Spirit's guidance. As we learn to pay attention we will notice that when we are making a choice that is according to God's will for us then the Holy Spirit will give us a real sense of the fullness and meaningfulness of that choice. It may also be similar to a sense of inner peace, joy and assurance. When we are making a choice that is against God's will then the Holy Spirit will give us a sense of being at odds with God and God's purpose for our lives. It will be similar to an experience of unease and disquiet, the opposite of inner peace, meaningfulness and abundance.

Sometimes the Holy Spirit will speak to us in a direct way. This will very seldom be a voice that we hear, but will rather be a definite thought that has with it the distinctive sense of authority and guiding light. We need to develop our sensitivity to this aspect of the Holy Spirit's ministry, which includes a patient and gentle seeking of guidance and an obedience to the guidance we do receive. Being moved by the Spirit's promptings does nudge us closer to God's heart.[11]

THE HOLY SPIRIT ACCOMPLISHES A ONENESS WITH MYSELF

Finally, the Spirit leads me into a real friendship with myself. This reconciliation with myself leads to my inner renewal, for when I receive God's Spirit then I am transformed into God's likeness. I become Holy, 'set apart', no longer conformed to this world but transformed by God. The divisions within myself, that made me unable to truly love, are transformed by the Holy Spirit, giving me an inner spiritual life, whereby all my faculties can be pressed into the service of love. This is not an overnight matter and certainly does require co-operation on my part.

The *unity within myself* that God created me to enjoy, but which was destroyed through sin, was re-established by Jesus in his birth and ministry, sealed in his death and demonstrated in the resurrection and is now *accomplished* for me when I receive God's Spirit.

Holy Spirit heart transplant

How does the Holy Spirit do this work of taking an ordinary person who has been spoilt by worldly things and make us holy? Much of scripture essentially says that we are given a 'Holy Spirit heart transplant'!

The prophet Ezekiel says that the Holy Spirit takes out a heart of stone and replaces it with a heart of flesh:

---

[11] Trevor Hudson has a helpful chapter devoted to Holy Spirit's guidance in decision making in *Holy Spirit Here and Now*, p. 81f.

> *'... a new spirit I will put within you; and I will remove from your body the heart of stone and give you a heart of flesh. I will put my spirit within you, and make you follow my statutes and be careful to observe my ordinances. Then you shall live in the land that I gave to your ancestors; and you shall be my people, and I will be your God. I will save you from all your uncleannesses... Then you shall remember your evil ways, and your dealings that were not good; and you shall loathe yourselves for your iniquities and your abominable deeds.'* (Ezekiel 36.23-31, selected verses)

Essentially the Holy Spirit will get it right to work with my inner being, the deep place within me where I carry my values, the inner core where I hold my priorities, the inner compass where I choose my allegiances, the wellspring of my life. This is the place called 'heart' in scripture and in most cultures.[12]

Without God at work in our hearts they are unresponsive, hard, immovable, cold, dumb, irreverent, without awe, selfish and insensitive – very much like a stone. But the Holy Spirit gets to work on this heart of stone and makes it come alive to God and to the needs of those around. The heart becomes warm and responsive, caring and compassionate, empathic and selfless, capable of awe and reverence, appreciative and kind, truthful and courageous, relational and loving, humble and faithful. This is a heart of flesh and is the result of the involvement of God's grace in our lives by his Spirit. This is the heart of someone in whose heart Jesus is not missing, but is present by his Spirit.

---

[12] It is interesting to note that neurologists point out that the heart is not just a pump but has such an advanced neurological network that it can be viewed as a 'brain' too – thus revealing the unconscious source of the metaphor 'heart' in most cultures.

Being born of the Spirit

One night Nicodemus visited Jesus and opened his heart to him and the conversation that followed became possibly the most compelling way in which Jesus ever spoke of our need for personal transformation by the Holy Spirit. Jesus said to Nicodemus that he must be *'born from above'* and *'born of the Spirit'* and *'Born again'* as the only way in which he can be part of God's Kingdom.

Jesus is saying that the only way to know the King of the Kingdom and to be true to his reign is to have the Holy Spirit bring about a rebirth experience in which we are inwardly transformed. The essence of Jesus' teaching here is that the Holy Spirit is able to make us into a new Christ-like person. This transformation is so radical that it can be said that the Holy Spirit has brought about a rebirth; that we have started over again with the Holy Spirit as the new life-giving centre of our lives.

Jesus' use of this imaginative idea of being 'born again' needs to be allowed to impress us if we are to rely on the Holy Spirit to do something remarkable within us. If the extent of the needed personal transformation does not overwhelm us then we probably have not had much insight into what Jesus is saying here. We may presume that we are born again when we haven't actually allowed the Holy Spirit to bring about our conversion.

So let our imaginations be impressed by this analogy: Before a child is born into the world she has eyes but cannot see and she has ears but cannot hear. The child exists but has not properly begun to live in this world. When the child is born she is able to truly use her eyes for seeing and her ears for hearing. In a very similar way a person who has not experienced spiritual birth has spiritual eyes but cannot see and spiritual ears but cannot hear. It is only after the Holy Spirit has given the person a spiritual birth that the person's spiritual senses can be used and she is able to see spiritual realities like the glory of God in this world, the Reign of God begun and the love of God come to us in Jesus. She is also able to hear the inward voice of God speaking his great words of love, personal forgiveness and call. A kind of spiritual respiration is set up between the person and God in which she breathes in the grace of God, she feels a peace and joy that is abundant and that passes all understanding, and most importantly she has a full and personal sense of God's love. The breathing out of this spiritual respiration is her daily growing in a real Kingdom consciousness, prayer and praise that is offered to God and a wonderful sense of communion with God grows. This respiration causes the newborn Christian to grow into Christ-likeness. In a spiritual sense the person did not live until she were born again, she only existed.[13]

---

[13] John Wesley made these points in his sermon 'The New Birth'. I have looked at the original sermon and at Clare Weakley's paraphrase of the sermon found in *The Holy Spirit and Power*, p. 44-45.

The Apostle Paul described this dynamic of personal transformation by the Holy Spirit as 'Resurrection Life'. In the next chapter this dynamic of 'resurrection life' will be unpacked in detail. This theme is of vital importance and deserves special attention because it is essential to appreciate the inspiring and meaningful dynamic by which the Holy Spirit makes us Christ-like!

The vital fruit of the Spirit

Let us reflect on some of the results of this personal transformation, this 'Holy Spirit heart transplant', this rebirth. Again this is an area in which the Apostle Paul has devoted much attention. He points out that the result of the Holy Spirit's presence in a person's life is complete moral renewal. Paul speaks of the Holy Spirit's work of nurturing the 'Fruit of the Spirit' within us: *'By contrast, the fruit of the Spirit is love, joy, peace, patience, kindness, generosity, faithfulness, gentleness, and self-control. There is no law against such things.'* (Galatians 5.22-23).[14] Linked with this is his emphasis that we are saved for good works (Ephesians 2.10, Titus 2.14, Galatians 5.6; Titus 3.8).

Love is the signature fruit of the Spirit

To be Christ-like is to be loving. Love that is prepared to suffer and sacrifice is Christ-like love. To become loving is to become Christ-like. This is the focus of Jesus' teaching and life, and is the focus of all the New Testament authors' and their lives. Love is the signature fruit of the Spirit – meaning that the essential result of the Spirit's work is to bring about love. The most important inner work of the Spirit in our lives is to fill us with love, to make us loving. True Godly love is given to us by God's Spirit:

> *God's love has been poured into our hearts through the Holy Spirit that has been given to us.* (Romans 5.5)

The Apostle Paul's prose about love, found in 1 Corinthians 13, is well known and read at many Christian weddings. He would be glad for its frequent reading and especially for the ways it can guide marriage to fulfil its potential. It is however important to appreciate that Paul wrote it for all Christians and wrote it with beautiful prose so that it would be memorable. We are now convinced that love is where true value is found, that it has definite qualities and is not just a warm feeling, that it is eternal and that it is the greatest of all life's forces.[15]

---

[14] See Romans 8.12-17, Galatians 5.24-26, Titus 3.1-3, Ephesians 4.25-31, 1 Corinthians 6.9-11 for more references to moral renewal.

[15] Take time to read 1 Corinthians 13 – even if you have read it many times. It would be good to make time to read the chapter before and after it too. Further, read Matthew 22.37-40; Galatians 5.22; Romans 13.8-10; Galatians 5.14; Romans 15.30; Colossians 1.8; Ephesians 3.16f

Making people whole

Part of the work of the Holy Spirit in making us loving is to make us whole. Here the Holy Spirit deals with the way in which our heart and head are at odds with each other, our will and our desires pull in different directions and our desire for spiritual growth and depth competes with our desire for superficial and instant pleasures. The Holy Spirit enters us and tethers these fragmented faculties together so that they may all serve God. The Holy Spirit presses our faculties into the service of Love. In this way we become whole and truly loving. I imagine it is like someone who walks into a field where there are horses in different parts of the field, some grazing, some playing, some fighting, some sleeping and then tethers six of them together so that they can be a team and pull a carriage in one direction.

Early in this guidebook we watched with a sadness we know well as Adam and Eve experience inner shame. Sin had spoilt their own relationship with themselves. We saw them ashamed with themselves, at odds with themselves, unhappy with themselves. We know that feeling. So, part of the Holy Spirit's mission is to restore us in this relationship with ourselves, to make us one with ourselves. The Holy Spirit will help us come to a place of peace and reconciliation with ourselves.

For some the Holy Spirit needs to do a lot of work to get us to love ourselves, to accept ourselves unconditionally. Many people have huge issues with their own bodies and need to learn to love their bodies and care well for them. Our cultural world view often separates body and soul and sees the former as unimportant. But this is both unbiblical and a mistake. Physicality will always be with us according to Scripture, since we will be given resurrected bodies, so it is good for the Holy Spirit to help us come into a good relationship with our current bodies. This does include befriending our sexuality and not pushing it into the shadow of ourselves.

Making people holy

Wholeness is linked with holiness so it would be good to appreciate the Holy Spirit's role even further now as we think about holiness and Christian perfection. 'I'm not perfect' is a phrase we like to use when we make a mistake, forget something important or overlook an important detail. 'You're not perfect' is a phrase we like to use to set us up to be able to criticise another persons' behaviour. But can we be perfect? The remarkable message of the Bible is that we can be perfect, and in Christ are perfect! We live with a worldview of personal growth as gradual and painstaking and so it is foreign to our ears to be told by the preachers and writers of the early Jesus movement that we are made perfect by Jesus. As you read on I pray that you will grasp the extent of the transformation we have by the Spirit of Jesus.

'Sanctification' is a theological word to describe what I am talking about here. It comes from the Latin words *sanctum facere* – meaning 'to make holy'. It is a word used to describe the activity of the Holy Spirit to make those who have been justified also holy.

I have already highlighted the Old Testament promise in Ezekiel 36 which promises a complete spiritual heart transplant. Jesus in the Sermon on the Mount said: *'Be perfect, therefore, as your heavenly Father is perfect.'* (Matthew 5.48). Paul is one of the early Jesus movement teachers and writers who emphasised this theme, more of which will be said later in the next chapter, but note for now that he says: *'So you also must consider yourselves dead to sin and alive to God in Christ Jesus'* (Romans 6.11), and: *'It is no longer I who live, but it is Christ who lives in me. And the life I now live in the flesh I live by faith in the Son of God, who loved me and gave himself for me'* (Galatians 2.20). John's letters are full of this theme, particularly his first letter, where he goes so far as to say: *'Those who have been born of God do not sin, because God's seed abides in them; they cannot sin, because they have been born of God'* (1 John 3.9).

Christian perfection has the same meaning as holiness and is at its heart the proclamation that as a Christian my sins have been truly forgiven and therefore I am made perfect through Christ's gracious forgiveness. Furthermore it proclaims that the Spirit's presence within me does mean that I don't need to sin, that I have actually been freed from the hold of sin on my life. Remarkably I am also freed from evil thoughts and intentions (e.g. pride, or an intention to hurt someone). These assertions may seem far-fetched. At this point it may be good to remember again the point Jesus tried to impress and overwhelm us with – that we need to be born again, and that after this new spiritual birth we need to grow up into the fullness of Christ-likeness.

Christian perfection does not mean that I am free of ignorance, or that I never make mistakes, or that I am perfectly strong and vital in my body, or that I am free of temptation. Also, Christian perfection does not mean that there is no room for growth in grace. What is important is that I am convinced that the Holy Spirit has made me into a new person![16]

Perhaps it is most meaningful to appreciate that the Greek word for perfect is *teleios*, which is a functional idea of perfection that relates to purpose – something is perfect when it fulfils and is used for the function for which it was planned, designed and made. A hammer is perfect for hammering nails and a screwdriver is perfect for turning screws. A hammer is imperfect for screwing screws and a screwdriver is imperfect for hammering nails. A human is perfect when fulfilling the purpose for which we were created.

True Christian holiness is not found in a retreat from the world into a separated life of private devotion. We should by now be very clear that the Holy Spirit makes Kingdom action possible. We grow in holiness therefore as we grow in loving action. The Holy Spirit is particularly involved at the point of engagement with our context – remember the Holy Spirit is where the action is. In 1739 in his preface to 'Hymns and Sacred Poems' John Wesley famously pointed out about the Gospel of Christ, 'Solitary religion is not found there. "Holy solitaries" is a phrase no more consistent with the gospel than holy adulterers. The gospel of Christ knows of no religion but social; no holiness but social holiness.'

Lifted by the tide

Gerald McCann with whom I used to hike and build trails in the Overberg was a great short story teller and he shared the following story which I would like to use to end this chapter. Like all stories that serve as metaphors and analogies

---

[16] For further reading on this important theme read John Wesley's sermon 'Christian Perfection' (sermon 35 in *Forty Four Sermons*). Alternatively read Chapter 12 (pp. 133-146) of *The Holy Spirit and Power* (a paraphrase of this sermon by Clare Weakley).

it doesn't answer all the questions, but its power is in its ability to capture our imaginations with a central and convincing truth.

> While walking beside the sea one morning, I came across a heavy, wooden fishing boat pulled up high above the water on rocky shingle. Two men arrived, intent on taking the boat into the sea to go fishing. For more than half an hour I watched them panting and sweating, as they struggled to get the craft down to the water, but their combined efforts were futile. They left worn out and disgruntled.
>
> That afternoon I returned. The tide was full. And there was the boat, still in the same place, rocking gently in the shallow, lapping waters. Only the slightest of shoves was necessary to help her to become fully afloat. No sweat; no violent effort; just the gentle surging power of the rising tide!
>
> *Not by might, nor by power, but by my Spirit, says the Lord.*[17] (Zachariah 4.6)

That which can seem too much for us, and is impossible with our own efforts, can be quite possible, and even easy, when the Holy Spirit is invited.

---

[17] Gerald submitted this illustration to 'Parables for Preachers'. I retrieved this from their 'Ultimate Illustrator' programme.

Missing Jesus?

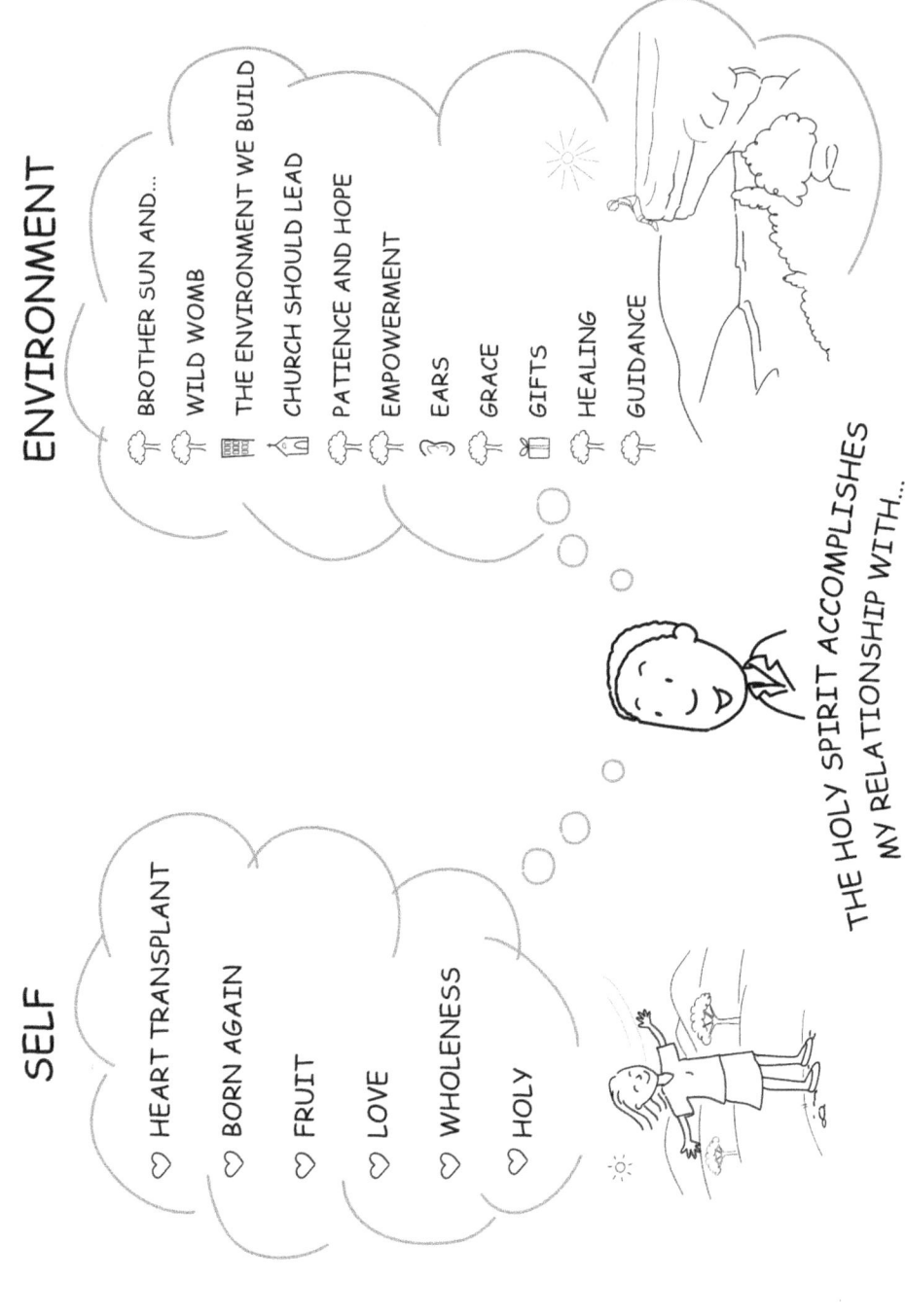

SUGGESTIONS FOR DISCUSSION, REVISION, REFLECTION AND APPLICATION

(These questions are intended for group work, but can easily be adapted for personal use.)

1. What is the most important message to you in this chapter? (Remember to also make a note of this on your 'God spoke to me' page.)
2. Icebreaker question: What movie have you seen lately that you would recommend? (The question must be answered quickly. As a group, do not spend longer than 5 minutes in total on this question.)
3. Read John 3.1-10
   a. Listen to the reading in a variety of translations. How does this help you to understand the passage?
   b. What would Nicodemus have needed to do to be 'born from above' or 'born again'?
   c. What is the role of the Spirit in this rebirth?
   d. Why does Jesus say that Nicodemus will not 'see' the Kingdom of God without being born again?
   e. What is helpful about likening the wind and the Spirit?
   f. What does it mean to be born of 'water and Spirit'?
   g. Someone says to you 'I'm born again' or, 'You must be born again', or 'Are you born again?' What goes through your mind? Why has this phrase developed negative connotations for some Christians? What would be an acceptable use and understanding of this phrase for you?
4. Below are a variety of suggestions and questions to aid your appreciation of this chapter. Do not attempt to do all of them! Choose those that are most appropriate to your unique situation and/or group. The questions are designed to help variously with revision, understanding, appreciation, reflection or application of the content.
5. The Holy Spirit accomplishes a life-giving relationship with my environment.
   a. What is the most important message to you in this section? If you are in a group gathering then pair up with a person sitting next to you and give 5 minutes to share this with each other. (Remember to also make a note of this on your 'God spoke to me' page.)

b. We all like nature – but do you see creation as part of your family? What difference would it make to see parts of creation as brother and sister?
c. In what ways do you live with an awareness of your dependence on the ecosystem?
d. What are the small ways you can make a Kingdom type of impact on your environment? Are you aware of big ways too? Do you ever pray for empowerment and enlightenment in this aspect of discipleship?
e. Name your hero organisations (they don't need to be Christian) that fight for social justice, economic justice, environment, anti-corruption, etc.
f. Discuss this statement from the guidebook: 'Where necessary the church must be prepared to join the power struggles of society so that progress can be made on these fronts. The church should not seek to keep a safe distance from immersing herself in these struggles, even for the sake of avoiding conflict within herself, but should always remember that our loyalty is to Jesus' Kingdom mission. Poverty in the world is the most awful dehumanising reality and the church really needs to stand firmly with the poor and against injustice, for it is injustice that causes poverty.'
g. Think about what SHAPE[18] you have for service in the Kingdom. Go through each of the five key elements below of how you are empowered for service. Once you have done so you will have a good idea of what your next step should be towards Spirit empowered service. What is that next step? Be prepared to share that with the group next week (if you are meeting in a group – otherwise share that with a confidant).
   i. Spiritual Gifts – What are you gifted by the Spirit to do? What can you do well that could serve God? Examples: Artistic creativity, Hospitality, Teaching, Organisation, Discernment. If you need help to answer this question you could ask someone who knows you well. You could also do a spiritual gifts questionnaire.
   ii. Heart – What are you passionate about? What has God given you a concern for? At the end of your life, what would you like to have done something about? Which need in the community around you disturbs you the most at the moment? Examples: Sharing Bible Knowledge, Building Community between previously alienated people, Evangelism, Poverty relief, Excellent Sunday Worship, Vulnerable children.

---

[18] S.H.A.P.E. is a registered trademark of Rick Warren and Saddleback Church.

iii. Abilities – What skills and abilities do you have? Our service can be greatly enhanced by our skills and abilities that we have acquired naturally or through training. Examples: Engineering, Excel spreadsheets, Catering.
iv. Personality – Are you orientated toward people or tasks? Do you prefer structured or unstructured environments? Answers to questions like these that relate to your personality are also helpful in discerning where and how you best can serve.
v. Experience – Which of your life experiences may God be calling you to use in the power of his Spirit? Examples: Death of a loved one, victory over addiction, struggle with mental health.

h. How do you discern the movements of the Holy Spirit in your life? How do you experience guidance from the Holy Spirit?
i. Share one area of your life at present in which you are seeking God's will.
j. In what one area of your life do you need to grow in order to become a believable witness to Jesus Christ? Can you trust the Holy Spirit in this area of your life?
k. Think about these words, 'You cannot understand God until you have obeyed Him. The only part of God that you understand is the part that you have obeyed.'
   i. What new act of obedience is required of you?
   ii. Are you aware of your specific areas of disobedience? What are they? Will you do anything about any of them?
l. Would you like to be involved with a healing ministry? What could you do to begin?

6. The Holy Spirit accomplishes a oneness with myself.
   a. What is the most important message to you in this section? If you are in a group gathering then pair up with a person sitting next to you and give 5 minutes to share this with each other. (Remember to also make a note of this on your 'God spoke to me' page.)
   b. Have you experienced a change in your heart through the work of the Holy Spirit? Would you share that with the group?
   c. In what one way would you most like to experience inner change?
   d. In what one area of your life do you experience temptation? How would you like the Holy Spirit to help you?
   e. In what one area of your life do you feel trapped by sin? Can you entrust this area to the Holy Spirit?
   f. Read Galatians 5.22-23.

      i. Which of the fruits of the Spirit do you think are lacking in your life?
      ii. Is there anything you need to do about it?
      iii. What can God do about it?

g. Do you have any difficulty with the assertion that to be Christ-like is to be loving? If so, what is the problem? What is helpful about seeing the two as synonymous?

h. Look again at the paragraph that started: 'Early in this guidebook we watched with a sadness we know well as Adam and Eve experience inner shame...' Which of the struggles in that paragraph apply to you? Will you speak to Jesus about this and invite his Spirit to help and heal?

i. How do you relate to the idea of Christian perfection? Can you accept this as possible for yourself? If not – are you underestimating the power of God?

GOD SPOKE TO ME ...

19

RECEIVING THE HOLY SPIRIT

'So I say to you, Ask, and it will be given you; search, and you will find; knock, and the door will be opened for you. For everyone who asks receives, and everyone who searches finds, and for everyone who knocks, the door will be opened. Is there anyone among you who, if your child asks for a fish, will give a snake instead of a fish? Or if the child asks for an egg, will give a scorpion? If you then, who are evil, know how to give good gifts to your children, how much more will the heavenly Father give the Holy Spirit to those who ask Him!' (Luke 11.9-13).

The story is told of a group of women that met for Bible study. While studying in the book of Malachi, chapter 3, they came across verse 3, which says: *'He will sit as a refiner and purifier of silver.'* This verse puzzled the women and they wondered how this statement applied to the character and nature of God. One of the women offered to find out more about the process of refining silver, and to get back to the group at their next Bible study. The following week, the woman called up a silversmith and made an appointment to watch him while at work. She didn't mention anything about the reason for her interest, beyond her curiosity about the process of refining silver. As she watched the silversmith work, he held a piece of silver over the fire and let it heat up. He explained that in refining silver, one needed to hold the silver in the middle of the fire, where the flames were the hottest, so as to burn away all the impurities. The woman thought about God holding us in such a hot spot, then she thought again about the verse, that *'He sits as a refiner and purifier of silver.'* She asked the silversmith if it was true that he had to sit there in front of the fire the entire time the silver was being refined. The man answered yes, that not only did he have to sit there holding the silver, but he had to keep his eyes on it the entire time it was in the fire. If the silver was left even a moment too long in the flames, it would be destroyed. The woman was silent for a moment. Then she asked the silversmith, 'But how do you know when the silver is fully refined?' He smiled at her and answered, 'Oh, that's easy – when I see my image in it.'[1]

This is what the Holy Spirit is doing – making us Christ-like, refining us so that we are true to the image of God.

THE RESURRECTION LIFE

As I sit to write this section I am daunted by the enormity of the task! The Apostle Paul summed up the Christian life by describing a dynamic that he named 'resurrection life'. For Paul, resurrection life is life in the Spirit. Resurrection life is what the Holy Spirit accomplishes within us. Resurrection life and the Christian life are synonymous. Essentially resurrection life sums up the saving significance of Jesus' birth, ministry, death and resurrection. It is an enormously important dynamic and I hope to convey it well. I have come to a retreat centre for four days to spend time on some of these chapters on the Holy Spirit.

Resurrection life – the essence

I will first describe the essence of the dynamic of resurrection life as simply as possible and then later unpack it more fully. In Jesus' death there is a power still at work that is activated through my faith in him, bringing about my death to sin. In Jesus' resurrection there is a power still at work that is activated through my faith in him, bringing about my new life of love.

Paul described what he experienced

Paul was a radically changed man who was aware that the Holy Spirit was still at work within him, which made him realise that complete transformation was the goal of the Holy Spirit's work within us. Paul had already changed from a murderous radical separatist Pharisee into a loving Apostle of grace – and the Holy Spirit was not finished with him!

Paul writes of this theme in all of his letters and it is a paradigm within

---

[1] I have known this story for many years. I do not know its original source. I downloaded it for the guidebook from https://dailysermonillustration.wordpress.com/2009/09/21/illustration-id-6909/ and the contributor in this instance was Tim Harrison.

which he functions as an apostle, pastor and theologian. He chiefly writes of this theme in Galatians, 1 and 2 Corinthians and Romans. The following passage is a good summary of this dynamic:

> *What then are we to say? Should we continue in sin in order that grace may abound? By no means! How can we who died to sin go on living in it? Do you not know that all of us who have been baptized into Christ Jesus were baptized into his death? Therefore we have been buried with him by baptism into death, so that, just as Christ was raised from the dead by the glory of the Father, so we too might walk in newness of life. For if we have been united with him in a death like his, we will certainly be united with him in a resurrection like his. We know that our old self was crucified with him so that the body of sin might be destroyed, and we might no longer be enslaved to sin. For whoever has died is freed from sin. But if we have died with Christ, we believe that we will also live with him. We know that Christ, being raised from the dead, will never die again; death no longer has dominion over him. The death he died, he died to sin, once for all; but the life he lives, he lives to God. So you also must consider yourselves dead to sin and alive to God in Christ Jesus.* (Romans 6.1-11)

As a pastor, Paul had seen many lives completely transformed through their decision to put faith in Jesus and so he writes confidently of this theme knowing that all of the churches to whom he writes will have people in them who are living examples of the dynamic of which he writes. At one point he boldly says: *'So if anyone is in Christ, there is a new creation: everything old has passed away; see, everything has become new!'* (2 Corinthians 5.17)

The true versus the false self

If you are like me, you may be thinking to yourself: 'I am not completely dead to sin – nor am I completely alive to God! Why are we modern Christians not like the Christians in Paul's day?' The reality is that the church in Paul's day also had people within it who struggled to entirely let go of the former life and wholly embrace the new life in Christ. This brings us to some of the inner lived dynamics of this resurrection life. So let's get into the gearbox of resurrection life.

Paul wrote of his own struggle in this regard and his memorable words are filled with pathos:

> *I do not understand my own actions. For I do not do what I want, but I do the very thing I hate… For I do not do the good I want, but the evil I do not want is what I do… Wretched man that I am! Who will rescue me from this body of death?* (Romans 7.15-24, selected verses).

We see here that we live in a conflicted state – the new life has been born within us, but the old life continues to have power. The new life that has been born is our true self, our self in Christ, the person we were meant to be had it not been for sin's deforming effects. This new life is also therefore our eternal self. The old self that still has some power is a temporary self in that it is a self that has developed because of sin – it was not the original person we were meant to be and it will not last eternally. This old self is therefore also a false self and a fallen self.

So there is this dynamic that I live with in the resurrection life – it is the dynamic of new life in Christ versus the old life of sin, the true self versus false self, the temporary versus eternal, the good versus the evil. Paul describes that there is the Spirit of God within who has me desire that which is good and loving and despise that which is evil and that the self that desires the good is my true self, my eternal and authentic self in God.[2]

What does this mean practically for you and me? We know this dynamic is

---

[2] Read Romans 7.15-24 to see one of the places where Paul unpacks these dynamics.

at work within us. Sometimes we are painfully aware of it as we live with regret at the good we knew we should do but didn't and the evil we knew we shouldn't do but did. At other times we are not quite so convicted, yet are still aware of tensions within between cooperating with God and resisting God. Quite simply, then, we need to intentionally partner with God's Spirit who is at work within us to live the good and faithful life. The beautiful thing is that God has given us his Spirit to prompt, nudge, encourage, remind, help and enable us into being our true and eternal selves. The precious reality is that a greater power is at work within us to bring about the new life in Christ than the old fading power of our sinful selves. We need to partner with the Holy Spirit within us – we need to be responsive to those promptings, nudges, encouragement, reminders and empowerment that the Holy Spirit gives.

Hello, my name is John and I am a sinner ...

Mostly we don't rely on the Holy Spirit's help and empowerment, believing rather that we don't need it, or forgetting how much we need it. We need to admit to our own weaknesses, frailties and vulnerabilities. It needs to be with us as it is with recovering addicts – the first step of the 12-step program of recovery says: 'We admitted we were powerless over alcohol – that our lives had become unmanageable.'[3] On our own we will not manage to overcome sin. Admitting to weakness, powerlessness and personal helplessness is the first step on the path to recovery from sin because without it we won't rely much on the Holy Spirit to be the higher power we need. Sin is addictive and so all Christians are actually meant to see ourselves as recovering addicts.

---

[3] This is the first step of the Alcoholics Anonymous 12-step programme for recovery.

Paul often confesses to weakness in his letters. At one point he confesses that he doesn't know how to pray! Each time he confesses to a weakness he highlights that he rather trusts God's Spirit than his own strength and that the results are then far more powerful and transformative.[4] Admitting to our own weaknesses and relying on the Holy Spirit is really the white-hot centre of the Resurrection Life. This aspect of the Resurrection Life dynamic plays itself out so often in Paul's own life that he says that the Spirit told him that God's power is made perfect in our weakness, to which he responds by bravely declaring: *'So, I will boast all the more gladly of my weaknesses, so that the power of Christ may dwell in me ... for whenever I am weak, then I am strong.'* (2 Corinthians 12.9-10)

In another instance he gives us an enduring image when he associates our lives with simple fragile clay jars that have within them a treasure. Normally a treasure would be placed in an unbreakable and beautiful box to keep it safe and to honour it: *'But we have this treasure in clay jars, so that it may be made clear that this extraordinary power belongs to God and does not come from us.'* (2 Corinthians 4.7)

RECEIVING THE HOLY SPIRIT
Inviting the Spirit

It should be clear that all of God's work in our lives is done through his Spirit and that God desires greatly that we be open to the work of his Spirit. God lovingly desires to fill, transform, bless and empower us by his Spirit. We express an openness by asking the Holy Spirit to be at work in us and through us. It is essential that we appreciate that we need to be open to the Holy Spirit on an ongoing basis and that our availability be something that develops and grows so that we experience more of his Spirit as we journey as disciples.

This question is often asked: 'Surely I receive the Holy Spirit when I become a Christian, therefore I don't need a further experience of the Holy Spirit, do I?' The answer is beautifully South African: 'Ja-Nee' (Yes-No).

Yes, we certainly do receive the Holy Spirit when we become Christians. We have seen that Jesus and his Spirit cannot be separated. It is by his Spirit that Jesus comes into our lives when we hear him knocking at the door and open up and invite him in. This moment of Jesus' entry by his Spirit may or may not be accompanied by a definite spiritual, physical, psychological or emotional experience.

It is however also important to realise that Jesus does want us to experience his Spirit in our whole beings (mind, body, spirit, emotions) and if we have

---
[4] See Romans 8.26-27.

not had the experience yet we should realise that it is his desire that we do experience him in a definite and special way. The Spirit's work of transformation is partly signalled by experiences in our mind, body, spirit and emotions. These experiences of the Holy Spirit are a gift of God's grace and are God's initiative and cannot be fabricated or forced in any way. But you can ask for them in prayer.

Ordinary and outstanding experiences of the Spirit

God's work with us by his Spirit are not various piecemeal experiences that break into our lives from the outside. The Spirit's work is constant because our relationship with the Father and Jesus is constant. The Spirit is constantly enabling that relationship. There may be experiences that stand out but those are exceptions.

It is perhaps good to think of a good marriage relationship in which the love and depth is constant and filled with daily unexceptional loving service to each other – but interspersed with highlight moments of delight when special experiences are shared. In the same way the Spirit is constantly at work to make the love of the Father and Jesus part of our lives. Interspersed into this work will be some outstanding moments of transformation.

So, yes, we receive the Holy Spirit when we invite Jesus into our lives. But no, you certainly do need to seek further experiences of the Holy Spirit.

Church history shows that great empowerment from the Spirit and great experiences of the Spirit can be given even to those in the very early stages of faith development. The work of the Holy Spirit is not dependent on being spiritually mature or advanced. This applies to all of the ways in which the Holy Spirit is available to work on our relationship with God, ourselves, other people and our environment. God is generous to all who wish to be used by his Spirit.

We are not capable of being properly aware of all the truly great things that God can do in us and through us by his Spirit. An ongoing seeking and expectancy of the work of the Holy Spirit will enable us to experience that adventure.

Personally, I am deeply confronted by how a lack of seeking of the work of the Holy Spirit seems to have resulted in a diminishment of blessings from the Holy Spirit in the life of the church and Christians. I ask myself what more could have happened in the life of individuals and congregations I have served in if I had had more responsiveness to the Holy Spirit. We can appreciate that the Holy Spirit wants us to be a willing partner and will not force a gift or experience on us.[5]

---

[5] After reflecting on the reason why miracles were not happening in the established church but were happening in the revival movement John Wesley wrote in his *Journal* on August 15, 1750 referring to scarcity of miracles in church history: 'That the grand reason why miraculous gifts were so soon withdrawn, was not only that faith and holiness were well-nigh lost, but that dry, formal, orthodox men began even then to ridicule whatever gifts they had not themselves, and to decry them all as either madness or imposture'.

How to make the invitation

Openness to the work of the Holy Spirit is practised primarily as an act of invitation on our part in which we ask the Holy Spirit to work in us and through us. Jesus emphasised this in Luke 11.9-13 (either read it in your Bibles now or at the top of the page at the beginning of this chapter). In this passage Jesus gives us a pattern in which God is a Father who has this wonderful gift to give his children, but who will not force the gift on any child. Jesus encourages his disciples to ask God for the gift so that it may be received.

You can ask for the Holy Spirit to work in your life in your own words, but if you would like a primer here are two prayers you could use:

> Abba Father, I thank You for your Spirit's presence in my life. But I need to experience You much more deeply. Breathe your own breath on me so that I may bring life to others. Release the power of your Spirit in my inner being, so that Christ may truly live in me. Will you also show me people with whom I can learn how to become open each day to the presence of your Holy Spirit. I ask this in the name of Jesus

through whom You promised me your own Spirit.[6]

Father, we thank you for your Holy Spirit who you send to us in the name of Jesus. Thank you Holy Spirit that you have been at work in my life. Please come now Holy Spirit and fill me with your glorious presence. Holy Spirit, bring the love of Jesus and the fatherhood of God to me.[7]

Over the years I have found that it is helpful to often pray that I will be used by the Spirit and useful to the Spirit. This has included praying that I will be present to God's presence and moved by God's moving; that I will be filled by God's Spirit; that God's Spirit would be at work in me and through me; that I will be responsive and sensitive to the Spirit; that I would appreciate the Spirit at work; that I would participate with the Spirit's work; that I would be anointed and enabled by God's Spirit; that I would be formed, informed and transformed by God's Spirit.

Paying attention to our bodies

Openness means that we respond to the Spirit's move within our bodies. This is where we experience the adventure of discipleship in the power of the Spirit. The Spirit may inspire a vision within us which we will notice is accompanied by an experience of an abundance of light, a buoyant attraction, a fullness in the chest. The Spirit may prompt us to action in response to need by bodily experiences like our stomachs turning with compassion, or an anger welling up from our gut about an injustice that needs to be exorcised. The Spirit may release our bodies and minds from an addiction and enable us to walk in faith, free from the practice that used to spoil our lives. The Spirit may give us victory over a bad habit and enable us to invest our time in healthier practices. As I invite you to pay attention to your body I know you will discover that the Holy Spirit has done work in you that you didn't know about, becoming part of your body, and in paying attention to your body you may well be attending to the leading of God.

Choosing love

Finally, openness to the Spirit is practised through being intentional about loving. We know that the Holy Spirit is the Spirit of Love and the Spirit's work is to make us loving. We do our part to ensure that we are being responsive to

---

[6] Trevor Hudson, *Holy Spirit Here and Now*, pp. 189-190.

[7] Paul Cameron, *Kingdom, Discipleship and Holistic Healing*, pp. 17-18. See www.paulcameron.org.za

God's Spirit through being determined to practise love. This determination will keep us questing for that which God wants to give us!

An open invitation

Openness to the Spirit will enable God to always be the One who gives shape, purpose, substance and wholeness to who I am. I would like to give you a clear picture of what this means in our lives. There are four unfinished statues of Michelangelo that are appropriately called *The Prisoners*[8] because they will stand forever imprisoned in the rock from which they were meant to emerge. Some researchers believe that Michelangelo intentionally left the statues unfinished as an abiding metaphor for the human journey of becoming what we are meant to be. The figures are very much alive and seem to be waking up and emerging from the marble to take their place in life – but a tragedy has interrupted their journey of transformation and they never do fully emerge and take their place in life. We are impressed at the muscles and strength of the figures and wish that they could have completed their journey of actualisation.

I offer *The Prisoners* to you as a distinct impression of how it is with us if we cease to be open to the Spirit. God gives us the freedom to resist his hand at shaping us, giving us purpose, substance and wholeness. If I should resist, then I remain unfinished as a person, half emerged as the person I am meant to be and unrealised in the glory that God created me to be.

You and I have a way to go, for God is not finished with us and the world yet. We can remain unfinished or we can let the Holy Spirit continue the work within and through us. Actively keep an open invitation to the Holy Spirit!

---

[8] *The Prisoners* also known as *The Slaves* are in the Accademia Gallery in Florence, Italy. These photos are taken from the accademia.org website, http://www.accademia.org/explore-museum/artworks/michelangelos-prisoners-slaves/

Missing Jesus?

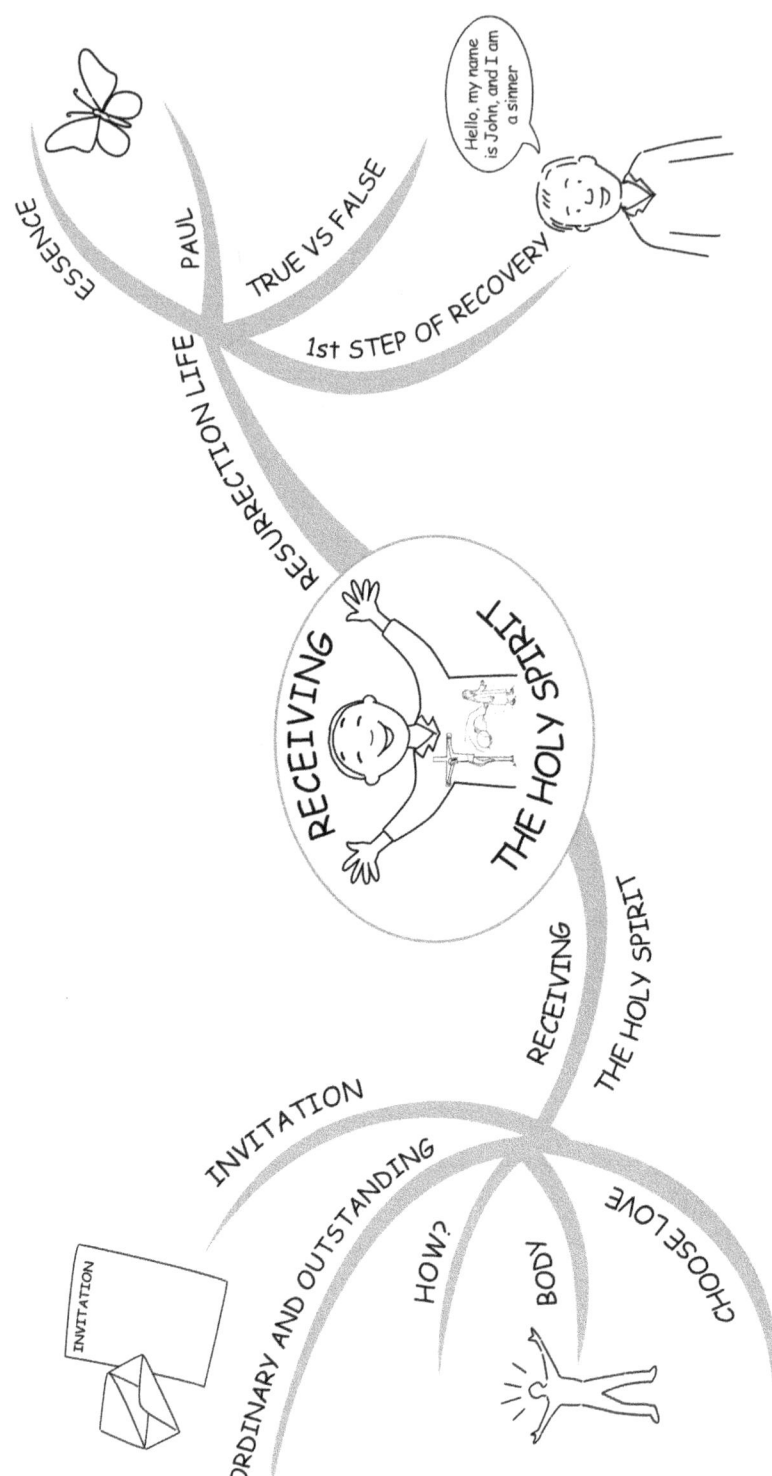

SUGGESTIONS FOR DISCUSSION, REVISION, REFLECTION AND APPLICATION

(These questions are intended for group work, but can easily be adapted for personal use.)

1. What is the most important message to you in this chapter? (Remember to also make a note of this on your 'God spoke to me' page.)
2. Icebreaker question: If you could choose your age forever, what age would you choose and why? (The question must be answered quickly. As a group, do not spend longer than 5 minutes in total on this question.)
3. Read Romans 6.1-11 together.
    a. Can you put the teaching of this passage into your own words?
    b. Describe your personal reaction to this teaching.
    c. What do you find most difficult to accept or relate to in this passage?
    d. Which part of the passage gives you hope?
4. Below are a variety of suggestions and questions to aid your appreciation of this chapter. Do not attempt to do all of them! Choose those that are most appropriate to your unique situation and/or group. The questions are designed to help variously with revision, understanding, appreciation, reflection or application of the content.
    a. What is the most difficult thing the Holy Spirit has prompted you to do? Did you do it? How did it go? Would you share your story with the group?
    b. How do you respond to the idea that real inner change is brought about by the Holy Spirit?
    c. Have you ever surrendered a stubborn sin to God and experienced a remarkable release? Remember this now – it is a testimony for yourself and others. Are you prepared to share this in the group?
    d. Describe someone you know who has been radically transformed by God's Spirit.
    e. Which area of your life needs to die?
    f. What do you think it means for you to become like Jesus? What kind of citizen, spouse, parent, person, friend, worker, employer and Christian would you be if you were like Jesus?

g. How would you describe your experiences of the Holy Spirit?
h. In which area of your life would you like to practise a greater openness to the Holy Spirit?
i. What would it mean for you to receive the Holy Spirit more deeply into your life?
j. In what new ways do you need the Holy Spirit at present?
k. Does anyone in your group want to be prayed for so that they may receive more of the Holy Spirit? If so, spend time praying for each other. You may gather round those wanting prayer and stretch your hands over them, or lay hands on them, and simply invite the Holy Spirit to be at work in the person. Alternatively, if you are alone, pray one of the prayers that is offered in this chapter.

GOD SPOKE TO ME ...

20

THE PRAYER OF THE KINGDOM

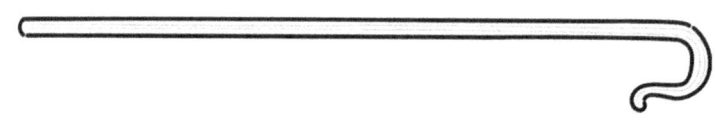

'When you are praying, do not heap up empty phrases ...'
(Matthew 6.7)

The film *Lion*[1] is based on the true story of Sheru (which means lion), a five-year-old Indian boy from a peasant family in a rural area who gets lost at a train station and who boards a train that only stops 1 600 km later in Calcutta. After a very dangerous year on the streets and in an orphanage in Calcutta he is adopted by a family in Tasmania. He grows up with that family and then in his adult years begins a long search to find his birth mother. His search lasts many years and often seems futile and even destructive. He eventually does manage to trace the place from which he got lost and returns there with the hope of finding his family. Miraculously he and his mother are reunited. Part of the tragedy of their separation for 25 years is that Sheru no longer speaks Hindi and so cannot communicate with his mother. One enjoys a long extended scene in the film of their reunification as they delight in being with each other again, even though they cannot speak to each other. He must learn his mother's language again if they are to ever communicate without a translator.

---

[1] *Lion* (2016). Directed by Garth Davis. Starring Dev Patel, Nicole Kidman, Rooney Mara. Based on the book *A Long Way Home*, by Saroo Brierley.

During this scene I was drawn to how it can be seen as a parable of our relationship with God. We all get lost in our relationship with God in one way or another. Primarily it is not actually our fault for we are born into a world that is distancing itself from God – a world that is like a train that is taking us away from God. In our journey through life we also go through experiences that hurt and damage us. Eventually we want to return to an experience of being found rather than lost, an experience of being at home rather than in a far country, of becoming whole rather than living with brokenness and damage. We may look for a long time in many places that don't lead to the 'homecoming' we need.

When that search leads to a real relationship with God then we begin a powerful and life-changing experience of his love, revealed to us in Jesus and experienced by us through His Spirit. As much as we may feel we have 'arrived' or 'come home' we soon realise that we have only come to the start of a new journey. We discover that we are almost deaf and dumb when it comes to the 'mother tongue' of speaking and listening to God. It is now necessary for us to learn this language of God – to discover the storehouse of literature, to hear and understand God's messages and to know how to open ourselves up to God and to express our love for God. This and the next chapter are about learning to speak and learning to listen to God.

These two chapters are about the rhythms, practices and disciplines of growing in intimacy in your relationship with God. The best way for me to be practically helpful in guiding you in following Jesus every day is for me to draw your attention to particular rhythms, practices, activities and disciplines that are broadly referred to as the 'Spiritual Disciplines'. The spiritual disciplines can be seen as disciplines of learning the mother tongue of God. Through these disciplines we get to know God, God's ways, God's voice and God's will. Through these disciplines we are able to enjoy an ever deeper relationship with God. Through these disciplines every day will be a day of following Jesus the Good Shepherd. Through these disciplines we invite the Holy Spirit to work within us.

Following Jesus every day is a journey of grace more than duty. These two chapters are about describing those disciplines and practices that open ourselves up to the grace of God – this is why these practices are called 'means of grace' by John Wesley and many other teachers.

Please do not think of 'grace' as just a theological idea, or merely the gift of forgiveness. Grace is a power and presence that is real. An experience of grace is an experience of God – an experience of grace is an experience of the Holy Spirit. In scripture 'grace' and 'Holy Spirit' often mean the same thing and the words can often be interchanged without altering the meaning of the text[2]. The 'means of grace' can therefore also be seen as 'means of the Holy Spirit' for they are the means by which the Holy Spirit works in us, for us and for the Kingdom. The Holy Spirit is powerfully at work when we practise the means and is more powerfully at work in our everyday lives because we have practised the means.

SPIRITUALITY, SPIRITUAL DISCIPLINES AND THE FOUR RELATIONSHIPS OF LIFE

What we pay attention to in these two chapters is in many ways the lived heartbeat of understanding, experiencing and participating in the life that Jesus offers the world. The Spiritual Disciplines are the practices of spirituality. I would like to avoid misunderstandings by briefly explaining the way in which spirituality and the spiritual disciplines are best understood.

---

[2] Look at Acts 11.23; Romans 12.6; 2 Corinthians 12.9. This was highlighted for me in Trevor Hudson's *Holy Spirit Here and Now*, p. 17f. He in turn learned this from Raneiro Cantalemessa's book *Come Creator Spirit*, Protea Books, Pretoria, 2003.

Richard Foster's opening words to his book on Spiritual Disciplines are an inspirational call to us all: 'Superficiality is the curse of our age… The desperate need today is not for a greater number of intelligent people, or gifted people, but for deep people.' Further, brokenness is also the curse of our age. All people to some extent and many people to a great extent have been deeply wounded, hurt, damaged and broken in their lives. Who is to blame is beside the point. We need healing. What the world needs is many more experiences that heal and make people whole. I believe that God's Spirit is inviting us to experiences and practices that lead to depth and wholeness. What is your answer to that call?

We are talking here about Spirituality. What is spirituality? In this guidebook I propose that we take the following as our definition of spirituality: **'Spirituality attends to the health of the four relationships of life'.** My spirituality is therefore determined by the health of my relationship with God, myself, other people and my environment. I am spiritually shallow and broken when these are shallow and broken. Growing spiritually is all about growing in **health** and **intimacy** in my relationship with God, myself, other people and my environment.

This definition means that everyone has spirituality. Growing spiritually is therefore everyone's business. It also highlights that a deeply spiritual person is not a person separated from the world; rather he or she is deeply involved in developing loving relationships. The Spiritual Disciplines are the means by which we grow in intimacy and health in the four relationships of life.

Take a look at the maze below. As in all such mazes you are able to see the 'Finish'. You are able to see your destination and what your destination is like. You are given a 'bird's eye view' of the 'Start' and the 'Finish'. The challenge is to find the way to the finish in the maze. This is a metaphor for the purpose of life. This metaphor brings the point home that we know what the purpose of life is and how to describe it, even though we have not got there yet. The purpose, the 'finish' in the maze of life, is our experience of full friendship with God, ourselves, each other and the environment.

I like this metaphor because it protects us from the ways we can sink into a pointless sense of 'I don't know what the purpose of life is'. Following Jesus is about choosing the best route to get to that finish. The Spiritual disciplines are the food for the long and winding road. If you partake of this food then your journey is going to be filled with early tastes and flavours of the banquet at the finish. We experience the blessing of friendship in the four relationships as a foretaste of the complete and undiminished blessing that awaits us at the finish.

THE SPIRITUAL DISCIPLINES ARE ABOUT GRACE, NOT WORKS

In an earlier chapter I spoke of faith as a five-step dance (belief, repentance, conviction, obedience and trust) which opens me up to a real relationship with God. The relationship is a free gift of God's graciousness to me. Faith opens me to receiving the gift. Without these steps of faith I am unable to receive or unpack the gift of salvation offered by God in Jesus. Now it is important to appreciate that the same faith that I first placed in Jesus for my salvation, by means of a decision for him, is continued through my use of the Spiritual

Disciplines as further means of receiving salvation from him. It is all based on the understanding that I cannot save myself through my own efforts. Salvation needs to be an 'inside job' that Jesus works in me by his Spirit, who I receive through applying the Spiritual Disciplines (means of grace).

While I continue to fight sin in my life with only will and determination, I am doomed to fail. During my youth I struggled unsuccessfully for a long time against a violent temper. I promised myself countless times that I would stop losing my temper – but I never succeeded. Then one night I lost my temper again and hit my fist through my bedroom window and cut myself so badly that I needed to be taken to hospital. Over the next weeks I prayerfully handed the matter over to God and asked his Spirit to change me from within and take away my temper. Months later I was amazed to realise that my temper had left me!

In my late thirties I became disheartened about my lack of self-control in certain areas of my lifestyle. I prayed about the matter often but this time I did not get the resolution that I had received in my youth. Then I discovered the contemplative practice of centering prayer. Once I started to regularly practise centering prayer a very deep inner transformation took place within me and brought about an almost complete change to the lifestyle matters I had struggled with for so long.

J. Heinrich Arnold writes, 'We ... want to make it quite clear that we cannot free and purify our own heart by exerting our own "will".'[3] Victory over sin, becoming more like Jesus, is the work of God's Spirit in me. My efforts must be on receiving his Spirit through the Spiritual Disciplines. Galatians 6.7-8 sums this all up well:

Do not be deceived; God is not mocked, for you reap whatever you sow. If you sow to your own flesh, you will reap corruption from the flesh; but if you sow to the Spirit, you will reap eternal life from the Spirit.

In the film *Lion* that I referred to earlier there are a number of scenes that show a brother that Sheru's parents also adopted from India. This brother, Mantosh, was adopted two years after Sheru. Mantosh had been brutalised and violated on the streets and in the orphanages of India and so is a deeply scarred, troubled and difficult child. In his adult years Mantosh often does not arrive for family dinners that he is invited to – but the place at the table is always set for him and the food is always dished up for him.

---

[3] Heini Arnold, *Freedom from Sinful Thoughts*, The Plough Publishing House, Walden, New York, 1973.

This is also a very powerful parable of God who is like a loving and understanding parent who always has a place for us at the table for fellowship with him. Can we each hear this good news? There is an open invitation and a place set for each one of us to have communion with God! Please view the Spiritual Disciplines as the meals that await you.

THE SPIRITUAL DISCIPLINES ARE ABOUT LIVING THE WAY JESUS LIVED

Jesus relied on Spiritual Disciplines to enable him to live the way he lived and do what he did. Jesus prayed, studied, memorised and meditated on scripture, fasted, embraced silence and solitude, practised service, worshipped with others in the temple and synagogue, kept faith with the religious calendar, nurtured a closeness with creation, especially mountains, gardens and wilderness areas, truly honoured the Sabbath, lived a simple life and practised sacrificial giving. These are the spiritual disciplines we know he practised. There are more that are not recorded in scripture but can be inferred from research of the wisdom tradition that he was part of – these would be the more mystical elements of communion with God.

If Jesus relied on Spiritual Disciplines then I am convinced that I also need to rely on them and make them a priority in my life. Part of my journey of following Jesus is to follow the way he lived.

THE SPIRITUAL DISCIPLINES DESCRIBED

The only Spiritual Discipline that I am going to describe in depth is the 'Lord's Prayer' – thereafter, in the next chapter, I will give brief descriptions of as many Spiritual Disciplines as possible. I suggest that you think of them as items on a menu and that you are free to choose whatever item that is going to be nutritious for you. You could imagine that the restaurant's name is 'Spirituality' and that you are doing what you can to care for your spirituality by choosing certain items from the menu.

The Lord's Prayer

Jesus intended this prayer to sum up his call to live with Kingdom Consciousness. In this prayer we are given a profound and beautiful guide to all our praying.

Jesus teaches this prayer in response to the disciples' request *'Lord, teach us to pray, as John taught his disciples.'* (Luke 11.1. Matthew 6.9-13 also records Jesus teaching the 'Lord's Prayer'. In that instance it is set in the middle of the Sermon on the Mount.) These Jewish men who had been following Rabbi Jesus around certainly did know how to pray – they would have been praying since childhood. They were not asking him for an ABC course in prayer, nor were they asking for advanced teaching. They were asking him to reveal to them what prayer he had personally developed and used to keep himself faithful to *Abba* and the Kingdom. Many Rabbis in those days had developed prayers that summed up their interpretation of the Torah (Law). There would be a moment when a Rabbi would teach his disciples the prayer he had developed. This was therefore one of the great questions a disciple would ask their Rabbi – and the answer would define much of the rest of the disciple's life.

Therefore, it is essential to appreciate that the 'Lord's Prayer' is more of a guide to our praying than a prayer as such. By this I mean that this prayer is not meant to be learned as a poem that I recite (which is unfortunately how most people use the prayer) but rather taken as a framework for my prayers. Mere repetition of this prayer is certainly not Kingdom praying. We are meant to pause often as we pray this prayer and then pray our own prayers that relate to the petition, word or phrase that we have paused at.

Using the Lord's Prayer as the foundation of your prayer life will certainly help you to be both balanced and healthy in your spirituality. Without this framework for praying, our prayers are often quite self-centred, lack worship and are dominated by what we need God to do for us.

The Lord's Prayer is a meeting place of God's mission in this world and my involvement in that mission. A meeting place between God's reign and my participation in that reign. A meeting place of God's Kingdom and my Kingdom Consciousness. It was Dallas Willard who helpfully described prayer as, 'Talking to God about what we are doing together.'[4] There is a partnership between God and us in building the Kingdom and Jesus offers us this prayer as a conversation guide for the ongoing work of that partnership.

I will be using the form of the Lord's Prayer that is prayed in most Protestant Churches today. It is a traditional reciting of the prayer based on the teaching of Jesus in Matthew. This version includes a doxology which was possibly not part of the version Jesus taught.[5] I am using this form of the prayer rather than the actual text from Matthew, since this is a chapter focusing on spiritual practices.

I have decided to step away from an instructional style for this piece on the 'Lord's Prayer'. In this way I hope to give you a feel for the direction in which your thoughts can go as you pause at each word, phrase and petition of the 'Lord's Prayer'. The words I offer are not prayers but they rather allude to the wellspring of the spirituality I think Jesus is calling us to in the 'Lord's Prayer'. My intention is to give you a primer for using the 'Lord's Prayer' as a guide to your prayers.

'Our'
I was going to start with *'My'*
and mainly think of *'I'*
but you have prompted me to start with *'Our'* and mainly to think of *'us'*
You have blessed me to remember that I am not your only child
I am part of your family.
And this is a family prayer.

---

[4] Dallas Willard, *The Divine Conspiracy: Rediscovering our Hidden Life in God*, p. 267.

[5] The doxology is 'For thine is the kingdom, and the power and the glory, forever and ever, Amen'. This may have been included in Jesus' teaching since it is found in some ancient manuscripts of Matthew. It is however not found in the oldest of the manuscripts. The doxology is a simplified version of the doxology David prayed in the Assembly when handing over the reign to his son Solomon – 1 Chronicles 29.11.

'Father'
The One who reigns is *'Our Father'*
A loving Heavenly Father
And a loving Heavenly Mother.
The tremendous gift of a personal relationship!
The Father always at work to free us from that which holds us captive and prevents our true worship.
The Mother nurturing, remembering, gathering and fiercely protective.
This prayer is the precious gift of hope for those who know these things – the Messianic community.
This prayer is the bold faith to join Jesus in calling God *'Father'* and being his obedient child.

'Who art in Heaven'
Heaven – that realm of your complete reign
So near and yet so far
The place and source of real hope, meaning and life for us all
Without *'Heaven'* there would be no hope for the world
Without *'Heaven'* there would be no vision which beckons our progress as humanity
But by your grace as Creator
And in your Kingdom come in Jesus
And in your Spirit of Love always at work and everywhere
Heaven touches earth
In so many places
That we may often live with a deep smile.

'Hallowed be Thy Name'
This is the moment of pure worship
In which I worship God for who God is
Not for what I get from God
But for who God is
The great *'I am'*
'Yahweh'
The name that is not a name
In this way, the name that is above all names
'I am who I am'
Holy, Holy, Holy,
Lord God Almighty

Who was and is and is to come!
You are worthy, our Lord and God,
to receive glory and honour and power,
for you created all things,
and by your will they existed and were created.[6]

'Thy Kingdom come, thy will be done, on earth as it is in Heaven'
The Kingdom
Is of supreme value
And I am called
To honour that Kingdom
In my context
Because it is here – not in a more comfortable place
That I must honour God's reign
That here too
In the crisis of the present moment
God's Kingdom must come
And His will be done
I may need to take up a cross of suffering
But herein is the meaning of my life
And herein is Life and Hope for the world.

'Give us this day our daily bread'
For the first time in the prayer
I am guided to think of our needs
Not my needs alone, but our needs, which include my needs
I pray desperately for my brothers and sisters
Who are starving
There is such simplicity of life in the phrase *'daily bread'*
And such freedom from anxiety about tomorrow in the phrase *'this day'*
And I remember the meals Jesus shared
Especially the famous ones
Which were feasts
With people he was trying to reach with the love of God
And I remember the most famous meal
Where he said of the bread
'This is my body broken for you.'

---

[6] These lines join us to the worship of God in Heaven. See Revelation 4.8-11 and other praise pieces that follow in the Revelation.

'Forgive us our trespasses'
We need grace
'We' need grace
I pray for God's forgiveness of my fellow humans
And for myself
There is no future worth living
Without the forgiveness of God
And time for repentance.

'As we forgive those who trespass against us'
I join the grace of God
And also forgive
Those whose wrong deeds
Have trampled over my life.

'And lead us not into temptation'
There is a battle against evil
And we need God's help:
To avoid falling for the temptations and enticements
To lead us around the traps
To overcome the obstacles
To avoid the addictions
To not lose faith, hope and love
And to not lose courage for the fight.
Jesus has won the decisive victory in this battle against evil
And has taught me this prayer that I may know his victory
And make his victory known.

'And deliver us from evil'
Good Lord
Deliver us from all that evil wishes to inflict on us
The violations, attacks, wars, enslavements, addictions, recklessness, hate, revenge, redress, corruption, destruction and godlessness.
Good Lord
Deliver us from the evil one
Good Lord
May we not shrink from any battle front you call us to
May we wear the armour you provide
And so be protected from evil.

'For Thine is the Kingdom, the Power and the Glory for ever and ever, Amen.'
Jesus' Kingdom
The Spirit's Power
And the Father's Glory
Are our true life
Yesterday
Today
And Forever
Amen.

In the next chapter we will explore more disciplines that support Kingdom Consciousness.

SUGGESTIONS FOR DISCUSSION, REVISION, REFLECTION AND APPLICATION

(These questions are intended for group work, but can easily be adapted for personal use.)

1. What is the most important message to you in this chapter? (Remember to also make a note of this on your 'God spoke to me' page.)
2. Icebreaker question: Do you know any humorous stories of children who learned the Lord's Prayer incorrectly? (The question must be answered quickly. As a group, do not spend longer than 5 minutes in total on this question.)
3. Read Matthew 6.9-13 and Luke 11.2-4. The differences between the two versions are not significant. Merely note them and talk about anything that you find interesting or important.
4. Below are a variety of suggestions and questions to aid your appreciation of this chapter. Do not attempt to do all of them! Choose those that are most appropriate to your unique situation and/or group. The questions are designed to help variously with revision, understanding, appreciation, reflection or application of the content.
    a. Respond to Richard Foster's reflection, 'Superficiality is the curse of our age... The desperate need today is not for a greater number of intelligent people, or gifted people, but for deep people.'
        i. Does this observation surprise you? Why/why not?
        ii. What would keep you from becoming a deep person?
        iii. How could you become a deep person?
    b. What is spirituality?
    c. Have you understood spirituality as something that engages you with the world or separates you from the world? Has that view changed? Discuss differing viewpoints in the group.
    d. What is the 'work' in the spiritual disciplines? What is the grace in the spiritual disciplines?
    e. How do you respond to the limited role of willpower? What is the problem with willpower? What good role may willpower play? What is a better path than a full reliance on your own willpower?

f. What about Jesus' life most demonstrates his dependence on the Spiritual Disciplines for you? Did Jesus have favourite Spiritual Disciplines? What might they have been? How was Jesus most helped by them?

g. To what extent do you see the power of the 'Lord's Prayer' as a daily guide to prayer? Would you adopt it as part of your prayer practice?

GOD SPOKE TO ME ...

21

INTIMATE LIFE WITH THE SHEPHERD

*The LORD is my shepherd;
I have everything I need.
He lets me rest in fields of green grass
and leads me to quiet pools of fresh water.
He gives me new strength.
He guides me in the right paths,
as he has promised.
Even if I go through the deepest darkness,
I will not be afraid, LORD,
for you are with me.
Your shepherd's rod and staff protect me.
You prepare a banquet for me,
where all my enemies can see me;
you welcome me as an honoured guest
and fill my cup to the brim.
I know that your goodness and love will be with me all my life;
and your house will be my home as long as I live.*
(Psalm 23, Today's English Version)

My intention in this chapter is to present to you a good list of Spiritual Disciplines. I will only offer a brief description of each discipline. The description will enable you to grasp the unique flavour and value of each discipline. If you are attracted to a discipline then please go to the website www.missingjesus.net, where I give you a comprehensive resource list including website links, books and portions of books for each discipline.

Here is my conviction about Spiritual Disciplines: I believe that the disciplined use of these means of grace will be sufficient to keep you close to Jesus the Shepherd for the rest of your life. Not only will these disciplines deepen your intimacy with Jesus, but they will also have a life-giving influence on every other aspect of your life. Often when I share this conviction I go so far as to say that these disciplines will probably enable you to die happy! Of course the circumstances of your death may prevent that – but the point I am trying to make is that these means of grace will be sufficient to see you through to the end of your life.

It is not necessary to use all of the disciplines that I describe here. As I said earlier, think of what follows as a menu presenting various options to you.

A LIST OF SPIRITUAL DISCIPLINES
Prayer as speaking to God

This has already been presented in the 'Lord's Prayer'. The importance of taking the Lord's Prayer as a guide to your speaking to God is that it will give proper order to your prayer. You will start with worship and then move on to God's will before focusing on your needs, rather than starting your prayer with your needs.

Too often we do not turn our thoughts into prayers. Too often we just think about things in our devotional time, without actually talking to Jesus about what is on our mind. This is the vital core of this discipline – the reality of being able to talk to God.

Centering Prayer

This is a deeper and more mystical experience and practice of prayer. There is a story of Mother Teresa's that gives me a sense of the depth of this kind of prayer. She was visiting in the USA and was asked during an interview: 'When you pray, what do you say?' She answered: 'I don't speak, I just listen.' To which the interviewer asked: 'And what do you hear God saying?' Her reply: 'He doesn't speak, he just listens!'

Centering prayer is not intended to replace the practice of speaking to God. Rather, it is a practice that will take you to a deeper encounter with God than what is possible through the use of words and the inevitable way the mind gets in the way when we use language. This prayer method is also referred to as Contemplative prayer or Christian Meditation.

In Christian meditation our goal is to empty the mind in order to fill it. In it we seek to be emptied from the confusion, busyness and noise around us so that we may become more richly attached to God, ourselves, other people and our context.

Interestingly, contemplative prayer was the main form of prayer within Christianity until the Reformation in the sixteenth century, after which such disciplines were sidelined by Protestant, Reformed and Catholic churches in favour of the intellectual disputes of doctrine. Fortunately, this tradition has been revived in the twentieth century through various ecumenical communities and organisations and also by teachers who have become known all over the world through their books and audio recordings.[1] What is now flowering is

---

[1] Here I am thinking of ecumenical communities like Taizé; organisations like The World Community for Christian Meditation and The Jesuit Institute; Centres of Christian Spirituality in most cities; teachers like Richard Rohr, Cynthia Bourgeault, John Main, Laurence Freeman, Basil Pennington, and Thomas Keating.

the awareness that contemplative spirituality is a practice that results in special experiences of union with God. At the beginning of the guidebook I highlighted that union with God is the first of the four relationships of life we were created to enjoy.[2]

Contemplative prayer is about finding the place of stillness within yourself where communion with God is deep, intimate and transformative. Contemplative prayer is about resting in God. It is about returning to the inner depths of my life, where I am known and loved by God more than by any other being in my life. A retreat director once described Contemplative prayer as 'resting in the smile of God'.

Prayer doodling

This childlike activity is particularly precious for adults because it refreshes our experience of being children of God. Another benefit is that it is clearly a method of prayer that encourages a sense of fun, keeping the door wide open for us to experience the goodness of God that makes us smile. Further, it invites the 'word weary' into a form of prayer that uses the right side of the brain.

Prayer doodling is a way of praying through drawing pictures and patterns – generally wavy lines with added flags, blossoms, shapes and other embellishments. Words, names and themes then get written along the lines or in spaces whilst you have a conversation with God.

Adult colouring-in books have become very popular recently and there are now many of these books that focus on Christian themes. This is similar to prayer doodling but leaves less room for your own originality.

Praying without ceasing

In 1 Thessalonians 5.16-19 we are invited to be the kind of people who are almost continuously in communion and communication with God:

Rejoice always, pray without ceasing, give thanks in all circumstances; for this is the will of God in Christ Jesus for you. Do not quench the Spirit.

---

[2] All of the writers I have just mentioned in the previous footnote assert the primacy of contemplative spirituality. I have been inspired recently by how strongly Rowan Williams makes the point in his book *Holy Living: The Christian Tradition for Today,* pp. 95-97: 'To be contemplative as Christ is contemplative is to be open to all the fullness that the Father wishes to pour into our hearts. With our minds made still and ready to receive, with our self-generated fantasies about God and ourselves reduced to silence, we are at last at the point where we may begin to grow… To put it boldly, contemplation is the only answer to the unreal and insane world that our financial systems and our advertising culture and our chaotic and unexamined emotions encourage us to inhabit.'

There are various ways to nurture this as a natural and unforced spiritual discipline. The idea really is to nurture a consciousness of God's constant presence by his Spirit and for us to be in a place that appreciates this. It involves disciplines that help us to appreciate that God is continually able to be at work within and through us.

Welcoming Prayer

The Welcoming Prayer is in my view a very advanced form of prayer that has a very high leverage to bring about personal transformation. It is only for those who have become familiar and proficient in the method of Centering Prayer. It is a method of prayer that is practised 'on the go' in our daily life and is particularly needed when you notice that you are getting emotional about something. It encourages you to welcome the emotions rather than to deny or repress them – and then some time later to let them go.

Examen of Consciousness

During a time of personal crisis, and the accompanying disorientation and confusion a few years ago, my spiritual director suggested that I end each day with the 'Examen'. The Examen is another great gift from St Ignatius of Loyola and is also a hallmark of Jesuit spirituality. My spiritual director, who was a Jesuit priest, told me that St Ignatius had told priests that this was the most important of all Spiritual Disciplines! I have followed my spiritual director's advice ever since and have certainly found it to be a very helpful practice to gain insight into what God is doing in my life.

The Examen of Consciousness is an examination (observation) of our consciousness and an awareness of God's presence and work in our lives. The Examen suggests a specific framework for this prayer and it is best practised at the end of the day.

Bible Reading (*Lectio Continua*)

Bible reading and the Lord's Prayer are the most important Spiritual Disciplines! In this discipline we are like Mary of Bethany who invited Jesus into her home and then sat at his feet listening to what he was saying. Her sister, Martha, chose to rather keep busy and then complained about Mary's just sitting there listening. Jesus' response was:

> *'Martha, Martha, you are worried and distracted by many things; there is need of only one thing. Mary has chosen the better part, which will not be taken away from her.'* (Luke 10.41-42)

In this discipline you invite Jesus into your home to speak to you as you sit and listen to him. Your access to get to know Jesus well is through the Gospels. This makes the systematic and continual reading of the Gospels the precious doorway of inviting Jesus into the home of your mind, heart and spirit.

The Gospels are not the only part of the Bible we should read, but they are the most important part for disciples of Jesus. Bible reading as a spiritual discipline involves structuring your daily devotional time so that it includes some time of reading scripture in a systematic way.

Lectio Continua refers to the practice of reading the Bible in a sequence over time, where each reading begins where the previous reading ended. I suggest that you aim to read through the whole Bible in the following way: Read a book of the Bible per month by aiming to read a chapter a day, but read a Gospel every alternate month (e.g. you would read Genesis, Matthew, Exodus, Mark, Leviticus, Luke, Numbers, John, Deuteronomy, Matthew, Joshua, Mark ...). In this way you honour the primacy of the Gospels for Christians. Once you have completed working through the Bible in this way you could start the process again, but now reading shorter portions and giving time for more reflection.

Too many Bible reading guides aim to complete the Bible in a year. The amount of reading is then quite onerous and most do not manage to keep up and then fail to achieve what they had aimed for. Bible reading is not an activity that should be surrounded with a sense of failure. Bible reading is a lifetime discipline – so why rush to finish in a year? I am not suggesting that it is an impossible challenge – many have done it. Nor am I suggesting that it is a wrong approach. What I am highlighting is that too many Bible reading guides are built on this approach and that it would be preferable to encourage a slow and savouring approach to Bible reading.

Many people use devotional guides for their personal devotions (e.g. *Faith for Daily Living, Upper Room*). These guides are beneficial for many people, but I do offer the following cautionary comments. Many devotional guides do not follow a systematic journey through the Bible, nor do they include much reading of scripture (e.g. sometimes only one verse is listed at the top of the page!). They are designed to tell you what to think about the verse by giving you their personal interpretation and story related to the verse. In this way it is too often the author of the guide, rather than scripture, which is the voice that addresses you in your devotion. To have someone else process the scripture reading for you, rather than you personally experiencing the encounter with God in the scripture passage, is like the groom kissing the bride through the veil! It is of far greater value to first sit with a verse or passage and believe that God has something very personal to say directly to you.

I hope that it is obvious that your basic Bible reading must include a prayerful response to what you have read. Next I describe various prayer methods to use with Bible reading.

Praying with Scripture (*Lectio Divina*)

'Let God have the first word in the day.' I have found this to be very good advice for the formation of my spirituality. I have been guided by this counsel ever since I heard it some years ago whilst I was attending a Christian writing workshop. I don't apply it in an obsessive way, but rather in a way that seeks to honour the principle. Each morning I start the day with devotion after a shower and breakfast. Each devotion will start with allowing God to speak to me from scripture. In this way I let God first speak to me before I speak to him. I also do not put on the radio, TV or phone until after my devotion is completed. In these ways I am seeking to live out a conviction that God must be given the primary place of formation in my heart and mind.

Lectio Divina (Divine Reading) is a gentle, slow and contemplative reading of Scripture that facilitates a scripturally grounded deep experience of communion with God. It is a very ancient spiritual discipline and used to be practised by all Christians. It involves four movements, namely, *Lectio* (listening and reading), *Meditatio* (meditation), *Oratio* (prayer) and *Contemplatio* (contemplation).

Using the Imagination in Praying with Scripture – Gospel Contemplation

This method is one of the great gifts given to us by St Ignatius of Loyola and has come to be appreciated as a hallmark of Jesuit spirituality. Many parts of scripture portray scenes that must be allowed to play out in our imaginations so it is somewhat obvious that we should use a spiritual practice like this. The genius of this method is that we are guided to place ourselves in the scene and perhaps interact with the characters, especially with Jesus.

Personality type and prayer

We all find it to be true that what works for one person as a spiritual discipline doesn't work for everyone. The reason for this is that certain spiritual disciplines suit certain corresponding personality types. Although we all do need to pray and read scripture, we could be greatly helped by discerning which Spiritual Disciplines are particularly valuable for our unique personality.

As you grow in the use of the Spiritual Disciplines you will find that some are more suited to your personality type than others. You will find that some are more fruitful than others. Suitability also varies with changing stages of life and lived experiences. Prayer does not have to be a 'one size fits all' activity. It is good to particularly emphasise the prayer methods, and any other spiritual disciplines, that are particularly powerful for your personality.

Chanting and psalmody

Stop! Before you skip over this section let me tell you something amazing. When you pray the psalms you are using the same prayers Jesus used! What is more, Jesus would not have simply read or recited the psalms quietly in his mind – he would have sung them.

You will notice for yourself that there is a significant difference to your experience of a psalm or any passage of scripture when you read it aloud. This spiritual discipline is about reading, singing and chanting aloud.

The corporate chanting of 'Siyakudumisa Thixo', the Apostles' Creed and other parts of the liturgy are included in this discipline and are very precious practices for many of us in Southern Africa.

Praying with icons

Icons are stylised paintings of Jesus and the scenes from his life. They can be very helpful in prayer because they give a visual medium to meditate on while talking to God. This is a very common practice amongst Eastern Orthodox Christians (e.g. Greek Orthodox, Russian Orthodox). It is becoming more popular in Western Christianity amongst Protestants and Roman Catholics. In this discipline the icon plays a similar role to a passage of scripture in that it is used by the Spirit to lead us closer to God and transform us as we meditate on it.

Visitors to the catacombs in Rome will see that the earliest Christians there clearly used icons as a devotional practice. Icons are as old as the New Testament and so they have within them the potential to connect us with the early faith of the Jesus Movement. There are also icons of the disciples and some Old Testament scenes.

Silence and solitude

Silence is also a form of prayer. I am making use of an evening's free time during a District Minister's guided retreat to do some work on this section of the guidebook. Our retreat leader, the Rev. Brenda Timmer, said earlier today that 'Prayer is when I am more than ordinarily aware of God – sometimes there are words, sometimes there are no words.'

The most effective allies of the devil in today's world are noise, busyness and crowds. These three allies succeed in keeping all relationships shallow and superficial. Silence and solitude appreciate that God's allies are quietness and aloneness.

In this discipline you are invited to spend time alone and in silence so that God, who generally speaks with a still small voice, can be heard. This time in silence can be a few minutes in your personal devotion. It can also be much longer in a silent retreat that can last from half a day to forty days.

Journaling

A journal is for some a very powerful means by which the Spirit of God achieves remarkable insights and spiritual breakthroughs. Journaling is a discipline of recording one's questions, insights, reflections, resolutions and other meditations as a disciple of Jesus.

The Spirit of God is particularly involved in the process of articulating one's thoughts on paper and this often leads to faster progress in our spiritual growth. It also helps one to remember what has happened in your spiritual journey. Someone said to me recently, whilst encouraging note taking as a means to remember, 'The shortest pencil is longer than the longest memory'.

I personally believe that recording all important insights in your spiritual journey is an essential discipline. I think of the Parable of the Sower (Matthew 13.1-9, 18-23; Mark 4.1-9, 13-20; Luke 8.4-8, 11-15) when I say this, believing that one of the ways in which I can make sure that seeds sown by God are able to take root, grow and bear fruit is through us recording the 'seed' in my journal.

Study

It is essential for Christian growth that the mind is not left out of the process. Without the mind learning the ways of Jesus, Christian discipleship will be impossible. The discipline of study is a discipline of applying yourself intellectually to the Bible and other books.

Books on spirituality are very helpful – please see the Bibliography at the end of this guidebook and also visit the website www.missingjesus.net for a list of recommended books and other resources. Biographies of Christians living faithful and missional lives are also very inspirational and challenging. Other resources like podcasts, webcasts, audiobooks, YouTube videos, etc. can be very fruitful sources.

In this discipline you are making time for researching, reading, listening, watching and learning in order to gain greater knowledge. This is the discipline of engaging the mind to matters of faith. Study fits well with the Apostle Paul's encouragement:

> ...whatever is true, whatever is honorable, whatever is just, whatever is pure, whatever is pleasing, whatever is commendable, if there is any excellence and if there is anything worthy of praise, think about these things. (Philippians 4.8).

Fasting

Jesus clearly believed in this devotional practice: He himself undertook a forty-day fast, which is the longest fast possible before it becomes life threatening. When teaching about fasting he said, *'Whenever you fast ...'* (Matthew 6.16); and he taught that fasting would be essential after his ascension (Matthew 9.15).

The most important goal of fasting is discernment. This is a discipline that enables our bodies to unclog and become more tuned in to God. Fasting is therefore particularly important during times of making important decisions. Furthermore, fasting empowers us to be set free from addictions, enables us to have empathy with those who starve and increases our effectiveness in intercessory prayer.

Physical health

Attention to the various aspects of physical health is an essential discipline for deepening your love for yourself. One of the four relationships of life is our relationship with ourselves and it is importantly life-giving to treat our bodies with care. Included in this discipline are good nutrition, physical fitness through exercise, vitality through sufficient sleep, avoiding all over-indulgence, avoiding dependence on substances (smoking, alcohol, drugs) and maintaining your correct weight.

Simplicity

This guidebook has detailed the values of God's Kingdom, which included the Kingdom way of relating to money and possessions. The discipline of simplicity is the spiritual discipline which enables us to embrace and live these teachings. This discipline of simplicity is therefore a vital lifestyle discipline for all Christians. It is this discipline that enables us to worship God with our lifestyles during the week, not just with our lips on Sundays. Without this discipline we would most likely be trapped by the worldly values of consumerism and greed that surround our daily lives. This discipline is founded on an inner simplicity of heart, namely a heart that is centered on God, a heart that is set free from anxiety about money and possessions.

This is a lifestyle discipline of practically pursuing the values of simplicity, sharing, generosity, sacrifice, selflessness and justice. It is a lifestyle that turns away from hoarding, clutter, pretentiousness, prestige, addictions, consumerism and debt.

Sabbath rest

The Bible opens with the creation story, and that story ends with *And on the seventh day God finished the work that he had done, and he rested on the seventh day from all the work that he had done. So God blessed the seventh day and hallowed it, because on it God rested from all the work that he had done in creation.* (Genesis 2.2-3). It is of great value to note that the first thing to be set apart as holy or sacred is a certain amount of time, namely the seventh day! The first distinguishing thing about God's people is that they keep the Sabbath.

Sabbath Rest is a spiritual discipline that honours this aspect of God's rhythm of life and of his expressed will for our lives. Perhaps this discipline, more than any other, appreciates our dependence on God's grace rather than on our efforts.

As Christians we are invited to honour the Sunday, as Jews were invited to honour the Saturday. The change of day does not change the possibility of blessing. For others who must work on a Sunday their 'Sabbath day' can be any other day in the week. The truth is that we don't 'keep' the Sabbath, it 'keeps' us! The Sabbath helps to 'keep us' humble, renewed, refreshed and grateful.

Covenant accountability

One of John Wesley's most important contributions to spirituality was his emphasis on mutual accountability amongst those in the Wesleyan revival movement. The heart of Methodism during the life of John Wesley was the Methodist Class Meeting. This was a small covenant discipleship support group where members were accountable to each other. They confessed their faults one to another, prayed for each other, and stirred up one another to love and good

works. Here the teachings of the Bible were examined in light of actual personal experience. Here leaders were nurtured and equipped. Members of each group held each other accountable for particularly the following three areas:
a. That of doing no harm and of avoiding evil of every kind
b. That of doing good by being as compassionate as is personally possible
c. That of keeping the Spiritual Disciplines.

Those of us who find ways to be held accountable for our Christian discipleship and devotional life will experience something of the power that the early Wesleyans and Methodists experienced through their own rigorous application of this discipline.

Service

In the moments before his arrest, Jesus sought to graphically impress upon his disciples a call he had offered many times before – the call to servanthood. He did this through washing their feet and then said: *'So if I, your Lord and Teacher, have washed your feet, you also ought to wash one another's feet. For I have set you an example, that you also should do as I have done to you.'* (John 13.14-15)

Service is so essential to the life of a disciple that it must be included as a Spiritual Discipline of its own – to ensure that we never lose sight of it. But more than that, service needs to be at the heart of almost everything we do: let us serve people in our personal prayers through praying for them; let us fast so that we can discern God's will for our lives as servants; let us study so that we can serve others with our knowledge; let us ask covenant accountability partners to hold us accountable to acts of service; let us embrace simplicity so that we can be free to serve. I hope you see how the practice of service needs to be at the heart of all the spiritual disciplines.

Further than that, we do need to ensure that our lives include other acts of practical service to those around us. In Jesus, we see that holiness did not mean separation from sinful humanity; in fact the opposite was the case: he showed the holiness of God's love by embracing and serving sinful humanity. Let us follow in his footsteps.

Certain acts of service are also needed as ways of repentance for specific sins within us. So, for example, if I am always needing attention I should repent of this through the discipline of specific anonymous or 'secret' acts of service where I won't get any acknowledgement, appreciation or attention for having done so.

There are two prayers that have tremendous power to nurture a servant lifestyle within us. The first is the prayer at the heart of the Methodist Annual

Covenant service. It is a prayer that is so inspired and wise that it will be a tremendous benefit to every disciple who earnestly prays this prayer often:

> I am no longer my own but yours.
> Put me to what you will,
> rank me with whom you will;
> put me to doing,
> > put me to suffering;
> let me be employed for you
> > or laid aside for you,
> exalted for you
> > or brought low for you;
> let me be full,
> > let me be empty,
> let me have all things,
> > let me have nothing;
> I freely and wholeheartedly yield all things
> to your pleasure and disposal.
>
> And now, glorious and blessèd God,
> Father, Son and Holy Spirit,
> you are mine and I am yours.
> So be it.
> And the covenant now made on earth,
> let it be ratified in heaven. Amen.

The second is one of the amazingly stirring servant prayers from St Ignatius of Loyola:

> Teach us good Lord, to serve thee as thou deservest;
> To give and not to count the cost,
> To fight and not to heed the wounds,
> To toil and not to seek for rest,
> To labour and not to ask for any reward save that of knowing that we do thy will, Amen.

Communion (Eucharist, Mass)

This means of grace has a place of priority amongst all the means of grace in that it is regarded by all Christian churches as a sacrament. This means that it is believed to enjoy a very particular blessing of God's presence.

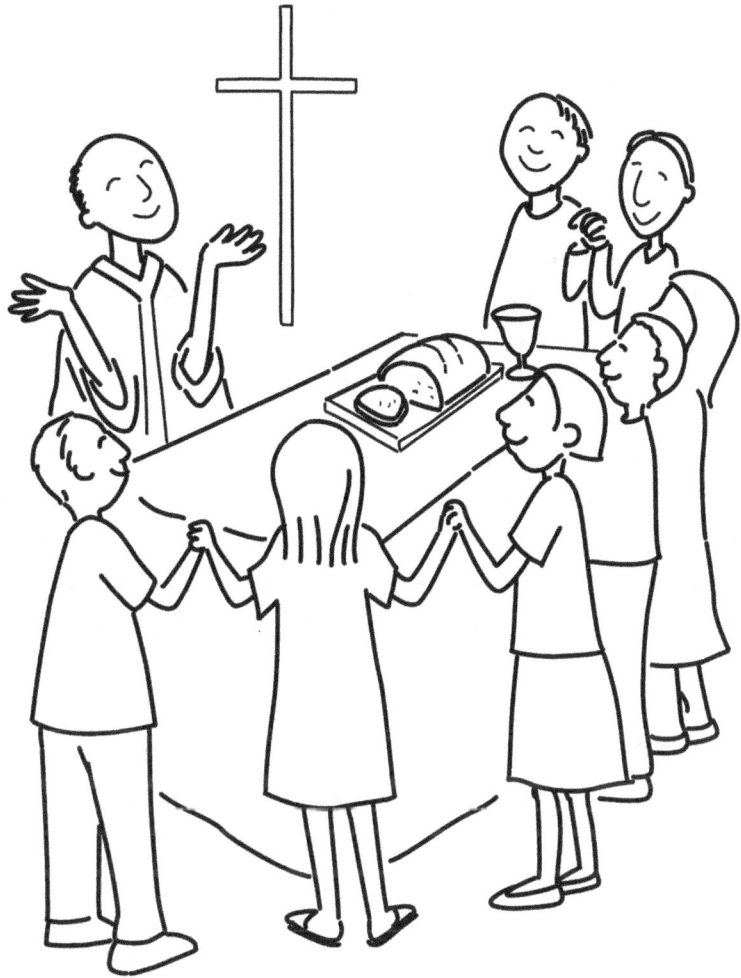

Partaking of Communion or Eucharist or Mass (different denominations have different names for the same act) as a spiritual discipline has a particularly powerful effect on the believer. Included in this is the discipline of making it a priority to receive Communion at least once a month (some traditions encourage once a week and have multiple opportunities in the week to receive the sacrament); the discipline of preparing yourself for the Communion service by some form of examining of your life; the discipline of paying particular attention to the liturgy and participating in it with full devotion; the discipline of receiving the elements with reverence, expectation, awe and faith.

Disciples of Jesus have been blessed by a tangible meeting with our Shepherd in this sacrament ever since Jesus' ascension!

Worship

Too many people come to a church service with the understanding that they are part of the audience in the gathering. One can understand this, since in both churches and auditoriums the congregation and audience sit in rows watching the front. But a service of worship is very different from a performance and if you want to use the analogy of a theatrical performance then the congregation are the actors who have gathered to give God our worship in response to his love for us. God is the audience. The worship leaders (musicians, choir, liturgist, preacher, etc) are also 'actors', perhaps similar to lead actors who carry the narrative forward. Embracing worship as a spiritual discipline will help us to be present and participative in worship services.

Key to appreciating this discipline is to appreciate how worship with a congregation is an essential discipline over and above worship in your own personal devotions. Certainly one is not able to have 'live' musicians leading you in worship when you are on your own – and therein is perhaps the point, that God desires that we do part of our worship together with other disciples because there are certain things we cannot do for him on our own. The book of Revelation does make known to us that our lives culminate in a communal act of worship.

Spiritual direction

A spiritual director is someone who listens to your own journey of discipleship and devotional life and then discerns what specific spiritual practices and spiritual understandings would be particularly helpful to you.

The particular power of spiritual direction is that the director is able to help us become aware of where God is and what God is doing within us, so that we can respond to him, participate with him and delight in him. The director helps discern the direction of God's moving in our lives.

If you cannot find someone who has been trained as a spiritual director then ask God to lead you to a person of wisdom who could meet with you regularly. Other options are to meet with a friend and help each other on the journey of spirituality.

Creation

Those who live in cities can get very separated from the beauty of creation – dramatic landscapes, contact with trees, encounter with wildlife and many other precious experiences. Some speak of 'Nature-deficit Disorder' (NDD) to describe the human cost of alienation from nature.³ This deprives our spirituality whilst God is beckoning us back to communion with him in his garden. We live in a startlingly beautiful world and appreciation of that beauty is an essential part of communion with God.

Creation has value in and of itself, not just as a provider of humanity's needs. Elizabeth Barrett Browning captured it well in her blank verse poem, 'Aurora Leigh': 'Earth's crammed with heaven/ And every common bush afire with God/ But only he who sees, takes off his shoes/ The rest sit round it and pluck blackberries...'. 'Creation' as a spiritual discipline prioritises connection with God in nature.

Creation is actually God's first act of revelation. Yes, before God spoke to individuals revealing his will to them, and before God's revelation was recorded in scripture, God spoke creation into being, revealing himself in it! This spiritual discipline of creation is therefore calling us to 'read' creation in order to meet God, just as we would read the Bible for the same purpose.

---

³ Richard Louv, *Last Child in the Woods: Saving Our Children from Nature-Deficit Disorder*, Algonquin Books, Chapel Hill, NC, 2005. Bill Plotkin, Richard Rohr and many others have all referred to the truth of this diagnosis.

God has used nature, most especially wilderness areas, to meet and form people. Scripture is clear on this point. It was in wilderness areas that individuals experienced God as the potter and they as the clay. It was in wilderness areas that some of the most profound encounters with God took place. It was precisely the very real human vulnerability in wilderness areas that humbled people into a state of awe and openness. Those who emerged as agents of God were often prepared for their role by spending time in the fierce landscapes of the wilderness areas of the Biblical lands. Examples of this are the people of Israel in the Sinai wilderness, and individuals like Jacob, Moses, Elijah, John the Baptist and Jesus and many others. As I said earlier in the guidebook, I call wilderness areas the 'Wild Womb' in which God forms us.

In many Biblical examples we see that time in wilderness areas was not a once-off event that set them on their path, but was an experience that they sought (or were pushed to) at various times in their life. Time out in a fierce landscape was vital for people who were God's agents in the world.

Sacrificial giving

The discipline of sacrificial giving is at its heart the exercise of a spiritual discipline that enables us to resist the way in which money and possessions can make us their captive. We know that money and possessions have spiritual power over us, seeking to entrap us and make us dependent on them. Although we need both money and possessions it is important that we resist the way in which we can become possessed by our possessions. The best way to fight back is to give sacrificially to God's work. In sacrificial giving we say to our money and possessions, 'I am in charge of you, you are not in charge of me, and I can give you away.' Our giving to God's work includes giving to our local congregation, but would also include other Kingdom initiatives that we are moved to do or support.

Christian Calendar

The Christian Calendar is also referred to as the liturgical calendar and it leads us through the themes of the Christian year, which is a cycle that starts with promise and journeys through fulfilment all the way to culmination. The most important festivals are Christmas, Easter and Pentecost. The journey of Advent helps us prepare for Christmas. The journey of Lent and then Holy Week helps us prepare for Good Friday and Easter Sunday. Pentecost is normally a journey that follows after Pentecost Sunday and is a season in which we seek to discern the move of the Spirit in our lives and in our world and offer ourselves to be partners with God.

I develop as a Christian when I pay attention to the developing story of the Christian year. The story of my life is enriched when I join faith with millions of Christians around the world and connect with the developing story of the Christian calendar. I make progress when I try and keep pace with the way in which the liturgical calendar progresses from promise to fulfilment. I don't have to always decide for myself what to focus on in my devotional life – I am often helped by submitting myself to the focus of the universal Christian journey.

You would practise this discipline by using a devotional guide that is designed and written for the Christian calendar. I also invite you to repeat the journey through particular parts of this guidebook at times in the Christian calendar that relate to the content. See 'How to Use the Book' for guidelines for its use in Lent, Holy Week, Easter, Advent, Christmas and Pentecost.

Memorisation

Jesus, and all students in his day, spent a large amount of their time memorising texts, passages and even books. Jewish rabbis in training committed the whole of the Old Testament to memory. Greek/Roman scholars in training memorised the whole of books like the *Iliad*. We overlook that it is in this activity that our contemporary world is so different from the world of antiquity.

Those who practise memorisation as a spiritual discipline say that there is a remarkable way in which the Holy Spirit brings the deepest part of ourselves into encounter with the deepest meanings of those passages of scripture. A further benefit for those who practise this discipline is that they are able to have better access to the wisdom and power of scripture when they are in need. Modern technology has made memorisation unnecessary since information is now very easy to store and access. Has this made us arrogant of the need for scripture to be installed in our spirits, minds and hearts?

Personal declarations

Some readers may find that this spiritual discipline is exactly what will work powerfully to ground you and orientate you to God's purposes. Personal declarations are strong, positive and present-tense statements about your life and your relationship with God. It is very important that your declarations are based on a responsible use of scripture and that you are convinced that the Holy Spirit has helped you formulate each declaration. Many people find that personal declarations help them to change the tone of their thinking and living from negative and reactive to positive and proactive.

The following quote from Henry David Thoreau sums up the power behind personal declarations as a frequent discipline: 'A single footstep will not make a path on the earth, so a single thought will not make a pathway in the mind. To make a deep physical path, we walk again and again. To make a deep mental path, we must think over and over the kind of thoughts we wish to dominate our lives.'[4]

It is also essential that you formulate a Rule for your life in which you define your priorities. (Some call this your personal mission or vision statement.) This Rule must be accessible and should be memorised and frequently visited. This Rule should be supplemented with annually set goals. These goals and plans should be viewed on a weekly basis in your planning for the week that lies ahead.

Rosary

There are some spiritual disciplines that are practised almost exclusively within the Roman Catholic and Anglo-Catholic community. It is worth exploring some of these disciplines if you have never been exposed to them. Disciplines such as the rosary (prayer beads) could well be very meaningful for you.

Twelve-step programme

Do not be surprised that I am including this as a spiritual discipline. A recovering addict will be convinced that the disciplined use of this programme is the narrow gate through which they are able to experience the incredible power of God to help them build a new and sober life. The principles and practices of the twelve-step programme are not only for substance abusers because all of us have addictions.

Seeking the suffering ones

I hesitated to include this as a separate spiritual discipline – after all, I could have included it in 'service'. However, the reality is that we spend so much of our time and energy trying to avoid a real encounter with people who suffer, it is necessary for many of us to intentionally engage with people and situations of suffering. In this discipline we make a special plan to go out of our way to engage with one of our suffering neighbours that are all around us. We seek to meet Christ within them, to seek to be Christ to them, and then to reflect on what changes this encounter should make to our lives.

---

[4] Quote accessed from '*goodreads*' at https://www.goodreads.com/quotes/1335615-a-single-footstep-will-not-make-a-path-on-the on 14th March 2018.

I also hesitated because I do not want to give the impression that this is an optional 'add on' in the menu of Christian spirituality. I hope it is clear by now that Jesus' Kingdom is fundamentally about transforming this world so that it is no longer a world that oppresses people and makes them poor and marginalised. We can only be faithful to this aspect of discipleship if we embrace a perspective 'from below': in the words of Dietrich Bonhoeffer, 'We have for once learnt to see the great events of history from below, from the perspective of the outcasts, the suspects, the maltreated, the powerless, the oppressed, the reviled – in short from the perspective of those who suffer.'[5] Our view of following Jesus needs to be constantly conscious of the plight of those who live under the boot of this world.

We will be fed in this perspective if it includes actual contact with suffering people and to this end I do hope that your journey through this guidebook has brought this about.

---

[5] Dietrich Bonhoeffer *Letters and Papers from Prison*, edited by Ebehard Bethge, Macmillan, New York, 1971, p. 17.

Celebration

If you, like me, think to yourself 'Celebration is really not needed as a specific spiritual discipline. That's like making "fun" into a discipline. Surely it will come naturally. And anyway, life is so hard on too many people that it is inappropriate to make a focus of celebration' – then it is most likely that you, like me, need to pay attention to this discipline.

In this discipline we are intentional and present in the enjoyment and celebration of life as God's gift to us. It is an act of faith in God's greatness, beauty and goodness as well as an act of permission to enjoy God and these gifts.

Community

God created us for community in the four relationships of life and it is in the experiences of this community with other Christians that we encounter first-hand how many of God's graces and how much of God's help comes to us through those with whom we are in community. It is essential therefore that we make time for gathering with other disciples for common activities of the church (such as prayer, worship, celebration, service, study, communion, fellowship). Face-to-face engagement is an enormous need in our current world of mostly electronic engagement. The Christian who believes that they don't need the church is a Christian who has closed the doors and windows of their life to the ways in which much of the fresh air of the Spirit would come to them.

Putting it all together

I used to wonder why we Christians seemed to need more time for prayer, Bible Reading reflection, quietness, worship, accountability and so on. Obviously a person who does not have a faith perspective is not interested in such things – but it sometimes seemed strange to me that we Christians are in such need of these practices. We are actually needy of them! Further, I used to wonder why it was that the longer one was a Christian and the more one lived the Christian life, so one's need for the Spiritual Disciplines grew rather than tapered.

I didn't really enjoy these questions and so often dismissed them until recently I had an 'aha' moment whilst reading Trevor Hudson's *Holy Spirit Here and Now*. He explains that a person who is following Jesus today is constantly entrusting to the Spirit their life, decisions, needs, weaknesses, sin, hopes, fears and more and so uses up more grace and is in far greater need for the Holy Spirit than someone who is not a follower of Jesus. Trevor offers the analogy of an aircraft that is racing down the runway before take-off and says that that aircraft is using up an enormous amount of fuel compared to an aircraft that is standing still in the hangar. In fact an aircraft that is being used is using up more fuel at every stage compared to one standing still in the hangar. Trevor asserts that:

> 'Similarly, when we are content to remain with our experience of God as it is, we park our faith in the hangar. But when we seek Christ wholeheartedly and want more of His Kingdom in our lives, we begin to move down the runway. As we do so, the Spirit of grace empowers us to take off. We begin to accomplish things that we cannot accomplish in our own strength.'[6]

So if you seek to follow Jesus every day and to be useful in his Kingdom then your need for his Spirit is great and your practice of the Spiritual Disciplines must be ample too.

At the start of this list of spiritual disciplines I suggested that you think of spiritual disciplines as items on a menu and that you are free to choose whatever item on the menu is going to be nutritious for you. Remember to go to the website www.missingjesus.net to find a comprehensive list of resources to use for each discipline. So here is a look at one glance at the offerings on the menu of the restaurant named *Spirituality*.

---

[6] Trevor Hudson, *Holy Spirit Here and Now*, p. 19. Trevor acknowledges that he learned this analogy from Dallas Willard.

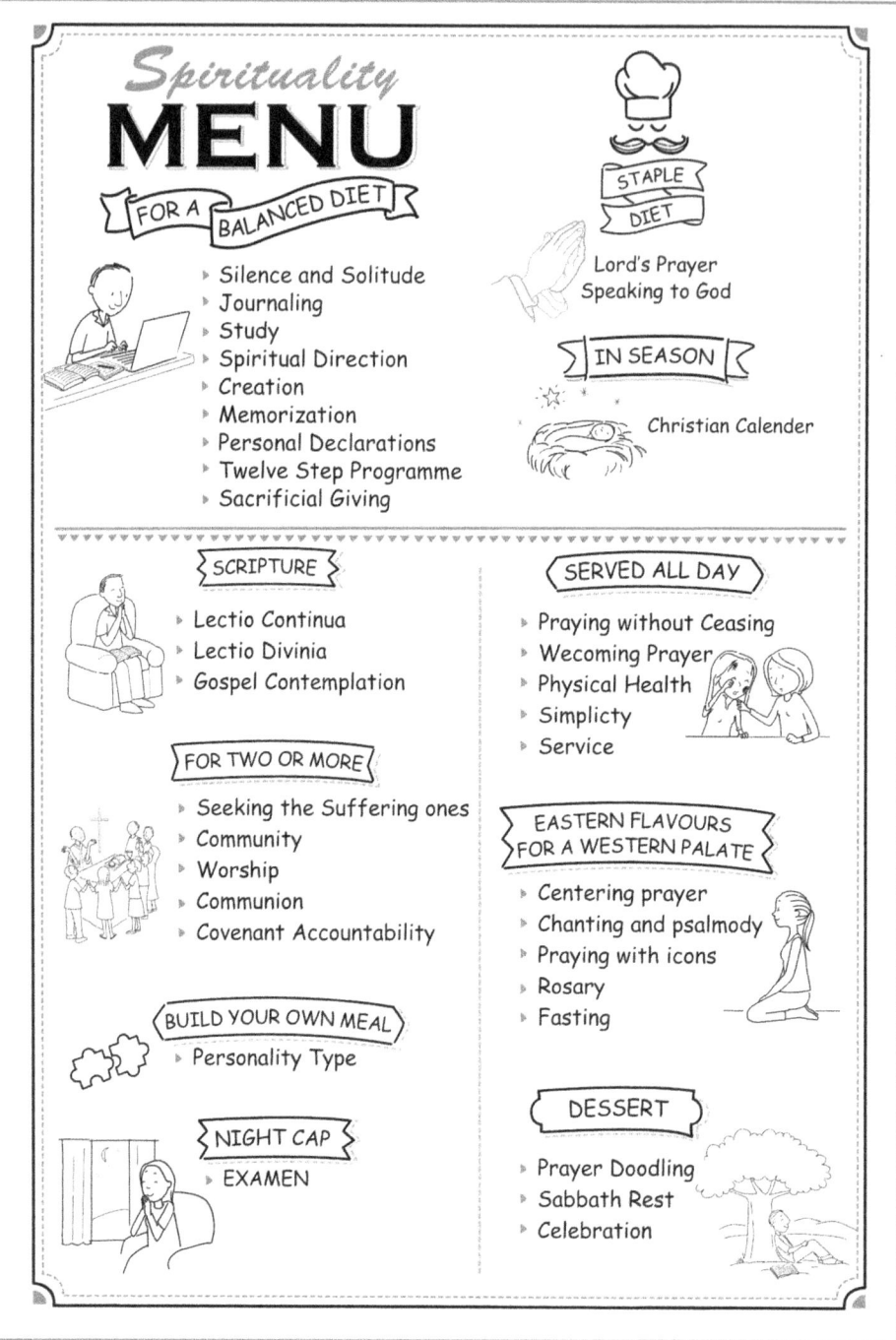

A closing metaphor

Sea Sailors of all times have had to deal with the problem of barnacles growing on the hull of the ship. In the old days of wooden sailing ships barnacles could quite quickly become prolific. Eventually the build-up of barnacles would make a ship very unyielding to the helmsman. It was essential to rid the ship of the barnacles and we can easily realise that it would be impossible to attempt to break each barnacle off of the ship. That would probably cause damage to the ship too. The captains however knew what to do – they would find a fresh water river, sail far up it and drop anchor. In this fresh water the barnacles would simply drop off.

In our journey through life there are many ways in which 'barnacles' develop on our spirits and make them unyielding to God's will. The good news is that direct painful removal of these barnacles is not actually the best remedy. The best remedy is to place yourself in the flow of the fresh water of God's Spirit. Use the spiritual disciplines suggested in this chapter as the practical means of daily exposure to the fresh living water of God's gracious and powerful Spirit and truth and you will notice that these barnacles will simply drop off you.

Dietrich Bonhoeffer – a lived example

My 'favourite' theologian has always been Dietrich Bonhoeffer. His writings are an incredible blend of intellectual vigour and mystical spirituality. In his twenties he achieved so much in the prestigious and competitive world of German academic theology. His life story became one of excitement and intrigue in political and religious matters. He even founded an 'underground' seminary for pastors. His ultimate courage enabled him to face martyrdom. Bonhoeffer is an inspirational disciple for every one of us.

Bonhoeffer was an incredible lived example of how the spiritual disciplines can keep us faithful to Jesus even at a time when most other Christians in the same context are falling away from faithfulness.

Dietrich Bonhoeffer was a Christian pastor and theology lecturer in Germany during the rise of Adolf Hitler and Nazism in the 1930s. During this time most Christians and most Christian denominations were Nazified and became what was called 'German Christians'. Bonhoeffer however was able to see the evil in these developments and he was able to be strong in the Spirit of God to resist. He was an almost lone voice on behalf of the Jews of Germany and involved himself in various endeavours to help Jews escape Germany. Eventually he became part of the military intelligence network that sought to assassinate Hitler. Bonhoeffer was arrested, interrogated by the Gestapo and executed in 1945.

Of the disciplines I have highlighted in this chapter I know that Bonhoeffer practised many of them regularly: Community; Praying the Psalms; *Lectio Continua*; Chanting; Prayer as speaking to God; Daily Holy Communion, especially when in community; Silence and Solitude; *Lectio Divina;* Confession; Covenant Accountability; Christian Calendar and of course Worship. These disciplines nurtured a daily relationship with Jesus and it was this relationship that was the wellspring of Bonhoeffer's life and witness.

It is vital that I make special mention of the spiritual discipline of seeking the suffering ones because this was central to why Bonhoeffer was faithful when others were not. Bonhoeffer understood that Jesus comes to us in the persecuted and that we stand where Jesus stands when we are in solidarity with suffering people. Bonhoeffer believed that if you wanted to know Jesus then you had to seek him from the perspective of the marginalised. Bonhoeffer therefore made it a priority of the church to protect the Jewish community even though anti-Semitism had been part of Christian thinking for centuries.

There is an indirect link with Africa that brought Bonhoeffer to recognise the vital importance of discipleship from below. During his time in the United States Bonhoeffer opened himself widely to the black perspective there. Specifically this was the people's liberation theology of Adam Clayton Powell Sr, the pastor of the Abyssinian Baptist Church in Harlem, New York and the scorching theological perspective of others in the 'Harlem Renaissance'. This, combined with black preaching and black spirituals, introduced Bonhoeffer to a Jesus that was completely different from the Jesus that had been shaped by his white, German nationalistic upbringing. Do not miss the vital point here – Bonhoeffer discovered a Jesus much closer to Jesus of Nazareth when he opened himself up to the perspective of those who suffer.[7]

The other spiritual discipline that I believe enabled Bonhoeffer to not be duped by the Nazi propaganda that had engulfed most of Christianity in Germany at the time was his commitment to study. Bonhoeffer made sure that he read and studied people who had not been captured by Nazism, that he was in community with critical thinkers, that he studied the newspapers and was vigilant about political developments, that he read widely enough to get alternative voices, that he reflected deeply on his context and assessed it thoroughly. The abiding impression I have always had of Bonhoeffer is that he saw the truth more clearly than others did. The discipline of study was core to this ability.

I have said that the spiritual disciplines will keep our relationship with Jesus so vital that we would likely be in a position to welcome death when that moment comes for us. Also, all through this guidebook I have reminded you that the purpose and end goal of life is full friendship and communion with God, each other, our environment and ourselves. Both these truths are profoundly evident in Bonhoeffer's own embracing of death and the state of his spirituality in the hideous context of his last weeks. Bonhoeffer said to those that were with him just prior to his hanging, 'This is the end – for me the beginning of life'. He asked that this message be relayed to Bishop George Bell of Chichester (Bishop Bell was Bonhoeffer's ecumenical partner and go-between for the German conspirators with whom Bonhoeffer had involved himself and Winston Churchill). We have insight into Bonhoeffer's spiritual state and the impact it had on his enemies in this testimony written years later by the camp doctor who witnessed his death:

> I saw Pastor Bonhoeffer… kneeling on the floor praying fervently to God. I was most deeply moved by the way this lovable man prayed, so devout and so certain that God heard his prayer. At the place of execution, he again said a short prayer and then climbed the few steps to the gallows, brave and composed. His death ensued after a few seconds. In the almost fifty years that I worked as a doctor, I have hardly ever seen a man die so entirely submissive to the will of God.[8]

---

[7] Allan Boesak gives detail about this important influence on Bonhoeffer's life in, *Pharaohs on Both Sides of the Blood-Red Waters: Prophetic Critique of Empire*, pp. 94-96.

[8] This quote comes from research done by Eberhard Bethge, who was a student, friend and covenant accountability partner of Dietrich's. He wrote the first and most exhaustive biography of Dietrich's life. The credibility of this quote, coming from the Nazi concentration camp doctor, is questioned by some today.

One of the fellow inmates, Payne Best, was an officer in the British Army and survived because the Flossenburg concentration camp where Bonhoeffer was hanged was liberated two weeks later. He wrote, 'Bonhoeffer was different, just quite calm and normal, seemingly perfectly at his ease … his soul really shone in the dark desperation of our prison. He was one of the very few men I have ever met to whom God was real and ever close to him.'[9]

---

[9] This is recorded in *The Venlo Incident: A True Story of Double-Dealing, Captivity and a Murderous Nazi Plot*, by Captain S. Payne Best. It was written soon after the war and is the most reliable account of Dietrich's last weeks.

SUGGESTIONS FOR DISCUSSION, REVISION, REFLECTION AND APPLICATION

(These questions are intended for group work, but can easily be adapted for personal use.)

1. What is the most important message to you in this chapter? (Remember to also make a note of this on your 'God spoke to me' page.)
2. Icebreaker question: If you could be an Olympic athlete, what sport would you compete in? (The question must be answered quickly. As a group, do not spend longer than 5 minutes in total on this question.)
3. Read Galatians 6.7-10 and answer the following questions:
    a. What does Paul mean when he refers to the following two important terms: 'flesh' and 'Spirit'? Be clear about what is included and what is not included in the terms.
    b. When is 'harvest time'?
    c. How do you 'sow to the Spirit'?
    d. How do you 'sow to the flesh'?
    e. Read verse 7. Is this principle always true?
    f. Think about your journey in life. When have you experienced the results of 'sowing to the flesh'? When have you experienced the results of 'sowing to the Spirit'?
4. Which of the disciplines are you quite familiar with and well-practised in?
5. Which are you unfamiliar with and would like to get to know better?
6. Is there a discipline that you are most curious about?
7. In which discipline would you most like to grow?
8. Which discipline do you think you most need?
9. Which disciplines suit your personality the best?
10. Which disciplines suit your personality the least?

Some important matters for the coming week:
1. Perhaps organise the disciplines according to those you want to practise a) daily, b) weekly, c) monthly and d) annually.
2. As a result of this 'Missing Jesus?' journey, have you committed yourself to a new act of service yet? If not, are you ready to take the step? What is the next step for you?

3. Is there a book on spiritual discipline/s that you are drawn to read? See the website www.missingjesus.net for the list.
4. Are there other topics you would like to read more about? See the bibliography for some suggestions.

GOD SPOKE TO ME ...

EPILOGUE

Ultimately the whole of creation will be transformed by the redemption that Jesus has sealed. Ultimately the Spirit of the Father and Jesus will fully accomplish what Jesus established. Romans 8.18-25 is a memorable passage that speaks imaginatively of this. Note how the Holy Spirit has accomplished this in part by making us the first fruits of the transformation, and will, by implication, accomplish it in full:

> *... creation waits with eager longing for the revealing of the children of God; for the creation was subjected to futility, not of its own will but by the will of the one who subjected it, in hope that the creation itself will be set free from its bondage to decay and will obtain the freedom of the glory of the children of God. We know that the whole creation has been groaning in labor pains until now; and not only the creation, but we ourselves, who have the first fruits of the Spirit, groan inwardly while we wait for adoption, the redemption of our bodies ... we hope for what we do not see, we wait for it with patience.*

In this passage something is being waited for that will bring about the fulfilment of life's purpose and an end to suffering. What, or who, is being waited for? All Creation waits for humanity to find the Shepherd we lost!

Our Bibles end with the book of Revelation. Revelation is an apocalyptic book which gives us insight into the continued battle God wages through Jesus against sin, evil and the deadly forces of destruction. We are given insight into the complete victory for God in Jesus that will mark the culmination of history. We are given apocalyptic insight into the cosmic significance of our participation in growing the Kingdom of God.

Revelation culminates with a vision of a universal invitation from Jesus to us and from us to Jesus. This mutual invitation is all about being found by the Shepherd we lost. Let us end our guidebook with this hymn of invitation and may all who have read this guidebook say 'Amen' to these words of Revelation 22.16-17, 20-21:

> *It is I, Jesus, who sent my angel to you with this testimony for the churches. I am the root and the descendant of David, the bright morning star.'*

Epilogue

The Spirit and the bride say, 'Come.'

And let everyone who hears say, 'Come.'

And let everyone who is thirsty come.
Let anyone who wishes take the water of life as a gift.

The one who testifies to these things says, 'Surely I am coming soon.'
Amen. Come, Lord Jesus!
The grace of the Lord Jesus be with all the saints. Amen.

APPENDIX 1
IDEAS OF THE ATONEMENT

Then he said to them, 'These are my words that I spoke to you while I was still with you—that everything written about me in the law of Moses, the prophets, and the psalms must be fulfilled.' Then he opened their minds to understand the scriptures, and he said to them, 'Thus it is written, that the Messiah is to suffer and to rise from the dead on the third day, and that repentance and forgiveness of sins is to be proclaimed in his name to all nations, beginning from Jerusalem.' (Luke 24.44-47)

Appendix 1: Ideas of the Atonement

'Ideas of the atonement' refers to the ideas, doctrines, theories, themes and motifs that Christians have about how we are reconciled to God through Jesus. Your own idea of the atonement will have an impact on every aspect of your relationship with Jesus and of the living of your life. It is one of those ideas that we carry that will give a certain flavour to everything else in our lives. I invite you to spend the next few minutes thinking about your view of the atonement – particularly in the light of all that Jesus reveals to us about God.

I believe that it should be beyond dispute that our idea of the atonement should be as faithful as possible to the essential meaning and drama of Jesus' birth, ministry, death and resurrection.

To help you in your thinking I offer you summaries of the main ideas of the atonement. The ideas I present here are the four main ways in which Christians have understood the saving work of Jesus' death. The view you hold will fit under the umbrella of one of these views. It might not fit exactly, but these four descriptions should help you see where your idea of the atonement fits within the theology of Christianity.[1]

1. CLASSIC IDEA

The starting point for this idea is that God created humanity to enjoy life in all its fullness and to experience a good relationship with God, other people, all creation and ourselves. Key to the starting point is that God is determined to fulfil this intention in spite of sin and evil, which have robbed humanity of it. God's love and power will not be thwarted. So God sends and uses many prophets, leaders, wisdom writers and teachers throughout history to fulfil his purposes in this world. Most especially God comes to us in Jesus who is full of the love and power of God and he personally has victory over sin, evil and death. He has victory over sin through remaining sinless and through freeing many from sin. He has victory over personal, spiritual, social, political, religious and all other evils. He has victory over death in raising people from death and in his own resurrection. This work of Jesus Christ brings to an end the rule of the objective powers of sin, evil and death, thereby ushering in a new dispensation. Jesus wins the decisive battle against sin, evil and death – their power is broken and the ultimate victory belongs to Jesus. Jesus gives his Spirit to us so that the battle against sin, evil and death may continue until the final culmination of this battle which will be the full establishment of God's reign.

---

[1] Each of these ideas have variations in the way in which they are described by different theological perspectives. There is no doubt however that these ideas can be grouped and summarised as I have done.

This view traces a continuous line of God's saving and atoning work in all of the aspects of Jesus – his birth, life, obedience, ministry, death, resurrection and in the gift of his Spirit to fight against and triumph over the sin, evil and death of the world. Jesus' death is viewed as the final and decisive battle against sin, evil and death and the victory won there is a victory for all time. Jesus' resurrection is a manifestation of this decisive victory over the powers of evil that was won on the cross. It is important to see that God overcomes evil not by a mighty and distant decree but by putting in a personal divine sacrifice. In this work of God we are reconciled to God – God is both reconciled and reconciler. Those who place their faith in Jesus receive this reconciliation from God and are released from the hold of sin, death and evil and are given power over these.

This is called the 'Classic Idea' because it is the standard idea of the New Testament, the early church and the church of the Patristic period. In fact this idea was the favoured idea for the whole Christian world for the first thousand years of Christianity. The motif of God's conflict with sin and evil fills every book of the entire Bible and is certainly the paradigm with which the story of Jesus is told in the Gospels.

The first sermons of the Apostles recorded in Acts give testimony to this theme. The rest of the New Testament is told in a victorious melody precisely because of the victory Christ has won and continues to win by his Spirit. Paul's writings taken as a whole certainly visualise our redemption by Christ as deliverance from the objective powers of evil. Paul typically speaks often of flesh, sin, law, death, demons, dominions, thrones, principalities and powers which rule in the world. These powers battle against Jesus and crucify him but in his resurrection he passes from death to life and is seen as the victorious Lord of Life. Christ puts all the enemies of God at God's feet so that he may rule over them. These powers are not wholly annihilated but the decisive victory against them has been won by Jesus. For Paul it is this breaking of the power of evil that constitutes the atonement between God and the world. Paul then devotes a large amount of writing to our participation in this victorious resurrection life.[2]

It was the great Church Father Irenaeus who in about AD 180 turned this scriptural motif of the atonement into a comprehensive doctrine. This idea came to define the atonement theories of most of the Church Fathers who

---

[2] The New Testament is a continuous description of this theme. It is best to just open your New Testament and read and notice it. If you would like to be pointed to specific places you could look for example at: Matthew 12.22-30; Luke 10.17-20; Mark 15.39; Acts 2.22-41; Acts 13.16-39; Romans 6.1-11; Romans 8.1-4; Romans 8.31-39; 2 Timothy 1.8-14; 1 John 5.1-12; John 16.25-33; 1 Corinthians 15; Colossians 2.15; Revelation 17.14; Revelation 19.11-21.

established the theological foundation of Christianity.[3]

It is important to note this continuity of interpreting Jesus' atoning work from the New Testament into the Patristic Period (Period of the Church Fathers). The Patristic Period would not have adopted an understanding of the atonement that was not deemed the prime scriptural view. Remember also that it was these very Church Fathers who were deciding which books would be accepted as official books of the New Testament. Christianity, which has acknowledged their authority in choosing the books of the New Testament could also respect their authority in choosing the truest atonement theory.

The Classic Idea remained dominant in Eastern and Western Christianity until it lost favour in Western Christianity to the 'Penal Substitution doctrine' in the 11th Century. The Classic Idea was revived in the 16th Century by Martin Luther, the great leader of the Protestant Reformation. This restoration of the idea did not last and it was only in the 20th Century that this idea has started to gain more recognition again, although it remains overshadowed today in Western Christianity by the 'Penal Substitution doctrine'.

It is important to note that even when it was not the dominant view the Classic Idea always informed the liturgy of the church, especially Baptism, Easter, Communion/Eucharist liturgies. The Classic Idea is also known as the 'Dramatic idea' or as 'Christus Victor'. This *Missing Jesus? Finding the Shepherd we lost* guidebook is closely aligned to this Classic Idea of the atonement.

2. PENAL SUBSTITUTION IDEA

The starting point for this idea is that there is a just order in creation which must be honoured. The order of creation demands that humanity obey God who is our creator. Humanity has not honoured this order in creation and now the God of this just order demands that humanity be punished. God is loving and wants to forgive humanity but God cannot violate the just order of creation. If God forgave sins without the demands of law and justice being satisfied then it means that sin would not be treated seriously and this would lead to toleration of sin and laxity in relation to the law. The law demands that a sacrifice is offered for sin but in this instance God desires to forgive the whole of humanity and so the sin is too great for an animal sacrifice to be

---

[3] The period of the Church Fathers, or Patristic period, runs from the end of the New Testament times (which is also known as the Apostolic period) to the Second Council of Nicaea in 787. The most significant of the other Eastern Church Fathers who described this 'Classic Idea' were Origen, Athanasius, Basil the Great, Gregory of Nyssa, Gregory of Nazianzus, Cyril of Alexandria, Cyril of Jerusalem. Chrysostom and John of Damascus. The most important Western Church Fathers were Ambrose, Pseudo-Ambrose, Augustine, Leo the Great, Caesarius of Arles, Faustus of Rhegium, and Gregory the Great.

sufficient. The sacrifice must be a human sacrifice, but not any human, a sinless human must be sacrificed. Nothing can be more reasonable than this demand for satisfaction of law and justice so that forgiveness can follow. God loves us so much that He sent His Son to be the sinless human and then be executed as the sacrifice for our sins. In this way God is both loving and just, paying the price for our forgiveness. In this way the honour due to God has been repaid and we humans may escape the punishment due to us. Through receiving Jesus into my life I receive the forgiveness of sins because He has paid the price for me.

The foundational paradigm for this Penal Substitution idea is found in the Old Testament sacrificial system in which prescribed sacrifices are made by people to God to give the honour that is due to him. In this Old Testament paradigm the law is the dominating factor and in this view the supremacy of the law determines that a sacrifice must be made to honour God. There are seeds of the idea in the New Testament although it is not nearly as pervasive there as the Classic Idea.[4] The Church Fathers Tertullian, Cyprian and Gregory the Great[5] started to work with this idea through emphasising that God must act in a legal manner. This was an important assertion that laid the foundation for the later flowering of the idea.

It was in the 11th Century that this idea was fully developed into a doctrine of the atonement by Anselm in his book *Cur Deus Homo? (Why the God-Man?)*. Anselm approached the matter from a high-altitude cosmic and rational perspective believing that a transaction had to be made between God and humanity that would satisfy the just demands of cosmic law. This doctrine found very fertile soil in the legalism of the mediaeval world and their theological fondness for the idea of penance. The idea flourished at a time when the notion of penance dominated Christian theology. Since then this doctrine has dominated Western Christianity's view of the atonement. This idea is also referred to by researchers as the 'Latin view' because of the way it appealed to the Latin judicial mind and the way in which it arose in Western Latin soil. This idea is also known as 'Vicarious Punishment', 'Vicarious Satisfaction', 'Substitutionary Atonement', 'Anselmian doctrine', 'Sacrifice' and 'Rational View'.

---

[4] The main New Testament passages believed to share this motif are: 2 Corinthians 5.21; 1 Peter 2.24; Galatians 3.13; Colossians 2.14 and Romans 3.24-26. These passages do not all necessarily need the Penal Substitution idea for them to make sense. For example, the very next verse after Colossians 2.14, namely verse 15, is a concise description of Jesus' victory over earthly and spiritual evil powers and is thus a testimony to the pervasive scriptural witness to what became the Classic idea.

[5] The writings of Gregory the Great present both the Classic and the Penal Substitution idea.

3. RANSOM

The starting point for this idea is that humanity is held captive by the devil because of our sin and that God wants to free us. God offers himself in Jesus to the devil in exchange for him setting humanity free. The devil accepts Jesus as a ransom for humanity and we are liberated. Jesus is given to the devil, in his death, as a ransom price to set us free. However Jesus rises from the dead and thereby escapes from the devil. In this way the devil loses both humanity and his ransom price. Through this ransom we are released from servitude to the law and sin. Because God in Jesus has paid the ransom we now belong to God.

The idea of ransom has its foundation in both Old and New Testament metaphors of God at work to save humanity and make us his own people again.[6] The Church Father Gregory of Nyssa developed the idea.[7] This idea did survive for a thousand years although not nearly as deeply and widely as the Classic Idea. The idea of ransom was also swept aside by Anselm's view.

4. SUBJECTIVE IDEA

The starting point for this idea is that the love of God is true divine love and is therefore gracious and without need. The sins of humanity have not caused a need for appeasement in God. The problem with sin is that it diminishes the abundant life God desires for us. So Jesus comes to lead us into that abundant life of joy. Jesus does this by being a teacher saving us from the ignorance that causes our sin. Jesus also does this by being the supreme example of an abundant loving life. God has sent his Son to demonstrate God's love, to be an example of how to live and to lead us out of our ignorance. In this way Jesus saves us through the effect he has on us. His love and example arouses a response in us of love and wise living in accordance with his teachings. Our response to Jesus leads to our sins being forgiven and us being reconciled to God. Jesus' death is a seal on his teaching and the supreme example of the love of God. Jesus' death saves us through the influence it has on us. When we look at the cross and see God's incredible love for us we are drawn into a relationship with God. Jesus is the starting-point of any human's consciousness of God. Jesus is the 'Pattern Man' and the ideal of all religion. Jesus is also the head of the corporate human body (in other words, Jesus is the head of all humanity) and when God looks at humanity He sees the head who is pleading for humanity's cause and this influences God's attitude to us because God sees the positive life-giving influence Jesus is having on humanity.

---

[6] See Matthew 20.28, Mark 10.45, 1 Timothy 2.6.

[7] Gregory of Nyssa fitted the Ransom view into the Classic view.

This theory also of course has seeds in the New Testament where the personal impact of Jesus on people is emphasised. This idea was also included in the writings of Augustine and other early church fathers without them fully embracing or articulating it. This subjective idea was properly developed by Abelard who was a contemporary of Anselm and it was a direct attack on Anselm's theory. Abelard found the idea of satisfaction to be impossible, because if humanity's sins before Jesus required such a great satisfaction to be paid to God how much greater would be the satisfaction owed to God for the sins against Jesus. Abelard's theory had to wait until the 18th century before it found a receptive audience.

It was during the Enlightenment of the 18th and 19th Century that this humanistic subjective view was promoted in opposition to the Penal Substitution doctrine. You may have noticed that this view is very much a product of the Enlightenment's reaction to aspects of Christianity that were deemed primitive, legalistic and anthropocentric.

You may have also noticed that this view does not stand out as clearly as the other two. This is precisely because it is a 'subjective' doctrine. The theology of the 20th and 21st centuries has reacted strongly against the theology of the Enlightenment and this succeeded in sweeping the subjective idea aside. This view is also known as the 'Moral Example Theory' or 'Moral Influence Theory' or 'Humanistic Doctrine'.

WHICH IDEA OF THE ATONEMENT IS MORE FAITHFUL TO THE GOD REVEALED IN JESUS?

Your own view of the atonement will be aligned to one of the views I have described above. Although all of the views have a Biblical foundation I invite you to make the following question the core question for your own review of your own view: 'Which idea of the Atonement is more faithful to the God revealed in Jesus?'

At the heart of the **Penal Substitution** doctrine is the acceptance of the complete supremacy of law and justice and the belief that God can only act within those confines. The Penal Substitution theory is based on the conviction that God must honour law and justice. Jesus however reveals to us a God who is willing to forgive without the demands of the law being met. Jesus' own ministry of forgiveness and healing is a demonstration of that. Jesus' teachings are full of references to God's freedom to be gratuitous. The parable of the workers and the hours in Matthew 20.1-16 is a special but not unique example of Jesus making this very point.

The Penal Substitution theory gives us a picture of God whose love refuses to forgive without punishment for sin first being suffered by a person who does not deserve it. Jesus however teaches us to forgive in a gracious and generous way and at the same time practises God's gracious and generous love. This matter really goes to the heart of what Jesus reveals to us about God and we would do well to remember at this point that the religious leaders of his day ended up executing him for these views. Clearly, Jesus understands forgiveness to be a gracious act, whereas the religious leaders of his day, and those who hold to penal substitution today, do not believe that forgiveness can be graciously given. It seems unacceptable to many of us today that a view of the atonement should oppose this aspect of Jesus' revelation of God. For this reason we cannot accept the Penal Substitution doctrine. This puts us in a difficult position because at this point in history it is the way most Christians think.

We must however accept that forgiveness is never free. There is always a price that is paid, but it is not a price paid to the demands of justice and law. If someone steals from me and I forgive them then I personally carry the cost of that theft without them having to pay for it. If someone lies about me and this damages my reputation and I forgive them, then I carry the humiliation resulting from what was said. Jesus' message and ministry of God's forgiveness of humanity was given at the cost of him personally carrying the consequence of that forgiveness – namely the execution on a cross. The essential reality to see clearly here is that Jesus' death is not given by God to satisfy the scales of the law. God is not submitting to the demands of the law but is rather paying the price of love and grace.

In declining the Penal Substitution idea we do not reject the idea of 'substitution' itself. Jesus' work of atonement is clearly something he does on our behalf and in our place. It is the 'penal' idea, namely the idea of Jesus satisfying the demands of justice, law, punishment or even anger, that is problematic.

The **Ransom** idea is universally sidelined because it is seen as taking the Biblical metaphor of ransom too literally and building too much onto the metaphor. It is accepted that reference to 'ransom' in scripture with regard to Jesus' death was never meant to be taken literally but was a metaphor indicating that there was leverage and great significance in Jesus' death.

The **Subjective** idea is problematic precisely because it is subjective and not objective. It is essential that we see that Jesus achieved a definite objective atonement that is available to all who place their faith in him. It is not enough to merely refer to Jesus as a convincing example.

The **Classic** Idea however honours the objective state of atonement that Jesus has made available to all through his victory over sin, death and evil.

This idea alone takes the objective reality of evil and sin seriously. The Gospels devote an enormous amount of time and space to describing the developing plot of the religious leaders against Jesus, and then to describing in great detail his dramatic last week, his arrest, trial, subsequent death and glorious resurrection appearances. It is at least a third of each of the Gospels that is devoted to this. All of this information is unnecessary to the Penal Substitution view but is essential in the Classic Idea. The Classic Idea exists because the Gospels are presenting Jesus as God's agent of good who is opposed by various forces of evil but who will not yield one inch to those forces. He stands his ground and is victorious against every enemy of God.

You may have noticed that the details of Jesus' own ministry and life are only relevant to the Classic Idea and the Subjective idea. In both the Penal Substitution and Ransom idea it is only important that Jesus existed as the God-man and that he managed to be sinless, but it does not matter what he taught nor that he blessed many with his healing ministry nor the type of community he developed through his social interactions and through his leadership. Surely this betrays or at least neglects too much of the meaning of Jesus!

The Classic Idea is completely consistent with the God revealed to us in Jesus. This view is faithful to the love of God that is on the one hand gracious, kind and generous and on the other hand fierce, determined and sacrificial in his opposition to sin, evil and the forces of death. The Classic Idea sings the great good news that an amazing revolution has happened in humanity's history – God has come to us and revealed himself to us in Jesus and in Jesus has taken the initiative and broken through the order of law and merit and has prevailed over the powers of evil, and created a new state of reconciliation between God and the world!

The Classic Idea alone includes the Holy Spirit in God's saving work. The Classic Idea reveals that the Spirit is given to enable us to be transformed as a result of the victory that Jesus has won for us over sin and evil. The Classic Idea is the only theory of the atonement to show that Jesus by his Spirit continues his battle against sin, evil and the forces that bring death to us and our world. This makes this paradigm obviously relevant to our experience of life for we know that these forces are objective realities.

The Classic Idea is the only view that shows the clear link between our personal transformation and what God has done in Jesus' victory. The doctrine of Penal Substitution however is not a doctrine that is able to link our personal transformation with what God has done in Jesus since in that doctrine Jesus' work is all about a transaction between God and humanity. Much of this guidebook has been devoted to this personal and societal transformation.

APPENDIX 2
THE GREAT OMISSION IN
THE GREAT COMMISSION

Now the eleven disciples went to Galilee, to the mountain to which Jesus had directed them. When they saw him, they worshiped him; but some doubted. And Jesus came and said to them, 'All authority in heaven and on earth has been given to me. Go therefore and make disciples of all nations.......'
(Matthew 28.16-19)

Jesus instructs his disciples to *'make disciples'* in Matthew 28.19. This is an important instruction from Jesus and is part of the directives that have come to be called 'The Great Commission'. Local congregations should be fulfilling this mandate yet we lack resources to help us to fulfil this assignment. There are many churches who want to offer courses that will help participants understand what it means to be disciples and will give them a forum to discuss how to practise what they have come to understand. There are many church-goers who ask for such opportunities. Unfortunately there is not much that is available that fulfils this need.

It is not as if there is nothing available. Let us look at what is on the menu: **The Alpha course**: This is a very popular course used by many churches and has made a very significant contribution to the evangelism and spirituality of many people. By this I mean that it has drawn a lot of people into a relationship with Jesus and has revitalised many people's spirituality. However, *The Alpha course* does not attempt to include Jesus' kingdom teachings in its curriculum and for that reason is not useful enough in making disciples, which in the great commission Jesus said includes *'teaching them to obey everything that I have commanded you'.* (Matthew 28.20)

One of the great strengths of *The Alpha course* has been the way in which it has given many congregations, most of them part of the mainline churches, a vehicle for evangelism and church growth. The other strength has been in its ability to spread the charismatic movement in the mainline churches which had up until then resisted that movement.

Disciple: Becoming Disciples through Bible Study: This is an excellent course published by Abingdon Press and distributed by Upper Room. It is a very comprehensive journey through the entire Bible and picks on 34 main themes of discipleship. *Disciple* is quite expensive for the South African context and it requires participants to commit for a whole year's journey. Neither of these two factors should discourage people since Christian learning is of such great importance and value. *Disciple* also has *'Second Generation Studies'* which include an excellent course *'Jesus in the Gospels'*. This also needs a whole year of study and can only be done once the first *Disciple* year has been completed.

Manna and Mercy: A Brief History of God's Unfolding Promise to Mend the Entire Universe: This is a really special and inspirational journey through the entire Bible that has been written and memorably illustrated by Daniel Erlander and is distributed in South Africa by my friend Alan Storey. Alan has also developed teaching videos to accompany the text. 'Manna and Mercy' is a bit like a graphic novel and has the intention of giving a summary of the whole of scripture through the lens of the twin themes of God's provision and grace and how that defines Kingdom living. It does this remarkably well but does leave out quite a lot of detail because of its focus on the twin themes.

Small Group resources: There are many resources available for small groups on many Christian themes but it is very noticeable that the menu on offer does not include studies aimed at gaining a good systematic understanding of Jesus' teachings of the Kingdom. Further, most small group resources are not substantial in terms of content. Also, most resources are from the USA and the exchange rate makes it difficult for small groups to keep buying their study material from them. Another problem is that the theological foundations of the organisations that produce most of the small group material is a narrow theology that at its roots does not appreciate the kingdom perspective of Jesus' teachings. The result of this is that the teachings in many of these resources don't really promote the journey of *'making disciples'* for the kingdom in a Southern African context.

In summary, it is clear to almost everyone involved in the local church that there are not enough resources for *'making disciples'* for us to be able to keep doing this important work. My prayer is that *Missing Jesus?* will be a vital addition to the very limited menu available to the local church.

There will never be a single book or course that brings our search for good discipleship material to an end – rather what we need is more nutritious items on the menu. Essentially the key to *'making disciples'* in the local congregation is in developing their members' intentionality and accountability around following Jesus. The better the menu is the better the member and the congregation are able to put into practice their good intentions.

RECOMMENDATIONS

'Just as the theme of God's Kingdom was central in the ministry of Jesus, the author succeeds in articulating the fundamental principles of Kingdom step by step for a plain person. Wessels does not shy away from his intention of inviting people to a radical transformation of consciousness which will lead to a transformation of the global world. If people were to experience this radical transformation the world would be a better place to live in.'

REV. GCOBANI VIKA
BA (RU), Mth (Edin). Methodist Minister

'*Missing Jesus?* is a timely corrective. The author reinstates the much-neglected teachings of Jesus and the kingdom perspective that permeates Jesus' ministry. Enlightening and inspired, the study excels in locating Jesus' kingdom/community consciousness in the communal life of the Trinity. Wessels ably shows that discipleship is multi-relational, a kingdom life.'

REV. DR TREVOR RUTHENBERG

'I truly believe that this resource has come at the right time for our Church, and the Church in general, especially in times where our understanding of Christ seems to be so much challenged by the different doctrines and theologies, driven by quick fixes and instant gratification.'

REV. SMANGA BOSMAN
BTh (Rhodes), BTh(Hons) (UNISA)

In this comprehensive work, John Wessels has drawn out facets of God's character I have not considered for years. Have I lost the Jesus of the Scriptures? Do I follow a Jesus I have moulded into a comfortable image? How much richer may my life be if I follow the true Jesus? This book presents a thought-provoking challenge for any Christ-follower who wishes to deepen or renew their faith.

MANDY HACKLAND
Christ-follower, blogger and author of
Hope Through Dark Valleys; *Witnesses*; and *An Interlude with God*

Too many people (even many Christians) are sadly missing Jesus from their lives and John Wessels wonderfully and comprehensively explains God's desire for each of us as disciples in relationship with God, with the community of

God's people, and with the world in which we live. This study guide is both a theological textbook and a practical handbook in this discipleship journey.

REV. DR ALAN BESTER
Resident Minister on the KwaZulu-Natal South Coast, MCSA
BTh(Hons), MA(Theol), PhD
Author of *Understanding Grief*

In this book John Wessels presents his understanding of the practices and teachings of Jesus of Nazareth, an intervention into human affairs that Wessels refers to as 'the Kingdom Consciousness Movement.' Drawing from the author's deep engagement with the New Testament gospels and extended service with South African Christians, *Missing Jesus?* should be a valuable resource for seekers of all kinds who wish to engage with Jesus' ministry.

CHRISTIAN A. WILLIAMS
Department of Anthropology, University of the Free State, South Africa
Author of *National Liberation in Postcolonial Africa:
A Historical Ethnography of SWAPO's Exile Camps*

Are you looking for God, for an authentic, living faith, for power to live as a citizen of the Kingdom of God? John Wessels has spent the last 18 years compiling and refining this compelling, practical guide to help readers find the missing Jesus and to surrender to His reign in their lives. Here is a guide book to help congregations, small groups and individuals both inside and outside the church to find Jesus the Good Shepherd.

BILL WEBSTER
BTh(Hons) UNISA
Retired Presbyterian minister and ex-teacher.
Editor of the Mowbray Tract Society for the past 18 years
and author of over 200 tracts on the Christian faith.

This is a must-read material, it covers all the aspect of the historical and the present Jesus. It will not only rejuvenate the reader, it will revolutionize the reader's thinking and attitudes towards self, others and Christ himself.

REV. FESTUS MARUMO

John covers a wide spectrum of basic doctrines of Christian belief. Having been a Christian and a Pastor for many years, it is easy to become familiar and even bored with theoretical doctrines and maintaining an institutional church. Yet, working through John's material, I was drawn into his invitation to engage these doctrines in very practical ways. Each paragraph opened points of reflection on what I believed or not. Furthermore, the questions posed challenged my lifestyle profoundly. I wholeheartedly recommend this book to anyone who is seeking a relevant faith within a damaged world.

REV. DR. BRIAN BURGER
Minister in the Methodist Church

John Wessels has written a comprehensive workbook on what it means to follow Jesus. His emphasis on the Kingdom of God goes to the heart of Jesus' message and ministry. John's intention is that this understanding will inform how Jesus intends for us to live in our world. As such this is a practical field book combining both responsible scholarship and pastoral wisdom. An invaluable resource not only for everyone seeking a deeper relationship with Jesus but a gift to the whole church.

REV. WAYNE BOUWER
Senior Minister at Hillside Vineyard and Regional Overseer
for the Association of Vineyard Churches

In an age of 'fake news' and 'alternative truths', this book speaks boldly and prophetically to those who claim to follow Christ, and unflinchingly calls them to drop their false narratives, and live instead to a higher standard of Christ's love and teachings.

STEVE BRIGGS
B.Com (Hons) MBA MTh

Our struggle with knowing the shepherd of our lives as Christian people is an ongoing reality. The fact that so many of us struggle with the complex realities of life both personally, in church, in community and within a wider world context points to our need to know and acknowledge the Shepherd of our Life. David clearly understood this reality when he begins Psalm 23 with the powerful statement of affirmation 'The Lord is my Shepherd'. Our Christian journey unfolds in knowing the Shepherd of our life as we experience all the realities of life (good-bad-brokenness-pain-joy-wonder- etc.) Missing Jesus will certainly enable the reader to discover the places in their lives that need to grow and develop to appreciate the powerful value of affirming Jesus as the Shepherd of our lives.

REV. SIMON PRINS
Pastor

I have had the privilege of being able to participate in a study at Trinity Methodist Church in 2016 and in a home group in 2017 both using a preliminary version of Missing Jesus. I personally benefited immensely from this book. Those with whom I interacted considered that a home group could use the book over and over again as so much is to be gained from considering the messages contained in the book and the benefit they obtained from using the book.

ROB THEUNISSEN

We so easily get distracted and forget that Jesus is our Shepherd, always caring for us and seeking us out when we have wandered away. This book reminds us that our relationship with Him and His Kingdom is more important than anything else in this life and in the next. If you realize that Jesus is missing in your life, or that you yearn to draw closer to Him, then reading this book will be of immense value to you.

REV. ANDREW SIEBÖRGER

(B.Sc Chem. Eng. B.Th.) and Sandy Siebörger (B.A. H.Ed.): Andrew's published books: *Grace Rediscovered, Grace-Side up, Here I am, Lord (ed.)*

I have always seen myself as somewhat more conservative in my thinking on the matters of God than John – and yet as I have now read his book – I realise that there is not much difference in our thinking besides matters that are secondary……..John has used his intelligence and his passion for Christ has come out. The teacher within him has been released in his writings.

REV. ALAN MOLYNEUX
B.Th (Hons)

In this book John has clearly given expression to his passion for growing maturity in spiritual life by crafting the material to take us much deeper than most material of this kind. I do believe that he has achieved this in the preparation of the material and I warmly commend this material for use in much needed deepening of spiritual life in groups, but also in individuals' lives. I especially enjoyed his stress on the Kingdom of God as being the essential focus in this journey of growth, empowering the reader for Kingdom-focused, missional action and ministry.

REV. DAVID NEWTON

THE 'MISSING JESUS?' WEBSITE

Please go to www.missingjesus.net, which I hope to maintain and update as a resource to help individuals, small groups and congregations with further resources for using this guidebook. Over time I hope to develop a resource there of:

- Practical help for individuals, congregations and small groups journeying with the guidebook.
- Lists of resources to help you journey forward with the themes of the book.
- Lists of resources for spiritual disciplines.
- Encouragement, equipment and inspiration to help restore the teaching ministry to the local congregation.
- Training videos.
- A questionnaire to assess your strengths and weaknesses in discipleship.
- Testimonies, reviews and recommendations.
- Ordering books.
- Publicising events that may be of help to you.

I have prayed and continue to pray that this journey will lead each reader to understand, experience and participate in the life that Jesus offers the world.

BIBLIOGRAPHY

The following books and articles were read to varying degrees in the writing of this guidebook. All of them are good for helpful further reading:

Aulén, Gustaf, *Christus Victor: An Historical Study of the Three Main Types of the Idea of the Atonement*, SPCK Classics, London, 1931.

Biko, Steve, *I Write What I Like,* Picador Africa, Johannesburg, 2004.

Bilezikian, Gilbert, *Community 101: Reclaiming the Local Church as a Community of Oneness,* Zondervan, Grand Rapids, Michigan, 1997.

Boesak, Allan Aubrey, *Pharaohs on Both Sides of the Blood-Red Waters: Prophetic Critique of Empire,* Cascade Books, Eugene, Oregon, 2017.

Boesak, Allan, *The Tenderness of Conscience: African Renaissance and the Spirituality of Politics,* Sun Press, Stellenbosch, 2005.

Bonhoeffer, Dietrich, *Ethics,* Macmillan Publishing Company, New York, 1955.

Bonhoeffer, Dietrich, *Life Together: The Classic Exploration of Faith in Community,* Harper Collins, New York, 1954.

Bonhoeffer, Dietrich, *The Cost of Discipleship,* SCM Press, London, 1937 (1958 translation).

Bourgeault, Cynthia, *The Wisdom of Jesus: Transforming Heart and Mind,* Shambhala Publications, Boston, 2008.

Bourgeault, Cynthia, *Mystical Hope: Trusting in the Mercy of God,* Rowman and Littlefield Publishers, Lanham, Maryland, 2001.

Bright, John, *The Kingdom of God,* Abingdon, Nashville, 1980 (first published 1953).

Buttrick, David, *Homiletic: Moves and Structures,* Fortress Press, Philadelphia, 1987.

Elkington, Robert Lionel, 'The Doctrine of Subsequence in the Pentecostal and Neo-Pentecostal Movements', Master of Theology Thesis, University of South Africa, Pretoria, 1998.

Cameron, Paul, *Kingdom, Discipleship and Holistic Healing*, self-published booklet, 2017.

de Gruchy, John W., *The Church Struggle in South Africa,* Wm. B. Eerdmans

Publishing Co., Grand Rapids, Michigan, and David Philip Publisher, Claremont, South Africa, 1986.

Erlander, Daniel, *Manna and Mercy: A Brief History of God's Unfolding Promise to Mend the Entire Universe*, The Order of Saints Martin and Teresa, Mercer Island, Washington, 1992. To use this resource you must go to http://www.mannaandmercy.org to place orders and also to see and order the teaching videos that Alan Storey has developed for studying this wonderful book.

Fee, Gordon D., *Paul, the Spirit, and the People of God*, Hendrickson Publishers, Inc., 1996. (This book is an accessible version of Fee's more thorough *God's Empowering Presence*.)

Fee, Gordon D., *God's Empowering Presence: The Holy Spirit in the Letters of Paul*, Peabody MA: Hendrickson, 1994.

Foster, Richard, *Celebration of Discipline – The Path to Spiritual Growth*, Hodder and Stoughton, London, 1989.

Fox, Matthew, *Original Blessing*, Bear and Company Inc., Santa Fe, 1983.

Gaybba, Brian, *God is a Community: A General Survey of Christian Theology*, UNISA Press, Pretoria, 2004.

Gaybba, Brian, *Soteriology: Study Guide 2 for THA301-T*, Department of Systematic Theology, University of South Africa, Pretoria, 1988.

Gaybba, Brian, *The Spirit of Love*, A Geoffrey Chapman book published by Cassell Publishers Limited, London, 1987.

Hudson, Trevor, *Friendship with God – How God's Offer of Intimate Relationship can Change your Life*, Struik Christian Media, Tyger Valley, 2015.

Hudson, Trevor, *Holy Spirit Here and Now*, Struik Christian Media, Tyger Valley, 2012.

Hudson, Trevor, *Invitations to Abundant Life: In Search for Life at its Best*, Struik Christian Books, Cape Town, 1998.

Hudson, Trevor, *Signposts to Spirituality: Towards a Closer Walk with God*, Struik Christian Books, Cape Town, 1995.

Hudson, Trevor and Kelsey, Morton, *Journey of the Spirit – Devotions for the Spiritual Seeker*, Struik Christian Books, Cape Town, 2000.

Kame, Greg, and Tshaka, Rothney S., 'Morality and Spirituality: The Missing Link for Economic Development in the 21st Century', *HTS Theological Studies*, 71(3),

2015. https://dx.doi.org/10.4102/hts.v71i3.2818.

Keck, Leander E., *Jesus in the Gospels,* Abingdon Press, Nashville, 2003.

Keener, Craig S., *The Historical Jesus of the Gospels,* William B. Eerdmans Publishing Company, Grand Rapids, Michigan, 2009.

Kendrick, Graham, *Worship*, Kingsway Publications Ltd, Sussex, 1984.

Kraybill, Donald, *The Upside Down Kingdom*, Herald Press, Scottdale, Pennsylvania, 1978.

Lewis, Greville P. ed., *An Approach to Christian Doctrine,* Methodist Publishing House, Cape Town, 1976.

McDowell, Josh, *Evidence that Demands a Verdict: Historical Evidences for the Christian Faith*, Here's Life Publishers Inc., San Bernardino, 1979.

Macquarrie, John, *An Existentialist Theology*, Pelican Books, Middlesex, 1973.

Maluleke, T.S., 'May the Black God Stand Please! Biko's Challenge to Religion', in Mngxitama, A., Alexander, A. and Gibson, N.C. (eds), *Biko Lives! Contemporary Black History*, Palgrave Macmillan, New York, 2008.

Maluleka, Tinyiko Sam, 'Christianity in a Distressed Africa: A Time to Own Up', in *Missionalia* 26.3 (November 1998), pp. 324-340.

Moltmann, Jurgen, *The Trinity and the Kingdom of God,* SCM Press, London, 1981.

Morphew, Derek J., *Demonstrating the Kingdom,* Derek Morphew Publications, Bergvliet, 2018.

Ndungane, Njongonkulu, *A World with a Human Face: A Voice from Africa,* SPCK, London and WCC Publications, Geneva, 2003.

Nolan, Albert, *Jesus Today: A Spirituality of Radical Freedom,* Double Storey, 2006.

Nolan, Albert, *Jesus Before Christianity,* David Philip Publisher, Cape Town, 1986.

Oosthuisen, Neil T., *In the Beginning: Allowing Genesis 1 – 11 to Address our Lives Today,* Chris van Rensburg Publications, Melville, 2006.

Peterson, Eugene H., *Reversed Thunder: The Revelation of John and the Praying Imagination,* HarperOne, New York, 1988.

Ralph, Margaret Nutting, *And God Said What? An Introduction to Biblical Literary Forms,* Paulist Press, New York, 2003.

Rohr, Richard, with Mike Morrel, *The Divine Dance: The Trinity and Your Transformation,* Whitaker House, New Kensington, PA, 2016.

Sakupapa, Teddy C., 'Ecumenical Ecclesiology in the African Context: Towards a view of the Church as *Ubuntu*', *Scriptura*, Volume 117, No. 1, pp. 1-15, June 2018.

Sobrino, Jon, *The True Church and the Poor*, Orbis Books, Maryknoll, 1984.

Sobrino, Jon, *Christology at the Crossroads*, Orbis Books, Maryknoll, 1976.

Storey, Alan, *Foundations for Discipleship: A Christ Healed Africa for the Healing of the Nations*, self-published, 2002.

Tshaka, R.S., 'The Christian as the Christ in Society: Karl Barth's Public Theology and its implications for Democratic South Africa', in L. Hansen, *Christian in Public: Aims, Methodologies and Issues in Public Theology*', African Sun MeDIA, Stellenbosch, 2007, pp. 127-140.

Tshaka, R.S., 'A perspective on notions of spirituality, democracy, social cohesion and public theology', *Verbum et Ecclesia*, Vol. 35, No. 3, 2014, Art. #1336, 6 pages. http://dx.doi.org/10.4102/ ve.v35i3.1336.

Tshaka, R.S. and Makofane, M.K., 'The Continued Relevance of Black Liberation Theology for Democratic South Africa Today', *Scriptura: The Journal for Contextual Hermeneutics in Southern Africa*, Volume 105, Issue 1, Jan 2010, pp. 532-546.

Tshaka, T., 'From Marikana to believers eating snakes, ants, underwear and rats cheerfully – black theology of liberation in a time of empire and life-threatening faith praxis', in M. Welker, N. Koopman, and J. Vorster, *Church and Civil Society: German and South African Perspectives*, SUN MeDIA MeTRO, Stellenbosch, 2017, pp.189-205.

Tutu, Desmond, *Rainbow People of God: South Africa's Victory over Apartheid*, Bantam Books, London, 1995.

Theological Education by Extension College, *Spirituality – Walking Closer with Jesus*, Course code 276, Practical Theology stream, Theological Education by Extension College.

Walker, Alan, *Breakthrough – Rediscovering the Holy Spirit*, Fontana, London, 1969.

Wesley, John, *The Holy Spirit and Power*, Logos International, New Jersey, 1977. (This book is a paraphrase of John Wesley's sermons on the Holy Spirit by Clare Weakley.)

Willard, Dallas, *The Divine Conspiracy: Rediscovering our Hidden Life in God*, Fount, London, 1998.

Williams, Rowan, *Holy Living: The Christian Tradition for Today*, Bloomsbury, London, 2017.

Wilke, Richard Byrd and Wilke, Julia Kitchens, *Disciple: Becoming Disciples through Bible Study*, Abingdon Press, Nashville, 1993.

Wimber, John, with Kevin Springer, *Power Evangelism, signs and wonders today*, Hodder and Stoughton, Kent, 1985.

Wright, N.T., *The Lord and His Prayer,* William B. Eerdmans Publishing Co., Michigan, 1997.

Wright, N.T., *Paul: A Biography,* HarperOne, San Francisco, 2018.

ABOUT THE AUTHOR

John Wessels BA, BTh Honours (Rhodes) is a Minister in the Methodist Church of Southern Africa (which includes South Africa, Namibia, Mozambique, Lesotho, Swaziland and Botswana). John is passionate about how Jesus is hope for the world now. Early in his ministry he became frustrated with the scarcity of resources that helped congregations present Jesus and his kingdom as real and life-giving in society. John is also passionate about Jesus' call to 'make disciples'. For these reasons he has consistently developed and taught the contents of this book in courses since the year 2000. Over the years since then he has often re-written, enlarged and refined the book. His aim was to create a book that is comprehensive, thorough and practically helpful. Now, nineteen years after the start of this project, he has decided it is ready for publication and is able to be used in a much wider context. It is John's prayer that this could be the tool the church needs to draw people into a deeper relationship with Jesus so that they can follow him more closely.

Please contact me, John Wessels, for the purchase of the guidebooks at info@missingjesus.net and at the www.missingjesus.net website. I can also currently be contacted at john@trinitylinden.org.za, or wesselsfamily@cybersmart.co.za and 011-8881740/1/2. If these details change then please contact your nearest Methodist Church to locate me in the Methodist Church of Southern Africa's directory. I can also be contacted to give advice on the use of the guidebook.

www.ingramcontent.com/pod-product-compliance
Lightning Source LLC
Chambersburg PA
CBHW081340080526
44588CB00017B/2697